alcott Parsons

DISCARD

The Sociology of Talcott Parsons

François Bourricaud

Translated by Arthur Goldhammer
Foreword by Harry M. Johnson

The University of Chicago Press
Chicago and London

Publication of this translation was made possible, in part, by a grant
from the MAISON DES SCIENCES DE L'HOMME, Paris

Originally published as *L'individualisme institutionnel*
© 1977 by Presses Universitaires de France

The University of Chicago Press, Chicago 60637
The University of Chicago Press, Ltd., London

Printed in the United States of America
85 84 83 82 81   5 4 3 2 1

FRANÇOIS BOURRICAUD is professor of sociology
at the Université René-Descartes.

Library of Congress Cataloging in Publishing Data

Bourricaud, François.
    The sociology of Talcott Parsons.

    Translation of: L'individualisme institutionnel.
    Includes bibliographical references and index.
    1. Parsons, Talcott, 1902–1979.   2. Sociology
I. Title.
HM22.U6P37313   301'.092'4   81-1348
ISBN   0-226-06755-6   AACR2

Contents

Contents

Foreword

In sociology today two somewhat distinct tendencies are all too common, namely, (1) either insistence on one of several unduly narrow or extremist "general" theories, or (2) undue attachment to particular methods such as "theory construction" and path analysis. Such methods are indeed valuable, but they cannot replace the sort of theorizing best represented by Durkheim and Weber and their most important recent heir, Talcott Parsons. François Bourricaud's book is especially timely, then, because with courtesy, breadth, and balance he helps to show how utterly premature it is, to say the least, to celebrate the demise of Parsons's influence in our field, as many people are doing. Bourricaud helps to establish the vital point that "general" theory is worthy of serious attention and should not be scornfully set aside in favor of "middle-range" theories alone. The latter are of course also important, but they will flourish better if they are developed consciously within a more comprehensive intellectual framework.

To be sure, Bourricaud himself stresses that his book is an "essay." Its special unity and contribution lie in its imaginative treatment of two interrelated themes: (1) the creativity of individuals within the more or less flexible and subtly changing guidelines of social structure, and (2) the nature of good sociological theory. These themes, however, are among the most important and far-reaching that could have been chosen.

With regard to the nature of good sociological theory, Bourricaud analyzes what Parsons meant by saying that sociological theory develops somewhat as the common law does. Let readers discover the main points of this analysis for themselves. Parsons's general theory of action relates "sociology" in a systemic and systematic way to the other social sciences and, to a lesser extent, to biology and certain cultural sciences. His version of sociological theory developed in tentative spirit within a series of interrelated paradigms. Parsons uses the term "paradigm" "simply to refer to an attempt at conceptually formal statement of the primary elements of a theoretical scheme and their relations to each other."[1] We might say, I think, that all the paradigms would ideally be so closely congruent or integrated with one another that they would constitute a single paradigm, complex yet much simpler than the actuality from which it abstracts selected aspects. The composite paradigm, then, together with the more general facts of varying complexity and scope that are discovered and integrated with its help, or that can be fitted into it from other sources, constitute Parsons's "theory." This theory he likens repeatedly to the vast and developing body of law called "the common law" (as opposed to the Continental Roman law tradition); the theory, like the common law, develops through the continual interaction between concepts and principles (the "paradigm" aspect) and empirical "cases" presented for "adjudication" (empirical problems and solutions).

In treating his two main themes, Bourricaud necessarily deals with most of these paradigms. In particular, he has fairly extended discussions of the four categories of function, social interaction, socialization, deviant behavior, social control, the pattern variables, the functional subsystems of the social system, the generalized symbolic media of interchanges between each pair of these subsystems, and the paradigm of both change in and change of the social system. These paradigms all combine the point of view of "actors" (i.e., the subjective point of view) with conceptual distinctions made by the scientist (the objective point of view). Further, the paradigms participate in an "analytical" theory as opposed to the type of theory called "philosophy of history." Max Weber's stand on this question was slightly ambiguous and has led to controversy, but Parsons maintained that Weber's practice definitely implied fundamental rejection of any radical difference between *Naturwissenschaften* and *Kultur-* or *Geisteswissenschaften*. In any case, Parsons himself went even further than Weber in the analytical direction.

With regard to the theme of "institutionalized individualism," Bourricaud analyzes both parts of this pregnant term. He treats with uncommon subtlety and understanding the meaning and operation of "institutionalized social structure." He recognizes Parsons's important distinction between internal and external environments. The units within a social system may be actors-in-roles or subcollectivities of the social system of reference. Institutionalized individualism refers to both types of units. Any unit must act in relation to the internal environment of the system, which consists of other units and the more or less commonly accepted and sanctioned social structure. This social structure conditions the action of units.

The external environments (note *plural*) of the units and of the social system of reference include not only other social systems but also cultural objects; the personalities of individuals, including the actors themselves; organisms, including those of individual actors; and the nonorganic physical environment. Individual units, then, must react to these environments as well as to the internal environment.

What of the individual in institutionalized individualism? Bourricaud comes back again and again, in different contexts, to the dilemmas and dialectics of freedom and constraint, social equalities and inequalities. He takes account of Parsons's evolutionary and, more broadly, comparative perspectives. He shows the difference between ideological distortion and what may fairly be called reasonable evaluation. Contrary to anarchistic and some other utopian opinion, social structures are not purely restrictive. They also provide individual units with possibilities of gaining and giving cooperation; therefore, of accomplishing much more for themselves and for others than the units could achieve as atomistic individuals and groups with no guidance from social structure. It follows, then, that the process of socialization does not put each generation into bondage and merely equip it with prefashioned blinders. Socialization, properly analyzed, is seen to enlarge our freedom of action. Further, it can be shown that certain evolutionary tendencies in social structure enlarge the net average freedom of individuals. Thus, social structure not only conditions the action of individual units but it also provides them with resources for making meaningful decisions with regard to one another. It does not determine those decisions.

In treating individuals, Bourricaud does not go into any detail about the personality. Instead, he treats various key roles of individual actors in industrial societies of the Western type. In keeping with the theme of institutionalized individualism, it was an appropriate decision, of course, to treat the area in which the social system and the personality interpenetrate most obviously, namely, the area of roles. Among the key roles Bourricaud discusses are socializer and socializee, citizen, employer and employee, consumer, and religious believer.

In the course of Bourricaud's exposition, he both illuminates the meaning of abstract concepts and shows their scientific usefulness. He makes good use of some (not all, by any means) of Parsons's empirical analyses. These have often been admired even when the admirers have not fully appreciated the fact—which Parsons rightly insisted on—that the (brilliant) analysis was made possible by the theory and was not only the result of "journalistic" intuition. We can say, however, that it is also true Parsons was like a great diagnostician in medicine, in that his powers developed in proportion to the development and excogitation and internalization of theory, to the point that undoubtedly he could often leap to empirical understanding and then afterward, if necessary, spell it out in terms of abstract theory. Further, once his theory had developed beyond a certain point, he could often convincingly say of somebody else's empirical analysis: "This may be so, but it is extremely unlikely in view of the following theoretical as well as empirical considerations."[2]

If one of Bourricaud's empirical examples does not work very well for some readers, probably another will. Some readers will probably not understand the point that values in medical practice have not recently changed, even though physicians are now in the process of making seemingly new decisions with regard to abortion and the termination of life.[3] But I think that few readers will fail to understand another empirical example, namely, the Judeo-Christian value system. Bourricaud admirably summarizes from various places Parsons's analysis of a range of possibilities in this system and shows that, although emphasis shifted from time to time from one possibility to another, we can still see that we are talking about the same system. This discussion, with these and other examples, is especially important because an important aspect of Parsons's sociological theory is his subtle yet strong analysis of the role of common value systems in social interaction: *subtle* because he avoids both the errors of extreme idealism and those of the Marxist theory that the "common" value system merely protects, advances, and "mystifies" the interests of the ruling class; *strong* because his theory helps us to make sense of history, that is, of the empirical interaction we study. This fundamental aspect of Parsons's theory he borrowed, of course, from the "fathers" of modern sociological theory, Durkheim and Weber; but Parsons developed the theory well beyond his forebears in the sociological tradition.

The nature of social and cultural constraint and of individual freedom is, of course, partly revealed in the course of developing good theory. At the same time, the nature of good sociological theory in its relatively advanced stages is what it is because of our growing understanding of the interdependence and interpenetration of different types of living systems and their internal and external environments. In explaining Parsons's paradigms (or most of them), Bourricaud also explains Parsons's objections to types of theory he could not accept.

Thus, Parsons's treatment of institutionalized individualism and his conception of good theory are explained in two ways: by examining the paradigms themselves, and by contrasting them in specific ways with unacceptable theories and types of theory. This aspect of Bourricaud's "essay" is one of the most interesting and can be studied with profit, I am convinced, by all other sociologists of whatever level or stage in their own intellectual development. I can suggest (but of course not summarize) the richness of this aspect by naming at least some of the most important theories and types of theory that are unacceptable. Thus, Bourricaud goes into some of the most important reasons for rejecting purely deductive statements of theory; vulgar functionalism; behaviorism of the type that stresses reinforcement or operant conditioning; one-sided theories that emphasize the ad hoc aspects of negotiation in social interaction and deny or play down social structure; cultural determinism; social determinism, of which Marxism is an example; utilitarian theory, from which Marxism did not entirely escape; so-called critical theory, with its ideological distortions regarding one-dimensional man and its utopianism; and somewhat similar theories of the ideological right, such as Sorokin's too narrow conception of religion and his distorted evaluation of our allegedly "sensate" values.

In Bourricaud's careful discussion, good points abound. He distinguishes different kinds of functional theory and explains why Parsons never espoused what he calls "vulgar functionalism" (despite the common charges of superficial critics). He explains how Parsons avoids circularity in his own kind of structural and processual analysis focused on functional problems; Parsons always dealt with the conditions in which norms might have functional consequences, conditions that might or might not be present empirically. Bourricaud's explanation of the concept of equilibrium is refreshingly free from very common misrepresentations. He explains brilliantly the idea of symbolic control. He shows that Parsons's paradigms are neither cynical nor unrealistic (again, despite common but gross misrepresentations).

Bourricaud, then, accomplishes a great deal. He warns us, however, that he is not trying to present a comprehensive summary of Parsons's theory. Indeed, there are gaps in certain areas, and what he does treat he makes no attempt to treat exhaustively. He is not particularly concerned with presenting the most recent versions Parsons arrived at in the course of defining and refining his various paradigms. We are certainly given enough information to see that the paradigms are interrelated and complement one another, but it is not part of Bourricaud's intent here to cover any one theme completely.

There are, of course, many outrageously inadequate secondary works on Parsons. For readers who may have been misled, it is perhaps necessary to reemphasize the point that this excellent book by Bourricaud is not and is not intended to be comprehensive. At widely separated stages in Parsons's intellectual development, he gave at least two somewhat different definitions of power. Unlike some less astute commentators, Bourricaud realizes correctly that the later definition is no less realistic than the earlier, and for his own purposes he makes good use of Parsons's analysis in both stages; but he does not enter into any discussion of the technical relation of the two stages to each other. Similarly, he takes material from several different discussions of the pattern variables, but he does not go into the reasons Parsons gives for dropping self-orientation/collectivity-orientation from the list; indeed, he does not even mention the change and its connection with the four-function paradigm (which was developed a few years later than the first presentation of the pattern-variable paradigm). Other examples of Bourricaud's legitimate selectivity for his own special purposes can be given. He treats the paradigm of sociocultural evolution, but he does not discuss the three stages or the rationale for Parsons's schematic division of evolution into these three stages precisely (e.g., instead of Robert Bellah's five). Again, although Bourricaud deals with the components and levels of social structure, he does so in scattered places, according to his contextual needs, and does not deal with them as a four-part paradigm whose rationale is suggested by the master paradigm of four categories of function.

Although what Bourricaud says about the relations among culture, the social system, and personality is very good, as usual, and will repay any reader's time, he does not go into the *sub*systems of culture or those of personality, and he does not deal with the "general system of action" as a system having the four functions L I G A. In what I say here, I cannot take the space to go into the interchanges between each pair of the subsystems of general action, but I should like to say enough to suggest the unremitting efforts Parsons made to refine, extend, and integrate his theory of action (which, as I have said, includes sociology). In his work after about 1953, the four-function paradigm (L I G A) became the basis for a reconsideration of the usual distinctions among culture, social system, and personality (although the word "usual" is perhaps too strong, since many people did not and many people even now still do not distinguish adequately between the cultural and the social systems).

At first, Parsons treated culture as the pattern maintenance (L) subsystem of "general action," the social system as the integrative subsystem (I), the personality as the goal-attainment subsystem (G), and what he called the "behavioral organism" as the adaptive subsystem (A). Later on, Victor and Charles Lidz suggested that the "action" level of living systems should not include the organism even insofar as the latter is modified by learning; they thought that the adaptive sub-system of general action needed to be redefined, and for this purpose they suggested that Piaget's psychology could be brought neatly into the theory of the "general action system." To maintain terminological continuity, they suggested that this A subsystem be called the "behav-ioral system."[4] (In effect, the G system, the personality, is the motiva-tional system of the individual, with subsystems identity L, superego I, ego G, and id A; and the behavioral system—A in general action, as we have noted—is the individual's cognitive system, including not only knowledge in the usual sense but also errors and nonempirical beliefs.)

Parsons accepted these changes after careful study; Bourricaud does not cover them here, and he does not deal with the generalized symbolic media of the general action system, which are involved in the interchanges of the component systems with one another (i.e., culture, the social system, the personality, and the behavioral system; Bour-ricaud, as already noted, does deal with the generalized symbolic media of the social system, which are involved in the interchanges within that system among its subsystems, namely, the fiduciary system, the societal community, the polity, and the economy).

Bourricaud also ignores the complexes of general action, each of which combines elements from the four subsystems of general action. Of these complexes, the cognitive complex has been treated at length by Parsons and Platt.[5] Victor M. Lidz has made a promising start in the analysis of the moral complex.[6] Stimulated in part, I believe, by the Lidz brothers' changed conception of the behavioral system, Parsons (in collaboration with Harold Bershady, Willy de Craemer, Renée C. Fox, and Victor M. Lidz, all at the University of Pennsylvania, where Parsons was a visiting professor) developed the paradigm of the "human condition"; in this still more comprehensive paradigm, the general action system (embracing, remember, culture, the social sys-tem, the personality, and the behavioral system) is the I subsystem, and the organism is part of G.[7] These developments probably occurred too late for Bourricaud to have considered them in this book; but, still more likely, they did not add a great deal that is relevant to his main foci of attention (the nature of sociological theory and the autonomy of the individual within the flexible and changing guiding framework of social structure and of culture more generally).

On the whole, I think Bourricaud emphasizes certain continuities rather than the discontinuities in Parsons's work. This is in harmony with the two basic themes of the nature of individualism and the nature of sociological theory. Bourricaud does recognize, of course, but does not stress, the tentative spirit of Parsons's formulations at every stage of his thought. Speaking in technical terms: as a scientist Parsons was an actor in the adaptive subsystem of the cultural system, taking fiduciary responsibility for the integrity and development of social science and of sociology in particular; and as such he personally was open to influences from other scientists and from other subsystems. I have deliberately mentioned the example of his acceptance of the Lidz brothers' rather drastic modification of the adaptive system of general action, now called the "behavioral system." Parsons's own tentative spirit and openness should be exemplary for the future. Many changes and additions will undoubtedly prove necessary. I have long wondered whether Parsons is correct in treating "land" (in the economy) as *both* a kind of commitment and the actual physical resources that are "permanently" (in a relative sense) reserved for productive purposes. After the Lidz brothers made their point that the "action" system, properly speaking, consists of interaction involving symbols and should not include the organism, I became convinced that the nonorganic environment should also be excluded. "Land" in the economic sense, therefore, perhaps should be regarded as the relatively stable commitment (or commitments, in the aggregate) of resources to productive use as opposed to consumption; and the actual physical resources themselves should be regarded as part of what Parsons in his latest work called the "adaptive subsystem of the human condition." This is only a tiny example. The future of sociology, I am convinced, depends, now, mainly on the correction, development, and further integration of Parsons's general theory of action, in the careful yet flexible spirit in which other responsible custodians (fiduciary experts) correct and develop the common law and strive to perfect its integration. Very important fields for future development are suggested by the present incompleteness of Parsons's paradigms. The inner logic of the theory suggests, for instance, that there ought to be generalized symbolic media and interchanges within each of the subsystems of general action other than the social system (namely, the cultural system, the personality, and the behavioral system). We know all too little about inflationary and deflationary processes in all generalized symbolic media. We should know more about the conditions in which such processes can be controlled and (the other side of the coin) the conditions where they cannot which lead to impairment of functioning or to important structural changes.

Despite its deliberate limitations, I think that this book by Bourricaud, now available to English readers in Arthur Goldhammer's excellent translation, is the best introduction now available to Parsons's
lifework. Its two basic themes provide nearly ideal occasions for Bourricaud to deal cogently with the most important misconceptions now
current regarding Parsons's work. After reading Bourricaud, sociologists will be more skeptical of charges that Parsons exaggerates
the degree of integration in social systems, that he had little interest in
social change and was even opposed to it, that he moved from ques-
tionable voluntarism in his early theory to exaggeration of the constraint of social structure later on.

Talcott Parsons himself was gratified by Bourricaud's book and
hoped that someone would translate it. It is done in the same generous
and reasonable spirit that Bourricaud praises in Parsons's treatment of
Durkheim and Weber. The first rule, says Bourricaud, is not to interpret in such a way as merely to provide yourself an opportunity to
show how much smarter you are than the author you are studying.
The second rule is to deal with apparent or real inconsistencies in the
light of the basic ideas, emphases, and trends of the author's work as a
whole. A third rule, we might add, is to take account of the successive
stages in the author's work and the reasons he gave implicitly or
explicitly for the changes he made in his earlier formulations. Bourricaud rightly says that Parsons was not out to prove himself a unique
genius; rather, he expounded his theory by carefully explaining both
its borrowings and its departures from positions that had been reached
or gained in the intellectual tradition he inherited. Moreover, he did
not develop theory for its own sake. He tried to illuminate empirical
problems, and he usually succeeded. He took up the important empirical problems that concerned Durkheim and Weber, such as: How
can we understand and reasonably evaluate so-called modern social
systems of the West? What is "capitalism"? How are "solidarity" and
"conflict" related? (He did not always agree with Durkheim or Weber,
we might add; but he was always careful to give his *scientific* reasons,
and he was always ready to reconsider in the light of rereading or of
further work of his own—usually both.) As Parsons continually went
back to Durkheim, Weber, and Freud (these three in particular), so we
shall continually go back to Parsons himself. And I have no doubt that
every reader of François Bourricaud's splendid book will return to it
often for its own sake and for guidance to Parsons.

Harry M. Johnson
University of Illinois
Urbana-Champaign

Introduction to Talcott Parsons

As I progressed in the writing of this book, my conception of its shape underwent a change. Originally, my intention was to bring up-to-date an introduction to the work of Talcott Parsons that I wrote in 1955. Over the ensuing twenty years Parsons had published a great deal, and his thought on important points had gained in breadth and richness. This branching out of his thinking, as I would be tempted to call it, is the essence of the Parsonian approach. Central to Parsons's work is the aim—which, I might add, is not a simple one—of combining two intuitions of society, one "active," the other "systemic." It might be said that his thinking has developed or, better, grown along a central axis, similar to the trunk of a tree, out of which branches and foliage grow and yet never lose contact with the central core.

I was persuaded to abandon my original intention by this very proliferation of Parsons's work. At the outset my idea was to place in the hands of the French reader a comprehensive and detailed introduction to this important and difficult thinker. But it became evident that this ambition was at once overweening and insufficient. To give a complete picture of what Parsons has published would require reading as wide as was Parsons's own attentiveness to the major developments in sociological thinking over a fifty-year period. Furthermore, even if this historical undertaking had been within my powers, I had decided not to limit myself to the bounds it would have laid down. Parsons's work has absorbed my attention as long as it has for only one reason: it seems to me to throw light on certain fundamental choices that every sociologist must face in thinking about the basic principles of his discipline.

Anyone who would comment on the work of a classic author—and Parsons is one, or at least in the process of becoming one—must answer three questions. First, he has to ask whether the work is consistent. Did the author contradict himself? Or was he content to repeat himself tirelessly? If he contradicted himself, was he aware of it? What do his contradictions mean, and how can they be explained? Second, the author must be situated in his historical context: What did he contribute that was new? Finally, the commentator must try to throw some light on the style and approach of his subject: Was he conciliatory, eclectic, trenchant, bold, or perhaps, at one time or another, all of these?

What strikes one at once about Parsons is the frankly academic character of his style. Cautious and heavy, its primary concern is to establish itself in relation to a catalog of authors and problems—in short, in relation to a tradition. Parsons never put himself forward as a genius: in this he showed a remarkable originality, which has inevitably done him a disservice in the eyes of his French readership. He was content to be a professor, proud of having spent his life within the precincts of a single renowned university. Was Parsons an establishment sociologist, as his critics charge? He was certainly an established sociologist, who enjoyed the benefits and endured the constraints of a web of institutional supports. He did his thinking in a context that combined the obligations of the teacher with those of the researcher, as a member both of an academic community (his university) and of a national and international scientific community; these dual roles were sometimes mutually beneficial, sometimes antagonistic. Parsons was as thoroughly an American professor of the period 1930–70 as Durkheim was a French academic of the early twentieth century. Of course the French university did not occupy the same place in French society in 1914 that Harvard came to occupy in American society in 1950. Durkheim was—perhaps—slightly further "left" in the French political spectrum than Parsons was in the American. Nevertheless, the fundamental outlooks of both men are similar—beyond the fact that they both refrained from partisan involvement in the strict sense, even while taking very clear stands in the major debates of their time. All in all, I am quite hopeful that I shall be able to prove, even to a reader who comes to the subject with the most unshakable prejudices, that the work of an "incurable theorist," as Parsons characterized himself, can be of help to us in understanding the problems of our modern societies.

I hope that I have not fallen short of my original goal, which was to provide the French reader with an introduction to a body of work that has been—despite the studies of Olivier Burgelin, François Chazel, and Guy Rocher—neglected or distorted to the point of caricature. Beyond that, I had another, even more important, reason for wishing to play the role of guide to Parsons's work: to further my own thinking in two related areas, in which Parsons moved with a great deal of assurance. When resolve flagged, I took heart from the knowledge that the work whose dynamic I was trying to unravel and explain was for me an invaluable source of insight into two central questions: What is the nature of sociological theory? And what is the relation between institutional conditioning and individual choice?

What, then, is the "general theory" that Parsons, beginning with his earliest works, worked patiently to elaborate? His insistent invocation of "theory" reflects his condemnation of the empiricism that was predominant among American sociologists in the thirties. For the empiricist, there are data; for Parsons, there are questions. To be an empiricist is to confuse facts and things, a confusion that makes itself felt particularly in the extreme forms of positivism, which combine a conception of knowledge as reflection with a strictly deterministic conception of action. Empiricists and positivists regard things as lying "out there." For Parsons, what counts is the fact. As a statement, it depends on a conceptual scheme; insofar as it is a true statement, it is given to us. The scheme and the particular facts pose questions and enable us to find answers.

In the social sciences the confusion of thing and fact is even more serious because the data these sciences treat are for the most part values, that is, preferences. One is correct in "treating them as things" if by that one means that they constitute the framework of action, considered to be beyond the power of the individual to modify at will. But to speak of values as things may lead to confusing physical nature with social nature. Accordingly, empiricism, particularly in its positivist version, is rejected not only on the grounds that it fails to recognize the hypothetical character of science but also that it ignores the *problematical* character of social order. To emphasize the importance of "theory" is to maintain that knowledge is in no way a copy or a reflection; more precisely, in the case of the social sciences, it is to recognize that questions are not raised by the things themselves but rather by our relation to things. Thus, in his early writings Parsons uses the term "theory" interchangeably with "frame of reference." By establishing a close connection between the two he avoids the dangers of dogmatic reification, against which one of his mentors, the philosopher Alfred North Whitehead, warned as "the fallacy of misplaced concreteness."

"Theory," in Parsons's sense, must satisfy two requirements: it must be relevant, and it must be verifiable—though verification, as we shall see, may take forms different from, and certainly less rigorous than, those prescribed by the canons of the logical-experimental method. A relevant theory is one that the observer finds significant in relation to his interests; but where a theory is concerned with actors and their behavior, it also has meaning for them, even if the interpretation suggested by theory differs from their own immediate interpretation. Every relevant theory is therefore an *abstract* theory, which takes into account only some of the data chosen by the observer and involving certain actors or certain acts—where it is of course understood that the pre-notions used by the actors themselves remain at some remove from the "scientific" representation given by the observer; the gap between the two can be bridged only by elaboration of the theory. But an abstract theory is not necessarily an arbitrary theory; science need not be a mirror image of the world. It differs from ordinary perception and intuition less by content than by approach. Classical economics, for example, is based on a small number of hypotheses about individual behavior, for which the authority is common sense. Choice and indifference are matters of experience, and the possibility of comparing two situations to determine which one is more satisfying is open to everyone. In general, however, we cannot state clearly our grounds for choice, indifference, or dissatisfaction. What distinguishes scientific hypotheses from commonsensical notions is that the former are explicit and few in number, and their mutual implications are clearly spelled out. Every theory is based on a selection of data and on the construction of hypotheses. This construction takes the form of an attempt to give answers to questions which step by step are made more relevant to the problems at hand. Indeed, relevance is not established by fiat. We may infer the relevance of a theory from its applications to a range of problems. Ultimately, these may be quite different from the problems considered during the initial stages of theory construction; as construction of the theory proceeds, it becomes possible to formulate problems in terms more appropriate to the initial situation than was possible at the outset.

Thus relevance is inseparable from verification. Hence the conditions under which a theory is verified, or at least verifiable, must be spelled out in detail. For Parsons, the criteria of scientific thought are everywhere the same, independent of the particular object of our attention. The celebrated distinction between *Naturwissenschaft* and *Geisteswissenschaft* is entirely relative. But the positivist, for whom knowledge is limited to logical-experimental truths, beyond which one assertion is as insignificant and uninteresting as another, runs up against an impasse. Can the sociologist lump together the ravings of a madman, the moral and religious beliefs of a man in the street, and his own assertions—which he presumes to couch in scientific guise, even if at times he is incapable of verifying them? Positivist science itself does not always come up to the standards set by the logical-experimental norm; rigor varies from one case to the next. Not only are some sciences "harder" than others, but even within a supposedly "hard" science there are relatively solid nuggets joined together by a connective tissue in some cases rather insubstantial.

The positivist tradition has popularized the model of mathematical physics, but an alternative model may be proposed. In attempting to characterize his role, or rather his personality, as a theorist, Parsons wrote:

> [Some have held that I am] primarily a talented and "stimulat-ing" essayist, writing on a variety of topics but without any genuine continuity or solidity of any kind—one might suggest an "esoterically academic" kind of journalist. [Others attribute] to me a kind of schizophrenic dual professional personality—on the one hand this kind of journalism, on the other hand a wholly unrealis-tic abstract kind of formalized theorizing, with the strong implica-tion if not assertion that the two personalities had nothing sub-stantive to do with each other. [1970a, pp. 867–68]

Defending himself a little later on against the criticism of George Homans, who charges Parsons with having built an enormous but empty and superfluous conceptual scheme, Parsons characterizes himself—not unsurprisingly for those who reproach him for his taste for formalization and would-be deductive theorizing—as "a compe-tent common-law appellate judge."

In a well-known essay, Lon L. Fuller[1] suggested a definition of the common law of interest to us precisely because Parsons makes explicit reference to Fuller's article and its influence on him in the essay cited above. What gives the judge his preeminent position in the common-law system is that common law is directly associated with the "process of resolving conflicts, which should be treated as a source of justice distinct from law, contract, and custom." Unlike continental European legal systems, the common law does not flow exclusively from the will of the lawmaker; in the commonly accepted interpreta-tion it is seen in part as "judge-made law." In consequence, it does not claim to be the embodiment of a rigorous deductive system in the manner of the Napoleonic and similar codes. The fabric of the com-mon law is richer but less tightly knit. It is also worthy of note that common-law procedure is resorted to in order to "resolve disputes that are *actually* brought to the attention of the judge. Common law does not lay down in advance rules for settling litigation but waits until cases have been brought before the tribunal for judgment." Finally, the common law prescribes a set procedure for the review of every case by a hierarchy of judicial bodies.

This comparison of the judge and the sociologist is in many ways surprising: unlike the judge, the sociologist cannot invoke the power of the state to enforce his judgments. But the appellate judge is not satisfied merely to issue a final decision; he does so in the name of a doctrine—in Fuller's words, "The judge gives the grounds for his decision." This is based on a coherent, or at least a compatible, set of assertions; the way certain cases were resolved by the judge in question or by his predecessors usefully illuminates and helps to decide similar cases. The common law is a way of resolving conflicts that "incorporates, consolidates, and derives law from judicial decisions." The common law and its underlying doctrine are inseparable from the process whereby the judge moves back and forth between "cases" and "principles." This process, moreover, is not circular but rather plays a part in enriching and elaborating legal doctrine.

Parsons, therefore, had every reason to reject the views imputed to him as to the nature of sociological theory. George Homans forcefully contrasted his own views on the nature of theory with those of Parsons:

> From my reading in the history and philosophy of science, I felt sure that a theory was a set of propositions, each stating a relationship between properties of nature. . . . The propositions were contingent in the sense that their truth did not follow automatically from postulates assumed *a priori,* as did the truth of the theorems of geometry. . . . A lower-order proposition in the theory represented an empirical finding. It could be deduced from higher-order ones under specified given conditions, and the deduction might make use of the rules of logic and mathematics. When the lower-order proposition was so deduced, it was said to be explained, so that a theory was also an explanation. From the higher-order propositions, under different givens, a number of other lower-order propositions could likewise be derived. . . . At the top of any theory stood one or more propositions of the highest order, in the sense that for the time being no proposition of still greater scope was known from which they could in turn be derived. . . . In other words, the highest-order propositions were logically independent of one another.[2]

Homans placed great emphasis on the necessity of empirical verification: Parsons surely would not have demurred. As for Homans's assertion that at the highest level of every theory are a number of mutually independent assertions, Parsons made just two points. First, he emphasized the advantage of using as few principles as possible. Second, he stressed the logical fecundity of the principles, and hence the advantage of drawing from each principle all its implications and of verifying the degree of independence of one principle from another. But this is all he says, and as far as I can see there is nothing in these two assertions to warrant the imputation to Parsons of the unrealizable ambition to deduce all the assertions of theory from a single principle.

Here, however, is the reproach leveled against him by Homans:

> Parsons . . . seemed to think that both the process of reasoning in a completed theory and the process by which that theory was arrived at worked in the same downward direction. He started with very general considerations and hoped to work downward to empirical findings. . . . Downward was the direction in which he thought the construction of a theory proceeded.

Parsons answers him thus:

> I do regard [the hypothetico-deductive method] as a legitimate goal for a course of development of theory, but to say that anything short of it is not theory at all is another matter. [1970a, p. 868]

Yet between theoretical knowledge on the one hand, and logical formalization and experimental verification on the other, the interconnections are many and complex; to weaken these ties is to risk sapping the sinew and rigor of theory.

The risk is increased to the extent that "theory" must refer to one or more distinct levels of representation and hence increases in ambiguity as the number of levels increases: the degree of rigor that may reasonably be required varies from level to level. Some theories give rather broad license to metaphor and imagery. Elsewhere, theorists have been successful in using the logical-experimental method to isolate quite specific relations. Even theories that meet the requirements of logical-experimental verification exhibit varying degrees of generality. Some are applicable to a small number of very special phenomena, while others claim applicability to broad areas of experience. In some cases, judicious generalization makes it possible to establish links between diverse theories and consequently to subsume a broad range of experience under a small number of general principles. In other cases, however, it may seem impossible to reconcile two theories, even though both appear to give good accounts of certain phenomena in their respective domains.

There is reason to wonder whether the word "theory" is perhaps too ambitious and ought to be replaced by "paradigm," a term recently made popular by the success of Thomas Kuhn's book.[3] What is more, Parsons has also referred to paradigms—though well before Kuhn and in a different sense: the interaction paradigm, for example, which is central to his theory, together with the paradigm of the four functions—A, G, I, and L—or the well-known "pattern variables," which are also characterized on occasion as paradigms. Associated with these, as it were, central paradigms are less sweeping paradigms relating to deviance, social control, socialization, professional authority, and medical practice. In every Parsonian paradigm we find the same characteristic approach: the illustrative example, the image, the model, the generalizing representation. Furthermore, though Parsons's paradigms differ in scope and content, they are not independent. It is perfectly clear, for instance, that the paradigms of medical practice, professional authority, and control of deviance constitute a cluster of closely related questions. Doctor, therapist, teacher, and parent all exercise authority in one form or another, among which a wealth of analogies and perhaps even identities are readily apparent.

Kuhn, for his part, places the paradigm at the center of what he calls "normal science," that is, "research firmly based upon one or more past scientific achievements, achievements that some particular scientific community acknowledges for a time as supplying the foundation for its further practice." Thus a paradigm is a conception predominant in a a particular area of science at a particular time. The question then arises whether the scientific marketplace tends naturally to be monopolized at any given moment by one particular paradigm or, on the contrary, whether no one paradigm ever prevails absolutely. Whatever the answer may be in general, Kuhn makes clear that, as for the major paradigms of science, given to us by history, "their success was sufficiently unprecedented to attract an enduring group of adherents away from competing modes of scientific activity. Simultaneously, it [the paradigm] was sufficiently open-ended to leave all sorts of problems for the redefined group of practitioners to resolve." A paradigm, therefore, would appear to be a novel and highly adaptable scheme that can be used to guide the practitioners of "normal science" on hitherto unexplored terrain. Kuhn, however, attributes to this model or pattern, which is accepted by a group of scientists, a generative capacity whereby, through replication of examples, it becomes possible to generalize the paradigm. Thus, "in grammar, for example, 'amo, amas, amat' is a paradigm, because it displays the pattern to be used in conjugating a large number of other Latin verbs, e.g., in producing 'laudo, laudas, laudat.'" This point takes us straight back to Parsons and his notion of the decision-making process engaged in by a judge under the common-law system: "A paradigm," says Kuhn, "is an object for further articulation and specification under new or more stringent conditions."

In comparing theory, even when renamed "paradigm," with judicial decision, as Parsons does—and, incidentally, as Kuhn also does—one is taking a considerable risk. The danger is that we will be led astray by the force of the imagery, by arbitrary comparisons, and by excessive generalization, and end up doing what Lévi-Strauss has referred to as "intellectual *bricolage*" [roughly "tinkering," though Lévi-Strauss's English translator considers the word elusive enough to leave it in French, and we shall follow his lead here—trans.] based on metonymy and metaphor. Listen to what Lévi-Strauss has to say about such "intellectual *bricolage*":[4] "The *bricoleur* is still someone who works with his hands and uses devious means compared to those of a skilled craftsman." What is characteristic of *bricolage* is that it sometimes results in ingenious constructions but, unlike the work of the engineer, is never the result of deliberately and rigorously defined operations. "The *bricoleur* is adept at performing a large number of diverse tasks . . . with 'whatever is at hand.'" He is thus never the master of his materials, whereas the engineer makes use "of raw materials and tools *conceived and procured* for the purpose of his project."[5]

Now the appellate judge, too, is someone whose job it is to reexamine cases that have already been dealt with by others before being brought to his attention. He must choose between lines of argument pleaded beforehand. The characteristic approach of both the judge and the theorist in working out an interpretation and arriving at a decision consists in establishing a paradigm through generative generalizations, beginning with the resolution of special cases belonging to the same family of problems, or syntagmatic series, as the case at hand. In what respect does this procedure differ from that used by the *bricoleur?* In essence, the *bricoleur* relies on metaphors and metonymies and remains "half-way between percepts and concepts." The ambiguity of metaphor makes it possible to compare heterogeneous elements and domains, as well as to reduce an overwhelmingly abundant and complex set of qualitative attributes to a single one of its aspects. Such a reduction is readily apparent in the statement, "The Indian potlatch is *like* the American custom of exchanging Christmas cards," or "capitalism is *no more than* the logic of profit and exploitation." When we say such things, we are behaving like Mr. Wemmick in Dickens's *Great Expectations,* who built himself a suburban "castle" with its miniature drawbridge, its cannon firing at nine o'clock, and its "bed of salad and cucumbers, thanks to which its occupants could withstand a siege if necessary."

But everyone—including Mr. Wemmick—is perfectly aware that the villa is not a *real* castle. Unfortunately for him, by holding fast to this chimera, through which [according to Lévi-Strauss—trans.] he establishes "paradigmatic relations between two equally unreal syntagmatic chains," Mr. Wemmick runs the risk of losing twice over, since "the castle never existed, and the villa has been sacrificed."

If the theorist is concerned to avoid a similar fate, he cannot be satisfied with saying, "How remarkable! The role of the doctor resembles the role of the father! Quite curious!" He must spell out the ways in which the comparison makes sense (and, conversely, the ways in which it does not); and once he has established the limits of the comparison, he must look for ways to define its content, for concepts to control its meaning. Analysis and comparison of different social roles may be carried out with reference to quite general dimensions of action, such as the competence of the actor, the nature of his commitment, and the character of his orientation, whether self-regarding or non-self-regarding. What enables the theorist to avoid the pitfalls associated with *"bricolage,"* therefore, is the rigor with which equivalences are defined. Emphasizing the rigor of the methods that distinguish scientific from associative thought, however, is not equivalent to asserting that the two are radically different. Nor does such an emphasis imply a belief that scientific thought starts from absolute ignorance and reflects omnipotence of Mind. As Lévi-Strauss puts it, "The scientist never carries on a dialogue with nature pure and simple, but rather with a particular relationship between nature and culture definable in terms of his particular period, civilization, and by the material means at his disposal." If science *constructs* experience, it does not *create* it—any more than the appellate judge invents the cases submitted to him for review.

To return to the conception that Parsons is defending, we may say that scientific knowledge is possible whenever the observer can manage to substitute his point of view for that of the actor through a series of decentering maneuvers. Verification, which brings into play a broad range of diverse techniques, may be defined as a systematic effort to establish distance between the observer and the actor and to question the observer's presuppositions. Thus, to ask whether scientific knowledge of social facts is possible is to ask under what conditions we can maintain an attitude of understanding and detachment toward others. We must understand the other person, and only by understanding him can we understand ourselves; we must also be capable of taking a detached stance if we mean to be "objective" about our fellowman. The scientific attitude is based on a set of rules and procedures that simultaneously determine our relation to ourselves and to the social object. The "observer equation" is especially hard to formulate when the observer is a sociologist, owing to the myriad interactions between ego and alter. [The terminology is Parsons's own: "ego" is "the actor who is taken as a point of reference himself," "alter" is "any given other individual actor" (1951a, p. 4)—trans.] In general, however, to know is to seek to establish control over the distance between ourselves and the object, whatever it may be.

Now, this formulation is quite similar to the one used by Parsons in defining "social relation." His analyses of double contingency and of the mutual dependence of ego and alter also raise, though in perfectly general terms, the problem of distance and its control. To understand the meaning of this we must go back to the origins of Parsons's work, in which a revolt against behaviorism was inextricably intertwined with a revolt against positivism on the methodological level. By behaviorism I do not mean, in this connection, a particular school of psychology, but the general outlook that dominated the United States in the 1920s, an outlook that denied any kind of validity to the actor's point of view. The actor was said to be conditioned by learning and by his environment. In this respect, according to Parsons, behaviorism was one of the two variants of positivism, where the other variant reduced human action to a set of inherited traits. In both cases consciousness was merely an illusion, just as knowledge was merely a reflection.

From the outset Parsons set himself resolutely against both of these views. The word "action," which he flaunted in the title of his first work, was launched as a battle cry against positivism. The discovery of the autonomy of the subject—that is, the conviction that the intentions and motives of the actor must be taken into account—was seen in two perspectives, associated with an inquiry into economic action on the one hand, and into the nature of collective preferences on the other. It was disappointment with the utilitarianism of both the English classical economists and the Spencerian evolutionary theorists that led Parsons to look in the direction of hypothetical sociology—which he was to broaden step-by-step into a general theory of action—for the framework within which individual initiative emerged. However inadequate the utilitarian model, its virtue was that it focused attention on the importance of individual choice. In utilitarian theory the actor has a place in an overarching process, a process which, though it transcends him, makes sense only in relation to him.

In no case is the sociologist justified in neglecting the point of view of the actor: this is the citadel within which Parsons established his individualism. But his was an individualism of a rather special kind, since he consistently maintained that the actors are interdependent, that there is a double contingency of ego and alter. Let me begin by recalling Jean Piaget's distinction between three types of sociological explanation: atomistic individualism, totalitarian realism, and relativistic interactionism.[6] Parsons, by his insistence on the importance of "understanding" (which makes use of subjective categories like ends, means, expectations, and intentions, though without claiming to grasp idiosyncratic—biographical, as it were—characteristics of the individual), marked his distance from totalitarian realism, against which he warned in his very first book. At this point it behooves us to take a glance at the description of the totalitarian realist approach given by Piaget, who regards the work of Durkheim as embodying its most complete expression. "Applying with the utmost rigor the principle of Auguste Comte, according to whom sociology must not explain the whole by the parts, but rather the other way round, Durkheim brought to light the fact that individual thoughts are fashioned by the entire body social in both its past and present aspects. But the fact that a collective whole is not identical to the sum of the individual parts of which it is composed does not imply that the whole as such is unanalyzable." Slightly later, Piaget gives a very clear definition of totalitarian realism: "The whole is an entity which, by imposing constraints, modifies the individuals and therefore remains heterogeneous to individual consciousnesses as they would be independent of their socialization."

Parsons would no doubt reject Piaget's interpretation of Durkheimian sociology, which, following Léon Brunschvicg, Piaget regards essentially as a "dogmatic theory of the *conscience collective*." More important, however, Parsons would condemn any form of "sociologism" or "reification" of society regarded as a closed and self-subsistent totality, which is supposed to impose constraints on individual behavior through transcendent norms and values. Ever since 1937 when *The Structure of Social Action* was published, Parsonian analysis has been directed against such a realist interpretation of constraint. To be effective, norms and values must be internalized. But the argument for internalization of norms and values that Parsons attributes to the Durkheim of *L'éducation morale* is not without its obscure points and traps for the unwary. Is the Durkheimian individual merely the carrier of the *conscience collective*, which, not being satisfied with the external sanctions of custom and law, manipulates him from within through the repressive agencies of the superego? At present, the most radical version of totalitarian realism is no longer to be found in the work of Durkheim or his followers, but rather in the work of sociologists who describe themselves as "critical." Here are two passages from the writings of Herbert Marcuse treating the status of the individual in "advanced industrial society." This society, which is explicitly reduced to "the technical apparatus of production and distribution . . . functions . . . as a system which determines *a priori* the product of the apparatus as well as the operations of servicing and extending it." "Mass production and mass distribution claim the *entire* individual. . . . The result is not adjustment but *mimesis:* an immediate identification of the individual with *his* society and, through it, with the society as a whole."[7] With Parsons things stand quite differently: norms are not dictates of some collective conscience controlled by the system of domination but rather are open to interpretation, if not outright challenge. They serve only as general guidelines. Unlike the culturalists, Parsons does not maintain that individual behavior is strictly determined by culture and the system of values. Unlike the critical sociologists, he does not imagine the existence of an evil genius whose function is to reproduce the existing system of domination by deceiving individuals about their own interests, using lies and fetishes. The relation between norms and values is very complex; controversial actions acquire legitimacy through the process by which this relation is established, whereby norms are specified and values modulated in ways that take account of the reservations and objections of the actors. The importance attributed by Parsons to the socialization process and the emphasis he places on deviance and its relations to social change indicate that he does not believe that the pattern of social evolution is unalterable and, further, that he views the intervention of individuals as something other than a mistake or an accident. Action would make no sense—there would be no action at all—if there were no actors, with their initiatives and their expectations, to which others may respond so as to confirm or reject the initial orientation. Understanding lies not merely in the relationship of the sociologist to the actor. We see understanding implicit in the spectrum of expectations that each actor forms of himself and the other actors in the system, the adequacy of which will vary from individual to individual. Social action is simply maneuvering by the actors, and such maneuvering would be impossible if they had no understanding of one another and of their various motives and intentions. Thus the actor, his partners, and the observer all participate in the process of understanding. The conditions of their participation vary from case to case, but they are qualitatively similar and always in correspondence with one another.

Society, though not a thing, may very well be an object. While it makes no sense to treat it as a closed totality, it does make sense to treat it as a fairly strict order, an attempt to achieve compatibility (rather than totalization) among several partial orders. The weakness of what Piaget calls "atomistic individualism" is the failure to recognize the fact of interdependence—to which Parsons affords full recognition. From the fact that the action process is a set of expectations, it does not follow that any given actor can entertain any conceivable expectation or that an actor will adequately foresee how others will respond to his initiatives. For both the observer and the actor the degree of regularity and predictability of expectations may vary. Furthermore, there may be significant differences between the predictions made by the actor and those made by the observer. The Parsonian individual is an actor, that is, he does not make his choices at random. These choices are governed by logical considerations, which may vary from case to case; the basis of the effective logic is to be sought in the interaction process itself, that is, in the range of conditions that enable the actor to obtain the outcome he prefers. If the actor paid no heed to any of the constraints imposed by interaction (which are spelled out in the theory of the four functions), he would have no prospect of attaining his goal. The Parsonian theory of action is functionalist to the extent—and only to the extent—that it seeks to establish a relation between the actor and his situation. In no way does it maintain that every society "functions" solely as a strictly integrated totality; such an assertion belongs rather to totalitarian realism. Parsons contends only that expectations and their realization depend on constraints defined by the order within which the actors coexist.

The expression "institutionalized individualism" sums up and reconciles the two aspects of Parsons's inspiration, the one emphasizing the objectivity of the social order, the other the activity of individuals. The phrase is one that Parsons himself uses; since it correctly represents the course his thinking has followed, it may be worthwhile to make a few further comments on it at this point in order to eliminate any possible ambiguity. Plainly, the phrase evokes the American institutional economists of the twenties to whose influence Parsons was exposed during his years as an undergraduate at Amherst. But Parsons's position is distinct from that of the institutionalists on several important points. He does not look upon institutions as isolated complementary data that the economist may incorporate into his analysis without regard to their interrelations. For Parsons, institutions are not aggregates but rather systems, in two ways: first, they occur in combination with one another in the context of certain problems, finite in number, which the functioning of any society raises for its members; and, second, they are differentiated internally in response to imperatives consistent with those that hold sway within the society of which they are parts or modalities. When Parsons invokes institutions, he differs from the empiricists for whom action is merely a set of ways of being or doing. The theory of choice and the "pattern variables" that condition choice, along with the theory of functions, that is, of the constraints imposed on the actors by their interaction, make it possible to study institutions in an analytical and comparative manner.

The Parsonian individual is therefore not a distinct consciousness who is supposed to make his choices on the basis of preferences independent of the preferences of his partners. He moves within an "action space," wherein he finds both support for his action and impediments to it—resources and constraints. Stated as generally as possible, institutionalized individualism is simply this: an actor who chooses among limited resources according to the various modalities of his coexistence with others. The compatibility of the choices and the coexistence of the actors constitute the central problem of the theory of action. Compatibility is all the more difficult to obtain because the constraints the actor must accept are radically heterogeneous. The logic of adaptation is different from the logic of cooperation, even if both are to be found in the division of labor, and even if both can in fact be reconciled within the value system that Parsons calls "instrumental activism," which he finds at work in industrial societies. Individual initiative thus gives rise to problems of two kinds, problems of arbitration and problems of combination. From this standpoint the process of legitimation is more important than the highly hypothetical state of legitimacy, which conservative thought improperly confounds with the social order.

Parsons's institutionalized individualism thus comes under the head of what Piaget calls relativistic interactionism. The major difficulty in this approach involves the way in which the interdependence of the actors is established and represented. This interdependence is clearly symbolic in nature, as Parsons has consistently maintained ever since *The Structure of Social Action*. It is true that the elucidation of the relation between the actor, the resources he has at hand, and the constraints imposed upon him confronts the human mind with the most taxing of all the challenges it has to face. But in the fight with the Angel, there is neither victor nor vanquished.

What Parsons is rejecting in Spencer's work is not the contention that mankind is changing, or even that it is progressing. It is rather the idea that change and progress are the necessary outcome of the calculations made over time by a collection of individuals motivated solely by a desire to seek their clearly understood interests.

Spencer was an extreme individualist. But his extremism was only the exaggeration of a deep-rooted belief that, stated roughly, at least in the prominent economic phase of social life, we have been blest with an automatic, self-regulating mechanism which operated so that the pursuit by each individual of his own self-interest and private ends would result in the greatest possible satisfaction of the wants of all. [1937, p. 4]

Parsons's mistrust of "generalities" regarding the origin and future of human societies is based on a conception of the role and limitations of theory. Sociological theory is not a philosophy of history in the vein of evolutionism or historicism. Nor is it merely a piling up of "facts." For the empiricist the mind is merely a passive instrument, which records a "reality" that is "out there." More than that, empiricism simply does not explain how the discrete impressions that the mind takes from experience are organized into a coherent, continuous whole—not merely an aggregate, but a *system*. Parsons, who rejected the empiricist outlook from the start, took as his point of departure the idea of the physiologist L. J. Henderson, who believed that "a fact is an empirically verifiable statement about phenomena in terms of a conceptual scheme."[2]

No observation would ever be made if the observer did not bring to the phenomena under study his "characteristic interests." The only way to verify any given hypothesis is to deduce from it, via an experimental procedure, a series of consequences that can be fitted into an overarching "frame of reference" that incorporates and transcends the hypothesis in question. Thus it is clear that the very act of observation involves not only hypotheses, deductions, and other formal manipulations made by the scientist but also his "characteristic interests," so that the notion of a detached individual observer, a purely passive mind, is scarcely compatible with what is generally taken for granted as the essence of scientific method.

Parsons goes beyond the contention that theory is not a mere copy of "reality" and is an "independent variable in the development of science," maintaining as well that "the body of theory in a given field at a given time constitutes to a greater or less degree an integrated 'system.' . . . Another way of putting this is to say that any system of theory has a determinate logical structure" [1937, p. 7].

Chapter One

The Starting Point

In 1937 Talcott Parsons published *The Structure of S Action.*[1] It was inevitable that the American reader of the late thi would find this a surprising work. Parsons emphasized the urgent r for "theoretical" inquiry. He embarked upon a discussion of a gr of European authors, maintaining that their quite disparate work c verged on a small number of consistent assertions.

In this first chapter we shall give an account of the course r Parsons's thinking took from his 1937 effort to the two works of maturity, *The Social System* [1951a] and *Toward a General Theory Action* [1951b]. The first few sections of this chapter are devoted *The Structure of Social Action.* Beginning with the section entitled "T Notion of System," we enter into an examination of Parsonian dc trine in its earliest, so-called structural-functionalist form.

Theory: What It Is and What It Is Not

The then-prevalent empiricism of the social sciences in America wa not the only target of *The Structure of Social Action.* Parsons set himself the task of bringing to light the social philosophy that was implicit in the work of sociologists of the day. This was the meaning of the famous question raised on the very first page of *The Structure of Social Action:* "Who killed Herbert Spencer?" That meaning is further spelled out in the interpretation that Parsons gives of Spencer's work and its influence. "[Spencer] believed that man stood near the culminating point of a long linear process extending back unbroken, without essential changes of direction, to the dawn of primitive man. Moreover, [he] believed that this culminating point was being approached in the industrial society of modern Western Europe. He and those who thought like him were confident that evolution would carry this process on almost indefinitely in the same direction cumulatively" [1937, pp. 3–4].

The expression "logical structure" basically implies the idea of heuristic power. "A scientifically unimportant discovery is one which, however true and however interesting for other reasons, has no consequences for a system of theory with which scientists in that field are concerned." Conversely, even the most trivial discovery may have truly revolutionary importance if its logical consequences have a decisive influence on the structure of theory. It may even happen that such a discovery has consequences well beyond the bounds of the field in which it was made. An observation that at first seems insignificant may lead to very important results in remote areas. Scientific revolutions, moreover, are not merely the result of logical attrition. New facts at first treated as superfluous may prove not to fit the Procrustean bed of the old theory. Reflection is stimulated not by the fact but by the paradox resulting from the juxtaposition of the fact with more important and better established theoretical statements. This asymmetry obliges us to examine the nature of the relation among the various propositions that constitute a body of theory. It then emerges that a theory is not merely a collection of statements, a compendium. It is a system equipped with a logical structure. Thus, "any substantive change in the statement of one important proposition of the system has logical consequences for the statement of the others. Another way of putting this is to say that any system of theory has a determinate logical structure" [1937, p. 7].

In any "theory," certain distinct types of intellectual operation are combined: deduction of consequences, generalization of principles, exploration of a certain "field" of related problems. Though distinct, these operations are related; do they constitute a hierarchy—in the sense that deduction is superior to the other two?

That such a hierarchy does exist is implicit in the discussion of "logical closure," toward which every system of theory is supposed to lead. But closure does not imply that a strict chain of consequences proceeds from a unique principle: "The general propositions which constitute a body of theory . . . are not, of course, deducible from any one—that would confine theory to one proposition" [1937, p. 7]. But a proposition associated with one area, A, which makes sense in its own sphere, may also make sense in another area, B. In that case we say that A and B belong to the same "system of theory." A "theory," therefore, is a collection of propositions concerning related but differentiated domains, among which the theory establishes a series of equivalences and differences with increasing precision.

Once the plurality of principles and the heterogeneity of sectors have been accepted, we must also recognize that the "tendency to closure" of a theoretical system is intrinsically limited by the growth and branching out of knowledge. Subjectively, the scientist encounters this limitation when he runs up against "residual categories," which, given a particular state of knowledge, indicate the resistence of certain "stubborn facts" to subsumption under the prevailing conceptual schemes. For any theory, certain facts that are scientifically valid will always remain unconnected with other facts and unrelated in any definable way to the body of theory itself. Though they may not contradict the theory, they refuse to enter into the framework that it lays down. If the demand for integration or closure were pushed to the limit, it would be necessary to say that propositions concerning such facts are not "scientific" in the strict sense. More reasonably, one might say merely that certain inconsistencies have emerged which, though they may not necessarily refute the dominant "theory," do however indicate the need for a reorientation of theoretical interests.

The relation between the body of theory and what we shall call "paradoxical facts" is expressed well by the following metaphor. These "unintegrated bits," Parsons says, "may be thought of as a 'spot' in the vast encircling darkness, brightly illuminated as by a searchlight" [1937, p. 16]. The same metaphor is more immediately comprehensible in its application to the relation between theory and that which is unknown—or dimly known. "Every system, including both its theoretical propositions and its main relevant empirical insights, may be visualized as an illuminated spot enveloped by darkness." But the image becomes far more striking when used to illuminate the relation between the paradoxical facts and an outworn "theory" that is itself slipping into the shadows. Here the theory lies in darkness and the paradoxical facts glow brightly. The critical area in which advances in knowledge are most likely to occur is the shifting fringe between the "residual categories" and the constituted theory. Indeed, "the surest symptom of impending change in a theoretical system is increasingly general interest in such residual categories" [1937, p. 18].

"The only theoretically significant statements that can be made [concerning paradoxical facts] are negative statements—they are *not* so and so" [1937, p. 19]. The residual categories may even take the form "neither . . . nor . . . ," simultaneously excluding two contradictory attributes. Parsons remarks that this is the case with Pareto's category of the nonlogical, which applies to actions not classifiable either as logico-experimental or illogical in the sense of being erroneous, insane, or absurd. Knowledge, however, does not advance by setting the residual categories apart in such a way as to restrict statements related to them to negation only, a procedure that would simply eliminate assigning attributes of any kind and enshrine the principle of noncontradiction. Once residual categories have been brought to light, they, too, display an order or structure, as Pareto's discussion of the nonlogical makes clear.

Countervailing the tendency to closure is the tendency to incorporate new facts. Theoretical systems are neither wholly open nor wholly closed, since paradoxical facts inevitably appear on their peripheries. They may be said to be "semi-open." Accordingly, theoretical systems partake of positive science on the one hand and of philosophy on the other. All we need do is make sure that we are aware when we are speaking as scientists, making statements based on observation and justifiable in accordance with logico-experimental canons, and when we are speaking as philosophers, attempting "to achieve a rational cognitive understanding of human experience by methods other than those of empirical science" [1937, p. 21].

Philosophy enters into the picture not only as a reminder that man has a past and a future but also in an analytic and critical role with regard to existing knowledge. The function of philosophy, then, is to scrutinize both the methods of positive science and the object a given "theory" claims to explain. For the philosopher the first step is to examine the validity of various methods of observation and experimentation. He may also want to inquire into the nature of the object treated by the scientist. Next, he will look into the conditions under which objective knowledge is possible. Critical reflection of this kind, which is distinct from methodological evaluation, goes back to Kant. "Kant," Parsons observes, began by saying that "it is a fact that we have . . . valid knowledge [of the external world]. And only then he asked, How is this possible?" Suppose that we have an "action schema" said to be objectively well-founded: we may then proceed to inquire into the conditions under which its objective validity is possible.

Is Kant's argument applicable to the case of the theory of action? Parsons pushes the comparison between the situation of the natural sciences and the situation of the sciences of action as far as he can: "If it were not a fact [that a science of action existed] . . . the whole 'action' schema would have to be discarded from scientific use" [1937, p. 24, n. 2]. In other words, Parsons does not claim that his schema creates or constitutes sociology. He does not hold that the subject begins with himself. The sociologist may call upon existing knowledge of social facts; even if such knowledge does not meet all the requirements of positive science, it has a validity of its own. But is this knowledge "scientific," in the sense that Newtonian physics was scientific for

Kant? In Kant's argument, moreover, the objectivity of physical science is accepted apart from any metaphysical commitment; does objectivity of knowledge in the action schema depend on the assumption that a science of action already exists? Or on the assumption that the existence of a science of action without a social order is as impossible as the existence of a social order without a science of action?

The Hard Core of the Theory

What do we know about the social order? When the first economists set about building their discipline, they sought to discover beneath the variety of the phenomena whose theory they hoped to elaborate a few simple and characteristic relations, relations that would make good sense to the actors and that could be combined to explain aggregate and complex phenomena, such as rents, wages, and profits. Parsons proposed to do the same thing for society.

It is possible to set forth a certain limited number of propositions concerning social action, quite abstract and quite unobjectionable at the outset, but justifiable only in the light of the applications to which they give rise. To begin with, we should mention that, as with the phenomena in general, the analysis of social action must be carried as far as possible, until we have achieved a meaningful theoretical scheme of the greatest possible simplicity. With this precept in mind, Parsons arrived at what he called the "unit act" [1937, p. 43], which can be used to explain the most complex phenomena. An act is a complex entity. At the very least it includes an agent, an "actor." Second, it "must have an 'end,' a future state of affairs toward which the process of action is oriented." Third, "it must be initiated in a 'situation' of which the trends of development differ in one or more important respects from the state of affairs toward which the action is oriented, the end." Thus, it is possible to distinguish the factors or constraints over which the actor has no control from those over which he has. The former we shall, with Parsons, call "conditions" of action; the latter, "means." Finally,

> there is inherent in the conception of this unit [of action] . . . a certain mode of relationship between these elements.
> That is, in the choice of alternative means to an end . . . there is a normative orientation of action. . . . The means employed cannot, in general, be conceived either as chosen at random or as dependent exclusively on the conditions of action, but must in some sense be subject to the influence of an independent, determinate selective factor, a knowledge of which is necessary to the understanding of the concrete course of action. [1937, p. 43]

Action, then, presupposes an actor or agent, a "situation" partially under the actor's control, and a combination of ends and means, which the actor is free to choose, subject to certain normative criteria. This definition has several important implications. First, action is a process. The actor may choose to enter into it or not, and, once begun, he may or may not choose to continue on the same course until he reaches his goal. Thus action has in a certain sense a probabilistic dimension. Second, action may be successful or unsuccessful. There is always some possibility that the actor will be mistaken, not only because he may be poorly informed as to some of the "conditions" of his situation but also because he may not have correctly anticipated the responses of the other actors to his initiatives. Action may give rise to "unanticipated consequences." Action is subjective: it is the work of an actor. But this does not mean either that every act is a singular process, absolutely sui generis, or that the only way to understand the features of any particular process is from within, from the actor's own point of view. When Parsons emphasizes the subjective dimension of action, he means merely that the motives of the actors must be taken into account. "The facts of action are . . . facts of the external world—in this sense, objective facts." But these objective facts include the attitudes and motives of the persons whose actions are under study [1937, p. 46]. Attitudes and motives are not, of course, external to the actor; but from the point of view of the observer they are, or should be, external. On the other hand, it would be impossible for the observer to make sense of the actor's behavior without thinking of it as a system in which ends or anticipations, conditions, and means—whether real, perceived, or imaginary—coexisted in tension with one another. To hold that action has an objective aspect is not to argue, as the behaviorists do, that the actor is a thing—or, in the extreme case, that there is no such thing as an actor; it means simply that the observer can—under certain conditions to be established by critical examination—arrive at a satisfactory understanding of the situation.

Parsons does not analyze the nature of the statements he makes in the second chapter of *The Structure of Social Action*, summarized above, but he does stress the importance of the distinction between using them "concretely" and using them "analytically" [1937, pp. 47–49]. A look at the problems involved in using the notion of an "end" will throw some light on the difference. "By the concrete end is meant the total anticipated future state of affairs. . . . Similarly, concrete means are those things in the situation over which [the actor] has an appreciable degree of control." Parsons observes, "The function of this concrete use of the action schema is primarily descriptive." To move to the level of analysis and explanation, attention must shift from the resources at hand and the goals desired to focus on the relation between what is anticipated and what actually occurs. This leads to the definition of what Parsons calls "an end in the analytical sense": "an end in the analytical sense must be defined as the *difference* between the anticipated future state of affairs and that which it could have been predicted would ensue from the initial situation *without the agency of the actor* having intervened." For the observer, the end is the difference or disparity between the anticipated state of affairs and the actual outcome, insofar as that difference may be imputed to the action taken by the actor.

Theory as a Point of Convergence

The difference between the end, or goal, of action and the initial state of affairs is embodied in the norm, and the time that must elapse between initiative and outcome is embodied in the "task." Norm and task are both subdivided into distinct stages, related to one another in that they all anticipate the same outcome. From the point of view of the person performing the "task," it consists of a series of real or potential actions, these bearing a clear relation to one another and making sense in some overall context. From the point of view of the observer, looking at how the task is performed and how the situation evolves, comparison of the expected and the actual behavior of the actors leads to conclusions as to the way they normally view their goals. The science of action looks first at the norms that govern the behavior of the actors and constitute the "structure" or "anatomy" of society. For objective knowledge of society to be possible there must exist a minimum congruence between the normative order imposed on the actor and the phenomenal order whose unfolding is reconstructed by the observer.

The theory outlined above is not based solely on common sense. Like the presuppositions of economic theory, the basic elements of the theory are drawn from earlier inquiries into the nature of man and the social process, in which they were implicit. Historically, these sources are quite diverse, with some elements coming from specialized fields of research and others drawn from the common values of the cultural tradition. "Just like the schema of classical physics, [the action schema] is deeply rooted in the commonsense experience of everyday life, and it is of a range of such experience that may be regarded as universal to all human beings" [1937, p. 51]. Thus science is not obliged to reject common sense, much less to proceed in a diametrically opposed direction. The scientist is content to select certain aspects of experience from which he claims to be able to distill, by methodical analysis, certain simple and controllable components. Economists do this when they theorize about the behavior of *homo oeconomicus*. And long before the economists, a similar approach was taken by philosphers and scientists, whose methods involved "a selective emphasis on certain problems and certain ways of looking at human action" [1937, p. 52].

Men in general have a dim notion of what action is, as, for example, when they say, "*I am doing* something," or some similar locution such as we find in all languages. This dim notion is not interpreted by all men in the same way, however. The European mind, according to Parsons, harbors a prejudice in favor of "atomism." By this he means not only that the European emphasis on clarity and analytical distinctions leads to a preference for elementary units of analysis of the simplest possible kind, such as unit acts, but also, in a quite different vein, that there is a tendency to regard complex social groupings as mere aggregates of elementary units. Characteristic of the "atomist" approach is the "strong tendency to consider mainly the properties of conceptually isolated unit acts and to infer the properties of systems of action only by a process of 'direct' generalization from these." This "atomistic" tendency comes into conflict with an "organic"—or "holistic"—tendency, which Parsons defines as "the spiritual absorption of the individual in the social unit," whether this be the "noble city" of the ancient Greeks, the Imperial State of the Romans, or medieval Christendom under the leadership of "those two aspects of God, the Pope and the Emperor." Running counter to this Greco-Roman and catholic tradition, "the primary source of this individualistic cast of European thought lies in Christianity. In an ethical and religious sense Christianity has always been deeply individualistic" [1937, p. 53], particularly in the time of the primitive Church, and later with the Protestant Reformation.

We are now in a position to describe the movement of ideas whereby science came, at the turn of the century, to set forth a doctrine of social action, the brainchild, in Parsons's view, of Pareto, Durkheim, and Weber. "In fact, by the nineteenth century a subsystem (or, perhaps better, an interrelated group of several sub-subsystems) of the theory of action dominated Western European social thought. It was built essentially out of the kinds of units described but put together in a peculiar way which distinguishes it sharply from the emerging system" [1937, p. 51]. The first attempt to elaborate a theory of action came in the form of utilitarian rationalism.

However acute were the conflicts that, as the historians tell us, pitted the various schools of thought and tendencies with a rightful claim to this appellation against one another, it may be said that four features are characteristic of the utilitarian approach: "atomism, rationality, empiricism, randomness of ends" [1937, p. 60]. Here, atomism indicates that the individual actor is the central reference of the system of action. Rationality means that action is based on calculation, or, more precisely, on comparison, first, of the different objectives pursued by the actor with one another and, second, of the means at the actor's disposal with the ends he can hope to obtain through judicious employment of those means. "Action is rational in so far as it pursues ends possible within the conditions of the situation, and by the means which, among those available to the actor, are intrinsically best adapted to the end for reasons understandable and verifiable by positive empirical science" [1937, p. 58]. Thus the utilitarian concept of rationality is at once normative and hypothetical. A certain range of methods is laid down as rational, and the individual actor may choose among these methods, combining his material and symbolic resources with an eye to achieving his objectives. Taken in this sense, reason is viewed normatively and has nothing explicit to say about the order of ends. To the extent that the province of reason is taken to include norms of only one type—for example, those defining technical efficacy or economic efficiency—rationality has, without explicit recognition of the fact, been made subordinate to an end, namely the achievement of a goal—any goal—chosen by the actor. The utilitarian schema may, therefore, be characterized as "empiricist" in that it will not "legitimate" the actor's ends, treating them rather as given preconditions; the utilitarian is content to ascertain that the ends in question are present in the mind of the actor or observable in his behavior. Utilitarian theory takes ends to be not merely given in advance but also random and arbitrary. It may happen that I prefer apples to pears. But no possible connection exists between this preference and any other that I may have, such as for redheads over blondes and brunettes, and in no sense can I be asked to account for my preferences: there is no disputing taste, or color either, for that matter.

Can hypotheses of this kind be used to explain the "social order"? Two attempts to do so that may fairly be characterized as utilitarian have been made: neither explanation can be accepted as correct. One such attempt was that of Hobbes, who held that individuals are locked in a struggle to the death in competition for scarce goods, from which he concluded that the only way to put an end to the "war of all against all" is for individuals to relinquish their liberty in favor of a political authority. In contrast with Hobbes's pessimistic individualism stands the optimistic individualism of Locke. Locke was able to arrive at comforting conclusions only because he had rejected the assumption of scarcity, along with the Hobbesian psychology of the passions. If one assumes that there are enough natural resources to go round and that individuals spontaneously wish to do good to one another, then it is perfectly possible to effect a reconciliation of conflicting interests, especially with the light of reason as a guide. Unfortunately, Locke's assumptions, both regarding Nature and regarding the passions, are quite as arbitrary as those of Hobbes. Since their respective positions represent two extreme views concerning the relation of the actor to his environment (moderate abundance in Locke's case, stinginess of Nature in Hobbes's) and motivational psychology (motives are aggressive and hostile for Hobbes, peaceful and altruistic for Locke), it follows that neither the optimistic nor the pessimistic version of the utilitarian schema gives a satisfactory answer to the problem of the social order [1937, pp. 89–95].

Is it possible to eliminate the difficulties inherent in both versions by defining rationality not as a hypothetical relation between action and certain conventional rules but rather as an adaptive relation of the actor to his surroundings? What makes such a shift from utilitarianism toward positivism possible is the paramount importance of the cognitive elements in the utilitarian scheme. If to act rationally means simply that the actor must evaluate the means at his disposal in relation to the ends he has set for himself, then to act effectively the actor must have knowledge both of the environment from which he draws his resources and of his own needs and capacities. Utilitarianism thus leads to viewing the situation instrumentally and the actor naturalistically. From this point, to make the transition to positivism it suffices to make the claim that action is entirely determined by the conditions uder which it takes place, a claim that robs the distinction between conditions and means of its significance. It is then asserted that action is rational to the extent that it is adaptive. If the actor fails to adapt rationally, he is held to have made a mistake or to have ignored important factors; though the actor may be unaware of the shortcomings in his knowledge of the situation, the observer is able to explain where he went wrong. Thus the positivist schema leads to "[abandoning] the subjective categories of the schema of action in favor of objective processes which may be thought of as influencing action by acting upon the actor without his knowledge or awareness of what is 'really' happening" [1937, p. 66]. But this solution of the problem does not withstand scrutiny; indeed, "in so far as the conditions of the environment are decisive it does not matter what ends [the actors] may think they pursue; in fact, the course of history is determined by an impersonal process over which they have no control. It should be noted that in the shift the subjective category of ends disappears and with it the norm of rationality" [1937, p. 113]. The utilitarian schema leaves the status of the ultimate ends in suspense, treating them as strictly contingent givens. The positivists completed the demolition of the utilitarian edifice by taking the view that ends are merely the products of heredity and environment. The baby was thrown out with the bathwater.

Sociological inquiry arises out of a critical examination of utilitarianism. For the French reader, used to thinking of Comte, Saint-Simon, and the socialists as the "fathers" of sociology, this line of descent has commonly been hidden from view. But Parsons regards Marx himself as a utilitarian [1937, pp. 109–10, 489–95], albeit a utilitarian of a rather special kind, who, presumably following Malthus and Ricardo, took an interest in the "division of society into classes of employers and laborers."[3] Marx does in fact belong to the utilitarian family (since he sees the springs of action in the interests of actors), but he also saw that a man's interests need not coincide with his subjective preferences, being in large part determined by the relations of production characteristic of the economic system. "The system [which is] itself the resultant of the myriad of individual acts . . . creates for each acting individual a specific situation which compels him to act in certain ways if he is not to go contrary to his interest" [1937, p. 492]. On this view of the matter, society becomes a gigantic machine spewing out unanticipated consequences that work against the interests of those who sought to bring them about.

This pessimistic verson of the utilitarian tradition, which Parsons associates with Marx, has the advantage over the optimistic version of bringing to light the fact that the social order is something other than a spontaneous harmony of individual preferences. But utilitarianism runs into further serious difficulties beyond those laid bare by the penetrating insight of Malthus and Marx, who saw the contradiction between individuals seeking their self-interest (the capitalist his profit, or the libido its gratification) and the laws of development that govern the demographic or economic system. Taking a more radical tack, it may be asked whether the concept of interest as worked out within the utilitarian tradition is consistent. Are interests randomly distributed and arbitrary? Some economists claim to believe that such is the case, and this view found particular favor with the marginalists of the neoclassical school. Yet Alfred Marshall, beyond doubt one of the high priests of marginalist orthodoxy, was forced, in constructing his theory of demand, to use a notion on the borderline of economics, the idea of "character and activity." "The concrete description of what types of activities and character [Marshall] had in mind is to be found principally in his picture of 'free industry and enterprise,' with which they are intimately associated. They consist in two sets of virtues; on the one hand, energy, initiative, enterprise; on the other, rationality, frugality, industry, honorable dealing" [1937, p. 135]. No theory of demand in the long period can ignore these factors, which play a part in determining the level of expectations and needs of the economic agents.

The narrowness of the utilitarian view was thus apparent to the economists themselves, at least to the most perspicacious of them. Pareto was particularly aware of this difficulty. Unlike Marshall, however, he no longer treated the problem as a side issue but in its own right, attacking it head on. Indeed, his *Traité de sociologie generale* begins with the distinction between logical or logico-experimental action and nonlogical action [1937, pp. 185–96; Parsons is here quoting Pareto—trans.]: "Logical actions are, at least in their principal element, the result of a process of *reasoning;*[4] nonlogical actions proceed principally from a certain state of mind *(état psychique),* sentiment, the unconscious, etc." The precise status to be accorded this realm beyond logic is, to be sure, far from clear. Pareto further complicates Parsons's problem when he states in the next sentence that "it is the task of psychology to be concerned with this state of mind."[5] Sorokin uses this statement to justify a reductionist interpretation of Pareto.[6] In Sorokin's view the residual categories are taken to be sentiments or instincts. This interpretation is rejected by Parsons, who disentangles the residual category from the nonlogical, in which he finds "two main groups of structural elements, those capable of formulation in terms of nonsubjective systems, especially heredity and environment, on the one hand; the value complex on the other" [1937, p. 268].

Under the head of the nonlogical come certain phenomena that are strictly social, not being explicable in terms of "error," idiosyncratic departures from rational norms, physical or biological determinisms, instincts, or interests. This subset of the nonlogical category contains collective preferences and beliefs. In order to highlight the social dimension of the nonlogical, Parsons relied on Pareto's concept of an essentially social form of utility, not reducible to an aggregate of individual ophelimities. "The *ophelimity* of a collectivity does not exist, but we may in a rigorous fashion conceive the *utility* of a collectivity."[7] To put it another way, although economics can never understand society in the same terms as it understands the individual, but can see it only as a collection of individuals, sociology can understand society, if not in the same terms as an individual, at least as a unity. But, Parsons adds, it can do so only on condition that "instead of regarding social action as a pure aggregation of individual preferences, we are able to identify the value complexes associated with it."

Though Durkheim's work is usually described as belonging to the positivist tradition, it actually marks the collapse of that tradition. Durkheim's target was not only the hedonistic and utilitarian version of positivism, which he argued in his first book could not explain the process of social differentiation and the division of labor; he also attacked, particularly in *Suicide,* positivism's most radical and narrowly focused versions. Against both he wielded his idea of the *"conscience collective."* [Parsons (1937, p. 309, n. 3) observes that the French word *conscience* may be translated either "conscience" or "consciousness." To choose one or the other, he says, "is clearly indicative of an interpretive bias." So we shall here follow Parsons in leaving the term untranslated.—trans.] Most commentators, of course, have interpreted the *conscience collective* in positivist terms, as though it were a "thing" that exerted pressure on individual consciences with all the force of a material constraint. But just as Pareto's residues are not "instincts," Durkheim's notion of constraint must be distinguished from physical force.

The usual interpretation of Durkheim can bring forth many citations from his works in its defense, yet it neglects the most essential part of his work. In industrial societies an organic solidarity is slowly built up by the establishment of certain obligations between individuals, which are enforced in two ways. On the one hand, there are sanctions, which are imposed on delinquent individuals. Only a representative of the public authorities may administer these sanctions. "To say that if a man commits murder he will die (probably) in the electric chair is very different from saying that if he does not eat he will starve. For in the former case he will not die unless someone *puts* him to death—his death is not an automatic consequence of murder taken by itself" [1937, p. 379]. Parsons, basing himself on a passage in *L'éducation morale,* takes this distinction between natural sanctions and social sanctions to be central to Durkheim's thought. On the other hand, penalties and punishments to be administered to deviants by the authorities are not the only basis of the social order. A complex, "individualistic" (in Durkheim's sense) social order would be unable to function if individuals were not capable of disciplining themselves, not "autonomous." In Parsons's view, "This means . . . that the normative elements have become 'internal,' 'subjective.' . . . [The individual] becomes, in a sense, 'identified' with them" [1937, p. 385]. In a note, he adds that "they are, in Freudian terminology, 'introjected' to form a 'superego.'" This assertion is the first and, in *The Structure of Social Action,* the only comparison between Freud and Durkheim.

Durkheim's break with utilitarianism and Spencerian evolutionism is complete from the beginning of *La division du travail social,* in which it is explicitly stated that the aim of the book is to lay bare the "non-contractual elements of contract," the nonnegotiated and noncalcu-lated foundations of exchange and the market. The repudiation of positivism is less clear-cut but, in the final analysis, equally unmistak-able, because if heredity and environment were strictly determining factors, then the individual's capacity to shape his own destiny and to discipline himself, essential to Durkheim's view, would be in-comprehensible.

As presented by Parsons, Durkheim's approach is quite similar to that of Pareto. Pareto had brought to light the category of the "non-logical," plainly a residual category since the utilitarian schema in both its narrowly economic version and its most general formulation left it out of account. Durkheim also devoted attention to the broad spec-trum of conditions neglected by the utilitarians, which he described as "non-contractual." Thus both authors were led to move beyond a strict utilitarian conception of action. In doing so they came to explore a realm that lay beyond calculation and was irreducible either to the logico-experimental category or to the domain of the contract: both men called this realm "society." Ultimately, Durkheim and Pareto could be seen to agree on what Parsons called the sociological theorem [1937, pp. 209–10], that is, the assertion that social reality cannot be explained simply in terms of determinants and conditions; in Parsons's view, both writers make this claim, though in different forms. Approaching the problem from the point of view of the rela-tion between means and ends, Pareto defined the social dimension as consisting of all ends that could be set over against individual preferences. "Durkheim . . . instead of generalizing the means-end schema . . . thought of the individual as acting in a social environment and went on to analyze the elements of this environment. . . . Then he came to the sense of moral obligation first as a motive for individual obedience to a given rule, and at last he came to see that the mainte-nance of a common system of rules rested on a set of common values" [1937, p. 710].

There is another point on which Durkheim and Pareto clearly agreed, relating not to the specific character of social action but to its structure or, as Parsons says, its anatomy: both men attached great importance to symbolism and ritual. "Do not urinate in the mouth of a river," declared Hesiod. In logico-experimental terms, this precept makes no sense. Yet while the connection between ends and means in an injunction of this sort is clearly arbitrary, it is still possible to treat it as the manifestation of certain "sentiments." This answer is unsatisfactory. The symbolic act of the neurotic who seeks more or less unconsciously to dispel his anxiety by performing certain ritual actions is different in kind from the act of the priest who performs a propitiatory sacrifice in behalf of the Greek fleet before it sets out to sea. Durkheim, for one, refused to allow a solution of the problem of ritual in narrowly psychological terms. He looked upon ritual as comprising a range of acts related in some way to the sacred. Alternatively, he said that these acts belong "to the serious side of life." Ritual is not mere acting out; it helps to reinforce the solidarity of the group by providing individuals with substitute means to secure or reassure themselves in the face of undertainties over which they have no control, while at the same time contributing to their sense of belonging to the same group and sharing the same tradition.

Max Weber's work is not part of the positivist tradition; its sources lay rather in what Parsons characterized as the "idealist" tradition—which was essentially German, drawing on both post-Hegelian and above all neo-Kantian sources—particularly in matters concerning the limits and validity of knowledge, the status of values, and the ends of human action. What first attracted Parsons to Weber's work was the contribution it made to the question of the origins of capitalism. As Parsons sees it, Weber began his work by attacking historical materialism—one more version of utilitarianism, though with a historicist cast. As a rival to historical materialism Weber put forward a theory of religion that focused on the relation between observances, values, and beliefs.

In Parsons's estimation, Weber's view need not be characterized as idealist. To begin with, Weber's stress on the need for methodical comparison of diverse societies, emphasizing what was unique and irreducible about them, helped to "vindicate the indispensability of general theoretical concepts for the demonstration of any empirical proposition in any field" [1937, p. 715]. Weber maintained his views as to the possibility of generalization in the social sciences against the "intuitionist" line taken by Dilthey, for example, who carried the dogma of individual uniqueness so far that it was no longer possible to conceive of any contact or communication between different individuals. Though Weber acknowledged the importance of "the subjective dimension of action" on which the "intuitionists" rightly laid stress, he opposed them in maintaining that "general concepts [are] essential to the concept of action since science and rationality of action are indissolubly bound up together." Last but not least, Parsons argues that Weber cannot be considered an idealist because he does not hold that institutions and conduct "emanate" from collective values and preferences in some sort of ideal procession. "Values exert their influence in complex processes of interaction, in which they come into contact with other elements of the system of action; they do not become real by themselves." In other words, a society is something other than a system of values; a system of values does not give rise to or engender a society merely by laying down what ought to be.

A central concern of Parsons in writing *The Structure of Social Action* was the problem of rational action. Action is first defined in utilitarian terms. But the utilitarian scheme comes to grief because the view it adopts is too constricted. The theory of action must recognize the existence of a consensus, a set of shared values transcending individual ends and interests. This consensus, however, must not be viewed as something fortuitous, much less as a contrived collection of "eternal objects" taken to exist "outside space and time."[8] Action is a process that takes place in a temporal dimension, though "physical time . . . a mode of relationship of events in space" is to be distinguished from "action time . . . a mode of relation of means and ends and other action elements" [1937, p. 763].

Parsons is convinced that the views of the three Founding Fathers can be brought into harmony; the theory he believes can be distilled from their work he characterizes as "voluntaristic." The term may be misleading, for it seems to suggest that an individual can effectively alter circumstances by an arbitrary act of will. This is not Parsons's intention; the point of voluntarism in his reconciliation of the work of his three heroes is that it runs counter to the various forms of the then prevalent positivism, toward which he made no secret of his hostility. "Returning to [the United States] I found behaviorism so rampant that anyone who believed in the scientific validity of subjective states of mind was often held to be fatuously naive" [1970a, p. 830]. The action concept was intended to counterbalance the enthusiasm for "behaviorism." Such enthusiasm went hand in hand with the belief that "scientific knowledge was a total reflection of the 'reality out there,'" which also had its heyday in the twenties; Parsons refers to this belief as "empiricism," and against it he maintained the necessity of "theory," that is, deliberate, or *voluntary,* exploration of an abstractly defined field with the aid of a coherent set of verifiable hypotheses.

The Three Levels of Theory

The history of the several approaches that were combined in the theory outlined above suggests that a theory is never unitary but is made up of different elements of varying degrees of generality and consistency. A theory is first of all a frame of reference, but it is not only that. It is also a collection of specific, individualized tools, useful within specifiable boundaries. Finally, a theory gives answers to questions concerning certain often noteworthy phenomena. In any theory, moreover, there is constant reference from each of these three levels to the other two.

Every theory incorporates a number of interdependent propositions. Parsons distinguishes three families of such propositions. To begin with, in the broadest sense there is a "frame of reference" within which particular items of knowledge are situated. "The spatio-temporal framework of the classical mechanics is such a schema," for example. "A similar schema in the social sciences is that of supply and demand in economics." But a schema of this kind is "descriptive," not explanatory. "The statement that a physical body at a given time and place has a given property, say a particular velocity, does not explain why it has this velocity. . . . The same is true of an economic fact, such as that the closing price of wheat in the Chicago market was $1.25 a bushel on a given day" [1937, pp. 28–30].

The same phenomenon may be related to more than one frame of reference. The choice of frame is arbitrary and reflects the preferences of the observer. Consider the case of a man who drowns. Such an event can be described in mechanical terms; by noting the velocity of the body at the moment it strikes the water, the observer can describe and even measure the force and direction of impact. But was the man diving for pleasure? Or did he hurl himself into the water with the intention of committing suicide? Or did someone push him? There is good reason for wanting to know what the man's intention was, particularly if his pockets are found to be full of stones. If he left behind a letter stating his intention to commit suicide, investigators would be able to decide between suicide and murder in classifying his death. Once classed as suicide, the event might be looked at either from the victim's standpoint, in terms of his motives or psychological state, or from the standpoint of the social group to which he belonged. Thus there is no one paradigm of social action but rather several frames of reference in keeping with the nature of the action.

"Descriptive frames of reference," Parsons argues, "are funda-mental to all science. But by no means do they exhaust scientific conceptualization. . . . Description [of the facts] within [the framework of a conceptual schema] has, in the first instance, the function of defining a 'phenomenon' which is to be explained." As for the explanation itself, it involves two different approaches, and it is important to distinguish between them. First, every phenomenon can be broken down into its elementary parts or units. "A steam engine consists of cylinders, pistons, driving rods, boilers, valves, etc. Similarly an organism is composed of cells, tissues, organs. A part in this sense is a unit, the concrete existence of which, aside from its relation to other parts of the same whole, is meaningful, 'makes sense'" [1937, pp. 30–31].

It may be said that the unit is the ultimate goal of the analysis, beyond which it would no longer make sense to speak of a phenomenon. But when we look further into the status of these elementary units, we come upon a difficulty that has to do with what is unclear about the contrast between the mechanical and the organic. We clearly sense a difference between phenomena that we see as "concrete" or "organic totalities," the elements of which cannot exist in isolation from one another, and mechanical phenomena, the elements of which can be separated without affecting the characteristic modalities of their existence, as in the case of a steam engine, which literally can be taken apart and then reassembled without altering its component parts. "Now," says Parsons, "precisely in so far as a whole is organic this becomes impossible . . . this is true whether it be an organism or some other unity, such as a 'mind,' a 'society' or what not. And in so far as this is true, the concept 'part' takes on an abstract, indeed a 'fictional' character. . . . Perhaps the classic statement of this point is that of Aristotle, that a hand separated from the living body is no longer a hand 'except in an equivocal sense, as we would speak of a stone hand'" [1937, p. 32].

Still, the distinction between the mechanical and the biological is relative. First of all, "a complex of actions can be analyzed into parts, such as rational acts and irrational acts, or religious and secular acts and the like. The test question is always whether we can *conceive* such an act as existing 'by itself,' that is as a 'pure type' without involving the other types from which it is concretely distinguished."[9] And to make clear that the requirements imposed on the analytical method are still the same, Parsons goes on to say "whether the concept refers to a mechanistic 'part' . . . or to an organic part . . . the *logical* character of the concept remains the same. It refers to an, actually or hypothetically, existent concrete entity."[10] What is required of the type is not that it should be real in the manner of a concrete object like a hand, which can only exist as the hand of a particular individual, but simply that it should make sense, that is, that its definition not involve a contradiction in terms. "This is true even if it is fictional, as are a 'perfect' gas, a 'frictionless' machine, etc. . . . So also are such concepts as a 'perfectly rational act,' a 'perfectly integrated group,' etc." The same may be said of such concepts as capitalism, democracy, or socialism.

Even a "pure type" is not a concrete reality, a closed totality. Its parts may be fitted into more than one whole. In order to eliminate any taint of organicism from his concept of the type, Parsons invoked the authority of Whitehead.[11] In *Science and the Modern World* Whitehead follows his discussion of the notion that biology is the study of "small organisms" with a suggestion that to relativize the opposition of part to whole it may be useful to look upon the event as the "ultimate unit of natural occurrence." Thus conceived, the event serves as a corrective to the positivistic notion of "fact," which usually carries with it a misleadingly precise attribution of spatial and temporal location—in other words, the trouble with the "fact" is that it is too intuitively concrete. Whitehead defines the event as something that "has to do with all that is given, and in particular with other events." What characterizes an event is that it offers two ways of access (prehension), intrinsic and extrinsic. On the one hand, its significance depends on the pattern of aspects of other events that it retains in its own appearance; on the other hand, its significance depends on the configuration of its own aspects that other events retain in their own appearance.

A "type" is an open class of relations, membership in which depends on the "intrinsic and extrinsic aspects" of the "events" or facts in relation to the type. Once types are fixed, however, it is clear that they establish quite general relations among the elementary units involved in them. Consider a piece of steel, for example. Certain secondary characteristics may be attributed to it. We may treat it as a mechanical system in equilibrium or, alternatively, as an entity made up of atoms and molecules. Neither of these types individually nor both taken together exhaust our actual or potential experience of the object. What is more, the equations of equilibrium rely upon notions such as mass, force, and velocity, of which no one experiment is sufficient to give an adequate grasp. The scientist looks upon each such notion as an *invariant* whereby a functional correspondence is set up between a variable (mass, velocity, etc.) and the range of values that the variable in question can assume during a given period of time. "We can observe that a given body has a given mass," writes Parsons, "but we never observe mass as such. . . . We may say that such and such a body *has* a mass of *x,* but not that it *is* a mass" [1937, pp. 34–35]. Now, these "universals" are connected with one another, being at least to some degree interdependent. The various types or systems in which they occur are determined by the whole range of their externally accessible attributes.

None of the above architectural levels of theory exists in and of itself. What is more, there is no reason to treat one level as though it were more "real" than another. "The distinction between type-parts and analytical elements has nothing to do with the relative degree of 'organicity' of the phenomena to which they refer." There is no reason to say that the notion of atom or mechanical system is more "real" than that of mass or acceleration—or, again, that the notion of capitalism is more "real" than that of the indifference curve. Whitehead's well-known phrase concerning the "fallacy of misplaced concreteness" is cited several times by Parsons; in the end it comes down to another way of formulating the concern to which Léon Brunschvicg gave voice in France when he warned against falling into the error he termed "realism of the concept." Theories are tools and should not be treated either as idols or as toys; to use an expression used more than once by Parsons himself, the theorist must avoid the pitfalls of "reification." The danger arises whenever entities or terms that make sense only in the context of a relation, a group, or a system are treated as having independent existence.

Can we escape the twin dangers of conceptualism—which takes words for things—and nominalism—which recognizes only immediate experience as real—by taking the position that science deals only with concepts that lend themselves to measurement? This extreme position was in fact held by the physicist P. W. Bridgman,[12] another of Harvard's luminaries in the early thirties. "A concept is nothing more than its corresponding set of operations." To this Parsons rejoined that measurement is not the only rational "operation." In the first place, two objects may be compared to determine which is the larger, even in the absence of any operationally defined unit of measure. Of course, such comparisons may fall short of stringent standards in respect of rigor: if there are a great many objects I may be unable to say by how much the size of A exceeds that of B, and if the difference between them is too slight, I may be unable to discriminate between the two at all. Still, the information at my disposal is not negligible. It does not follow from the fact that I do not know how to subject a phenomenon to measurement that I know nothing about it. I can compare it with other phenomena, establish an ordering of different phenomena in accordance with some kind of criterion, or assign each of several phenomena to different "classes" or "categories."

Initial Results

In order to arrive at a judgment as to whether the "theory" that Parsons derives from the work of Durkheim, Weber, and Pareto lives up to the standards that he himself laid down, and to answer the further question whether it marks an advance over the highly general action schema [1937, pp. 43–51] in which action was viewed as the elaboration by an actor in a given situation of a chain of links between ends and material and symbolic means, we shall now focus our attention on the following problem: if we press further along the lines laid down by Parsons himself in comparing the three great European sociologists, do we find that their work lends credence to the notions of unit act, system of action, and analytical elements?[13] "The 'smallest' unit which can be *conceived* of as concretely existing by itself is the 'unit act.'" Our capacity to conceive such a unit is determined by two characteristics of the act itself. First, the act must make sense to the actor—even if the sense for the actor is different from the sense the observer makes of the same act. Second, it must be possible to impute to the unit act certain observable effects, which may be quite different from the actor's objectives.

The task of theory is not limited to identifying the elements of which systems of action are made up—although that is an important part of theory's function. But theory must also explain how the properties of these elements give rise to the novel characteristics of the system. We see this clearly in the distinction between microeconomics and macroeconomics. This distinction gives rise to a problem: given a large number of economic acts, each of which, taken individually, meets the criteria of economic rationality, a rational economic order does not necessarily follow from their juxtaposition. Phenomena such as the deflationary spiral illustrate the paradox inherent in the structure of collective action, whereby economic agents will often act in such a way as to bring about an end result that goes against their individual goals. During a period of crisis, for example, bank depositors hoping to improve their liquidity positions will precipitate a run on the banks and thereby drain cash out of the economy, leading to disruption of the entire system of production.

The difficulty of arguing from the elements of the system to the system as a whole is as great in the case of social action as in the case of economic action. This delicate question of transition is treated by Parsons not in terms of aggregation but, in a frankly metaphorical fashion, in terms of the "web." "A given concrete unit act is to be thought of, then, as a 'knot' where a large number of . . . threads come momentarily together only to separate again, each one to enter, as it goes on, into a variety of other knots into which only a few of those with which it was formerly combined enter with it." Each knot symbolizes the condensation or coming together of a number of individual acts or events. If we follow out any one particular thread, we find that it proceeds from one knot to another. Moreover, in each knot it is found in combination with other threads, and these vary from knot to knot. To unravel the skein it is not enough to isolate the individual threads. We must also identify the forks and branches, the critical points at which a particular element leaves one combination to enter another. It is therefore incumbent upon the analyst who is trying to isolate the elements of the system not to treat them as self-sufficient entities—he must beware of what Parsons calls the "'mosaic' fallacy" [1937, p. 741].

Thus the unit act is not an atom in the empiricist sense of the term, whereby the social fabric is reduced to the sum of physically observable and measurable interactions of concrete actors. The unit act is the central knot of relations without which the event would make no sense to either the actor or the observer, where, as always, actor and observer may make sense of the event in quite different ways. As for the system of action, the actor sees it as a set of constraints, an external "environment" in which his action is performed; though the system is made up of unit acts, in his eyes it cannot be reduced to a mere sum of such units. The theory of action in a sense proceeds in a manner analogous to the way theories are formulated in physics. A pendulum is made up of atoms and particles, but there is good reason to distinguish between the pendulum as a physical system, which is defined by a set of properties—relations between mass, acceleration, and the like—and the system defined by the properties of atoms and elementary particles.

As for the underlying or "structural" properties of social systems, they are of two kinds: properties of social relations, and properties of groups. Social relations have to do with the expectations to which the mutual interrelations of the actors give rise.[14] Social relations, in turn, give rise to groups, and the question is then to understand how the social relations serve to establish and maintain the cohesiveness of these units.[15] Weber's distinction between *Zweck-Rational* and *Wert-Rational* is applied to social relations, while groups are, at least at first, viewed in the light of the *Gemeinschaft-Gesellschaft* distinction that Parsons borrowed from Tönnies.

As a result of borrowing these distinctions and systematizing the

fundamental ideas they summarize, Parsons came to lay the foundations of a kind of combinatorics of action. "Sociology," he writes
[1937, p. 768], "is the science which attempts to develop an analytical
theory of social action systems in so far as these systems can be understood in terms of the property of common-value integration." What is
striking about this definition is that it emphasizes two things: first, that
integration is the social function par excellence, and, second, that
common values are essential to integration. On this view of the matter, every society would seem to be nothing other than a system of
values, and every system of values would seem to be integrated. Some,
in fact, hold that this is the essence of Parsonian sociology—which
they take to be a windy, repetitious idealist platitude erected by a
doltish American, much given to sophistry, on the corpses of the three
great European sociologists, of whom he was the belated and self-
appointed champion. I shall endeavor to show that the truth of the
matter is quite different, that one can and should hold that common
values do exist, and that one can do so without falling into the trap of
culturalism and vulgar functionalism.

The Notion of System

For many of Parsons's early readers the importance of his first book
was obscured by the success of the structural-functionalist methodol-
ogy, then much in vogue, and this despite the fact that there is very
little in common between the discussions of method found in *The
Structure of Social Action* and the methods of the structural-
functionalists.

Parsons suffered a fate comparable to Durkheim's. Durkheim's
concept of constraint and his stubbornness in "treating social facts as
things" earned him a reputation as the leading theorist of "totalitarian
realism," the defender of a concept of society as a self-sufficient reality
closed in on itself. Parsons himself attempted to show that this interpretation neglects important aspects of Durkheim's work.

Just as Durkheim's work has been attacked as the archetype of
"sociological realism," so Parsons's work is said to embody
"structural-functionalism" in its most extreme form. "Structural-
functionalism" seems to be understood in several more or less compatible senses. The term has first of all been taken to extend the views
of certain anthropologists, most notably Malinowski and Radcliffe-
Brown, as to the priority of the social whole over its parts, that is, over
individuals or, better still, over individual activities. Second,
structural-functionalism is said to take the view that social norms are

strictly determined by the functioning of society. Accordingly, a normative system is considered to be explained once it has been shown how the norms in question ensure the functioning of the society taken as a whole. This being the case, it is easy to understand why structural-functionalism should have been regarded as a conservative ideology, for such a view would imply that the structure of society was determined by the need of society to "reproduce" identical copies of itself for an indefinite length of time.

Was Parsons a structural-functionalist in any of the above senses? To my mind, he never held the view that society is a closed totality, or that individuals and their activities are strictly determined by the normative system, or that society is a structure capable of reproducing itself again and again. In what sense may Parsons legitimately be described as a "structural-functionalist"?

Whatever answer we eventually give to this question, we would do well to approach Parsons in the same spirit in which he approached Durkheim—a spirit of "generous interpretation." The first rule of generous interpretation is to refrain from attributing to the author under scrutiny only those views that he must have held if the commentator is to be successful in refuting him. The second rule is that, when the author held views open to conflicting or contradictory interpretations, the commentator should choose those interpretations to which the author explicitly attached the greatest importance. Parsons, for example, believed that Durkheim could be rescued from the charge of totalitarian realism because the theory of moral education, which stands in contradiction to the contention that society can be reduced to the "order of things," was given a high priority in the French sociologist's work. On the other hand, Marx, in Parsons's view, cannot be saved, because his ideas—ultimately untenable and absurd—concerning the nature of sociological knowledge and social action derive from his unshakable conviction that the structure of "bourgeois" society is strictly determined by the struggle-to-the-death arising out of the division of society into the two universally antagonistic classes, the exploiters and exploited. Naturally, if Marx and his followers were to abandon their one-sided conception of exploitation and class struggle, they would be entitled to "generous interpretation" as well.

We shall apply these rules of exegesis to Parsons himself. To recapitulate, the rules are the following: avoid polemic; establish an order of precedence among the various positions taken by the writer; correct, if necessary, the less important of these positions in certain respects, in order to preserve the consistency of the work as a whole.

In this connection the notion of system is of crucial importance. It is based on analogies of three kinds: economic, biological, and cybernetic. The notion of social system nevertheless retains its distinctive character. A society, of course, is neither a market, an organism, nor a servomechanism or thermostat. From economics Parsons took the idea that the social system should be treated as a network of interdependent exchanges. From biology came the idea of a regulation effected by way of symbiosis between internal and external environments. The cybernetic analogy places the accent on the importance of symbolism and information in mechanisms of social control. These various views were reconciled through the notion of action, or interaction, whereby the ideas of strategic interdependence, adaptive regulation, and symbolic hierarchy were linked together.

For the moment we shall content ourselves with describing the notion of system in purely formal terms. To begin with, the notion of system implies interdependence. Pareto saw this clearly, as his treatment of the problem of ritual indicates. Three elements are involved in the analysis of ritual: a state of mind A, with certain intentions (such as obtaining a cure), acts B (such as saying prayers), and sentiments, which are frequently expressed in the form of theories C (God cannot refuse what I am asking of him). B and C can be understood only through observation: they may take the form of actions or verbal statements of various kinds. The observer can do no more than infer A. For Pareto the problem is to understand how the three elements are related. On the commonsense view of the matter, the tendency is to explain that actor X performs act B because he held opinion C (which expresses sentiments of which X himself was unaware, in a way that usually eludes the commonsensical understanding). Although the naive observer takes the relation BC too literally and accords it undue importance, there is no reason to deny that it does exist and is important. But AC and AB must also be taken into account. Of even greater interest is Pareto's suggestion to consider all these relations together. "Before the invasion of the Greek gods," he says, "the ancient Roman religion did not have any theology C; it was confined to a cult B. But the cult B, acting on A, strongly influenced the actions D of the Roman people. More than that, when the direct relationship BD is given, it appears to us moderns as manifestly absurd. But the relationship BAD may on the contrary have been in certain cases highly reasonable and useful to the Roman people. In general, the theology C has a direct influence on D even less important than on A." In other words, the relation between the state of mind A and its various effects B and C is no longer understood in abstract terms. A has now taken its place in a set of elements to which D has been added, though D was not noticed at first by the historian of religion, who considered only the effects of the ritual on A and C, without taking into consideration its effects on the customs and general equilibrium of the society. The transition from the initial formulation, A, B, C, to the new formulation, A, B, C, D, does more than call our attention to the possibility of acquiring further information about the new element D. D is not an arbitrary element: it is the state of the system at a particular moment. Thus introducing D into a relation leads us to take into account the influence of the system as a whole on the other element in the relation; we are led to analyze not only the question of dependence but also that of interdependence. The whole is no longer thought of as an independent principle standing over and above the elements, regarded as subordinate to it, but rather as a complex web of exchanges and relations [1937, pp. 193–96].

Besides interdependence, the notion of system also implies differentiation. Every social act is differentiated or differentiable, whether from the standpoint of the actor or that of the observer. As the case of the drowned man makes clear, the observer may interpret the act in more than one way. From the standpoint of the actor the act involves more than one interest, and among these several interests he must strike and maintain a more or less precarious balance. At the outset, Parsons introduces a distinction between two kinds of acts—or, as he will later call them, "social roles"—which distinction may also be applied to each role individually: instrumental activities on the one hand, and symbolic activities on the other. This distinction is introduced in connection with the analysis of the medical profession, which extends the analysis of ritual. The doctor-patient relationship is neither purely technical nor purely economic and cannot be reduced to a relation of exchange. The fees paid to the doctor do entitle the patient to claim a certain portion of the doctor's time and attention. But health matters always involve an expressive dimension, at once personalized and institutionalized. Consider, finally, the norms that govern the medical profession: these are compounded of criteria of several kinds, involving more than one type of rationality.

That the rationality implicit in therapeutic action is not reducible to technical or economic logic is, of course, clear, but that is not all. No one criterion is responsible for the form taken by therapeutic rationality, which is rather the result of a *combination* of criteria. The medical profession embodies rationalities of several different kinds. To begin with, medicine is an applied science: what it does may therefore be justified on the grounds of efficacy. The doctor claims not only to possess objective knowledge of disease but also to be able to cure the sick. He practices an art or a technique and is interested in "basic science" only insofar as it has therapeutic application. But the doctor is not a technician in the same sense as an engineer who builds a bridge. In many cases, by far the most common and important ones, the patient can be cured only if he cooperates with the doctor in his treatment—first by going to see him, and then by following his advice, that is, by displaying confidence in him. Then, too, the importance of psychosomatic and other factors relating to mental health shows that the efficacy of therapy depends not only on technical control over a cause-and-effect sequence but also on the interpretation and manipulation of certain symptoms by both doctor and patient. Along with technico-instrumental rationality, medical practice makes room for a symbolico-expressive rationality, insofar as the physician is forced to admit that certain symptoms make sense, though they do not reflect any simple organic "condition." In many cases of neurosis, treatment is, of course, possible only if the therapy succeeds in "revealing" to the patient the meaning of his symptom. More than that, though, any kind of therapy that involves serious risks to the patient brings him into a complex and potentially dangerous relationship with his doctor, which the patient can control only by achieving mastery over his emotional responses, not always an easy matter.

Parsons's thinking about the symbolic dimension of illness led him to the work of Freud. Indeed, Freud is a major figure missing from *The Structure of Social Action*. In the preface of the second edition, published in 1949, Parsons laid the groundwork for accepting the celebrated Viennese pioneer into the pantheon of Founding Fathers. "A major one-sidedness of the book is its relative neglect of the psychological aspects of the total conceptual scheme.... Here, at least, one figure in the same generation as the others, that of Freud, looms up as having played a cardinal role in a development which ... must be regarded as a vital part of the same general movement of thought" [1937, p. xvi]. Freud's contributions were actually of two kinds. First, he stressed the importance of symbolism: neurotic symptoms must be interpreted both by the observer and by the patient as substitutes for forces and relations not immediately evident. Second, Freud drew attention to the importance of internationalization and introjection of social norms. In this respect Freud reinforced the work of Durkheim, and Parsons notes considerable agreement between the teaching of the two men as to the nature of norms. The source of the obligation attaching to a norm lies in the feelings of shame or guilt to which violating it gives rise. But to say that norms have a psychological dimension and are closely related to propensities and attitudes is not the same thing as saying that they are purely subjective in nature or that they strip the actor of all autonomy.

A Case Study in Structural-Functionalist Analysis: Medical Practice

The therapeutic "situation" may be characterized as a zone of uncertainty within which relations of power arise between doctor and patient, involving risks of abuse and exploitation on both sides, though in quite different ways. Conflicts do in fact occur between doctors and patients. They result from the patient's lack of power and from the limits imposed on the doctor's exercise of his power by the state of the medical art. The patient is *dependent,* not only because his condition makes it impossible for him to discharge his responsibilities to his family, his colleagues, or his wife, or in some cases even to take care of himself, but also because he cannot understand or explain what has befallen him and, above all, cannot cure his ailment himself. In such a situation the patient's anxiety may increase to a point where he is incapable of taking a detached and critical view of the matter in which he is so deeply involved. He may also come to place his faith in anyone who offers the prospect of help and thus to regard the doctor as an all-powerful healer. Parsons here makes the observation[16] that, just as the uninitiated believe that advances in theoretical knowledge are automatically translated into corresponding advances in the state of the curative art, so, too, may the expert come either to exaggerate his own powers or, alternatively, to minimize them on the grounds that, since the diseases that actually come to his attention are in many cases incurable, there is nothing he can do. "'More' is definitely known than before, but hope has been destroyed" [1951a, p. 448]. Then, too, as the powers of the physician and the surgeon increase, more and more opportunities to exercise them present themselves, but along with these opportunities go new risks, and subjectively the medical practitioner thereby comes to experience graver and more agonizing doubts as to whether intervention is wise. If it is a question of risking potentially dangerous surgery, subjecting a young patient to a prolonged course of treatment, or dealing with a person with whom the doctor is emotionally involved, extrinsic affective considerations come into play, and if the case happens to be one of such complexity that diagnosis and prognosis are necessarily uncertain, these factors take on even greater significance.

The relationship between the doctor and the patient is asymmetrical, and this opens the possibility of various sorts of material or symbolic exploitation. There is, however, one point of reference that both doctor and patient share: health, the common goal, over which there is no conflict. Socialists believe that the profits of the "capitalist" are taken out of the hide of the "workers." But the health of the patient is not acquired at the expense of the doctor, or vice versa. The doctor does, of course, earn his living from his patients' illnesses. But his cash reward is extrinsic to the therapeutic process; the physician would cure the patient just as well if he were paid by a third party, or even if he were not paid at all. Wages, on the other hand, are an essential constituent of the capitalist mode of production. No wages, no capitalist.

The physician is a technician with competence extending over a more or less broad range of skills, who is concerned to cure his client of what ails him. The patient is "patient" in the sense that he must bide his time in the confidence that the technician can cure him of his disease. The differences in the situation of the one and the other often lead to quite contradictory expectations. The "function" of the normative system is to try to reduce the possibilities of abuse inherent in this situation—though not always with success, for there are "bad" doctors and "bad" patients; the well-known rule of professional secrecy (which is the counterpart of the patient's obligation to "tell all," including the most intimate and shameful details of his personal life, if these might be useful to the physician) is designed to govern a relationship that could, if left to itself, easily go awry in some way or even become explosive. What makes this corrective possible is knowledge of the goal of the therapeutic relationship. By accepting the primacy of the common end—the cure of the illness—doctor and client are able to face up to the dangers inherent in the situation in which both are involved.

The functional *interdependence* of the actor and his situation is ensured by a normative system that takes primacy over the needs of the various categories of actors involved in the relationship, by the integration of the microsociety consisting of doctor and patient, and by a certain inertia of the cultural tradition. But this interdependence is neither perfect nor complete. There are "bad" practitioners and "bad" patients, and the cultural tradition, which is supposed to justify the duties imposed on doctor and patient alike, is far from stable. The current debates over abortion and euthanasia are reason to doubt that medical ethics are quite so universally sanctioned as Parsons, in 1951a, was able to imagine they were. Also worthy of note is the process that has led to a greater differentiation of roles and division of responsibilities within the medical profession, illustrated by the difference between the general practitioner and the specialist. Medical competence has come to involve more technical knowledge than it once did, and some depersonalization of the therapeutic relationship may also have taken place. Finally, the growth of "third-party payments" (from private insurance companies or social security) has introduced another element into the doctor-patient relationship, with an associated trend toward imposing limits on the patient's freedom of choice and the doctor's professional independence.

I concede that structural-functional analysis may result in tautology or become caught in a vicious circle. But there are precautions that may be taken against such risks. Rather than look upon norms as peremptory imperatives, precepts that ensure the smooth functioning of the therapeutic system, the sociologist may look instead at the problems associated with their implementation and effectiveness. If the norms are taken to be directly effective and fully legitimate, the sociologist will naturally tend to focus on them in place of actual behavior, which then becomes an unnecessary, redundant element. But he can escape from this untenable fiction by using norms as a starting point from which to begin research into the *disparity* between the ideal or desirable state and the actual behavior of the actors, or, perhaps better, into the conditions under which the norms might be effective. Sociological analysis begins with the *tension* between the way the role is actually performed and its normative definition. How is the doctor induced not to take advantage of his power? How does the patient manage to face up to his powerlessness? Interdependence is not a vicious circle; it is a dynamic relation between permanently established norms and a situation that can never be defined in any one-sided fashion.

The Actor's Situation and Its Characteristic Dimensions

Stress has been placed on the importance of the notion of "situation." The situation may be thought of as consisting of a number of constraints that impose limitations on an actor's freedom of choice, while at the same time providing him with a stockpile of resources that may be combined in a variety of ways. Every situation has a structure; resources and constraints are not distributed at random. They fall into three major categories, each with its own logic: "Action systems," Parsons reminds us, "are structured about three integrative foci, the individual actor, the interactive system, and a system of cultural patterning. Each implies the others and therefore the variability of any one is limited by its compatibility with the minimum conditions of functioning of each of the other two" [1951a, p. 27].

There are two conditions or prerequisites for a system of action to exist and remain stable, relating, first, to the psychological motivation of the actors and, second, to the symbolic significance of their acts. "A social system cannot be so structured as to be radically incompatible with the conditions of functioning of its component individual actors as biological organisms and as personalities, or of the relatively stable integration of a cultural system" [1951*a,* p. 27]. As for the first condition, which we shall call the "motivational prerequisite," Parsons does not set up a one-to-one correspondence between motives and acts. He does not say, as Malinowski does, that "society must satisfy certain individual needs." He maintains only that, in order for a society to exist, its members must be motivated to perform certain roles and submit to a certain discipline. Furthermore, the motives that he brings to light are no more the subjective reflection of the social organization than the social organization is the crystallization or condensation of individual desires. Motives are *learned* in a dynamic process, which does not exclude the possibility of time lags, mistakes, or novel discoveries. To say that actors are motivated is to say that they have previously been "socialized"—whether efficiently or not. Socialization implies a degree of *plasticity* in the actors, since they will learn, and thereby increase the range of attitudes available to them, only if they are motivated. It also implies some *responsiveness* in the actors, because it is through their reaction to or anticipation of different kinds of reward that the actors are motivated to learn and persuaded to forgo certain types of behavior (along with the satisfactions associated with them) in favor of new types. Finally, it implies the possibility of success or failure, since we can never be sure of having been adequately socialized and may be motivated to do or expect what we ought not do or expect.

Moreover, "from the point of view of the functioning of the social system, it is not the needs of all the participant actors which must be met, nor all the needs of any one, but only a sufficient proportion for a sufficient fraction of the population." This proposition adds substance to the no doubt true but empty assertion that there is a relation between motives and behavior, introducing two criteria by which structural-functionalism may be distinguished from vulgar functionalism. Malinowski was satisfied with the assumption that there is a correspondence between needs and institutions. In point of fact no such correspondence can be taken for granted; its existence is problematic and raises questions concerning conformity and deviance on the one hand and change on the other.

Parsons's concept of the situation leads neither to psychologism nor to any of the several forms of culturalism. Doctor and patient both carry on a cultural tradition that places a high value on health and, in consequence, on obedience on the part of the patient and attentive service on the part of the doctor. Is this cultural tradition sufficient to explain how the therapeutic relationship functions? Clearly, the cultural tradition is indispensable to the functioning of the relationship: it is a prerequisite. It fulfills the social function of legitimation and the psychological functions of motivation and orientation. The prerogatives of both doctor and patient in the therapeutic interaction are prescribed by tradition. In short, it is the culture that gives ultimate meaning to the situation: it thus constitutes a second prerequisite, which we shall call the prerequisite of significance.

The culture is therefore inseparable from the processes of motivation and interaction. As something learned, it is assimilated in the course of an interactive process by individuals with motives and sanctions for what they are doing. Nevertheless, culture is not reducible to a process of motivation or to a process of interaction. It is possible to decipher a religion or a work of art from within, I should be tempted to say, by treating them as novel systems whose meaning can be restored only by discovering the immanent code contained within the message itself. Alternatively, we may scan a given canvas or listen to the preaching of a particular prophet with the intention of relating what we see or hear to the broad range of meanings that we associate with the experience of the artist, the religious virtuoso, or human beings in general.

In looking at the relation between norms and roles on the one hand and motives on the other, a reductionist approach runs the risk of breaking the objectivity of social roles down into a number of distinct, randomly distributed motives. This has two consequences for the relation between values and norms. In order to relate beliefs to the situation it is tempting to view the former as a reflection of the latter. But values and symbols make sense apart from the interactive process. Whitehead speaks in this sense of "eternal objects" in a passage cited by Parsons: "They consist . . . of objects not of indefinite duration but to which the category of time is not applicable" [1937, p. 763]. Musical forms and styles of poetry are values of the kind Whitehead has in mind, which "haunt time, [like color] . . . it [color] comes and it goes. But where it comes, it is always the same color. It neither survives nor does it live. It appears when it is wanted."[17]

No one of the three frames of reference mentioned above takes precedence over the other two. Each one is "open" to the others, which constitute what we may refer to as its "environment." Each frame exerts an influence on action. Rules, motives, and orientations are all important to the actor, who has real resources of various kinds at his disposal, usable for maintaining his independence. This much is brought to light by the analysis of institutions. From the standpoint of the observer, institutions appear to be a "complex" of roles. The doctor is at one and the same time an expert in the instrumental domain and an expert in the expressive domain. Consider the case of the relations between a professor and his students, which may be compared with the relations between doctor and patient. The role of a professor is a "bundle" consisting of three parts. The professor is first of all a teacher. He conveys previously acquired knowledge. But in large modern universities the professor is also a researcher. He takes part in the process of discovery of knowledge. Finally, the professor helps to transmit the values characteristic of his profession to his "youthful" students or fellow research workers: independence of mind, analytical rigor, belief in the values associated with the pursuit of knowledge. The three parts of the role are different from one another. At one time or another quite disparate interpretations of the professorial role have been put forth, and the character and style of these interpretations have depended largely on which of the three parts was deemed the most important. We find the heterogeneous character of the role reproduced a fortiori in the institution. But this heterogeneity must be kept within limits if the institution is to remain intact. Thus we encounter the problem of "integration." It may be said that integration is ensured by constraints that impose limits on the permissible variety of the elements constitutive of the institution, thereby ensuring that those elements are compatible with one another.

The term "integration" should in no way be regarded as synonymous with "assimilation" or "identification." Individuals whose action is governed by a set of institutional norms cannot be treated as though they were joined together by emotional ties or shared objectives. Nor is the actor enclosed inextricably within his role as was Nessus in his burning tunic. Beyond the variety of orientations characteristic of each role taken individually, there is a variety of motives and values associated with the role as well, and the actor has the opportunity to decide the relative weight to be given to each. The relation between the actor and the institution is to be thought of not in terms of unilateral dependence but rather of relativistic interdependence. The adjective "relativistic" is intended to emphasize that no one of the three points of view—culture, personality, society—is more "total" or "concrete" than the other two. This is what Parsons means when he says that sociology is an "analytic," that is, abstract science, and that society is not a thing but a collection of partial relations compatible under certain conditions.

Chapter Two

The Alternative Orientations of Action

The two sides of Parsons's ambition are reflected in the titles of the two books to which we shall now turn our attention. He continued to work toward fulfillment of his original intention, which was to lay the theoretical foundations of sociology. This is the plan that underlies *The Social System.* But he also set out to make a place for sociology within a larger framework, that of the theory of action. This is the aim of *Toward a General Theory of Action.*

What Is Social Action?

"'Action' is a process in the actor-situation system which has motivational significance to the individual actor, or, in the case of a collectivity, its component individuals" [1951*a*, p. 4]. From this definition several propositions follow: (1) Action is a process. It is a history; it has a dynamic. (2) Action takes place in a heterogeneous setting consisting of more than one actor (at a minimum, the pair ego-alter), together with physical and cultural objects, which do not "respond" to or anticipate ego's expectations as ego responds to and anticipates the expectations of alter. (3) Action is a system whose elements are the reciprocal expectations of the actors. (4) Action makes sense to the actors, taken together or individually (though an observer in possession of complete information might not agree with any part of the interpretation).

In the foregoing propositions we see clearly Weber's influence on Parsons. "The concept of action," Weber wrote, "includes any human behavior to which the actor attaches a subjective significance. . . . Because of the subjective meaning attached to it by the actor, action is social to the extent that it takes account of the behavior of others and adapts itself, so long as it continues, to that behavior."[1] In commenting on his translation of the first part of *Wirtschaft und Gesellschaft,* Parsons explains why Weber's term *Handeln* should be rendered in English as "action," a term applicable to "all the concrete phenomena of human behavior" but only insofar as they are accessible to the "understanding," in Weber's sense of the word *Verstehen,* that is, with the aid of subjective categories.[2]

In regard to *Verstehen,* Parsons points out that in Weber's sense the understanding involves more than an individual actor's awareness of his own motives or his ability to predict the consequences of his acts. Understanding another person is not, or in any case, not merely, a matter of finding out what is on his mind, what he means to say or do. The word "understanding," Parsons says, must be taken in a more technical sense, connoting two things. First, understanding involves the use of "subjective categories" (ends, means, project, aim, meaning). Second, these subjective categories have a certain universality. What is singular in the intention of an individual actor is of no use to us in trying to understand that intention. It is rather the relevance of one or more analytical categories (such as rational action, etc.) that can help us to unravel the tangle of motives behind a concrete act.

Parsons gives as a justification for his translation of *Handeln* as action the fact that Weber distinguished *Handeln* from *Verhalten,* a more general term applicable to the behavior of living beings in general, "whatever the framework for analyzing that behavior." He goes on to say that he might just as well have used "conduct" as "action." Obviously he regards the difference between the two as insignificant. His only concern is to avoid the suggestion of interpreting the Weberian notion of *Handeln* in narrowly behavioristic terms.

Narrowly behavioristic: the qualifier bears repeating—for the term "behavior" occurs frequently in "Values, Motives, and Systems of Action." "The theory of action," in the words of Parsons and Shils, "is a conceptual scheme for the analysis of the behavior of living organisms."[3] But the behaviorism of Parsons and Shils is of a rather special kind. Here is the way they describe it:

> There are four points to be noted in [our] conceptualization of behavior: (1) Behavior is oriented to the attainment of ends or goals or other anticipated states of affairs. (2) It takes place in situations. (3) It is normatively regulated. (4) It involves expenditure of energy or effort or "motivation" (which may be more or less organized independently of its involvement in action). Thus, for example, *a man driving his automobile to a lake to go fishing* might be the behavior to be analyzed. In this case, (1) *to be fishing* is the "end" toward which our man's behavior is oriented; (2) his situation is the road and the car and the place where he is; (3) his energy expenditures are normatively regulated—for example, his driving behavior is an *intelligent* means of getting to the lake; (4) but he does not spend energy to get there; he holds the wheel,

presses the accelerator, pays attention, and adapts his action to changing road and traffic conditions. When behavior can be and is so analyzed, it is called "action." [1951*a*, p. 53]

The distinguishing characteristic of the theory of action is that not only is actual and observable activity taken into account but so also are intentions and aims. The theory of action as set forth here by Parsons and Shils stands not only in the tradition of Weber but also in the line of Paul F. Lazarsfeld.[4] It may also be linked with various schools of psychology that flourished in Austria and Germany in the early years of the twentieth century. In a manner reminiscent of the Wurzburg school, Lazarsfeld calls attention to those approaches to psychology that use experimental techniques and provide some way of gauging the importance of ends in determining how the actors behave as well as ways of understanding "the successive transformations of their intentions, the influences that bring the act to its conclusion." To what Lazarsfeld calls the "empirical analysis of action," Karl and Charlotte Bühler contributed their insights into the origins of motives and the importance of motives in shaping "the perception and outlook of the subject." The two Viennese psychologists called attention to attitudes such as "satiety, functional pleasure, and the autonomy of the subject." The Gestalt psychologists, as well as Kurt Lewin during the Berlin phase of his career, also made a contribution to the action paradigm by calling attention to the notions of task and frustration, that is, to the interruption of action by interposition of an obstacle.

In the utilitarian scheme, the observer views the conduct of the actor in terms of his intentions and calculations. Psychologists in the early part of this century spoke of aims and attitudes. Parsons generalized both approaches and combined them in his theory. For his basic notion Parsons chose the idea of expectation, assuming that the actor can foresee certain events and their consequences and that he has an interest in achieving certain goals and enjoying the fruits thereof. Thus expectations, like attitudes and calculations, are intermediary and subjective; they enter into the action process itself, not as mere epiphenomena but by helping to give meaning to the process in the eyes of the actors themselves, or, more generally, in the eyes of persons affected by the process. Parsons's use of the idea of "expectations" is best understood by way of comparison with the idea of "intervening variables," which were introduced into psychology by certain researchers, such as Tolman,[5] who used them with greater frequency as he moved further away from his initial allegiance to behaviorism.

Historically, what is important about the notion of an intervening

variable is that it first appeared in psychology in the most strictly
positivistic of contexts, the psychology of learning. Experimental conditions by themselves prove to be insufficient to explain why certain
dogs and apes learn more quickly and surely than others. Some attention must be paid to the subject, both to its present state (dispositions)
and to its past experiences. But this approach is faced with two difficulties, the acuteness of which is made clear by the cautious attitude
adopted by an "orthodox" behaviorist like Hull. First, how can we be
sure that the factors singled out to explain the behavior of the subject
have not been chosen arbitrarily from among the whole range of possibly relevant factors? Second, if the aim is to arrive at intervening
variables that are something other than entelechies, variables of which
operational concepts may be made, then ways must be found to link
those variables to specific characteristics of the environment and to
unequivocal features of conduct, using rigorously defined and experi-
mentally controllable functions. Tolman, however, does not limit his
claims for his method to its applicability to the case of rats in a maze,
under strict experimental conditions. By identifying individual values
and beliefs in matters of cuisine and ambience, he asserts, one may
give an adequate account of a subjects's choice of one restaurant over
another. Tolman is well aware of the difficulty of "describing a standard experiment in which a measurable variation in the behavior of
the subject could be said to correspond to a given intervening variable."[6] There is nothing to indicate that this difficulty is lessened when
attention is shifted from rats to men. Lazarsfeld emphasizes this point
in his summary of Tolman's notion of an intervening variable: "We
have grave doubts whether such a procedure is feasible even with
animal experiments. And we are confident that it is the wrong idea as
far as the study of human behavior is concerned."[7]

Not even Tolman's rather widely ranging version of positivism was
able to establish an "operational" relation between the various stimuli
(taken to represent the environment) and responses (or observable
aspects of action), even with the aid of intervening variables, in-
ferentially assumed and granted rather ambiguous status as
"hypothetical constructs." Could one avoid the embarrassing impasse
into which Tolman stumbled? Or was any theory of action in which
intervening variables played a key role likely to wind up in the same
dead end?

Taking a totally different stance, Parsons's theory replaces the
intervening variables by norms, which specify the conditions under
which social action takes place. Central to pattern variable theory, this
approach emerges earlier in the discussion, in Parsons's introduction
of the notion of social system.

To be more than a mere rhetorical flourish, the word "system" must mean something beyond a collection of elements. What needs to be understood is the way in which the elements of the system are *related*—this being the case, it is pointless to ask whether the "system" or the "element" is the more fundamental concept.

> A social system consists in a plurality of individual actors inter-acting with each other in a situation which has at least a physical or environmental aspect, actors who are motivated in terms of a tendency to the "optimization of gratification" and whose relation to their situations, including each other, is defined and mediated in terms of a system of culturally structured and shared symbols [1951*a,* p. 6]

This passage reminds us of the three levels of reference intrinsic to every system of action—culture, personality, society—and introduces them as, and in terms of, relations: motives, roles , and values, that is, are all relations, and, what is more, they are related to one another. There are relations, for example between social interaction and culture and personality, although the former cannot be reduced to either of the latter. Reductionism is explicitly ruled out: Parsons condemns three "heresies," namely, "culturalism" (i.e., the reduction of the social fact to pure symbolism), "psychologism" (i.e., the reduction of social relations to the motivations of the actors), and "sociologism" (i.e., the view that actors and ideas, beliefs, and ritual can be treated as pure reflections of the "infrastructure" or as aspects of the division of labor).

To say that action is a system of norms or conditions does not preclude our saying that it is also a system of choice—provided, of course, that we give an appropriate meaning to the word "choice." In the works he wrote after 1950, Parsons tended to favor "orientation" or "selection" over "choice." Similarly, "goal" was preferred to "end." The words "choice" and "end" belong to an earlier vocabulary, that of *The Structure of Social Action*. The first pair of terms accentuated the subjective will of the decision maker, who called his own signals and was fully aware of his preferences. The switch to "goal" and "orienta-tion" marks the transition to a new framework. The actor still has a destination, a goal, but there is nothing to say that he actually arrives there or that the path he takes is the quickest and most direct. More important, "orientation," like Kurt Lewin's terms "vector" and "va-lence," suggests that the situation itself provides the actor with the occasion for and content of the choices he makes. The elements of the social system are choices made with reference to orientations that exist prior to the actor's arrival on the scene. The actor is not free to do as he pleases; he must operate within a web of constraints. But these constraints are not one-dimensional: they present themselves to the actor as a series of choices that he must make between alternative possibilities. Action is accordingly both constrained and free: constrained, insofar as the situation determines the conditions under which action takes place, and free, insofar as those conditions take the form of choices between alternatives.

Every action involves choice, and therefore motivation, too, is a matter of choice. Not only do we choose one motive over another, but our motives themselves are a product, a crystallization of a series of choices made as we grew up. There are basically three "orientations." I may seek to set up a relationship with an object (physical, social, or cultural in nature); we then say that this is an "object of my desire" (a "cathected" object, in Parsons's terms). Accordingly, it has an immediate influence on my emotional equilibrium. Or I may seek to define the properties of an object: to say what it is, to explore its relations with other objects or with myself, or to determine the conditions of its emergence or disappearance. Following Parsons, we shall call orientations of the first type "cathetic," orientations of the second type "cognitive." Since it is impossible to have both orientations at once, the actor must choose between them. When confronted with an object, will he try to approach it or avoid it because it inspires either desire or aversion in him? Or will he seek to investigate it so as to relate it to familiar aspects of his own life? Once we have recognized that motivation always involves both cognitive and cathectic aspects, we can then ask which of the two has priority: does the presence of one mean that the other must be entirely absent, or are combinations of the two possible, and if so, how?

Here we come to the third aspect of motivation, the "integrative" orientation, in connection with which Parsons speaks of "selective ordering." Most critics of Parsons have imputed to him a kind of obsession with "harmony" and "integration." If we focus on his own use of the word "integration" rather than on that of his critics, we find that he gave it two distinct, though rather clearly related meanings, neither of which has much to do with the conventional image of Parsons as a complacent champion of the status quo. First of all, integration, thought of in terms of "selective ordering," is a response to the fact that the energy of a human actor is limited. As the supply of energy is insufficient to allow response to all the stimuli impinging upon the actor, he must make some kind of selection. Now, the actor does not make this selection at random. Both his prior experience and his current partners will have an effect on the choices he makes. Thus motivation always entails evaluation, the purpose of which is to establish a list of priorities, a "selective ordering" of the various cathectic and cognitive orientations [1951*a*, p. 7]. Now, in choosing his object-orientations, and hence in making the evaluations in terms of which the choice of an object-orientation becomes possible, the actor can envision a certain level of ego-gratification only in terms of the relations between ego, the actor himself, and his situation, which includes ego's relations with one or more alters. In making these choices he may err in two ways. Ego may be mistaken, first, as to his own interests and desires. He may also wrongly anticipate alter's response to his initiatives. Thus in establishing priorities for the use of his resources, given a range of alternatives and the attendant risk of dissipating his energies, the actor must consider the need to maintain his own sense of wholeness, that is, his personal identity as well as the likelihood of his enlisting the help of others. Accordingly, the presence of some degree of integration and cohesiveness is a minimum condition without which there can be no actor, in the sense of a unified personality. At the same time we can see why this indispensable integration is reflected in the form of a "selective ordering" of orientations.

Need-dispositions in their "orientational" aspect are "expectations" that lay the groundwork for future choices, both immanent and remote, and thus enable the actor to exert control over the future. In view of his need-dispositions, the actor will judge some anticipated situations to be preferable to, more "gratifying" than, others. This will give him an incentive to explore certain anticipated situations and to make certain kinds of predictions concerning matters of interest to him (or for the sake of his intellectual curiosity). We may think of expectations as verifiable or, alternatively, as "falsifiable": they are "hypotheses" an actor makes with regard to the behavior of other actors. If action is to make sense to the actors, they have to have the capacity to communicate with one another about its significance, more rapidly, if possible, than the requirements of logical-scientific discourse allow. At this point Parsons proposes, in a manner reminiscent of George Herbert Mead, a distinction between sign and symbol. What distinguishes the symbol from the sign is that the significance of the former, unlike that of the latter, is not dependent on a constant and steady stimulus; "The sign is part of a situation which is stable independently of what the animal does; the only 'problem' presented to him is whether he can 'interpret' it correctly, e.g., that the black panel means food, the white one no food.'" In social interaction, moreover, the problems that arise are different from those faced by the rat in a maze (and also from those faced by the physicist in trying to unravel nature's laws). Indeed, "alter's possible 'reactions' may cover a considerable range, selection within which is contingent on ego's actions. Thus for the interaction process to become structured, the meaning of a sign must be further abstracted from the particularity of the situation. Its meaning, that is, must be stable through a much wider range of 'ifs,' which covers the contingent alternatives not only of ego's action, but of alter's and the possible permutations and combinations of the relation between them" [1951a, p. 11].

With his well-known remarks on the ability to "take the role of the other," Mead seems to reduce this social relation to an indefinite series of substitutions of ego for alter and vice versa. Still, he does call attention to the question of how we learn to "decenter" ourselves, to assume different points of view. He thereby brings home the problematical character of our relationship with alter. Though he claims to treat the problem not in philosophical but rather in "objective" and "scientific" terms, we again come back to the classic question of the "social order" [1937, pp. 89–95]—or, perhaps better, the question of the conditions under which ego and alter may reach a consensus.

The capacity to take the place of another person, whether in fact or in imagination, depends on symbolic communication, on mutual comprehension of intentions. Thus ego and alter have a basis of common understanding. This does not imply identity in their points of view or in their thinking, but it does ensure complementarity by means of word, deed, or symbolic interaction. We may look upon this common understanding from more than one angle and at different levels. For instance, from the attitudes of ego toward alter in the total field of their possible relations there must be distilled or filtered out a finite number of gestures and words. From another angle, we may look at beliefs about the social order, not necessarily empirically true but taken by those who hold them to be essential underpinnings of society: in other words, what Parsons calls "ideology" [1951a, pp. 349–51]. Such beliefs establish a code, or perceptual grid, that imposes limitations on social perception and experience, to which they impart a predetermined form. Thus the common basis of mutual understanding among the actors intervenes between each individual actor and his situation, shaping the actor's anticipations and enabling him to predict the behavior of others while at the same time enabling others to predict his behavior. Only selection makes prediction possible, however. Our expectations of others—and their expectations of us—commit us to a given course of action or oblige us to behave in certain ways only because such expectations enable us to make choices. The notion of choice is inseparable from the notion of value, to which Parsons attaches considerable importance. "An element of a shared symbolic system which serves as a criterion or standard for selection among the alternatives of orientation which are intrinsically open in a situation may be called a value" [1951a, p. 12]. In other words, values are not things, or even objects,[8] but terms of reference in the evaluation process, which has four main characteristics. First, this process is expressed in terms of the elements of a "symbolic system." Second, it involves problems not amenable to treatment by logico-experimental methods. Third, these problems are quite general in character. All men in all societies must face them, though the solutions given may vary widely from one case to the next. Finally, these problems are not independent of one another but form a system. That collective preferences are at once systematic and shared was seen clearly by Max Weber,[9] who believed that existence is in certain ways enigmatic or scandalous. To understand their predicament, human beings resort to symbolism, transposing the riddles of existence into the key of mythology or ritual. Birth and death, growth and decline, suffering, and the blindness of fate are among the eternal themes on which a systematic analysis of values might be based.

Evaluation, therefore, is an "attribution of meaning," a *Sinngebung* in Max Weber's terms, that enables an actor to make his way through life's obscurities. But the "criteria" or "standards" that govern our evaluations are not God-given. Values are neither alien nor transcendent; on the contrary, according to Parsons "a value pattern ... is always institutionalized in an *inter*action context" [1951a, p. 38]. Insofar as the value specifies in more or less precise terms what is desirable, suitable, or obligatory, it helps ego not only to know himself but also to know what he can and should expect from alter. Thus every evaluation process has two dimensions. It reflects the need-dispositions of the subject; from alter's standpoint, on the other hand, evaluation defines the conditions, that is, the norms, to which the interaction is subject.

The Pattern Variables

There are two equally legitimate standpoints from which to view the interaction process. One is microscopic and involves the analysis of roles; the other is macroscopic and involves the analysis of institutions.

> A role ... is a sector of the total orientation system of an indi-
> vidual actor. ... An institution will be said to be a complex of

institutionalized role integrates which is of strategic structural significance in the social system in question. The institution should be considered to be a higher order unit of social structure than the role, and indeed it is made up of a plurality of inter-dependent role-patterns or components of them. [1951a, pp. 38–39]

The problem is to understand how the elements (interpersonal relations, roles, institutions) are organized in more or less coherent, durable, and extensive "integrates."

Taking qualitative and quantitative aspects of these three variables together, the two terms "solidarity" (which is applicable to those groups that Parsons calls collectivities) and "anomie" (applicable to certain other groups) sum up the various possibilities. Solidarity and anomie may take different forms, but they are always subject to certain fundamental constraints; these constitute primary points of reference in the interaction process. These constraints may be described as alternative or two-pronged choices. What interests us here is not the contingent content of these choices but rather their form [1951a, pp. 58–59]. Interaction, whether it involves roles or institutions, takes the form of a series of choices or, rather, of selections of one or the other of two possible alternatives. The theorist's task consists of two parts. He must first try to identify what the possible alternatives are and may then go on to investigate the compatibility conditions that determine how the various possibilities may be combined.[10]

The problem is laid out in similar terms in "Values, Motives, and Systems of Action" [1951b] which Parsons wrote in collaboration with Edward Shils.

An actor in a situation is confronted by a series of major dilemmas of orientation, a series of choices that the actor must make before the situation has a determinate meaning for him. The objects of the situation do not interact with the cognizing and cathecting organism in such a fashion as to determine automatically the meaning of the situation. Rather, the actor must make a series of choices before the situation will have a determinate meaning. Specifically, we maintain, the actor must make five specific dichotomous choices before any situation will have a determinate meaning. The five dichotomies which formulate these choice alternatives are called the *pattern variables* because any specific orientation (and consequently any action) is characterized by a pattern of the five choices.

Three of the pattern variables derive from the absence of any biologically given hierarchy of primacies among the various modes of orientation. In the first place, the actor must choose whether to accept gratification from the immediately cognized and cathected object or to evaluate such gratification in terms of its consequences for other aspects of the action system (i.e., one must decide whether or not the evaluative mode is to be operative at all in a situation). In the second place, if the actor decides to evaluate, he must choose whether or not to give primacy to the moral standards of the social system or subsystem. In the third place, whether or not he decides to grant primacy to such moral standards, he must choose whether cognitive or appreciative standards are to be dominant, the one set with relation to the other. If cognitive standards are to be dominant over appreciative standards, the actor will tend to locate objects in terms of their relation to some generalized frame of reference; if appreciative standards are dominant over cognitive, the actor will tend to locate objects in terms of their relation to himself, or to his motives.

The other pattern variables emerge from indeterminacies intrinsic to the object situation: social objects as relevant to a given choice situation are either quality complexes or performance complexes, depending on how the actor chooses to see them; social objects are either functionally diffuse (so that the actor grants them every feasible demand) or functionally specific (so that the actor grants them only specifically defined demands), depending on how the actor chooses to see them or how he is culturally expected to see them.

It will be noted now that the three pattern variables which derive from the problems of primacy among the modes of orientation are the first three of the pattern variables as these were listed in our introduction; the two pattern variables which derive from the indeterminacies in the object situation are the last two in that list.

At the risk of being repetitious, let us restate our definition: a *pattern variable* is a dichotomy, one side of which must be chosen by an actor before the meaning of a situation is determinate for him, and thus before he can act with respect to that situation. We maintain that there are only five *basic* pattern variables (i.e., pattern variables deriving directly from the frame of reference of the theory of action) and that, in the sense that they are *all* of the pattern variables which so derive, they constitute a system. Let us list them and give them names and numbers so that we can more easily refer to them in the future. They are:

1. affectivity-affective neutrality
2. self-orientation–collectivity-orientation
3. universalism-particularism
4. ascription-achievement [Parsons later (1967, p. 195) changed his mind and decided to use the terms "quality-performance" in place of "ascription-achievement." In what follows, we shall use the terms that Parsons ultimately preferred, and we shall also use

a slash rather than a dash to separate pattern-variable components:
thus, "quality/performance"—trans.]
   5. specificity-diffuseness.

Thus the pattern variables are in fact a priori conditions imposed on
interaction. Elsewhere, Parsons and Bales argue that these conditions
are indeed a priori because "no hierarchy is given by the biological
nature of the actor." There are two possibilities: either the actor is
condemned to live amid chaos, constantly threatened with the danger
of behaving in self-destructive ways, or else he will attempt to make
sense of his experience with the aid of certain categories, which enable
him to find his proper place, both in relation to himself and his drives
and in relation to others.

What is noteworthy about these categories, however, is that they
confront the actor with a choice. Parsons's notion of choice has two
quite disparate sources. In neoclassical economics, the economic actor
is thought of as having a personal "preference schedule," on the basis
of which he is able to choose among goods of different kinds as well as
between physical commodities and currency and between consumption and saving or investment and saving. His ability to make such
choices is an expression of his freedom. And yet he is compelled to
choose, as it were, because the quantity of goods and services at his
disposal is limited. Given an actor together with his subjective preferences, and a situation in which resources are scarce, and assuming that
the actor will discriminate between goods and services according to
the degree of satisfaction they will bring him as determined by his
personal preference schedule, then it is clear that choice is merely a
method for optimizing resource use. Like the neoclassical economic
actor, the Parsonian actor is also compelled to choose because his
resources are limited. But in the case of the Parsonian actor, choice
does not take the form of an optimizing calculation.

Parsons's concept of choice was also influenced by Weber. Weber
held that, in spite of the fact that values are chosen by the individual,
they remain arbitrary. Values can be asserted and put to the test but
not proven. Strictly speaking, there is no way for the proponent of the
"ethics of responsibility" to prove to the proponent of the "ethics of
absolute values" that prudence and concern about the consequences
of one's actions—for oneself and others—should be considered more
important than total, irrevocable commitment; by the same token, the
Christian is unable to convince the Confucian that one should turn the
other cheek. But choices have their logic, and even arbitrary values,
once chosen, have relatively constraining consequences for those who
hold them. Weber was quite sensitive to the need for compatibility

among one's choices. This was a point he stressed against those who might forget that an ethic "is not a cab which one can have stopped at one's pleasure; it is all or nothing."[11] As for collective values, Weber was equally at pains to emphasize their arbitrariness. Puritanism is neither truer nor better than Buddhist mysticism. But if a society "chooses" Puritanism, it rules out certain other choices that would have been compatible with a choice of Buddhism.

Choice, as Weber understands it, is an arbitrary selection of ultimate preferences, subject to the requirement of verifying in detail that the consequences of the initial commitment are mutually compatible. The old saying "You can't have your cake and eat it too" puts the point succinctly. You may be fond of cake or not. You may eat it or not (though you are more likely to eat it if you are fond of it than if you are not). But it is not within your power—being forbidden by the reality principle—to eat your cake and still have it, inviolate and whole, in your cupboard. The compatibility requirement is fairly stringent. The more basic the actions or events on which choice is brought to bear, the more stringent the compatibility requirement becomes. If, as I am writing, I ask, "Is it raining or not?" the question makes sense. So does the question, "Shall I eat this piece of pie or save it until later?" The questions are so phrased that I cannot simultaneously choose both answers. It is raining, or it is not. I will eat the cake, or I will not. Let us next consider statements of a more complex kind, including information as to time, place, and so on. For example, consider the statement "I like pastry," or "the Atlantic climate is unstable." It is, of course, possible to object that statements of the form "X is a glutton," "the Atlantic climate is unstable," and the like cannot be held to be true along with their negations, "X is not a glutton," "the Atlantic climate is not unstable," or whatnot. But even though X is a glutton, the observer cannot predict whether he will choose an éclair or a baba au rhum; in fact, the observer will be unable to predict whether X, on this particular day, after a fairly heavy meal, will prefer a little dry cheese to pastry or not. By the same token, the observer cannot say whether it will rain today in London or not. It does not advance matters much to observe that, until we have arrived at some suitable index of meteorological stability, it is impossible to decide whether the Atlantic climate is stable or unstable anyway. Before we can even specify such an index, we must say what indicators make it up and show that to some degree they are compatible. Compatibility in this sense is quite different from compatibility in the purely logical sense, which involves only logical predicates and their mutual implications.

In Parsons's conception of choice, the stringency of the compatibility constraint depends on the complexity of the action. In the domain of unit acts (which it is tempting to call the atoms of interaction), choice is described in strictly dichotomous terms. Parsons makes this point crystal clear in the three passages we have cited. His argument boils down to two assertions: (1) the actor has at hand a stockpile of resources and possible uses for them; (2) given a context and an actor, there always exists a point of reference, which the actor may or may not take as a norm for his action. Looking at the aggregate, which involves a large number of unit acts and individual actors, we discover that a single actor may simultaneously adopt more than one point of reference (depending, in particular, on the number of different groups to which the actor belongs). From the macroscopic standpoint, the compatibility principle requires the existence of either an explicit aggregation procedure or a set of unconscious mechanisms for coordinating the either/or choices made by the individual actors in response to the alternatives facing them.

Does the theory of pattern variables explain how individual choices are coordinated so as to give rise to collective choices? As we shall see shortly, the only way to do this is to look at individual choices as flowing from dynamically interconnected strategies and plans of many kinds. From the standpoint of a static equilibrium, that is, at the moment of choosing, the choice appears to strike a balance between costs and benefits. Sacrifices are always involved. If I opt for a universalistic solution, I must forgo the particularistic one. But foregoing the latter *today* may promise that *eventually* certain benefits will accrue for my enjoyment. Socialization is based on a logic of this kind, involving tradeoffs and compensations; these take place constantly, not only among the members of the family within which socialization is being carried out, but also within the mind of the individual being socialized, who must make tradeoffs between one phase of his development and another (some bygone, some yet to come).

Given an actor, ego, engaged in an interaction process, the pattern variables are merely points of reference that ego may or may not apply to his relationship to alter. These points of reference, it should be added, constitute a system; they enter into all the dimensions of action—motives, roles, and values. In *The Social System,* as well as *Toward a General Theory of Action,* the pattern variables are introduced in a deductive form. They are "derived," or derivable, from the frame of reference, which is the most inclusive category of the general theory. The theory begins with a pair of actors, ego and alter. It is assumed that they are potential participants in a transactional process. In addition, they are assumed to be responsive, to have an interest in possessing certain goods, and to be motivated by their anticipations of their partners' reactions to their own initiatives. Finally, the theory stipulates that the resources available to the actors are limited. It then follows that ego and alter both must make certain choices, the logic of which results from the structure of the interaction.

Before turning to the question of whether this deduction or, as Parsons says, "derivation" of the pattern variables (which are thus treated as a priori conditions of interaction) can be taken seriously as establishing an axiomatic theory of action in general,[12] we can safely pause to notice that Parsons's approach is in fact an attempt to codify certain theories and concepts that to a certain extent were used in methodical ways by the founding fathers of sociology. Ever since Tönnies, the distinction between *Gemeinschaft* and *Gesellschaft* has held a preeminent place in German sociology. Nevertheless, this distinction was in a sense overdetermined: Tönnies proposed to use it to account not only for the structure of societies in general but also for the rationalization process said to be responsible for the rise of modern social forms. Weber incorporated the *Gemeinschaft-Gesellschaft* distinction in his own work, but used it on two different levels. In his most lengthy discussion of the topic,[13] he used it as an analytical tool to account for the gradual "disenchantment" *(Entzauberung)* of human societies. But the *Gemeinschaft-Gesellschaft* distinction already figured among the "fundamental concepts of sociology" treated in the first chapter of *Economy and Society*. Weber believed the distinction to be based on two pairs of attributes in combination: calculation as opposed to sentiment, and collective ownership by more than one individual as opposed to apportionment of the surplus, with its attendant risks of conflict.

At once too crude and too rich in meaning, the distinction between *Gemeinschaft* and *Gesellschaft* will not do. Accordingly, it needs to be analyzed into its constituent elements: the pattern variables. "The theory of pattern variables originated in an attempt to interpret the problem of the liberal professions. Quite plainly, the capitalism-socialism dichotomy was useless for this, and for that reason I turned to the well-known central distinction in German sociology, first set forth by Tönnies and later used by Weber, between *Gemeinschaft* and *Gesellschaft*" [1970*a*, p. 843]. By all appearances the distinction between community and society seemed relevant to the analysis of the liberal professions. "I took as my point of departure the problem of individual interest, as opposed to the public interest, even if the latter was not the overall public interest, the interest of the whole collectivity in the sense of the socialists. ... The physician declares that he regards the well-being of his patient as of paramount importance. In view of this criterion, it is legitimate to set medicine and the other liberal professions on the side of *Gemeinschaft.*" Though this line of inquiry at first seemed to augur well, things quickly went awry.

The fact is that the importance attributed to science, the universalistic character of the knowledge applied to problems of health exhibit all the characteristic traits of modern societies, which Tönnies and his followers would have classified under the head *Gesellschaft.* Tönnies' dichotomy did not represent the two extremes of a single variable but rather resulted from a confusion of several analytically independent variables.

For each pattern variable, an antecedent—often several of them—may readily be found in the classical literature. The self-orientation/collectivity-orientation dichotomy, for instance, harks back to the distinction between individualism and altruism; more generally, it has to do with the attempt to distinguish between what is determined by ego's inner state and what is under the influence of alter or the collectivity. Roles involving responsibility or representation are affected by this pattern variable. The affectivity/affective neutrality dichotomy is clearly Durkheimian in origin. Provided the terms are interpreted broadly enough, this variable is relevant to problems of discipline, mastery, and control, where the question, regardless of the type of activity involved, is to determine whether or not ego's emotional reactions will pose a problem. The specificity/diffuseness dichotomy figures in Durkheim's analysis of the two types of solidarity.[14] Quality/performance is a reformulation of Linton's distinction between ascribed status and achieved status. The distinction between universalism and particularism can be traced back equally to Weber and Durkheim. The assignment of bureaucratic roles must be carried out in accordance with criteria of competence, taking no account of kinship ties or clientele relationships. Similarly, in a regime of organic solidarity, as Durkheim describes it, the compensation awarded each participant in an interaction is said to depend on his *contribution;* all the participants have equal standing in the relationship.

If we think of the founding fathers of our discipline as having cleared the terrain, then the pattern variables serve to mark out the boundaries of the ground they cleared, the limits of the field of sociology. In one sense they provide us with a detailed survey of the territory conquered. Significant landmarks were turned up as modern societies emerged out of traditional ones, and these were recorded by our illustrious forebears. In some cases, however, the maps they left of their explorations are rather unintelligible. Order needed to be brought to the confused landscape, and for this it was useful to work out what the frame of reference was, to distinguish between different levels of action (personality, culture, society), and to treat action in terms of a series of dichotomies.

If one follows Merton in using the term "codification" to mean an effort to systematize the empirical generalizations suggested by an investigation of apparently disparate forms of behavior,[15] then the theory of pattern variables may be considered an example of codification—although in Parsons's exposition, the theory is presented in deductive form, that is, both as a set of propositions derivable from the frame of reference and as a point of departure from which new statements concerning social action may be derived. Let us suppose that some satisfactory relationship between the pattern variables and the frame of reference has been established. We then need to ask what the usefulness of the pattern variables might be. This question is treated in *The Social System* (pp. 111–14) and in *Toward a General Theory of Action* (pp. 247–55). Roughly speaking, to show that the pattern variables are of general import, it is enough to demonstrate that they provide a full complement of tools for analyzing motives, roles, and values.

At this point, it will be useful to take a new tack, beginning this time with the double contingency of ego and alter. A well-known example of double contingency is provided by the phenomenon of the division of labor.

> Nobody ever saw one animal by its gestures and natural cries signify to another, this is mine, that yours; I am willing to give this for that. . . . But man has almost constant occasion for the help of his brethren, and it is in vain for him to expect it from their benevolence only. . . . Whoever offers to another a bargain of any kind, proposes to do this: Give me that which I want, and you shall have that which you want.[16]

We give and receive not only goods, labor, and cash but also feelings and attitudes. If I show love for someone, I expect to be rewarded with love in return, and if I give someone something, I expect that person to return the gift in kind. From this it does not follow that "social exchange" of feelings and attitudes can be reduced to an exchange of goods and services. In both cases, however, a relation, or, rather, a set of reciprocal relations is instituted, though of course ego and alter do not always enjoy equal status in these relations. To analyze these fundamental forms of double contingency we may use the affectivity/affective neutrality variable in conjunction with the specificity/diffuseness variable. Since each of the two possible values of the former may be combined with either possible value of the latter, we obtain a table with four entries: these are the four ways in which ego may be related to alter [1951*a*, p. 108]. Following Parsons, we shall call the first of these four types of relationship "receptiveness-responsiveness," which Parsons describes as "the disposition to be receptive to and respond to alter's attitude of expectation of mutual gratifications within a specific sphere or context." We shall call our attitude toward alter "approval" when we "aprove alter's action within a specific sphere conditional on his performances in terms of a standard." These two attitudes are *specific,* since they apply to a specific area of interaction. Whereas the first of them engages ego's affectivity, however, the second does not involve ego emotionally in his judgment of alter's performance. Next, we shall use the term "love" to denote "the disposition to be receptive to and to reciprocate a diffuse affective attachment to alter and accept the obligation of loyalty accompanying it." Finally, we shall use the term "esteem" to refer to the "disposition to evaluate alter as a total personality relative to a set of standards." Love and esteem are contrasted in the same way as affectivity and neutrality, or, again, in the same way as hot and cold, but they share as a common feature their inclusion of both parties in a diffuse bond of solidarity, whereas "receptiveness-responsiveness" and "approval" (the former "hot," the latter "cold") establish specific, reciprocal ties between ego and alter.

This mapping of "the major types of value-orientation of personal attitudes" lays the groundwork for an analytical treatment of social roles. We shall encounter such a treatment when we come to investigate the theory of social control. In Parsons's well-known analysis of medical practice [1951*a*, chap. 10], the theory of pattern variables is used to elucidate the relationship between the physician and his patient. What is striking about this analysis is, first of all, the care with which Parsons situates the doctor-patient relationship in the several contexts (cultural, interpersonal, and social) in which it develops. He begins by describing the cultural tradition that serves as backdrop to the professional practice of medicine and goes on to show how the "interests" (in the Weberian sense) that underlie medical practice combine a theoretical with a practical orientation. Unstable and tenuous in the extreme, this amalgam can be realized in practice only if the physician's actions are guided by the appropriate pattern variables. Parsons explains how medicine is dependent upon a specific state of scientific knowledge and linked to popular traditions and beliefs. Progress in anatomy, for example, was long impeded by the prohibition of dissection. Similarly, Pasteur in the nineteenth century ran up against traditional ideas about spontaneous generation. In the next stage of his analysis, Parsons turns to an examination of the "social structure" constituted by the physician and his patient. He explains in detail why the two partners cannot enter into a straightforward "face-to-face" relationship. There is, in fact, no way to "control" the risks of "exploitation" by one party or the other unless the roles of both are specified, in certain critical respects, by means of strict and explicit norms. More fundamentally, only if certain conditions are fulfilled is therapeutic intervention possible; certain precautions must be taken if recovery is to follow a normal course. The patient's incapacity to help himself and his anxiety about his condition would mark him out as a hapless victim for the machinations of the unscrupulous physician if there were no stringent code of ethics designed to protect the patient—for the most part successfully—against just such depredations. Looking now at the physician, we find that he, too, is subject to a variety of pressures. What is more, he must be on his guard against attempts by the patient to *seduce* him, taking the word "seduce" in its broadest possible sense, not merely in its sexual aspect. The patient, likely to be affected by the vicissitudes of his malady and frequently prone to take his doctor for a surrogate father or spouse or even, more generally, for a savior, may well project very intense emotions onto the physician. Such projection or transference may thwart the therapeutic process.

Accordingly, without norms there would be a danger that the therapeutic relationship would degenerate into one of cynical exploitation of the patient by the physician, or into one of manipulation of the physician by the patient by means of emotional blackmail that would prevent effective treatment from being undertaken. The context within which these norms are specified is defined by the pattern variables. The physician's role is universalistic; put differently, the medical practitioner *must not* give consideration to any private ties he may have with his patients, but *must,* rather, treat them as "cases" or instances of well-defined nosological types. This is why medical ethics do not allow the physician to give medical care to his spouse, his children, his parents, or even his intimate friends. Second, because the physician may be obliged to require his patient to take great risks or make large sacrifices, he must be on his guard against "seduction" by the patient. Even if he feels personally "involved" in the course of the illness or the fate of the patient, the doctor must take an "affectively neutral" attitude. Third, the prestige attaching to the physician's role is independent of such attributes as age or reputation for wisdom. Prestige comes rather from the physician's manifest competence, which is warranted by a diploma or certificate issued either by the medical profession itself through its duly authorized agencies or by such public institutions as universities or boards of medical examiners. Fourth, the physicians' competence is specific. Too broad an interpretation of medical competence, transcending the bounds of health concerns proper, would threaten to undermine the affective neutrality of the physician. To transform the doctor—especially the general practitioner—into an adviser or confessor of some sort would tend to run counter to the universalism essential to his outlook.

Finally, the physician is under a clear imperative to provide a "service": his role is collectivity-oriented. This phrase calls for clarification. The collectivity in question is primarily, if not exclusively, that consisting of physician and patient. But there is also a need to protect the interests of third parties, such as relatives, and some control must be exerted over their possible wish to interfere in the treatment. More than that, the therapeutic process and its outcome depend on conditions in the wider society, which is necessarily affected by medical treatment. Sometimes, as in the case of epidemics, these social effects may be dramatic, while at other times they may be diffuse and barely noticeable. Yet the health of our neighbors and fellow citizens is never a matter of indifference to us, for it affects the quality of our own lives. One final point is that increasingly often the physician performs his role in an organizational setting. Even if the organization is private, it will usually receive some public funding. As Parsons uses the term here, however, the "collectivity" is not limited solely to the doctor-patient pair, or even to the institutional framework in which their interaction takes place. It is defined, further, by the normative bond that associates them in the execution of a common task. Physician and patient form a "collectivity" in the sense that they are joined together in their common goal of bringing about a cure of the patient's ailment. This common goal legitimates their expectations of one another and establishes a firm basis of procedure. The physician—like the attorney and the educator—has a special role, due to his dedication to healing, in virtue of which his role is distinguished from that of the businessman, the merchant, or the bureaucrat.

Let us now consider the following question: Which pattern variables are relevant to the definition of the patient's role? We shall begin by describing the patient's situation [1951a, p. 436]. If the physician is a "technician" whose services are sought out by the client, the patient may be described as passive and dependent. He cannot overcome his difficulties on his own: hence he is in need of help, and help of a specific kind—technically effective and morally disinterested, or at least well-intentioned. Since, however, the passivity that makes the patient dependent on others (he is bedridden and cannot take care of himself) can also be the source of significant secondary advantages (people minister to his needs, tell him to stay in bed, overlook his moods), his condition must be verified, certified by someone. Otherwise, anyone could declare himself ill in order to shift the burden of the healthy persons's responsibilities onto others. Then, too, there is the possiblility that the assistance the sick man needs to get well will be offered to him by charlatans intent on exploiting his ignorance and disorientation. Hence his obligation to seek medical care—which stems not only from his obligations to others (his children, his spouse) but also from his general obligation to himself to maintain his good health, since health is in itself a good thing, and to refuse to seek medical care may in extreme cases be taken as a form of suicide—goes hand in hand with an obligation to turn to a competent provider of such care, a trained physician and not a quack. Given the characteristics of the patient's situation, Parsons has no difficulty showing that pattern-variable components—namely, affectivity, quality, and particularism—may be used to define the role and expectations of the patient, just as universalism, affective neutrality, and performance make it possible to define the role of the physician.

Using the above analysis, we can also restate the problem of the complementarity of expectations, or "double contingency," and the problem of the "reciprocity of orientation" of ego and alter. The meaning of these phrases is clear: ego and alter cannot even enter into a relationship unless they simultaneously accept the same norms and partake of the same values. But this may be misleading if it is interpreted to mean that the content of the roles of ego and alter is the same, or that both submit to the authority of identical values, though, of course, the two roles are complementary. Doctor and patient need not, and in fact do not, behave in the same way. Each interprets the meaning of the word "health" differently. That their expectations are complementary in no way implies that these expectations are the same. Still more important, the fact that ego and alter stand in a relationship of reciprocity to each other does not mean that one may be freely substituted for the other, or that they stand on an equal footing.

In Parsons's work reciprocity does not imply equality between the participants in an exchange, nor does it imply quantitative equivalence of that which is exchanged. To the extent that the Parsonian notion of reciprocity is derived from the Durkheimian model of the division of labor, role differentiation and specialization are implicit in it. But Parsons also takes account of the integration of roles in a hierarchy. The patient's need to be protected against potential abuse or exploitation by the physician is a consequence of the technical competence of the latter. This competence affords the doctor a specific advantage over the patient, an advantage that carries with it rather extensive powers. The patient *must* in large measure trust the physician's diagnosis and accept the therapy prescribed because doctor and patient have quite different responsibilities and jobs to perform, both in the qualitative sense and in view of their different positions in the hierarchy.

The usefulness of the pattern variables in the analysis of values has yet to be shown. The classical sociologists, particularly Durkheim, stressed the importance of values, though they did not always clearly specify their content. Nor did they always indicate precisely how the common values actually govern the behavior of the actors—how the conformity of individual behavior with the ideals prescribed by these values is actually brought about. Weber did make some progress toward a systematic treatment of common values in his treatment of such problems as death, suffering, and fate as seeds around which meaning might crystallize for an individual trying to make sense of his experience. He based his comparative study of the world's major religions on two dichotomies: innerworldly/otherworldly and asceticism/mysticism. In Puritanism, for example, an innerworldly *(innerweltlich)* orientation is coupled with an ascetic orientation, whereas Buddhism combines otherworldliness with mysticism.

Weber sought to discover what system of ethics underlies economic behavior by investigating the meaning assigned to another world in which the world of ordinary labor, this world, is incorporated. Suppose that, instead, we try to understand directly how our experience of the social world acquires meaning by virtue of certain dichotomies that exist in our minds. Two particular dichotomies are pertinent to this question: universalism/particularism (which we shall abbreviate U/P), and performance/quality (Per/Q). U/P enables us to determine how values are assigned to roles and statuses. Per/Q is relevant to the establishment of a hierarchical ordering of individuals and groups: in establishing such a hierarchy, we may give precedence either to the intrinsic attributes of the actors—what they are—or to their contributions—what they do.

Combining each of the two terms of one variable with each of the two terms of the other, we obtain four pairs in all. Let us suppose, for example, that a value-orientation is described by the combination of universalism with performance (U-Per). Then roles, status, resources, and rewards will be assigned and evaluated in accordance with principles independent of the persons involved either in making the allocation or in receiving the assignments (in view of the primacy of U) and in accordance with the contributions actually made by the actors (in view of the priority of Per). Is the combination U-Per stable? To answer this question, we may ask what happens when U is associated with Q (roughly, ascription [quality]). As before, roles and status are allocated in accordance with principles that are the same for all. But the value attributed to the actor no longer depends solely or principally on his actions. No longer is he "the person who performed such and such an act" but rather "the person who has such and such a status." When the value-orientation is described by U-Per, initiative, self-assertiveness, and mobility are valued. On the other hand, when the value-orientation is described by U-Q, then rank and honorific status (*Ehre* in the language of the Junkers) are valued.

Without, for the moment, going into the highly complex conditions that govern the way these orientations are actually incorporated into the social system, we may ask whether the pattern variables preserve their identities when they enter into combination with one another. Universalism, when associated with achievement, signifies that the attributes of a given actor are evaluated independently of the relation in which that actor stands to the person evaluating his actions. When the actor is no longer indentified with his actions but rather with his status in a hierarchy, can it be said that his independence still holds? Nothing prevents us from judging a Junker in accordance with the universalistic criteria that define the category of Junkers. But to judge in this way might undermine the status hierarchy. Under these circumstances, a danger of conflict is inherent in the value system.

Let us now turn to the other half of the U/P dichotomy, particularism. We find particularism in combination with either achievement or ascription. In both cases, roles, status, and sanctions, both positive and negative, will be attributed to ego and alter in the light of their relation to one another. When the value-orientation is described by P-Per, however, the common values will apply to the achievements (not to say successes) of a generalized, idealized alter; when the orientation is described by P-Q, on the other hand, it will be the qualities and attributes of alter that matter.

The Scope and Meaning of the Theory

The list of pattern variables spells out the fundamental dichotomies on which the system of action is based. I shall pass over the question of whether the list is exhaustive, as Parsons and Shils claim. As for the independence of the variables upon which they lay equal stress, the point is indeed of crucial importance. If, for example, universalism were allowed to occur in combination only with certain of the other variables, such as specificity, affective neutrality, and achievement, then plainly the number of permissible combinations would be severely reduced, and we would find ourselves back in the predicament of having only a single dichotomy of the *Gemeinschaft-Gesellschaft* type, which is precisely what Parsons wished to avoid. This is what happens, for example, when one attempts to characterize the common values of industrial society by drawing a contrast with traditional society. In the one case we find affective neutrality, universalism, specificity, performance; in the other affectivity, particularism, diffuseness, quality. Where roles or motives are concerned, however, there is no problem combining universalism with diffuseness, or specificity with affectivity (just as we have already seen, in considering the level of values, that we could equally well have universalism in conjunction with quality or particularism in conjunction with performance). The universalism/particularism dichotomy, for instance, is appropriate in considering the role of the artist [1951a, pp. 408–14]. For the artist's expressive technique is subject to the definite rules of a strict discipline and aims at communicating with a public. To that extent, the artist role is characterized by universalism; on the other hand, the spectator who experiences the emotions that the artist intended to express is characterized by particularism. In contrast to the role of the scientist, the role of the artist may be described as "hot," that is, characterized by affectivity; this legitimates the expression of the "need-dispositions" of the artist, although that expression may, of course, take a stylized form.

Each term of each dichotomy can therefore be combined across the board with any of the others. This does not, however, mean that all the theoretically possible combinations are equally probable. To investigate the compatibility conditions governing the stability and viability of the various combinations of variables, we must deal with a number of questions that go beyond the analysis of the variables themselves. As we have already seen, the coupling of two variables may give rise to tensions. When universalism occurs in conjunction with ascription, many problems arise, as was the case, according to Parsons, in Germany before the Nazis came to power. There, the characteristic qualities of the actor and, above all, his position in the hierarchy proved to be impediments to the application of universalistic criteria. "Implementation," however, of universalistic values (even leaving aside for the time being the problem of the compatibility of universalistic with other criteria) presupposes a certain interrelation between roles and motives. These, as we have seen, cannot be reduced to values, nor can they be reduced to the pattern variables. Take

American society, for example. As Tocqueville saw with great lucidity, the value-orientation in the American system is characterized by universalism and performance. To begin with, this value-orientation is incorporated in the structure of professional roles. Careers are open to talent: in the United States, from colonial times on, the application of this precept has been facilitated by the absence of aristocratic and corporative traditions. To explain how universalism and performance are implemented in the American value system, we must look at the activities in which this particular combination is embodied, so to speak, as well as at what sanctions are applied; on the other hand, we must also look at sectors not characterized by this combination of variables.

In a later work,[17] Parsons tells us that the notion of society is to be distinguished from the notion of social system. A society is characterized by a high degree of self-sufficiency and independence of the environment. The question of the compatibility of the elements of the social system with the pattern variables is thus more than a question of logical consistency. The relation between the social system and its internal and external environments will also be germane to the question of compatibility. This explains why certain combinations of variables are more likely to occur than others. The pattern variables are not to be confused with the society itself: arguments of two kinds may be adduced to show why this should be so. First, society is a system, the elements of which cannot be associated in an arbitrary manner. Second, the social system involves not only regulated transactions among the actors taking part in it but also transactions between the actors and their environments, which the social system makes possible.

What, finally, is the status of the pattern variables? Are they essences, forms of sociability—or purely conventional constructs? To answer that they are essences or forms is to give a "realist" cast to the theory of action, where the "realism" in question is based either on the small group or on culture. Both of these interpretations are unacceptable. As we have seen, values do not operate autonomously; it is impossible to explain the functioning of any society as an automatic and immediate response to the imperatives of the *conscience collective*. By the same token, there is no reason to treat directly observable groups as though they were self-sufficient entities. To be sure, a group is something other than a collection of individuals: it is a patterned set of roles played by individual actors. Accordingly, no group is characterized by the presence or absence of any one variable such as universalism, specificity, etc. If one must insist on the "reality" of the group (for polemical purposes, such an insistence may well be useful as a reply to the claims of certain "reductionists"; in the final analysis, however, to say that the group is real is not to say that it is more real than the individual but rather that the social system is different from the personality system), then it must be added that the reality of the group is not the same as the reality of the pattern variables. The reality of the group is merely a constraint imposed by the requirement that certain pattern variables be compatible with one another.

A nominalistic interpretation of the pattern variables, on the other hand, is clearly ruled out by the passages we have cited. There we saw that the pattern variables were introduced not as hypothetical constructs but as necessary conditions without which interaction would be impossible, as norms governing the manner in which interaction takes place. This does not mean that we must regard them as Kantian a prioris. Think, instead, of the so-called oppositions in phonology, as defined by Nicolas Troubetzkoy: "A phonological opposition is a phonic difference that may, in a given language, be used to differentiate one mental signification from another."[18] I shall say nothing of the distinction between phonics and phonology other than to mention that it is useful for distinguishing between the acoustical material, the sounds of human language, and the phonic images of which the words of a language are composed. We may, then, refer to the roles as the "distinctive features" of the social system, and to variables as the "distinctive features" of roles [borrowing again from the terminology of structural linguistics—trans.]. The observed differences between two roles, or between two types of roles, enable us to explain how ego and alter can give different interpretations of their behavior.

Now, in linguistics, the "sign" can be analyzed as a sequence of "non-significant distinctive features."[19] In other words, phonological oppositions are different in nature from phonic oppositions, which are nothing more than "the material components of the sounds of human speech." We may ask, however, to what extent Parsons's dichotomies also exist outside the mind of the actor, even though it is indeed true that the actor uses those dichotomies to construct a series of "distinctive oppositions" by which one role may be distinguished from another, thereby obtaining a better comprehension of a process that is under his control though he has not "produced" it.

Here we can do no more than treat this question superficially in passing. An adequate treatment must be deferred until we have discussed the phenomena of development and regression in terms of both the social system and the personality system.[20] Only then shall we be in a position to appreciate fully the nature of the pattern variables as defined by Parsons. Before looking into how the system of distinctive oppositions is constructed, however, we shall mention some of the difficulties that Parsons runs into as a result of resorting to what Martinet (in discussing the work of Troubetzkoy) has called "binary apriorism." Parsons's assertion that the oppositions or dichotomies characteristic of the system of action are of the form "either ... or ..." lands him in the same predicament the great Russian linguist faced when he introduced the notion of correlative oppositions. The "correlation property" involves the opposition between the presence and the absence of a phonic quality that differentiates several pairs of phonological units (in French, e.g., the presence or absence of nasal resonance differenciates between a as in "bas" and $\tilde{a}$ as in "parl*an*t," or between e as in"est" and $\tilde{e}$, the nasal vowel sound in "v*in*" or p*ain*").[21] Thus the universalism/particularism opposition might be called "correlative," since it indicates the presence or absence of a set of features that can be used to differentiate between several pairs of social roles. Whenever an opposition is not correlative, it will be treated, roughly speaking, as a disjunction, a "simplistic"[22] procedure, to be sure, but one that can be made considerably more precise by introducing another distinction, between proportional opposition and isolated opposition.[23] "An opposition is proportional if the relation between the terms is identical to the relation between the terms of other oppositions belonging to the same system."[24] Using only the strict concept of correlative opposition, the relations $p:t$ and $t:k$ have nothing in common with any other oppositions involving p. Using the notion of proportional opposition, however, it is possible to show that, between the terms of the series p, t, k, there exist the same types of relations as between the terms of this series and the terms of the correlative series b, d, g. In other words, $p:t, t:k, k:p$ as $p:b, t:d, k:g$.

Assume, next, that there is a feature or set of features whereby it is possible to establish a correlative opposition between two roles. Let us borrow, for purposes of illustration, Radcliffe-Brown's well-known analysis of the role of the maternal uncle in South Africa.[25] Between the maternal uncle and the nephew a correlative opposition can be shown to exist, characterized in some cases by the presence, in others by the absence, of tender relations. Two further observations will enable us to make the extent of this opposition more precise, however. First, the maternal uncle/nephew opposition is connected with the father/son opposition. "In groups where familiarity characterizes the relationship between father and son, the relationship between maternal uncle and nephew is one of respect; and where the father stands as the austere representative of family authority, it is the uncle who is treated with familiarity."[26] More generally, the nature of these oppositions is determined by the matrilineal system of filiation in the former case, the patrilineal system in the latter. One result of this analysis, not immediately apparent, is that it becomes possible to undertake a systematic comparison between the role of the father in the matrilineal system and the role of the father in the patrilineal system, by way of the proportional oppositions between the father and the maternal uncle and the son and the nephew in both systems of filiation.

In this way binarism may be saved, but only if it is possible to construct proportional oppositions from a given set of correlative oppositions. Now, this construction is possible only if the categories of features to which the oppositions refer are themselves defined in an unequivocal way. This is the case in linguistics, where "the material components of the sounds of human speech (whether the vibrations of the air corresponding to these sounds, or the positions and movements of the organs producing them)"[27] can be classified objectively.

Suppose that the pattern variables are invariants of every system of action, although it is difficult to see how we might view them as nonsymbolic "material components" analogous to the "sounds of human speech." A major problem remains. These oppositions must still possess the same value[28] in whatever context they may appear—or, at the very least, it must be possible to introduce a series of regular correspondences between one use and another. When we come to discuss the problem of social stratification, the importance of this problem will emerge with particular clarity, as will the difficulty of giving a satisfactory solution to it.

Elsewhere I have referred to the theory of pattern variables as a "set of axioms for action in general."[29] The claim was excessive: Parsons's assertions regarding action do not have the rigor of Peano's assertions about natural numbers. If we agree, nevertheless, to talk about a set of axioms, we must understand that the word axiom is to be taken in its modern rather than its traditional sense. Traditionally, an axiom was a self-evident truth. That universalism and particularism stand in mutually exclusive opposition is not a self-evident true proposition about action in the sense that, in Euclidean geometry, it is self-evident that through a given point in a plane it is possible to draw one and only one line parallel to a given line in that plane. Gonseth has written that "a set of axioms states that certain relations among elements given *a priori* are possible." Here we see clearly the point of using a set of axioms in the modern sense of the term. The purpose of doing so is no longer to apprehend categorical truths but rather to make explicit notions that at first were only dimly perceived. An axiomatic approach aims at bringing to light the initial *terms* and *propositions* and the *relations* between them, and it proceeds along two paths at once.[30] For one thing, one tries to set forth noncontradictory principles on which to base a theory. As Gonseth put it, the axioms are used simply to establish what relations are possible. To that end, one tries to reduce the theory at hand to a prior theory, which is assumed to be consistent. Then the consequences of the theory in question can be spelled out, and one can work downward toward the empirical data by constructing a model, that is, a set of hypotheses that must be both verified and at the same time shown to satisfy the relations set forth by the axioms.

With any set of axioms it is possible to work both upward and downward. Parsons's approach is to do both together. His purpose is to boil down certain vague notions drawn from common parlance to a few basic terms: role, actor, situation. Once these terms have been defined, a set of preliminary propositions may be compiled: (1) the situation has a meaning for the actor; (2) the situation consists of physical objects, symbols, and other actors; (3) the actor chooses from among the various elements, material and symbolic, where the stockpile of all resources is finite. The pattern variables set up primary relations among these terms, specifying how ego, alter, and the situation are all contingent upon one another.

Suppose this set of propositions is noncontradictory; then we may say that any proposition that can be shown to follow from them has been "derived" from the general theory. But it is not enough for a theory to be noncontradictory. It must be applicable to a specific domain. If this is the case, we say that the axioms are "realizable"[31] in terms of a model, that is, a concrete theory—a theory pertinent to a specified domain.

Can it be said that Parsons's primitive terms and propositions are beyond criticism from the standpoint of consistency? Unlike the primitive terms used by Peano, such as "zero," "number," and "is a successor of," the primitive terms introduced in *The Social System* and *Toward a General Theory of Action* do not lend themselves to operational definition. We need not even go so far as to compare Parsons's axioms for action in general with the theory of numbers. They do not stand up well in comparison with the axioms used in the theory of consumer's behavior, which successfully set forth restrictive conditions under which the consumer may maximize his utility function. It may be asked further whether the notion of choice, taken in the strict sense to refer to a choice of one of two possible alternatives, is compatible with the notion of symbol, taken (far less rigorously) to mean a substitute or equivalent.

Still, as I shall argue here, even when its weaknesses have been recognized, there are at least two reasons why the theory should be invaluable as an analytical tool. In the first place, the theory enables us to make certain fundamental statements about man's "unique position" in the world, and in so doing to make clear what we mean in saying that man is a social animal. Even if we adopt the familiar standpoint of contemporary social science, according to which such assumptions are unnecessary, we cannot regard it as unimportant whether the social actor is held to be jealous or benevolent, or whether socialization is seen as purely repressive or, in contrast, as a growth process. The advantage of clarity and formal tidiness is apparent when we survey the confusion that surrounds contemporary debate in such disciplines as the sociology of education or politics. The hypotheses put forward by rival schools within these disciplines strike one as arbitrary and tenuous. Not that facts are wanting. But the factual information adduced is hard to interpret in the murky light cast by pseudohypotheses that amount to no more than commonsense clichés or piquant paradoxes. Parsons's approach has the merit of forcing us to lower our masks, to lay our cards on the table rather than keep our aces up our sleeves. The great virtue of any attempt to axiomatize or formalize a theory, even if it is unsuccessful, is, or rather should be, that it forces all of us to pay careful attention to what we are saying and to distinguish between proof and ad hoc argument. Such intellectual hygiene is of particular importance in sociology, a discipline in which labor and thought are lavished on prejudices—both our own and those of other sociologists—these being the raw material of our industry. Criticism—"the examination of pretentions," to borrow from Kant— begins with formalization.

A second argument may be put forward in support of what Parsons attempted. A theory is not to be judged only in itself (most notably for consistency) but also in relation to other theories. Does it do a better job than its rivals of answering the questions that typify the "state of the art" at a given moment in the history of a science? If we agree, furthermore, that every science needs a frame of reference within which each researcher working in a particular field may, if need be, provide a definition of each term that he uses, at least in principle, then theory is indispensable, and the alleged vanity of theory is no excuse for trying to do without it.

Finally, any theory that aims at a high level of generality consists of a hard central core together with more peripheral propositions, with some degree of coordination between the one and the other. By focusing attention on the links between the center and the periphery, we can gain some idea of how the theory came into being. We may also gain insight into the interaction between the formative intuitions of the central core of the theory and the intractable problems and paradoxical phenomena that turn up on the periphery—a two-way interchange as a result of which the theory was molded into shape and given genuine content.

Chapter Three

The Social System

Social action is "a process in the actor-situation system which has motivational significance to the individual actor," who chooses *his* orientation in terms of the binary pairs of attributes that characterize his own motives and the anticipated responses of his partners [1951*a*, p. 4]. What distinguishes this point of view from the individualistic approach is that here social action is not said to be determined by individual preferences in aggregate. The tastes of individuals are not regarded as randomly distributed; they have a structure. The choices confronting ego do not merely reflect his subjective condition. They are implicit in the environmental constraints that impose limits on action and confront the actor with a situation the consistency of which is reminiscent of that of nature itself.

There is good reason to doubt that economic action involves only random choices.[1] Scarcity obliges the economic actor to forgo the consumption of certain goods and to combine the resources that he does use according to set rules. Prices are fixed so as to reconcile the individual preference schedules of the various parties involved in the exchange. Similarly, the cost of a factor reflects the sacrifice or expense involved in its use. If we assume that the economic actor will attempt to situate himself at a point lying on the highest indifference curve within his reach, it follows that there are prices at which he will not buy, and costs that he will not accept (even though the projected cost falls within the bounds fixed by his budget). What is random is merely the consumer's schedule of ultimate preferences. The theoretical task with which Parsons, who wished to "generalize" economic theory,[2] was faced was to show how an analysis in terms of consumer tastes might be extended by an analysis in terms of collective values, without reverting to a model based on an aggregation of individual characteristics.

At no point in his writings, however, does Parsons abandon the notion that social action always makes sense to the individual actor.

This does not imply that social action has any immediately apparent meaning, or that its meaning is the same for all the actors involved. Nor does it imply that the meaning ascribed to social action by an observer will coincide with its meaning as understood by all, some, or even a single one of the actors. Parsons goes no further than to assert that the categories appropriate to the interpretation of action are subjective categories (meaning, intention, or project, in which the double contingency of ego and alter is implicit). Thus it is never legitimate to look upon collective values or norms as pure constraints, as physical objects—nor is it legitimate to look upon them as ruses of Reason.

In Parsons's view, then, social action is not determined either by individual preferences in the aggregate or by blind environmental pressures affecting the actors. One way to approach the subjectively meaningful, yet stable and consistent, structure of relations affecting social action is to focus on the "group." The elements of the group are interacting individuals, that is, individuals playing roles. The group is the most appropriate context in which to study interactive processes, which acquire a normative structure from the pattern variables. Once this study has been carried out, we will be in a position to define the notion of function more precisely.

Functional Analysis of the Small Group

Imagine a group consisting of a dozen or so people gathered around a table to discuss a problem submitted for their consideration:

> Each member receives some impression or perception of each other member distinct enough so that he can, either at the time or in later questioning, give some reaction to each of the others as an individual person, even though it be only to recall that the other was present.[3]

From the standpoint of the observer, each participant's actions are characterized by the frequency and quality of his contributions, and in particular by the way his contributions fit into the network of communication established within the group. Each participant thus assumes a role, that is, takes up a position with respect to each of his partners. These positions are to some degree differentiated from one another. It is possible, moreover, to predict the order and interrelationship of the actions of the group: interaction is a *process*.

The observer may, with good reason, look upon interaction as a behavioral system based on binary alternatives. The sociologist, however, will go even further and try to discover the underlying conditions that determine the process. The sequence of events in the interaction process is not arbitrary. The process follows an orderly course. Transition from one phase to the next may give rise to tensions so powerful as to threaten a fundamental change in the relations between the participants, and possibly even the disintegration of the group. But despite changes in the moods of the participants, the difficulties may in due course be resolved. Despite momentary tensions and unforeseen difficulties, the structure of the group may endure. In that event the group may be said to be in equilibrium. This does not mean that it is completely static or even that its various states will follow a repetitive cycle. It merely means, as Bales puts it, "that there is a more or less regular turnover of phases back to a steady state. . . . The successful transition through any particular phase may be regarded as one of the functional prerequisites[4] to the maintenance of the interaction system in a kind of equilibrium." By studying these functional prerequisites we can understand the nature of the system and of its characteristic processes.

Bales's system of classification, which is based on two dichotomies, makes it possible for the observer to keep track of the group process. This may be viewed as a transactional process involving exchanges among the actors and between individual actors and their internal and external environments. The same idea is sometimes expressed in other terms. Interactions, for example, are sometimes described as "problem-solving processes," that is, processes in which the group tries to find the solution to some problem or, more dramatically, the way out of a crisis associated with social or practical problems of one kind or another. When the problem of the moment is one that concerns physical resources, the actor may try to solve it by using his know-how to bring about certain changes in the environment. Behavior of this sort is practiced by craftsmen and other skilled workmen when they try to find novel ways of assembling the pieces that go into whatever it is they may be working on. Students presented with standard types of mathematical problems face a comparable situation (though not an identical one, since the raw material on which the student works consists of concepts and relations): they have to figure out ways to cope with preordained problems, the terms of which they are not free to change or conjure away.

Broadly speaking, the external environment of the group is composed of all those constraints with which the actors cannot cope merely by modifying their relations to one another. The execution of practical tasks depends on the relations between the actors set up by the division of labor. It also depends on the support they lend one another. In other words, the execution of practical tasks depends on how the actors interact and cooperate.

Accordingly, the question of group interaction is more than a question of adaptation to external constraints. Interaction sets up a network of relations between ego and alter. This causes changes in each actor's level of satisfaction, or "deprivation-gratification balance," as Parsons puts it in *The Social System*. Certain problems, moreover, become the focus of interaction. Dealing with and solving these problems will thus become collective goals. For the individual, success or failure in achieving or approaching the goals he has set for himself will give rise to tensions that will not only affect him intimately but also bring him into close association with, or opposition to, other individuals involved in the same process. Finally, both the outcome of the interaction and the course it follows will be remembered by the participants, thus adding to the fund of common experience. Group functioning is thus more than just task performance; nor can it be described simply in terms of interpersonal feelings of attraction and aversion.

Analysis of interaction as a temporal process leads to the same conclusions.

> The process tended to move qualitatively from a *relative* emphasis on attempts to solve problems of *orientation* ("what is it") to attempts to solve problems of *evaluation* ("how do we feel about it") and subsequently to attempts to solve problems of *control* ("what shall we do about it"). Concurrent with these transitions, the relative frequencies of both *negative reactions* (disagreement, tension, and antagonism), and *positive reactions* (agreement, tension release, and showing solidarity), tends to increase [1953, p. 141]. . . . We note joking and laughter so frequently at the end of meetings that they might almost be taken as a signal that the group has completed what it considers to be a task effort and is ready for disbandment or a new problem. [1953, p. 143]

Accordingly, it may be said that a normal course of interaction consists of four phases, which occur in the following sequence: (1) the group situates itself with respect to its external environment; (2) the group constitutes itself as internal environment by specialization of roles; (3) the participants express their feelings about themselves, one another, and the group as a whole, evaluate the various aspects of the task, and determine the contribution that each participant is to make to its overall performance; (4) they determine whether the cohesiveness of the group has emerged from the meeting unchanged, diminished, or enhanced.

Parsons gives the following account of Bales's work [1953, p. 64]:

> The essential approach [taken by Bales, says Parsons] was to think of the small group as a functioning social system. It was held

that such a system would have four main "functional problems" which were described, respectively, as those of *adaptation* to conditions of external situation, of *instrumental* control over parts of the situation in the performance of goal oriented tasks, of the management and *expression* of sentiments and tensions of the members, and of preserving the social *integration* of members with each other as a solidary collectivity.

The functional problems faced by the group are of a natue determined by the need for two kinds of differentiation: synchronic (specialization of roles) and diachronic (specialization of phases). These two needs are counterbalanced by a third, complementary requirement: that the cohesiveness of the group be maintained at a level compatible with the other functional requirements. The capacity of the group to satisfy the requirements of differentiation and cohesiveness simultaneously determines the extent to which it will be able to exert control over its functioning and development. Responsibility for the control function is borne by the *leader* of the group on behalf of the other members and under their scrutiny.

The investigation of small groups did more than allow an integrated presentation of the interaction paradigm first introduced in *The Social System*. It also made possible a more precise description of the relation between ego and alter. Interaction involves both task and dialogue. In the one as in the other there is an exchange process, an inside and an outside. This exchange process involves dependence, cooperation, and antagonism—all at once. We can press the analysis further in two different directions. As we shall see later on, the ideas developed above will enable us to propose a theory of socialization, which will provide useful insights into the nature of collective norms and values. This theory will help us to escape the false dilemma of having to choose between the idea that norms and values come to us from above, on the one hand, and, on the other hand, the idea that norms and values are purely and simply constraints, determined either by the imperatives of biology or by the nature of the environment. The analysis of small groups also throws new light on certain mechanisms of social control and gives useful hints for setting forth a theory of social control that avoids the pitfalls of the oversocialization paradox and the problems of utilitarian individualism.

We can give a preliminary illustration of the outlines of this theory by looking at the case of the nuclear family. Reduced to essentials, the nuclear family consists of four role-types, distinguished from one another on the basis of generation and gender. The significance of generation from the standpoint of social role is primarily biologically determined. The helplessness of the child, particularly the infant, rules out any semblance of intergenerational equality during this first phase of the socialization process. Sex, however, is not a fact of nature in the same sense as age. The parents are both adults, but they have been socialized in different ways to perform opposite sex roles. The children of both sexes, however, are equally helpless at birth. Sex-role differentiation within the family is an example of characteristic differentiation, which tends to occur in *all* systems of interaction, whatever their composition. In particular, differentiation of this type, involving the instrumental-expressive dimension, is quite apparent in the small discussion groups studied by Bales, which are of approximately the same size as the nuclear family.

According to our hypothesis, it is this type of differentiation that gives rise to *leadership* phenomena in all small groups; the question is not why we observe leadership in the family, since the family is a group, but rather why it is the woman who assumes the essentially expressive role. We can explain this allocation of roles by sex in the following way. Since it is the woman who brings the child into the world and takes responsibility for its early education, an exclusive bond develops between mother and child. As a result of this exclusivity, the male, freed of responsibility for these biological functions, is able to specialize in the instrumental role [1953, p. 23].

The nuclear family is a system composed of four roles (one of which may not be filled): there are two parents, one male and one female, and two children, one male and one female. As usual, we may characterize these four roles in terms of a pair of dichotomies: expressive/instrumental, power/lack of power. Thus far we have treated the family system as though it were—in itself and for itself—a unit. In fact, although the nuclear family is often described as an "elementary" or basic unit, it actually consists of four subsystems: the parents/spouses, the children (who, besides being children of their parents, are siblings of each other), the men (the father and his son or sons; in the case of more than one son, the boys are of course brothers of one another), and the women (the mother and her daughter or daughters, sisters to one another). Furthermore, the family unit engages in a series of exchanges with the working world: the father/husband is also the family breadwinner. Finally, the nuclear family exists only for a limited period of time: eventually the children will leave home, and the parents must grow old and die by themselves.

A self-destructive mechanism is at work in the nuclear family. Every group composed of mortal individuals must necessarily vanish one day. But the nuclear family faces extinction for a somewhat different reason: the incest taboo, which prevents the children from taking either parents or siblings as sexual partners, forces them to leave their parents' home to seek mates elsewhere and establish homes of their own. The nuclear family expels its children from its bosom when they turn adult. Accordingly, a particular individual is likely to be a member of two nuclear families: the one into which he or she was born—the arena of his or her childhood—which may be called the family of orientation, and the one in which he or she becomes in turn a parent, which may be called the family of procreation.

Like any other group, the nuclear family is a differentiated system. What is more, the differentiation we find in the family is not randomly distributed. It is based on dichotomies of sex and age: male/female, parent/child. There is, however, a more general dichotomy, expressive/instrumental, which will enable us to shed a good deal of light on the two foregoing pairs, on the basis of which (allowing for the restrictions imposed by the incest taboo) the fundamental family roles (i.e., father/mother, son/daughter, brother/sister) are defined. Accordingly, we shall pause to consider the distinction between an instrumental and expressive function.

An instrumental function is one concerned primarily with the relation between the group and its external environment. In other words, an instrumental function is focused on the adaptation of the group to the situation and on the attainment of given goals, gratifications, and consummatory states. By contrast, an expressive function is concerned with the harmony or solidarity of the group, the relations of the members of the group to one another, and the stress and role-adjustment problems they experience as members of the group.

We can analyze the expressive/instrumental dichotomy in functional terms. Instrumental activity involves a combination of adaptive and goal-seeking functions (A and G). Adaptive behavior on the part of the actor is carried on in conjunction with goal-attainment by the collectivity. Expressive activity involves the integrative (I) and latent pattern-maintenance (L) functions. It is broadly integrative, aimed at establishing group solidarity and, from the standpoint of the individual, at bringing about role-adjustment by matching motivation to role requirements. Alternatively, we could analyze the expressive/instrumental dichotomy in terms of the pattern variables, namely, affectivity/affective neutrality and universalism/particularism. This, however, raises the problem of whether it is possible to establish a correspondence between analysis in terms of pattern variables and analysis in terms of functions. We prefer to postpone examination of this problem until later.

Functionalism Revisited

Thanks to the theory of the four functions, the abstract principle of interdependence acquires a specific content. To say that we are members of a social system means that: (1) we are bound by certain constraints that the location of the system vis-à-vis its specific environments imposes; (2) we accept the obligations that the task to be accomplished jointly imposes on all the members of the group; (3) transactions and interchanges with our associates and companions affect us both positively and negatively; (4) we have an interest in maintaining, reinterpreting, or replacing the norms that govern our behavior and make it meaningful. These four propositions set forth the relations between the actor and the social system, looked at from the standpoint of the actor. Looking at the same relations from the standpoint of the system, we again find the four system functions with which we began: adaptation, goal attainment, integration, and latent pattern-maintenenance.

The theory of the four functions of the social system is both a codification and a generalization of earlier results. Under A and I, for instance, we can readily make room for Bales's categories, which involve the supply and demand of information, suggestions, and evaluations on the one hand, and the expression of disagreement, hostility, or sympathy on the other. The distinction between A and I emerges clearly from Bales's work, in which the sphere of tasks is set apart from the sphere of feelings and their expression. It was Parsons, however, who introduced the distinction between A and G, which we do not find in the work of Bales. The L function is reminiscent of the emphasis on consensus in certain of Bales's categories, particularly those connected with the final phase of the meeting. But Bales treats the problem as one of interpersonal attitudes rather than as a distinct state or function of the social system.

The four functions are built up out of two dichotomies: internal/external and instrumental/consummatory. Of the first pair, we need only say that the distinction is a standard one in the sociological literature, most notably in the literature pertaining to small groups. The second pair recalls the venerable distinction between means and ends, which occupied Parsons's attention in *The Structure of Social Action*. If the consummatory state has priority, there are two possibilities. Either that state may be defined in terms of data external to the system of interaction, in which case we speak of collective goal-attainment, or it may be defined in terms of the relations of the members of the society to one another, in which case we speak of integration. Similarly, when instrumental action has priority, it may be based on external data, in which case we shall speak of adaptation. Or it may involve cultural values, taken as points of reference with respect to which the action is oriented, in which case we speak of latent-pattern maintenance.

In a more recent work we find an even more radical generalization of the notion of function, now said to be "a central notion for the comprehension of all living systems."[5] It is useful in two ways. First, whether the system in question is a society or a living organism, the idea of function enables us to distinguish between "it" and "the rest" of the universe, the environment. The idea also helps us to understand the process whereby the system itself becomes differentiated. In effect, at any given moment a living system is defined in terms of the difference or set of differences by which it may be distinguished from one or more environments. On this view of the matter, death may be defined as a limiting case, in which no further differences between the organism and its environment can be perceived. But the organism-environment relationship is not one of pure exteriority, because regular exchanges do take place between the two. Like every living organism, the social system is an "open" system that communicates with the external world across boundaries, which to one degree or another are permeable. These transactions with the "outside" world have to be regulated, of course; a second problem has to do with the continuity of the system over time. Continuity is not to be confused with identity. A social system is not now what it once was or some day will be, any more than an organism remains the same throughout its development. Just as the *identity* of the system, its distinctiveness in relation to its environment, is maintained by regulating the transactions that take place between the interior and the exterior, so the *continuity* of the system depends on mediated transactions (anticipation, conservation, memory) between different points in time. These processes will follow a certain course, which may be compared to the successive phases in a group discussion as analyzed by Bales or to the programmed sequence of biological functions in the life cycle of an organism. "Thus food intake must precede the internal process of oxidation, which in turn produces organic energy." In other words, an arbitrary choice of means, in the narrow sense, does not automatically bring about what, in a broad sense, we have been calling adaptation. To give a biological example of what we mean, suppose that the environment contains a wide variety of nutrients that would in theory satisfy the needs of a certain living organism. Of these nutrients, the organism will select only a limited number and may at different times choose different nutrients. Activity of this sort is what we have been calling goal-selection (G). This is to be distinguished sharply from adaptation (A), which pertains to the *overall* relationship between the actor (or organism) and the environment.

With the theory of the four functions we can give a pluralistic analysis not only of the social system but of any system of action. The most important sociological theories of the nineteenth century, those of Comte and Marx, became ensnared in an endless debate as to which was the "dominant factor": Do ideas determine the course of the world? Do the relations of production determine all social relations? As we shall see later, one advantage of Parsons's theory is that we may spare ourselves the tedious job of composing exegeses on such points as the meaning of "the final analysis" wherein the relations of production are said to be all-determining or the "relative autonomy of the political." For now, let us try to understand the significance of the distinctions among the four functions. Being completely general, the theory is applicable to the personality as well as to culture and society. Parsons makes this application in an article entitled "An Approach to Psychological Theory in Terms of the Theory of Action," in which the four functions of the psychological subsystem are listed in an order different from that in which they occurred in the small group. Here, our attention is directed first to the function designated G, "the tendency or drive to attain goal states." Goal-seeking of this kind is true exploratory behavior and not merely trial and error. The purpose of such behavior is first to anticipate and then to attain a certain consummatory state. Suppose that a relation is established in the actor's mind between a consummatory state and a symbolic object (physical or cultural). That relation will tend to become stabilized. This tendency illustrates a general principle of inertia, according to which "a system will tend to continue with its direction and potency unchanged unless it is deflected or otherwise changed by the impingement of some other process (in the system or in its situation)."[6] Inertia increases when a gratification relation (optimal or suboptimal) is established between the actor and some aspect of the situation. The system and its environment are always changing, however. Therefore, it is highly unlikely that the social system will settle into a state of static equilibrium or that the individual will remain totally unperturbed. The principle of inertia does not mean that stability is the rule but rather that action, like motion, is oriented by a goal-seeking drive aimed at attaining a consummatory state that approximates the desired goal more and more closely. Matters are complicated by the fact that in a given situation different patterns of goal-attainment and object-gratification choices may lead to the same consummatory state. It is because such alternative goals exist that the actor must make

choices. This accounts for the existence of the dichotomies characteristic of the action process, as noted above. If, somehow, the actor
happens to be confronted with but a single goal, choice is no longer a
necessity, but the price he must pay for this simplification is a stiff one:
he is now utterly dependent for gratification on one object. These
observations put us in a position to examine the distinction between
adaptation and goal-attainment from a genetic standpoint. When we
do this, we find that G is more highly differentiated than A, which is
only "a generalized capacity to meet the exigencies imposed by an
unstable and varying situation" [1959, pp. 631–33]. If we now shift
our point of view and use the language not of the theory of action but
of sociological theory, we may say that G, the "political" function of
the social system, is more highly differentiated than A, the "economic" function. This is because G sets up complex relations between
the actor and the situation, subject to rather flexible regulations, while
the adaptive response (A) to the situation is one-dimensional.

The two functions discussed in the preceding paragraph have to do
with the relations between the system and its environment. Like any
system of action, however, the personality system does not respond
directly to each environmental stimulus. When a stimulus is received,
a response must first be selected from among those that have previously been learned. The response that is actually made will be determined not only by the circumstances but also by the need-
dispositions of the actor. According to Parsons, one can speak of a
system of action "in the technical sense [only] so far as the relations
[that constitute it] are organized through *learned* patterns of orientation."[7]

When we consider the personality, the problem of culture and
learning—the accumulation and management of symbolic capital, as it
might be called—is one with which we must deal in "functional"
terms. Parsons refers to this as the "latent pattern-maintenance" function. The problem is twofold. Symbolic capital lends itself to a variety
of uses, among which choices must be made: the meaning that our
symbolic capital has for us is a result of our own choices, of what is
sometimes called "a strain toward consistency." The mere availability
of symbolic capital is not enough, however. A decision must be made
to mobilize it, to commit it to some specific application. Here we
encounter a second aspect of the "functional problem" of culture: the
tension-management function, which has to do with the regulation of
motivations.

A fourth and final "functional problem" remains. To describe it,
Parsons used a word that is more often than not misunderstood: inte-

gration. Like the latent pattern-maintenance function, the integration function has to do with problems that arise because of the properties of the system itself (personality or society) rather than the environment. Here, however, the problem has to do not with symbolism and norms in themselves but rather with the individuals who play certain roles, subscribe to certain values, and manipulate certain symbols. Parsons puts it this way: "From the point of view of the unit in a system, a culture pattern has in the first instance cognitive significance; it is content in the sense of information, to be learned in the double sense of comprehension and motivational commitment" [1959, p. 636]. In other words, if the cultural model is to have meaning for the actor, he must learn it. At the same time, the actor himself is enriched by what he learns; learning changes the image he has of himself as well as others. Now, each actor is an object for the other actors in the system. In particular, Parsons says, alter becomes an object for ego to the extent that ego treats him as an object of cathexis. "By system integration we mean the mutual cathectic adjustment of these units to each other in the perspective of the internal harmony or, as is often said for social systems, solidarity or cohesion of the system." From the standpoint of the individual actor, integration merely refers to these primary interpersonal relations, which may be either positive or negative in character. From the social standpoint, integration refers to the relational nexus that comes to be established among the members of the group as they adjust their affective attitudes to one another; these mutual affective adjustments (or, to use another term, affective self-expansions) may bring different members of the group together or set them against one another. "Cathexis," as Parsons uses the term, means neither pure attraction nor pure aversion. Alter is desired, loved, or hated to the extent that he stands as the symbolic representative of certain values defined by the culture. The integration of the social system cannot be deduced from the spontaneous attraction of one individual for another, any more than the voluntary attachment of an individual to another person or to an object is determined solely by that individual's temperament or psychology.

The theory of the four functions does more than make a pluralistic analysis possible. It also sheds a good deal of light on the nature of functional analysis. "For a considerable time, Merton and I came to be known as the leaders of a structural-functional school among American sociologists. Developments since the emergence of the four-function paradigm have made the designation 'structural-functional' increasingly less appropriate. First, it gradually became clear that structure and function were not correlative concepts on the same level—as, for example, universalism and particularism are in the pattern-variable formulation. It became evident that function was a more general concept defining certain exigencies of a system maintaining an independent existence within an environment, while the cognate of structure, as a general aspect of such a system, was process" [1970*a*, p. 849]. At bottom, the very concept of a system of action is at stake when the term "process" is substituted for the term "structure." A closed system surrounded by impermeable boundaries may legitimately be treated as a structure, that is, a stable set of relations among the elements of a self-subsistent entity. If, however, the system is open to one or more environments, which may themselves be subject to exogenous changes, then its structure can no longer be studied independently of the processes that impinge upon it, that is, independently of the transactions that take place between the system and its environments.

Discussions of functionalism are frequently encumbered by a number of ambiguities to which Kingsley Davis has usefully called attention. The movement generally known as "functionalism" originated in work of quite diverse inspiration. Is the term "functionalism" more widely accepted than "structural-functionalism"? As Davis points out,[8] "Radcliffe-Brown's distaste for Malinowski's functionalism is well known, and is hardly stronger than that of nonfunctionalist Kroeber." Malinowski was accused of "naturalistic psychologism" by Radcliffe-Brown who, as a loyal disciple of Durkheim, abhorred this particular heresy. Such culturalists as Benedict and Kluckhohn, in the enemy camp insofar as they may be regarded as Malinowski's heirs, have suspected Radcliffe-Brown's functionalism of being an avatar of Durkheimian sociologism. In Davis's judgment functionalism is less a doctrine than a method, which boils down to two precepts, in reality little more than elaborations of the hoary principle of interdependence: "to relate the parts or elements of society to the whole, and to relate the elements to one another." But, Davis asks, is this not what every science does?

In essence, functional analysis is just the analysis of interdependence in general, the model for which Parsons found in Pareto's conception of the social system. Mention should be made of two remaining difficulties. The first has to do with the nature of the model of interdependence. Is this just an intuitive notion, rather like the vague concepts of "concrete totality" or "total social fact"? The second problem has to do with the teleological implications associated with the concept of function. Raymond Boudon has shown that certain functionalists, Parsons in particular, are quite capable of avoiding this pitfall.[9] When Parsons investigates the "functions" of the nuclear family in industrial society, for example, he does not try to say what the use of the family as an institution is, nor does he try to spell out in any direct way what consequences the family as an institution has for the way industrial society functions. What he does do is merely to ask whether a certain system of kinship, that of medieval Europe or ancient China, for example, is or is not compatible with the conditions under which personnel are recruited in a modern bureaucracy or industrial firm and with the way capitalist firms are managed. The intuitive approach of Radcliffe-Brown, who defined the function of "any recurrent social activity" as "the part it plays in social life as a whole,"[10] is prudently set aside; instead, Parsons makes a judgment of the probability of finding a social system in which attributes of several different kinds coexist. Boudon describes the differences in the following terms:[11]

> In modern functionalism we do not characteristically find that research is focused on determining what functions are fulfilled by the various elements of the social system. . . . Modern functionalism is, or tries to be, rigorously analytical. Its approach is to show either the necessity or the impossibility of the simultaneous occurrence of certain elements in a social system.

"Necessity" and "impossibility" are probably rather too stringent requirements where concrete elements, customs, or forms of behavior are concerned. As Boudon observes, Parsons's analyses demonstrate impossibility (e.g., it is impossible to have a family structure like that of ancient China or medieval Europe at the same time as a productive structure like that of the United States in the twentieth century) far more frequently than they demonstrate necessity. Hempel independently arrived at very similar conclusions. "Functional analysis is the observation of a system S (whether a living creature, a personality, or a social system) characterized by a set of recurrent activities." This qualification plainly takes in the notion of the social system as Parsons understands it, in view of the principle of inertia. Given such a system, consider one of its features: a social usage, as Radcliffe-Brown likes to say. Let this feature or usage be designated by i. Characteristically, the functionalist approach is to "identify the contribution of i to the preservation or growth of the individual or group in which it occurs."[12] To gauge the "contribution" of i, we need to have a thorough knowledge of the way S functions and, in particular, of what is meant by "recurrent activities of the system." Furthermore, we must agree upon the meaning of the phrase "normal functioning of S," and to do this we must investigate the specific conditions, both internal and external, under which such "normal functioning" is observed. Until we have precise answers to such questions, we have no way of judging the contribution of i to S. In particular, we have no way of judging whether or not i is replaceable, that is, whether or not its presence is necessary if S is to function. If it is possible to replace i by i' or i'', and so on, the contribution of i can only be stated in comparative terms. Does S "function" better or "more normally" with i or without i? With i' or i''? Can we say that the occurrence of i' or i'' in S corresponds to distinct states S1, S2 of the system S? Or does the absence of i—or of i' or i''—mean that the system under observation has changed its identity, so that we may no longer refer to S but must instead speak of a radically new system, P, Q, or R? If i', i'', and so forth belong to a specific family of features, can we say that S1, S2 are distinct states of the same system S? If i, i', i'' do not belong to the same family, it may be (though it need not be) the case that in making successive observations we are looking not at different states of the same system but at different systems altogether.

We shall return to this discussion below.[13] Even at this stage, we can distinguish three quite different versions of functionalist analysis, which we find throughout Parsons's work, sometimes in pure form, sometimes modified, sometimes in combination with one another. The first is just the old theme of generalized interdependence. The interdependence of the elements of the system, on this view, is supposed to ensure equilibrium. This vague statement was as far as Parsons went in an essay he wrote in 1945.[14] But with the introduction of the four-function paradigm came a change of perspective. In his post-1955 analyses of the various subsystems of the social system, in particular the economy and the polity, Parsons tried to give a picture of the intersectoral linkages. In addition, he gave much more precise indications of the way in which the elements of the system of action are interdependent. In earlier work, he had been satisfied for the most part to assume this interdependence. The best-known version of functionalism, however, is the one set forth by Merton,[15] which Hempel and Nagel have criticized. Characteristic of this version is the effort to impute, as rigorously as possible, to each feature, custom, or practice its effect on the functioning of a supposedly stable, cohesive system. In Parsons's work, however, this approach is hardly of paramount importance: we find scant mention of it except in his early essays on the institution of the family, dealing with sex and age, all written prior to 1950.

There is a close connection between the two versions of functionalism described above, which I shall call the generalized interdependence model and the teleological imputation model, respectively. The reason that such a close connection between the two exists is the following: we can impute to a given feature i in a system S its effect on the functioning of the system because that system is in a state of equilibrium or tending toward such a state. The third version of functionalism, the four-function theory, is quite different. In this version the four functions are unequivocally held to be distinct, even independent of one another. Parsons compares them to the dimensions of a four-dimensional space: "These four dimensions are conceived to be orthogonal; their values are independently variable in the sense that change of state with respect to any one cannot be interpreted to have an automatically given relation to change of state in any of the others (except so far as this relation comes to be known and formulated as a law of the system). It is also true that maximization of all four, and probably of any two, is not possible in the same state of a given system" [1959, p. 631]. Quite clearly, interdependence is no longer taken for granted. The interdependence of two or more functions is taken to be a relation characteristic of the particular system. The theorist cannot assume that such relations exist; instead, he must state hypothetical relations as far as possible in a parametric form suitable for subsequent experimental verification.

At this point a relatively precise definition of the notion of equilibrium can be given. In its most general form, the principle of equilibrium holds simply that every system exhibits a tendency to maintain the status quo, "unless and until it is disturbed by some influence from outside the system. Furthermore, if such a disturbance occurs, tendencies will be set up to bring about the state in which the system would have been had the disturbance not occurred" [1959, p. 631]. Inertia together with restorative forces that tend to maintain the system in its "normal" condition: these are the components of the principle of equilibrium. It remains indeterminate, however, unless we can specify, and if possible measure, the forces capable of disturbing the inertia of the system as well as those capable of impeding the restorative mechanisms. And even this is not enough. We must also determine the critical threshold levels below which exogenous forces will not affect the behavior of the system; in addition, we must determine what level of disequilibrium is required to bring the restorative forces into play, and the maximum degree of disturbance that those forces can handle.

The functions are independent of one another, or, as Parsons says, "analytically distinct," provided that their simultaneous values are compatible with the maintenance of the social system. Inter-dependence is therefore not a hierarchical, totalizing principle. It should be interpreted in much narrower terms, merely as a condition of coexistence. A second important consideration is that the functions that regulate the transactions between the system and its environments are symbolic processes. That action may be symbolic in nature is nothing very new: certainly any reader of *The Structure of Social Action* would be aware of it. But the idea has important consequences for the interpretation of Parsonian functionalism. If functions are symbolic processes, then functionalist anaysis need not be based on either the unrealistic premises of individualistic utilitarianism or on the teleological premises of biological totalism. The criticisms of Nagel and Hempel are far more telling against the first two versions of functionalism than they are against Parsons's symbolic functionalism, assuming, of course, that at the appropriate time we can come up with a reasonable interpretation of symbolism.

The "Oversocialization" Debate

In sharp contrast to the legend of the functionalist Frankenstein, the theory of the four functions in no way seeks to impose on us a vision of a one-dimensional, fully integrated society. The functions, like the pattern variables, should be viewed as fundamental dimensions of action, out of which a wide variety of roles and institutions may be constructed and made compatible with one another.

Two kinds of accusations have been leveled against Parsonian functionalism. The first of these need not detain us long: this is the charge that the four functions are like biological functions. Carried to an extreme, the charge is that adaptation, integration, and the preservation and propagation of the cultural heritage are carried out in the same way by bees, apes, and humans. These functions are supposed to provide for the indefinite reproduction of a given "structure" or "type." Parsons, according to this line of criticism, is supposed merely to have adapted the ideas of vitalists influenced by creationism. This indictment is linked to another, not logically unrelated to it. This second arraignment is developed at some length in an article by Dennis H. Wrong, treating the so-called oversocialized conception of man in Parsonian sociology.[16]

To begin with, Wrong arms himself with the views on Hobbes and the problem of order that Parsons himself set forth in *The Structure of Social Action*. "Let me pay tribute," he writes, "to [Parsons's] recognition of the importance of the Hobbesian question—'the problem of order' as he calls it. . . . Parsons correctly credits Hobbes with being the first thinker to see the necessity of explaining why human society is not a 'war of all against all.'" After stating the problem in very clear terms, however, Parsons and his disciples waste no time disposing of it, according to Wrong, who cites Francis Sutton to the effect that "to a modern sociologist imbued with the conception that action follows institutionalized patterns, opposition of individual and common interests has only a very limited relevance or is thoroughly unsound." To this, Wrong retorts that in the eyes of functionalist sociologists "human society is not essentially different [from the society of bees], although conformity and stability [in human society] are maintained by non-instinctive processes." This is the view that Wrong imputes to Parsons, while at the same time reproaching him for having swept under the rug the Hobbesian problem, the importance of which he had recognized in his earliest published writings.

This evasion of the issue is said to have been facilitated by the psychological theory invoked by Parsons. Wrong argues that this theory led Parsons to explain conformity by means of socialization and later, using an ad hoc theory of internalization, to reduce socialization to a mere question of conditioning. "So long as most individuals are 'socialized,' the Hobbesian problem is not even perceived as a latent reality." In short, *homo parsoniensis,* according to Wrong, is a conformist whose behavior as an individual merely copies or reproduces the social norms.

This interpretation, which Parsons flatly rejected, reopens a classic debate on the relation of the individual to society. Some commentators have rather too hastily dismissed such questions as "false problems." Poorly formulated or inadequately resolved problems, perhaps. But by evading the issue we neglect a central point: the problematical character of the social order. *The Structure of Social Action* adverts to the paradox that lies behind all sociological and political reflection: on the one hand, human society (as opposed to insect society, for instance) is composed of more or less autonomous individuals; on the other hand, however, the whole that is human society is greater than the sum of its individual parts. In *The Structure of Social Action* both these propositions were defended in the terms common at the time, such as totality, structure, element, and the like. But the element in question—though utterly unlike the individual as conceived in the utilitarian tradition, the individual who chooses between greater and lesser degrees of pleasure and pain—is not subsumed under, or submerged in, a concrete totality: the element is the *actor,* who chooses between alternatives defined by his situation. The quotation from Max

Weber that serves as an epigraph for Parsons's first book, moreover, leaves no doubt as to the importance of such categories as means and ends, both for understanding the meaning the actor attaches to his own action and for explaining the consequences or results of that action for his partners.

"To my knowledge," Parsons wrote, "I have never abandoned the perspectives which were thus worked out in *The Structure of Social Action*."[17] To the extent that he kept faith with the unit-act schema, Parsons must be termed an individualist, as he expressly wished. Just what sort of animal the Parsonian individual is remains to be seen.

There is no action without actors: true enough, as far as it goes. But for action to be possible, what qualities must the actors have? This is the question that the theory of functional prerequisites of social systems was designed to answer [1951a, pp. 26–36]. These prerequisites suggest an axiomatic treatment of natural man, just as the pattern variables lay down a set of axioms for action in general. When all is said and done, sociology seems to stand in need of a basic character-ization of natural man as much as does political theory. In order to determine the scope and content of the social contract, theorists used to begin by endowing the individuals who would eventually become parties thereto with certain passions and interests and with some ca-pacity to foresee the course of events and to exert control over nature. The theorist could then decide whether a given constitutional ar-rangement was or was not legitimate and useful. It may be objected, however, that the sociologist begins with society as a given. This is true. Still, his next step must be to ask under what conditions—that is, under the impulsion of what interests, in view of what aims, and with the aid of what mental equipment—the individual can be required or induced, constrained or motivated to take part in social life. A set of axioms describing man in a state of nature is therefore not less indis-pensable to sociology than to political science.

The functional *prerequisites* of society, in Parsons's view, are accord-ingly none other than the attributes of *homo parsoniensis*. Now, these attributes are not established once and for all, but are rather thought of as a system of dynamic relations which can be used to explain learning and socialization. *Homo parsoniensis* is a responsive being: he feels pleasure and pain—not merely in response to physical objects but also in response to his partners. As a responsive being, he will see a positive and a negative aspect in every occurrence. An individual who is responsive is not indifferent: he will not ascribe the same value to all events. He has the capacity to make evaluations. When we say that

homo parsoniensis makes choices, however, we may also mean that he
has the capacity to analyze a situation into its elements and then re-
combine them in a new way, in accordance with the logic laid down by
the pattern variables.

Let us call this latter capacity "combinatorial"; I grant that no express mention of such a capacity is made in *The Social System,* at least
not with the same degree of explicitness with which the responsiveness of the individual is described. But if we turn to one of Parsons's
more recent essays, we can read of the three major influences on his
thinking in the area of psychology: Tolman, the Gestalt psychologists,
and Freud. Of Gestalt psychology he says: "I was greatly impressed by
Wolfgang Koehler's study of the mentality of apes and of the factor
which he called 'insight,' which he imputed to his ape subjects. The
generalization of the theoretical point of view implied there in the
subsequent work of Koehler himself and of Kofka impressed me very
much" [1974]. What Wolfgang Koehler refers to as "insight"[18] is one
of the factors that can be used to explain a monkey's ability to solve a
problem set by the experimenter, the one element that cannot be
reduced either to instinct or to conditioning. To speak of insight, then,
is to endow the animal with the capability of discovering novel solutions to problems. In *homo parsoniensis* the aptitude of the monkey to
combine and innovate of which Koehler speaks is incorporated and
generalized.

Responsive and flexible, *homo parsoniensis* is an animal capable of
learning. Accordingly, Parsons's theory of socialization[19] may serve as
a touchstone for evaluating Dennis Wrong's argument. Before deciding that the individual is oversocialized, we may ask about the nature
of the process by which he becomes a member of society. At the end
of this process, the adult who has assumed full membership in society
must shoulder many responsibilities: he is a producer, the head of a
family, a citizen, perhaps a member of a political or religious group. In
short, an individual becomes a member of society by virtue of his
capacity to play and to learn a variety of roles. We thus come back to
the central paradigm of interaction, which claims to describe the relations between ego and one or more alters.

But socialization itself is a form of social interaction: it is not only a
learning process but also a genuine interplay between teacher and
pupil roles, because interaction refers to intangible as well as to tangible aspects of the relation between ego and alter. Behaviorism, in its
narrower versions, tends to treat such encounters in purely tangible
terms. But ego and alter are not merely individuals; they are persons
playing roles. For the analysis of the social system, the pertinent point

of reference is not the actor of the general theory, of whom we need recall only that he is responsive, flexible, and educable, but rather the actor playing his roles. Accordingly, interaction may be defined as a nexus of roles involving many actors, or, again, as the process by which those roles are played out. Socialization, which involves contact between the child and his father, mother, brothers, and sisters, may in this sense be analyzed as interaction of a particular kind.

A particular kind: the qualification bears repeating. The socialization process raises problems of two sorts. First, because of the inescapable fact that the young child is helpless, we must ask how best to view socialization as an interaction: as an exchange between partners whose contributions may be differentiated but who are in principle equal associates; or, alternatively, as a hierarchical interchange in which the relations between the actors are asymmetrical and the responsibilities and capacities of each are, for the time being at least, different. At this point in the argument, we may pause for a moment to discuss the two different conceptions of interaction just introduced. Although the two are not mutually exclusive, trying to reconcile them inevitably raises difficulties. As we have seen, interaction may be described either in unrealistic, egalitarian terms, or in naturalistic, hierarchical terms. On the former view of the matter, status differences will be deemed unjust, unless they stem from explicit stipulations by the parties to the social contract, as is the case, for instance, with the difference in status between officials and citizens in democratic regimes (this, of course, has nothing whatever to do with the family), or unless the differences in status accurately reflect differences in the contributions to the general welfare as between various individuals. If, on the other hand, we take the naturalistic, hierarchical view, we will attribute status differences to one or another of the enduring reasons for the superiority of one individual over another, such as differences in the level of knowledge, capability, or experience. On this view of the matter, the relative status of individuals is a part of the "nature of things"; the lower-status individual is said to benefit by trusting to the advice of his betters, who are always ready and willing to assist. As we have seen, the therapeutic relationship between doctor and patient may be regarded as paradigmatic in this regard.

The second rather than the first paradigm is more appropriate to the case of socialization. We now come to the second of the two difficulties that crop up, as we said earlier, in the course of analyzing the socialization process. The term "interaction" is not applicable to just any sort of relation between ego and alter. For "behaviorists" and "objectivists," there is always a temptation to reduce interaction to the circulation of commodities and rewards of a tangible kind or to concrete spatial displacements. As Parsons uses the term, however, interaction is possible only where expectations are present and only by virtue of communication: thus it is both normative and symbolic. The theorist may treat this system of communication and nexus of expectations in two different ways. On the one hand, he may seek to describe its logic or structure. This is what Parsons does with his theory of pattern variables. But if he takes only this one approach, he will inevitably find himself in the predicament to which we alluded earlier: the pattern variables only lay down a priori conditions for interaction. Can we rest content with this view alone? A second approach comes to mind at this point. Could we not improve our understanding of the pattern variables by trying to figure out how they originate? With the highly abstract approach taken by Parsons, however, the only way to do this is to investigate the process whereby the actor acquires his capacity to play different roles, that is, the socialization process, according to both the egalitarian and the hierarchical paradigm.

One difference between an interaction of the doctor-patient type and the socialization process (i.e., the various phases of the relation between the child and its parents and siblings) is that in the first case the ego-alter relationship develops in a context of existing norms and values, whereas in the second case norms and values arise out of the relationship itself. The question to be asked about the socialization process is the following: How does the child learn "adult" norms and values?

This question would be quite misleading if, in keeping with the most egregious practices of anthropomorphic teleology, we were to look upon the socialization *process* as the means by which the individual achieved a socialized *state*. Such a view would incline us to utter the tautology that the child learns the norm in order to accede to adulthood. The mistake here lies in thinking that, once the individual has become socialized, his state is one of repose or inactivity; in fact, socialization is a dynamic process, one of progress, or perhaps of regression. Beset by a variety of dangers in his initial state of helplessness, the individual was in a position where he might have been overwhelmed. By the time the socialization process has been completed, he will have learned new capacities and increased his capital stock of roles. He will not only have widened his field of action but also increased his very capacity to act, that is, to take the initiative and to innovate. We need not hold that he is free in any fundamental sense of the word (Parsons always rejected the idea of "free will") to maintain that his dependence has been diminished and his control over the environment enhanced. He will have increased his autonomy, in other words.

Another, equally striking fact must be set down alongside the increased autonomy of the individual (even if we take the word "autonomy" in its quasi-behavioristic sense to mean "room for maneuver" or "margin of liberty"): namely, that the end of the socialization process in the life of an individual is marked by the moment when that individual is able to comport himself as an adult, that is, as an individual with the degree of functional autonomy normal in the society under study. The child's departure from the home of his parents signifies that now "he is old enough to take care of himself." The paradox of socialization is that somehow the individual moves from a situation of dependence to a position of increased autonomy and differentiation from others. The concept of "identification," as it is widely interpreted, masks this paradox. Socialization does indeed make the individual similar to the other members of the group, most notably his parents. But this does not mean that he becomes identical to them: the son does not grow up to be indistinguishable from his father. Similarly, internalization does not make the actor consubstantial with the norm he has internalized. The most that can be said is that an actor who has internalized a norm is affected by his fulfillment of the obligations imposed on him by that norm, without regard to any possible response to his behavior, either positive or negative, by alter. The notion of internalization focuses on the process whereby ego takes the place of alter and imposes on himself the sanctions that alter would have imposed had he witnessed the actions of ego. "The eye was in the tomb and stared at Cain."

Only by using a relational concept of socialization can we avoid confusing similarity with identity. There is no reason to assimilate the actor to the norm, or the socializee [the neologism is Parsons's— trans.] to the socializer. If we do, the relation between the individual and the *conscience collective* becomes incomprehensible, and we can say nothing at all about the process by which a mutual relation is established between actor and norm, model and learner.

Here Parsons alludes to the work of Freud, who understood the genetic dimension of the identification concept and avoided the fallacy of identifying socializer and socializee. Freud first describes identification as "the earliest manifestation of an affective attachment to another person." He then goes on to distinguish between identification with the father, "the person one would like to be," and identification with the mother, "the person one would like to possess."[20] For the time being we shall say nothing of identification of this second type, which might be termed "identification through possession." Identification of the first type, with another person one would like to be, can appear in quite different guises. Identification need not even be with another *person,* as in the case of the child who thought he was a cat (or, rather, who behaved as though he wanted to be seen as a cat). This child meowed, crawled on all fours, and refused to eat at the table. Urie Bronfenbrenner has discussed this type of identification:

> Moreover, there is the further question of what aspects of the model are being emulated. At times [as in the example of the boy who thought he was a cat, mentioned above], it is the overt behavior of the model which is being adopted. In other instances . . . identification would appear to include internalization of the motives as well as the overt behavior of another. Finally, in [Freud's] later writings it is not the parent's ego with which the child identifies but his superego, his idealized standards for feeling and action.[21]

Thus it is not alter's Ego but his Superego that ego takes for his model in the identification process [to avoid confusion between Parsons's use of the term "ego" and Freud's, I have used capital letters when referring to Freud's notions of Ego and Superego.—trans.]. In giving an interpretation of the process of indentification in terms of relations, Parsons goes even further than Freud in that Parsons does not restrict the content of the Superego to moral rules imposing, as we might think, almost palpable constraints on the action of the individual. In Parsons's view the Superego is to be understood far more broadly, as a whole set of relations between the personality and the common culture: "Freud's view was too narrow. . . . Not only moral standards but *all the components of the common culture* are internalized as part of the personality structure."[22] Two observations are called for by this considerable broadening of the Superego's scope. In the first place, as Parsons sees it, the Superego surveys the entire range of activities of the individual personality. The Superego is not merely the normative system; it is imperative that we incorporate symbolic and expressive dimensions into it as well. By making the Superego coextensive with the "common culture," we extend the concept to embrace not only ideas or notions but also feelings and their expressions, however vague, which are part of our cultural capital. Consequently, the Superego now becomes more than just an arbiter between right and wrong. As Parsons understands it, the Superego is a repository of value-orientations upon which the individual may draw in trying to decide how to orient his actions, that is, in trying to set the terms of his relations with his partners. Socialization does not make ego "like" alter or cause ego to "identify" with alter's Superego. Such expressions are metaphors. What socialization does teach us is how to recognize the norms and values that mark out the boundaries of our field of action.

About these kinds of moral standards, we know two things. First, we know that they are defined relative to the interaction process: "Neither what the human object *is* . . . nor what it *means* emotionally can be understood as given independently of the nature of the interactive process itself; and the significance of moral norms themselves very largely relates to this fact." Second, we know that these standards are *learned.* Parsons immediately observes, however [1964, pp. 23–24], that the learning involved is of a very special kind, since the learner, unlike Skinner's pigeons, is conditioned not by physical rewards but by the attitudes of educators, parents, therapists, and so forth in response to his efforts and initiatives. These attitudes function as "sanctions." Socialization does more than equip the person being socialized with the limited set of methods; what is acquired through socialization is rather a general aptitude to apply and interpret procedural models, and even to use those models in innovative ways. These skills can be transferred from the learning situation to other, objectively comparable or symbolically analogous situations.

The socialization is neither the product of inculcation by the teacher nor the replication of a model by the student. It is primarily a process, a genuine interaction between socializer and socializee. There would be little sense calling socialization a process, though, if socializer and socializee remained unchanged from the beginning to the end of their relationship. Not only does socialization change the subject by teaching him new standards of behavior and judgment—"denaturing" him, as Rousseau might say; more important, as teacher and pupil come to understand the norms governing their behavior in new ways, the relation between their respective roles also changes. Socialization is an interaction during which new roles are learned and new norms comprehended.

Finally, roles and norms are *related,* by definition. To learn to play the role of son is also to learn to play the role of father. Not that a person can be his own father in a physical sense; but he may feel or sense that in certain circumstances his father should not behave in the way that he himself is behaving, or as he might wish his father to behave. Similarly, learning the boy's role involves making at least an implicit distinction between it and the girl's role. Socialization makes individuals more similar by enabling them to understand one another, but it does this by differentiating one from the other. So socialization is not homogenization. Nor is it a matter of filling our heads with immutable images of our ideal selves. What socialization does do is to provide us with a repertory of simple models and formulas, which we may subsequently generalize and apply to a wide variety of different situations. We thereby acquire the ability not only to identify ourselves with others but also to differentiate ourselves from them.

Thus in the case of the boy vis-à-vis his mother, the learning of his sex categorization enables him to understand and accept the fact that with respect to sex he is different from her. The standards of proper behavior for both sexes are shared by the members of both, but their *application* is differentiated. The usage of the term identification has often been ambiguous, since it has been used to imply a likeness both of standards and of application. [1964, p. 28]

The individual does not learn his social roles as a sponge soaks up liquid [1955, p. 74]. "What is internalized is a reciprocal ego-alter role-interaction pattern. Therefore, in internalizing 'alter' as an object, ego also internalizes alter's orientation toward himself as an object (subject of course to possible distortions). The internalization of the nurturant 'caring' mother includes the internalization of the object of care. . . . Thus the idea of the internalized object as in some sense a 'mirror'image' includes the idea of a 'hall of mirrors' effect, namely the reflection inside the reflection inside the reflection, etc." The relational nature of internalization enables us to understand the phenomenon of narcissism, which occurs when ego takes himself to be the object of what he believes to be alter's desire for him. Looked at in this way, moreover, internalization reveals the paradoxical nature of the relation between the actor and his roles: "When a person is fully socialized . . . it is not so nearly correct to say that a role is something an actor 'has' or 'plays' as that it is something that he is" [1955, p. 107].

In order for the actual behavior of the actor to coincide fully with his roles, that is, with his expectations of his partners' behavior or expectations, two things are necessary: first, roles and motives must mesh perfectly; and second, the actor must be in a state of equilibrium so that he can at all times be what he is supposed to be and do what he is supposed to do. Such a state of affairs is purely hypothetical and could exist only in a society in which social deviance would be no problem. In other words, from the standpoint of general theory, motives (i.e., elements of the personality system that interfere with the social system or systems) are neither more nor less fundamental than roles (i.e., aspects of interaction involving both ego and alter). Both roles and motives are merely ways of looking at action as a process. Still, regardless of the disparity or dissonance between roles and motives, "the crucial components of that aspect of the structure of personality which interpenetrates with systems of social interaction are *the same* as those composing social systems" [1955, p. 107]. Substantialism in all its forms is thus rejected: "society" does not absorb the individual or dissolve him as though it were a chemical bath of some sort—any more than individuals "produce" society directly out of their desires and wishes. Roles and motives crystallize, as it were, in individuals and interactions, compounded under certain conditions out of the fundamental passions of *homo parsoniensis.*

Like any other interaction, socialization can be understood only as a *process,* that is, a sequence of interrelated changes in the relative positions of the actors involved. Socialization leads to changes in the roles we play and the status we enjoy. We are no longer the same people doing the same things after socialization as we were before. Along with these changes go changes in our capabilities, powers, and possessions. These changes in what we *have* bring about changes in what we *are.* To revert once more to Freud's formula, every man wants to be his father and to keep his mother for himself. These goals can be achieved only if they are repudiated or transferred to new objects. There are two reasons for making such a transfer: first, there is the implacable biological pressure of maturation (we literally cannot help growing up); and second, there is the symbolic understanding we have of the process and of what is at stake, an understanding which in many cases is woefully inadequate. Socialization may be seen as a change in ego's status that is brought about by a reordering of his assets, symbolic and real. Adulthood brings with it aptitudes that enable an individual to shoulder responsibilities vis-à-vis his own children in the same manner as his parents did toward him in the past.

The Dialectics of Socialization

Narrowly construed, socialization is the process by which the child becomes an adult who is in turn capable of producing a child, where the verb "to produce" may be taken in biological, psychological, cultural, and social senses. Three aspects of this process are of particular importance. First, it is impelled by an exogenous force, the biological development (maturation) of the individual. Second, it is discontinuous, proceeding by distinct stages. Third, it results in, or at least makes possible, increased autonomy for the individual, by incorporating him in ever more comprehensive systems of interaction. A schematization of this kind obviously owes a great deal to Freud, though on at least two points—bisexuality and the nature of the Superego—Parsons parts company with Freud. It is also reminiscent of Piaget,[23] particularly in regard to the transformation and universalization of norms during the course of socialization. In both Freud and Piaget, Parsons found what I shall refer to here as a dialectical conceptualization of socialization; "dialectical," in this context, means that certain results of the socialization process are unintentional, unwilled, and yet have profound effects on the ultimate relations between the actors involved. Utterly helpless to begin with, the newborn child establishes with its mother its first social relationship. The symbolism characteristic of this relationship is oral, since the mouth is at once the organ that contacts the mother's breast, the orifice through which nourishment enters the child's body, and the organ of crying, which the child can use to attract its mother's attention. The mother-child system thus constituted is in fact the first social system in which the individual takes part. This system determines the range of social experience available to the infant. It is built around a need of great emotional intensity, the more so because the child is dependent on the mother's willingness to provide gratification. The infant is consequently liable to experience very intense feelings of frustration. This social protosystem is to all intents and purposes a closed system, consisting exclusively of mother and child. Its symbolism is quite limited in scope (and not very informative about the "objective" needs of the child), but stridently insistent upon the urgency of the need for attention or assistance.

The next question to ask is how this miniature social system becomes differentiated. How, in other words, is greater complexity introduced into the mother-child relationship? The answer is that the initial relationship undergoes "binary fission." To begin with, the child is absolutely dependent on its mother. Gradually, however, this dependency is reduced by the development of the child's physical capabilities. Eventually, the child acquires the capacity to do things that once were beyond its reach, moving from total helplessness to partial autonomy. At this point the needs for protection, attention, and assistance cease to be the sole motivations of the child's personality. The child will seek to assert that personality through independent behavior. When the child does assert itself, it discovers that there are two possible orientations, dependence and autonomy, and a wide range of available choices of behavior is thus opened up. This is where the genetic principle of "binary fission" comes into play: from the earliest stages of development the individual must confront the "logic of alternatives." As the range of motivations in the child's personality grows broader and more diverse, the mother's personality system adjusts to the change. During the early phase of its existence, the infant, Parsons would say, is more a "possession" than a "social object" and receives care and nurturance from its mother. As it grows older, it becomes a "love-object," in important, specific ways. No longer does the mother respond solely to the child's sporadic, intense expressions of need for food and sleep, which are expressed with particular vehemence when immediate relief is not forthcoming. Now she begins to respond to her child as an independent and already individualized source of demands for attention addressed exclusively to her [1955, p. 70]. Characteristically, the expression of this love is or becomes *conditional*. The forms in which the love of the mother is expressed and the intensity of that expression come to depend on the nature of the "independent initiatives" taken by the child. Depending on its behavior, therefore, the child will now receive either positive or negative sanctions, reward or punishment, whereas previously whatever it received from its mother was given without any demand for reciprocity. The lack of reciprocity had no effect on the "preordained program" of care and attention. Love thus broadens the basis of the relationship between mother and child, into which a provisional system of mutual dependence and reciprocity has been introduced.

With regard to the first two phases of the child's development—the anal phase and the oral phase, to use Freud's terms—we shall focus primarily on the lessons to be drawn concerning the socialization process. In the first place, the existence of such distinct phases makes the socialization process appear to be a series of crises. Each crisis is resolved by the elaboration of a more complex and differentiated system of relations. In moving from one stage to the next, the socializee moves from a lower to a higher level of performance. Thus socialization is not merely a process of differentiation but also of upgrading. Progress, however, is not automatic. Upgrading requires that certain conditions be fulfilled, and quite often this is not the case. Some of these conditions relate to the physical growth of the child; others have to do with the mother: she must be a "good mother," as one says, that is, she must combine in suitable proportions a reassuring, nurturing attitude with a motivating love. The socialization process requires not only a "socializee" but also a "socializer" conscious of his or her responsibilities. Between socializer and socializee there must exist a consensus, or in any case mutual confidence, if not as regards the details of each stage in the process, then at least as to its general orientation: both parties must see socialization as playing some part in the "upgrading" of the socializee. The process faces many pitfalls: the socializer may expect too much too soon of the socializee, for example; or the socializer may be concerned more with his or her own convenience than with the best interests of the socializee. On the other hand, the socializee may drag his feet, balk at a certain hurdle in the development process, or even regress to a more primitive stage of gratification, to the detriment of his own progress.

The Oedipal crisis may be defined as "the process of transition from integrated membership in a two-member (autonomous) interaction system where power and instrumental-expressive differentiation are fused, to integration in a four-member, or basic role, system, where these two axes of differentiation have become segregated out from each other. In personality terms we regard it as the process by which in the internalized object aspect ego differentiates from a two-unit personality structure to a four-unit structure, by a process of bifurcation, on the instrumental-expressive dimension, of each of the earlier two into two more, making four altogether" [1955, pp. 77–78]. The Oedipal episode is an essential step in the broadening of the child's social horizons, characterized by bifurcation of roles and attitudes. "The pre-Oedipal mother-child system represented a two-member system, with a 'you,' a 'me' and a 'we' and the residual category of 'non-we.' Now father and mother are differentiated out from the earlier 'you,' and 'self' (and/or sibling of own sex) and 'sibling of opposite sex' are differentiated out from the earlier 'me.' There is the further implication that an elaboration of the structure of 'we's' takes place. There is still the old 'we' of 'mother and I.' If the child is a boy, however, there is 'father and mother,' 'we males,' i.e., father, myself and brothers and 'those females,' mother and sister(s). There is the we of myself and siblings regardless of sex. Finally, there is the overall 'we' of the family as a whole over against the non-we of non-members of the family. We-ness, then, has become a *hierarchy* of two levels, with a superordinate we-system, and a series of collectivity sub-systems, taking the possible permutations and combinations of the four basic roles, namely six" [1955, pp. 78–79].

The Oedipal phase, when envisaged as a learning process, may be regarded in essence as a confrontation between the child and a new-comer to the scene: the father. Intruding upon the intimacy of the exclusive mother-child microsystem, the father brings with him new constraints of an unfamiliar kind, since they come from outside the family, from a mysterious world far from home of which the father is the representative. The father's intrusion means that relations between the mother and the child must be redefined: no longer can the child lay exclusive claim to the mother, who must in certain respects be shared with the interloper. This new dichotomy in the adult world is not the only result of the "binary fission." The child must also define itself as either boy or girl; in other words, the child must choose either the side of the mother or the side of the father. Another consequence is that the male child, say, will have to make the same discrimination between his brothers (who are like himself and his father) and his sisters (who are like his mother, i.e., unlike himself and his father). This disjunction in the social world is symbolized by the presence or absence of a penis. To have or not to have a penis thus becomes the determinant both of one's own identity and of one's relations with alter, hence on two counts an essential component of personal security.

As we have seen, in the oral phase the child's need-dispositions are of two kinds, emphasizing either dependence or conformity, which occur in conjunction with two need-dispositions on the mother's side, nurturance and love. In the post-Oedipal child, we may now say, "security" and "adequacy" characterize the two need-dispositions, the former corresponding to a feminine dimension of the personality, the latter to a masculine dimension (the first articulated with the mother's nurturance, the second with the tendency to conformity on the side of the father). Masculine and femine in this context are not to be thought of as physical characteristics: they are to be interpreted as role-expectations associated with the internalization of certain objects and must not be isolated from the context of the process that gives them their meaning. The feminine dimension of personality is merely the desire of the individual to be taken care of as the mother takes care of her child or to adopt toward alter such an attitude of caring, solicitude, and devotion. Accordingly, it is by virtue of the socialization process, from which all of us learn how to interact with others, that we are all to some degree bisexual, as opposed to Freud's "assumed constitutional bisexuality" [1955, p. 83]. Not only is the masculine/feminine dichotomy used to distinguish traits that, taken in themselves, may be found in the adult behavior of either sex; it also over-determines those traits by classifying them as either masculine or feminine, when in fact they were acquired during the prior [i.e., pre-Oedipal—trans.] phase of development. Each phase contributes to the development of the personality by generalizing the results of the previous phase, in so doing not only consolidating but also reinterpreting those results.

This interpretation of the socialization process emerges from Parsons's discussion of sanction-types and their interrelations [1955, pp.

84–87]. The importance of this discussion is that it helps us to form a picture of the socialized individual, so that we can understand both the springs of his action and the nexus of relations through which he exchanges rewards and punishments with his partners. What Parsons does is to associate a specific sanction-type with each of the four types of "need-dispositions" encountered above [namely, nurturance, security, adequacy, and conformity—trans.]. Thus there are four sanction-types in all: response, acceptance, approval, and esteem. Response is the "attitude of readiness to provide segmental gratifications, to serve as a consummatory goal-object, or to serve as the direct agent of the availability of such objects" [1955, p. 86], and "is the sanction-type most appropriate to the nurturance need." "Acceptance—which at an earlier stage we called 'love'—is (in social system terms) acceptance in terms of solidarity of membership in a collectivity, the diffuse symbolic expression of the attitude of belongingness," associated with the "security need-disposition." Third, approval is the "attitude appropriate to the positive sanctioning of functionally specific instrumental performances, in terms of their effectiveness or efficiency," which is associated with the "adequacy need-disposition." Finally, esteem is the "attitude of positive overall evaluation of a person, a collectivity, or other object, in terms of universalistic standards by which it is measured in comparison with other objects, independently of its belongingness in a particular relational system," which is associated with the "conformity need-disposition."

As we have said, the sanction-types must be considered in conjunction with the corresponding need-dispositions. We explained earlier that two of the need-dispositions, security and adequacy, are already present during the oral phase. It may be useful at this point to say an additional word or two about these particular needs. To quote Parsons once again, "Security is that aspect of the earlier undifferentiated autonomy need-disposition which concerns the relational aspect of the significance of the cathected mother-object." The goal is to strike a balance between autonomy and dependency. "Adequacy, on the other hand, refers to the autonomous *performance* aspect, the need and disposition to *do* specific things which are expected and acceptable" [1955, p. 84]. Once again, the goal is to strike a balance between dependency and autonomy. But now the balance to be struck refers not to the mother-child microsystem but rather to the new demands associated with the broader context symbolized by the father. Thus security comes under the head of the integrative function, adequacy under the head of the adaptive function.

We learn about more than just the socialization process from the discussion of the sanction-types. The list of sanction-types tells us what the nature of the interaction process must be if the socialized individual is to remain socialized. Specifically, the process must ensure that participants obtain "segmental gratifications, relatively independently of their conformity with normative standards" [1955, p. 84]. Here we touch upon the deep roots of solidarity, which is based on a different principle from that which holds sway in the domain of exchange (whether the latter principle is one of equality or inequality). Response is something I am entitled to expect from alter, and I am entitled to expect gratification from that response. This is the first requirement of civility, which we experience in its raw form, so to speak, in the nurturance relation. The acceptance or love sanction in its positive form carries with it acceptance of the whole person rather than of individual needs or appetites in search of "segmental gratification." Approval and esteem are sanctions that put ego on notice that alter may stand in judgment of him; this judgment may pertain either to specific contributions (approval) or to overall conformity with the norms (esteem).

In order for the socialization process to proceed normally, three conditions apparently need to be fulfilled. First, something must impel the individual to strive to achieve a higher level, wresting him from the grip of self-gratification: this is the erotic function—in Parsons's sense of the word. The guidance of a devoted adult is also necessary: this is the pedagogic function. Finally, the individual must be willing to go beyond immediate gratification: this is the cathartic function. Eroticism is an indispensable ingredient to the extent that it induces us to form attachments to other people apt to serve as role-models. Along with these models we gain a sense of our own ideal ego-image, and meeting the requirements of that ideal enhances our sense of adequacy, of being able to live up to the expectations that other people, as well as ourselves, are entitled to have of us. Thus the erotic function refers not to a specific gratification but rather to a diffuse need-disposition, which is generally far broader in scope than the physical erotic instinct, being instead a more and more generalized symbolic mode of expression.

In psychiatry, transference, that is, the formation of an affective attachment to the psychiatrist by the patient, is an important factor in treatment; I hope it is not too audacious to compare this to the love of the mother's love or the esteem of the teacher's esteem, which are important factors in child rearing and education, respectively. To carry on with this analogy, notice that it would be dangerous for the psychiatrist to allow his patient to fall in love with him, for this would risk arresting the therapy at the transference stage; similarly, the teacher must keep his pupil at a respectful distance. By the same token, in the socialization process the mother must not allow her child to wall himself off from the world in an exclusive relationship with her. Adulthood means leaving the group that first provided the security that every individual must have and acquiring the capacity to deal with all kinds of other people, in particular people who are not one's parents. Hence schooling, like any learning process, does away with the need for itself. Just as psychoanalysis must one day be "terminated," so must every person one day reach the point where he or she is ready to leave the bosom of the primary family group. This catharsis, as we called it a moment ago, imposes complementary obligations on teacher and pupil. The teacher must remember that his pupil will not be his "child" forever. At the same time, the pupil must assert his independence without forming Oedipal reactions of recrimination and hostility.

In choosing an interactive theory of socialization, Parsons moved away from the particularly crude brand of functionalism that is commonly imputed to him. There is no reason to look upon stability or continuity as explicit or latent ends that "society" (or the "system") somehow lays down by manipulating the actors. Socialization does not teach the individual any particular form of behavior. It teaches him, rather, how to orient himself relative to his actual or potential partners in the interaction process by laying down a frame of reference in very broad and general terms.

The ability to properly use the distinction between universalism and particularism is a criterion by which one may judge whether or not an individual is socialized. Parsons has given us a definition in logical terms: "Universalism . . . is the consideration of objects as related to one another by abstract similarity; e.g. object D or E or F (not and) is a man. . . . [P]articularism is the consideration of objects as related to one another by common membership in one group; e.g. objects A & B & C make up family I. A & B & C are particularistically related as members of the family. . . . We could not say A or B or C is the family I; we must say rather A & B & C is the family I. Thus particularism denotes a conjunctive relationship of terms. . . . [Whereas] universalism denotes a disjunctive relationship of terms" [1955, p. 120].

The universalism/particularism dichotomy enables us to distinguish between particularistic membership groups and universalistic reference groups by observing whether or not there is some extrinsic criterion common to all the individuals under consideration. We shall return later to this dichotomy, at which time we shall be in a position to cast a little light on two particularly vexing questions. First, there is the problem of solidarity: is solidarity always of the "conjunctive" type? Under what conditions are conjunctive and disjunctive types of solidarity compatible? Second, disjunction may create situations of exclusion. Under the logic of universalism, individuals not possessing a given attribute are not, as a group, defined by that attribute. But are they, and can they be, excluded from a group consisting of individuals from whom they differ only by virtue of that attribute, and with whom they otherwise coexist and interact? Exclusion based on pure disjunction gives rise to serious problems when the individuals thus set apart continue to live in close physical proximity. Taking this into consideration, we shall be able to throw a good deal of light on the problem of stratification, which is just a large-scale process of inclusion/exclusion. We shall also gain insight into the relation between mechanisms of social broadening and certain other mechanisms of avoidance and separation. The broadening mechanisms impel the individual to enter into an ever more complex and extensive nexus of relations, while the mechanisms of avoidance and separation, the most striking of which is the incest taboo, tend to "dissolve" the individual's early attachments, exposing him to the harsh rigors of interacting with all sorts of other people. Thus it is far from true to say that socialization encloses the individual in the society from which he happens to have sprung; in fact, socialization forces him to move beyond that society.

Deviance and Control

However socialized—or socializable—*homo parsoniensis* may be, he is nevertheless liable to deviant behavior. He may try to escape the authority of the collective norms and fail to carry out their precepts. He may even actively rebel against them and work to undermine existing norms or to replace them with new ones. As a first approximation, we may interpret deviance as a failure of socialization. Ultimately, however, this view proves to be far too narrow. In the first place, individuals will continue to behave deviantly well after the circumstances that gave rise to their deviant behavior have changed. Then, too, not only can deviant behavior alter the relations between the ill-socialized or desocialized individual and the society around him, it can also give rise to social movements far-reaching in their consequences and cause profound changes in the structure of society.

As we have seen in the case of socialization, the interaction paradigm can help shed some light on the nature of deviance [1951*a*, p. 251]. Thus we would do well to take another look at ego, alter, and the relationship between them. To oversimplify, assume for the moment that there is one and only one context for the interaction between ego and alter (i.e., no third party intervenes between the two, for the time being, and that stable, explicit rules govern their relationship. So long as the expectations of both partners remain complementary, that is, mutually contingent in a strict sense, the two-element microsystem they constitute will remain in equilibrium. Now, these expectations, as well as the values associated with them, may well be affected by the actions of ego or alter, or perhaps by both of them. If the change in expectations exceeds a certain threshold level, it may cause ego to become frustrated. There are three elements involved in this situation. Two of them are actors or social objects, in Parsons's terms; the third element consists of rules and values of various kinds, with respect to which each actor orients his own and his partner's actions.

The source of deviant behavior is to be looked for primarily in the socialization process itself. Socialization does not merely bring about a change in the status of the socializee. It also calls into question the whole relationship between socializee and socializer, as well as the interpretation of the norms that govern that relationship as seen by both parties. At each stage in the process ego will make new demands on alter, which alter may try to avoid. This leads to regression; the individual falls back into perceptual and behavioral modes less differentiated than the situation calls for [1955, p. 181]. At each point in the process where transition from one psychological stage to another is required, the more the socializee is asked to sacrifice and the greater his hope of obtaining immediate gratification by reverting to an earlier stage, the greater the danger of regression. Another possibility is that ego's high expectation level will cause alter to overestimate his strength. Assuming a level of maturity beyond that which he has actually achieved, alter may react to the challenges that the socialization process lays down with attitudes that may seem to be sophisticated but that, unfortunately, his level of emotional and intellectual development cannot sustain. Precocity of this sort, and inflationary borrowing, so to speak, against nonliquid assets, is the opposite of regression, which might be thought of as an underemployment of current assets. Too little or too much, too soon or too late: these are risks inherent in the socialization process, which threaten to destroy the reciprocity of the relationship between ego and alter (the one asking too much or for something new, the other offering too little or the wrong thing for that particular stage in the process), at the same time shaking the foundations of the normative system itself.

Changing attitudes toward ego on alter's part will be sources of frustration for ego, and three major factors will affect the way ego deals with the new situation. First, there are his motives: goals to be attained and needs to be gratified. Second, there is his attachment to alter: ego places a certain value on the fact that alter takes a particular attitude toward him. Finally, from his prior relations with alter, ego will have formed an idea of what is "normal," which will govern the transactions between them. Thus we may sum up by saying that frustration with alter will force ego to question his own motives, his relationship with alter, and the rules that govern their interaction. "He can restructure his own need-dispositions by inhibition and one or more of the mechanisms of defense, such as simply repressing the needs which are no longer gratified. He can, secondly, seek to transfer his cathexis to a new object . . . and, finally, he can renounce or seek to redefine the value-orientation with which alter is no longer conforming" [1951a, p. 252].

If the socialization process has gone smoothly, such restructuring of the relations between ego and alter can be carried out without serious difficulties. If I have a friend who is allergic to tobacco smoke, for example, I can either refrain from smoking or stop seeing him. If my friend insists that I give up either smoking or our friendship, choosing becomes unavoidable. As painful as it may be for me, I will find that the more clear-cut my preference is, the more decisive I will be in choosing. Things may not always be so simple, however. "Ego may not abandon his cathexis of alter by substituting an alternative object, but may retain his cathexis, but this cathexis can no longer be 'undisturbed.' Ego must have some reaction to the frustration which alter has imposed upon him, some resentment or hostility" [1951a, p. 253].

In such a situation, ego's motives will be characterized by more or less marked ambivalence, while the ego-alter relationship will be one of conflict. Ego may continue to have motives for loving or admiring alter, and yet his frustration will give rise to negative, even hostile, attitudes and lead to emotional conflict between him and alter. Moreover, ego may lose confidence in the congruence of his expectations with the rules governing his interaction with alter, because he will have ceased to follow the rules himself. Thus it is not only ego's motives that are tinged with ambivalence but also his attitudes toward alter and toward the orientations (norms and values) with respect to which ego and alter define their relationship.

Ambivalence is always psychologically costly. Accordingly, there is pressure on the actor to get out of an ambivalent situation. On the other hand, ego will attribute a certain value to both sides of his ambivalence, although the value attributed to one side can be quite different in nature and degree from the value attributed to the other side. The child, for example, may want to cling to motives learned during an early stage of development while at the same time holding on to its mother's love; but the mother, now that the child is a "big boy," wants him to relinquish gratifications that he has outgrown. The child must face up to this conflict, torn as he is between his regressive tendencies and the need to grow up, which need is made clear to him by his mother's use of the language of "conditional love." We are inevitably ill-equipped to cope with progress since we cannot comprehend its meaning in the light of past experience alone.

There are two directions in which we may look for a way out of an ambivalent situation. "[Either] ego will continue to be attached to alter and/or to be motivated to conform with the normative pattern in question, [or] ego will tend to abandon his attachment to alter . . . and to refuse to conform with the normative pattern" [1951a, p. 253]. The first of these alternatives reflects what Parsons calls the "conformative need-disposition," while the second reflects the "alienative need-disposition," which indicates estrangement from the norm or the person symbolizing the norm. In deviant behavior, which is always ambivalent to some degree, elements of both conformity and alienation are involved. Such a combination may be quite unstable; still, we may assume that either conformity or alienation has priority, at least genetically.

An actor may either actively seek or passively accept a certain relation to the norms (or to the persons embodying them). On the one hand, I may try hard to prove that I am beyond reproach in every respect, that I do everything alter expects me to do—and a little bit more besides. On the other hand, I may do just what is asked of me, no more and no less, in just the way I was told to do it. We may call the former case an instance of compulsive conformity, the latter an instance of compulsive acquiescence. Let us turn now to the other side of the conformity/alienation dichotomy, namely, alienation. Again there are two possibilities. I may take every opportunity to flaunt my opposition to the norms or authorities and to rebel against them. Or I may simply refuse to cooperate, feign ignorance, avoid living up to alter's expectations, and decline to sacrifice opportunities for self-gratification in favor of collective goal-attainment as specified by the norms. We shall refer to the first alternative as rebelliousness, to the second as withdrawal [1951a, p. 257].

Thus, by combining the two dichotomies alienation/conformity and activity/passivity, we arrive at four types of deviant behavior. This, of course, recalls the conceptualization we developed earlier of the interaction process. Ego and alter depend on each other by virtue of their reciprocal expectations. Since every actor is responsive to the initiatives and responses of his partners, and since every actor takes initiatives in the hope of eliciting certain responses from his partners, the causes of conformity and alienation must be sought in the emotional impact on ego of his partner's expectations and of normative requirements, which may affect the way he views his own capacities and his relationship to alter. If the normative requirements are too stiff, the actor may ask whether it makes sense to try to meet them. Is there any hope of measuring up? If ego does what alter expects, will alter reciprocate by doing what ego expects of him in return? From the standpoint of the personality, the cause of alienation is what Parsons refers to as "disillusionment." Analytically, disillusionment consists in mistrust of others (whom ego perceives as threatening, abusive, or treacherous) and a fearful attitude toward life. As for conformity, its roots must be sought in ego's dependence on the norm or the authority in which the norm is embodied.

When one treats deviant behavior as a process, a particular form of interaction, as we have done, it is natural to look to deviance as an archetype of ego-alter conflict. Parsonian sociology, according to some, is a sociology of consensus and ignores conflict. Rather than indulge in useless exegesis to refute this assertion, we would do better to examine the following two propositions, which lie at the heart of Parsons's discussion of conflict. When there is conflict, at least one of the parties will claim, with one degree of justification or another, that a legitimate norm, germane to the situation at hand, is being violated, ignored, or wrongly applied, while the other party—the accused, as it were—will adduce other norms or possibly even the same norm but with a different interpretation. If it were unimportant to achieve or maintain a consensus at the termination of the conflict, the question would come down to one of physical violence pure and simple. Conflict is not vaguely synonymous with opposition in general, however. Nor is the best way to understand what conflict is to focus on quarrels over the distribution of the profits of a cooperative venture, or on battles for control of the means of production. Instead, we must turn our attention to a simpler and more fundamental situation. In the course of interpreting social deviance as a kind of interaction, we defined conflict as the primordial situation in which ego and alter must decide which rules are applicable to their relationship. Accordingly, it is unnecessary for the time being to decide what kind of situation it is and what kind of relations it involves (two-person zero-sum game, cooperative game, etc.).

Parsons focuses on the socialization process, in the context of which divergent, sometimes bluntly contradictory interpretations of the fundamentally important norms are given by the participants. This approach runs into serious difficulties, however, as the proponents of the oversocialization thesis have clearly pointed out. Parsons puts conflict at the heart of the socialization process. Well and good. But to the extent that the socialization process is a biological process, its goal is for ego to achieve adulthood. In the end papa turns out to have been correct; the little boy's fate will be that of all little boys: he will settle his conflict with his father and become in due course a father himself. This being the case, is it possible, if we view conflict from the standpoint of socialization, to regard it as anything but a transitory episode, which must ultimately be resolved by accession to a higher stage of cooperation?

One possible answer to this question is to observe that adulthood is not without conflicts of its own. What is more, the successive phases of conflict-resolution are defined by capacities specific to certain stages of individual development, and these capacities may always be put to alternative uses. The end-result of socialization, therefore, is not a stationary state in which the individual can enjoy what he has amassed in tranquillity. It is not unreasonable to say that the goal of conflict is its resolution, in the sense that the goal of every intentional process is its outcome. But this outcome is not a static state, and it would be more appropriate to term the resolution of the conflict a settlement, in the sense in which the term "settlement" is used in diplomacy.

Conflict and deviance are therefore strict correlates of consensus and conformity. The most delicate point, however, is to judge whether the foregoing theory of deviance, based though it is on the interaction paradigm, is fruitful for sociological analysis. Parsons, who is at pains to remind his readers that social facts must be built up out of the meanings the actors attach to their actions, has consistently and insistently made statements concerning processes that entail changes or reversals in meaning as seen by the actor; obviously, these statements beg for clarification.

At first glance, deviant behavior may be considered a form of rational action. Deviance occurs in situations in which the actor cannot simultaneously meet the requirements of the norm and the demands of his own sensibility. The first dilemma he must face is to decide whether to give priority to his own motivations or to the prescriptions laid down by the norm. Ego's dilemma is thus one we have already encountered in the form of the affectivity/affective-neutrality dichotomy. Let us suppose that the actor chooses the path leading to deviant forms of behavior. He will then have to confront two new dichotomies: conformity/alienation, activity/passivity. The deviant actor seeks an optimal, or at least a satisfactory, compromise between his own motives and the collective norms. But deviance cannot be adequately treated in terms of calculation. Is the situation of the deviant actor comparable with that of *homo oeconomicus* faced with a choice between apples and pears, who will select a quantity of each determined by substitution rates that reflect both his preference schedule and the relative scarcity of the goods?

No. Deviance is not a matter of strictly rational choice, for not all the consequences of deviant behavior can be predicted or controlled by the actor. One may be right to choose deviance over conformity. But deviance often proves a slippery business, both for the deviant and for others. What distinguishes deviant behavior from rational choice is normative ambiguity and motivational ambivalence, in consequence of which the actor not only cannot do what he wants to do but does not even know what it is that he wants. In situations of deviance, as we have said, the norms are ambiguous, amounting to little more than vague homilies: "Do the best you can." The scrupulous actor will ask himself, "Am I doing enough?" Motives are fraught with ambivalence: in other words, the same goal is simultaneously invested with positive and negative characteristics—loved and hated. "There is still the need to love or admire alter, but there is also the product of his frustration in the form of negative and in some sense hostile attitudes toward alter" [1951*a*, p. 253]. From a synchronic point of view, ambivalence leads to instability. From a diachronic point of view it leads the actor to alternate between one side of a dichotomy and another. He both loves and hates alter. Initially he will exhibit love, only to replace it by hatred in a subsequent phase, to be followed still later by a return to love, and so on indefinitely. The upshot is that alter's image in ego's eyes becomes confused—unless ego deliberately limits his field of vision, seeing himself as the person he would like to be, or, in the manner of a paranoiac, as one who is threatened by the hostility of others.

We have been treating deviance in interpersonal terms. But can we view deviant behavior as a true social fact in light of the interaction paradigm? The answer is yes, owing to the cumulative aspect of deviant behavior. A cumulative process is one in which a system is displaced from its initial position in the absence of any automatic mechanism for restoring the system to its original state. The disturbance may then be amplified, if the effects of its various components reinforce one another. Suppose, for example, we look at a particular pair, ego and alter. If ego behaves deviantly, he will change the initial situation by modifying not only his own expectations but alter's as well. For instance, suppose that ego feels alter has been too severe in judging his performance. "Ego," Parsons writes [1951*a*, p. 255], "will react to this with resentment, which, however, he will repress and become compulsively anxious to secure alter's approval. . . . This in turn has its effect on alter. . . . Ego has now put him in a position where it is more difficult than it was before for him to fulfill ego's expectations; the same level of approval which would have sufficed before is no longer sufficient."

This situation is quite similar to that observed by Peter Blau[24] in an office in which information was passed from a "senior" official to his more competent "junior." With this information in hand, the junior could then make the right decisions, and in exchange he offered deference and gratitude to his senior, thereby reinforcing the status of the latter. Blau's analysis, however, focuses on what determines the terms of trade whereby supply is balanced against demand, assuming a constant rate of substitution between information and deference for the two men, while Parsons concentrates on the effects of the transaction on the norm, resulting first in alienation and finally in desocialization. The form desocialization will take depends on the relation between each actor and his partners as well as between the actors and the normative system. Suppose, for example, that ego is out of step with the norms. All he wants from alter is to be left alone. Suppose, on the other hand, that ego is a hyperconformist, an obsessive. He will then stubbornly try to get a critical or reluctant alter to grant him his due. Finally, the nature of the ego-alter relationship will depend on alter's motives and attitudes. Alter may have been socialized in such a way that his actions will not disrupt the normative system. But a socially deviant ego may well find himself involved in a relationship with a socially deviant alter.

How does deviant behavior produce cumulative desocializing effects? It should first of all be noted that it is far from always the case that deviance has such effects. Take, for instance, the case where both ego and alter are "alienated" with respect to some norm. They may quietly agree between themselves to "get by" doing as little as they possibly can since they have a common interest in keeping the true state of affairs concealed. Thus in the short term, at least, their deviance has no effects that extend beyond the two deviants themselves. For deviance to take on a social dimension, it must have consequences outside the sphere in which it originated. This can happen in at least two ways. On the one hand, certain "solid citizens" may be disturbed or outraged at the sight of deviant behavior of some kind; they may regard such behavior as a form of "social pollution." "Respectable" members of the middle classes, for instance, might find the sight of a hobo worrisome or (if many hoboes are about) even frightening. They can then either move out of the "slummy" area, in which they no longer feel at home, or try to get the police and other authorities to enforce law and order. On the other hand, the deviants themselves may realize that they pose a problem for others and try to resolve it by taking farsighted action not immediately relevant to their own particular interests.

The preliminary analysis of deviance as a disruption of the interaction process can be extended by a further analysis of deviance as a social problem, once we have grasped the *symbolic* import of certain acts. These acts perform a regulatory function at the highest level of the system. Accordingly, disruption of them can lead to dislocation of the entire social structure. Under what conditions is such "nuclear fission" most likely to occur [1951*a*, p. 287]?

Imagine a group in which several individuals exhibit an alienative need-disposition in conjunction with a positive commitment to their alienated attitude. Under these conditions, group cohesiveness can be maintained only if "normal" individuals, that is, individuals who continue to accept the authority of the norms, try to restore their effectiveness: this means silencing the rebellious members of the group. If the "normal" members are not overwhelmed by the rebels, there is a danger that they will become "conformists." Thus a conflict arises in which the definition of the norm is at stake. Will it be respected or challenged? Splits will develop in the group over this conflict, and potential leaders will come into competition with one another. Because of the danger of reverting to a "war of all against all," increasingly strict disciplinary measures are called for.

Deviance simultaneously gives rise to conflicts over *power* and *authority*. Pitting the champions of the established order against its opponents, deviance also raises a challenge to the values that underpin the normative system, directed against their tenuousness, obsolescence, or inadequacy. Social deviance is not merely revealing, it is explosive. In effect, deviance gambles on a shift in hostility from inside the group to outside, and from top to bottom. Compulsive conformists, like rebels, also try to dominate and mobilize passive or indifferent members of the group. The more they can prove their superiority over their opponents, the more likely they are to be successful in doing so. Rebels and conformists clash over their relative prowess, and the stakes for themselves and for the group as a whole are extremely high.

In the classic work of Fraenkel Brunswick and Theodor Adorno, this pattern was referred to as the "authoritarian syndrome." It is central to social deviance as a process and gives that process its cumulative and self-destructive character. A group split into active and passive components (where the active component comprises those who are in command, or at least take initiatives, while the passive component comprises those who obey or follow orders), the active component of which is further split into a group of compulsive conformists and a group of rebels, can only evolve in one of two ways: catastrophic violence can erupt, or the group can dissolve. Furthermore, it is reasonable to hypothesize that complex causal connections exist between these two processes; the exploration of these connections is the subject matter of the sociology of conflict.

As we have seen, however, radical confrontation between ego and alter, that is, conflict, originates with the norm, which one upholds while the other tries to evade its authority. Therefore, conflict may have as an unanticipated consequence a redefinition of the norm, or normative change. What happens in effect is that the conflict calls the normative system itself into question by revealing its "factitious" nature. One side, feeling that the norms are under attack, will undertake to defend or refurbish them, while the other will denounce the constraints imposed by the norms as unrealistic or downright abominable. More generally, once the existence of social deviance has been brought into the open, the question of legitimacy arises. At this point it is no longer just one rule or custom that is under attack but the normative system as a whole. "The legitimation of a deviant pattern immediately shifts it from the status of an individual to that of a collective phenomenon" [1951a, p. 292]. A wide-scale process of legitimation-protest is thus set in motion; such processes are the mechanisms of social change par excellence. It is not difficult to see that such processes are ambivalent in nature; in other words, they are likely to produce unanticipated consequences, which, as we have seen, are inseparable from social deviance itself. This ambivalence affords the deviants some room for tactical maneuver. On the one hand, they may try to depict their cause as a just one by emphasizing how their practice differs from what is normally done and by showing how it is at variance with the official norm. On the other hand, they may try to "turn the tables on the wider society" by showing that the official norms themselves are at variance with the values that the authorities profess to be upholding. Thus the analysis of deviance not only suggests a way of analyzing social change but also helps us to identify a problem of singular importance: the structural mismatch between norms and values, a mismatch that can be overcome only by a sporadic infusion of charismatic symbolism, and even then not entirely.[25]

Is there any way to bring deviance under control before it becomes a cumulative process that can result in social conflict and destruction of the normative system? In other words, is there any way to limit the scope of social deviance and attenuate its effects? Can the deviant or near-deviant individual be resocialized? Let us turn once again to the interaction paradigm for answers to these questions. Ego and alter respond to each other's initiatives and reactions. Each can anticipate what the other's expectations will be. Available to both are sanctions, which they may actually apply or merely use in a symbolic way, for making threats or promises. It is this repertory of sanctions that enables each partner to exert some control over the behavior of the other.

Let us next assume that, for one partner or the other, the code of sanctions has become incomprehensible or unacceptable. Let us further assume that one of the two, due either to his present role or his previous socialization, has an interest in putting his partner's behavior "back on the right track." What resources does he have at hand for accomplishing this end? Situations of this sort must be faced by parents, teachers, psychotherapists, and physicians, for example.

As we have already seen, the doctor-patient relationship is built around a zone of uncertainty over which both partners would like to exercise control. Sickness creates a situation that may be looked at from two different points of view. On the one hand, it raises problems of an instrumental or technical nature, the solution of which requires a certain competence on the part of the doctor and some delegation of authority by the patient, who in his eagerness to get well transfers responsibility for certain decisions to the doctor and agrees in advance to abide by what the doctor decides. Sickness, however, also has a second dimension. The patient temporarily finds himself in a state of helplessness and dependence. Since a high value is placed on health, particularly in societies like ours, in which activist individualism is predominant,[26] the patient is motivated, or even morally obligated, to "do everything within his power in order to get well." The doctor can use this motivation of the patient to manipulate him (in fact, the patient's motivation is of two kinds: biologically based, because illness is or may be painful, so that the patient is willing to take an active part in any treatment that offers relief; and culturally based, because the presumably autonomous adult cannot accept, or, worse still, connive in, a prolonged state of incapacitation due to illness without risking a loss of standing). The will to recover, like the child's or adolescent's will to grow up, is indispensable to the socializer; without that will, the doctor would find it difficult to influence his patient's behavior (or, analogously, the teacher or parent to influence the child's behavior).

Paramount among the resources available to the socializer is the docility of the socializee. Necessary though docility may be, however, it is not enough. If the patient believes that the doctor has ulterior motives in prescribing a certain treatment, such as to hold on to his patient as long as possible, then the patient may not be willing to cooperate. School discipline and the hardships of study would be difficult to bear if the student felt himself a victim of persecution justified only by his adversary's superior strength. Thus successful socialization depends on the fulfillment of a second condition, namely, that, in the eyes of the socializee, the socializer be seen as a disinterested and competent individual, a person worthy of confidence not only because of his superior wisdom but also because he has the best interests of the socializee at heart in doing what he does.

What Parsons calls "fiduciary" roles are roles based on some degree of explicit delegation of powers, a delegation that ultimately rests on trust. In such cases alter will do for ego what ego would not be able to do as well without his help. In certain areas ego may not be ready to make choices, lacking the necessary knowledge or will, so that alter must decide for him. Three factors help to foster the trust on which such a delegation of powers is based. First, ego must be convinced that his interests are not in conflict with alter's. This condition is not met in the case of labor-management relations, where the worker is right to suspect his employer of wanting to pare away his wages to the bare minimum, especially if it is true that the capitalist's profit is and can be nothing other than what he takes out of the worker's hide. But in the case of the doctor and his patient, the situation is quite different: in no sense can the physician be said to be the "class enemy" of his patient. Second, there are certain institutional guarantees—in the case of medicine, for example, a culturally sanctioned code of ethics, medical traditions, and laws—that protect the patient against possible attempts to take advantage of his helpless condition. Finally, there is an impersonal mechanism, which Parsons, borrowing from the Freudian lexicon,[27] calls "transference," that creates a kind of community of interest between ego and alter.

From the standpoint of common sense, it may be difficult to believe that the patient suffering from tonsillitis who goes to an eye, ear, nose, and throat man for treatment actually invests this specialist with an extremely intense emotional significance, projecting onto him a whole range of fantasies in which hostility and dependency are mixed in an ambivalent combination. Indeed, in many cases the therapeutic relationship is a purely technical and instrumental one. Whenever the expressive aspect of health comes into play, however, whether on the part of the patient, the doctor, or both, then the problem of transference takes on considerable importance. In fact, "It became clear that the psychoanalytic relation presented the extreme . . . example of this relationship, and that the vast and vague range of psychosomatic relationships fitted into this" [1970a, p. 837].

The phenomenon of transference is bound up with symbolism. I "project" my hopes and fears onto the physician because I look upon him as a person who mediates between me and the sphere of health, a zone of uncertainty to which I am acutely sensitive. The doctor, like the father,[28] is a symbol or image. This symbol consists of many component parts, and using these components the subject can set up relations between aspects of his psychology (e.g., instrumental, expressive, cognitive, affective, active) and areas of his life relatively remote from the sphere of action directly concerned (such as the relations between the domestic and professional life of the subject, as in the case of the father symbol, where the father stands both for the head of the family and the head of the firm in which he earns the family's livelihood; or, to take another example, the physician symbol, which intervenes between sexual intimacy and individual responsibility). But in transference, whether it involves the father, the teacher, the therapist, or, more generally, the socializer, the role of symbolism is larger still. Symbolism holds up a *model* of what we will eventually be or do—or ought to be or do—when we are adults, or what we would be or do if we were truly adult.

If we define social control as "those processes in the social system which tend to counteract the deviant tendencies" [1951a, p. 297], we readily see how control is distinguished from manipulation. In order for control to be possible, the agent or "agency" exerting it must have at hand resources stockpiled during an earlier phase of socialization, an arsenal of symbols and models amassed prior to the agency's involvement in social control activities. Without such a stockpile the agency could not play its proper role, because the necessary degree of trust and understanding would be lacking. The socializer cannot rely exclusively on his skill in manipulating other people. Control depends on prior socialization and on the cultural capital accumulated through socialization. Though it may be analyzed as an ego-alter interaction, social control presupposes a preexisting stock of resources, amassed prior to the relationship between ego and alter.

Just as the deviant individual finds himself enmeshed in a series of unwanted consequences brought on by his actions, so the socializer must work with existing sanctions not necessarily of his own choosing. The most he can do is to try to make the available sanctions compatible with the ends he is pursuing when he uses them. To begin with, ego can offer support to alter. The "primary direct significance" of support is "in relation to the anxiety component of the reaction to strain, to give a basis of reassurance such that the need to resort to aggressive-destructive and/or defensive reactions is lessened. . . . The stability of the love attitudes of the mother in critical phases of socialization is one fundamental type of case" [1951a, p. 299]. Similarly, the supportive teacher will not take an overbearing attitude toward his pupil and will be careful not to drum into the pupil's head the idea that he will never amount to anything. Instead, the teacher will try to make the student's task easier by explaining difficult points and offering reassurance when the student reveals shortcomings or failures, as well as by reminding the student that practice makes perfect. In other words, the teacher has the right, if not the duty, to interpret performance norms so as not to jeopardize the student's chance of future development. But even this relaxation of the normal standards is not enough, for it pertains only to instrumental action. Here, what Parsons calls "permissiveness" [1951a, p. 300] comes into play in order to allow alter to preserve his self-image and ensure that he does not become "demoralized." When we adopt an attitude of permissiveness, we are authorized to regard as "natural" certain types of behavior that otherwise would be deemed immoral. Like support, permissiveness involves a lowering of standards, but in the case of permissiveness we are concerned not so much with standards relative to specific achievements as with a generalized mode of existence relating to all aspects of alter's personality.

The two control mechanisms just described help ego to adjust to the prevailing norms and values. They presuppose a certain aloofness on ego's part with regard to the actions and methods of alter, a "detached concern" in ego's attitude, as Renée Fox has put it, as well as a common commitment on the part of both ego and alter to work together in a task that transcends the self-interest of either of them. Let us salute in passing our old friends the pattern variables: affectivity/affective neutrality, self-orientation/collectivity-orientation, quality/performance, specificity/diffuseness. Ego has available two strategies for putting alter "back on the right track." The first of these is "denial of reciprocity," whereby ego tries to make himself into the symbol or concrete embodiment of the values that he intends to teach or to impose on alter. Occasion to resort to such a strategy may arise when alter tries to take advantage of an attitude of "support" or "permissiveness" on ego's part in order to behave in a deviant way with impunity. A doctor, for instance, cannot allow a patient to treat him as a "buddy" without running the risk that the patient will use this familiarity to bargain over the terms of his own treatment. Similarly, a psychoanalyst cannot permit his client to exhibit love or hatred for himself without running the risk of playing into his client's fantasies. Denial of reciprocity, then, is a way for the socializer to let the deviant individual know that they are not "birds of a feather." In doing so, the socializer calls upon the deviant socializee to overcome his narcissism and model himself after the role-model held out to him by the socializer, either because that model is representative of a higher stage of development or because it embodies qualities the deviant individual once possessed and would like to regain.

The socializer stands before goals of two sorts, which he must somehow combine. On the one hand, he must make himself into a role-model with which other people can identify; this he will accomplish by making judicious use of permissive and supportive attitudes, thereby bringing the norms down to the level of the socializee. It might be said that, in psychological terms, the role of the socializer is almost maternal. To compromise on the norms, however, is not the same as to degrade them. Denial of reciprocity (which relates to the symbolic status of the socializer, whereas permissiveness and support relate to the symbolic status of the deviant) helps win respect for the norms that the socializer is responsible for inculcating.

Ego's first goal is to eliminate the disparity between what the norm requires and what alter actually does, and in attempting this he must confront the twin dangers of excessive laxity and excessive strictness. Moreover, even if ego wished to force alter to conform by exerting continuous, external control over his behavior for an extended period of time, he would be unable to do so. Ego is not a policeman; his influence is in the nature of a "self-liquidating mechanism." To put it another way, the control ego exerts over alter is limited by the fact that both are autonomous individuals. Hence ego will attempt only to anticipate what rewards alter might expect in the real world, given the reality principle. Ego's ability to manipulate alter is doubly limited. One limitation stems from the requirement that nothing he does casts doubt on the fundamental benevolence of his attitude. Literally speaking, there is no such thing as "conditional" love. If alter really believed that ego might abandon him at any moment, the resulting insecurity would destroy his confidence in ego. A second limitation on ego's manipulations stems from the fact that he must not take undue risks with the capital alter has invested in him. His most effective lever for influencing alter comes from such palpable progress as the latter may make as a result of following ego's instructions. Manipulation is a ruse of Reason, one more resource to be used, but within strict limits: not manipulation but the reality principle determines the ultimate outcome of both the educational process and medical treatment. Neither a demiurge nor an evil genius, the socializer does not somehow use devious devices to whip the deviant back into shape and keep him there. Wisely, he will remain modest for himself and emphasize the natural rewards (health, maturity) that fall to his docile charge, saying with the physician, "I treated him, God cured him."

This motto of the *naturo vis medicatrix* is intended to remind us that social control is more than manipulation pure and simple. The distinction between symbolic sanctions and "real rewards" brings us back to a point made earlier in connection with socialization. To explain how, with adult guidance, the child manages to traverse all the phases of the socialization process successfully, we may first of all look to the impetus given him by the *vis a tergo* of his biological maturation. Similarly, at the termination of the socialization process, when deviant behavior threatens the normative order, control is restored by making use of real rewards and punishments. When we consider social life, whether from the standpoint of the socialization process by which its rules and disciplines are learned or from that of the mechanisms of control by which deviance and abnormality are corrected, we perceive a constant intercourse between a world of symbols and a world beyond symbols, where the latter never exhausts the boundless creativity of symbolic expression.

More Theory

In the few remaining pages of this already lengthy chapter, we intend to examine two questions. First, Is the theory of pattern variables compatible with the theory of functions? If not, must Parsons's theory of action split at the seams into two distinct parts? Second, Does the paradigm that emerges from the study of socialization, social control, and deviance meet the requirements laid down by Parsons?

The problem of the relations between the pattern variables and the functions was first raised in *Working Papers* [1953]. The explicit aim of that work was to compare the preliminary results of the general theory with the findings of microsociology as it was then practiced by Robert F. Bales. For example, "adaptation implies adjustment of the system to the reality principle and methodical transformation of the situation lying outside the system.... The orientation of action must therefore be mainly cognitive, and the relation of the actors to the objects universalistic, i.e., it must take account of the relations of the object to other objects, or of its membership in a class of objects with definite and predictable characteristics. Secondly, if the situation is actually to be mastered and not merely accommodated to, the actor's attitude must reflect the specificity of his interests." In the same way, it is possible to show that the adaptation requirement can be satisfied only if the objects are treated not as symbolic constellations of attributes but as cause/effect or means/ends chains. Finally, an achievement orientation must correspond to an attitude of reserve or inhibition, defined as affective neutrality.

Because Parsons uses the language of variables and of functions, Robert Dubin[29] has asked whether it might not be a good idea to recognize the existence of two Parsonian theories of action rather than one (in which case Dubin wishes to state his preference for model 1 over model 2, the latter being "overgeneralized" in his view).

In answer to Dubin, Parsons acknowledged that the pattern variables split into two broad categories.[30] Certain of them relate to the orientation of ego with respect to alter, certain others to the modalities of the social object, that is, the modalities that determine ego's perception of alter. The first category includes the two pairs affectivity/affective neutrality and specificity/diffuseness. The second category includes universalism/particularism and quality/performance. Parsons also says that while the pattern variables make it possible to obtain a systematic understanding of the relations between ego and alter, they are insufficient for understanding the system of action as such. Indeed, a system of action is not characterized solely by the orientations of the actor (ego) and the modalities of the object (alter). "It is also a *structured* system with analytically independent aspects which the elementary pattern variable combinations by themselves do not take into account" [1967, p. 195]. In other words, the functions are not reducible to any combination of pattern variables. Each function combines two variables, but "across the board." To clarify what we mean by this, let us consider the integration function, I. "It is dependent on the *matching* of the function of the object for the 'needs' of the orienting actor with the functional meaning with which the object is categorized" [1967, p. 204]. If ego approaches alter with a diffuse attitude, he will no longer be free to classify alter as a social object in an arbitrary way. To use the terminology of dueling, if ego attacks in the quarter of diffuseness or affectivity, alter will parry with particularism or quality. Using the term "system of action" implies that we take into account not only the stability of the expectations ego and alter have of one another but also the consequences of those expectations for the system as a whole. If the system, as distinct from its constituent elements, is to have a genuine existence of its own, its identity must be preserved even though the relationship between ego and alter may vary considerably over time. What is more, the preservation of the system may constitute a goal of sufficient importance to govern that relationship. The system thus has a specific character as distinct from its elements: the functions are not reducible to the pattern variables. The functions introduce an order, a coherence among the elements; the elements may be looked at in themselves one by one and may vary independently of one another.

Strictly speaking, then, the action system is distinct from the interaction system [1967, pp. 207–10]. The four-function paradigm is structurally and temporally more comprehensive than that which focuses on the complementarity of the expectations of ego and alter. It is true, of course, that the problem of complementarity arose prior to the view of the system of action in terms of functional problems and was essential to the elaboration of that view in connection with both the personality and the social system. In answering Dubin's criticisms, Parsons had this analytic-regressive approach in mind when he expressed the hope that his paper would be "a considerable forward step in the systematization of both the pattern-variable scheme and its grounding in the general frame of reference of systems of action."[31]

By now it should be readily comprehensible that, as we suggested at the outset, Parsonian theory is not purely deductive, at least not if "deductive" is somewhat crudely interpreted to imply that concepts somehow have the miraculous power of engendering other concepts. The pattern variables do not *engender* the system functions, and the theories of socialization, social deviance, and control are engendered by neither the variables nor the functions. It would be pointless to argue that these three "medium-range" theories are merely timid codifications, whereas the pattern variables and the functions are contentless abstractions. What Parsons actually holds out to us is a series of paradigms that fairly cry out for generalization; once they have been appropriately analyzed, it becomes apparent that their structures are comparable, if not identical.

The meaning of the term "paradigm" is far from clear.[32] It is used in three related senses, and we may ask whether these different senses are compatible. In the first place, a paradigm is an illustrative example in which certain relations are exhibited in condensed form. Second, a paradigm is, to some degree, general in nature, applicable beyond the sphere in which it was first elaborated: for example, some of the hypotheses put forward in the study of the doctor-patient relationship are applicable in the case of the teacher-pupil relationship as well. At the risk of repeating ourselves, we will point out once more that it is not being claimed that doctors are the same as teachers or that students and patients are identical. The assertion is simply this, that such notions as permissiveness, supportiveness, cooperation, and inequality of status are useful in both situations for explaining how role-adjustment is carried out. While on the subject of paradigmatic generality, it may be worthwhile pointing out that paradigms are not all general to the same degree. Parsons, for instance, refers to both the "therapeutic paradigm" and the "interaction paradigm." The latter is obviously more general than the former. Finally, a paradigm is an image. The whole cast of the treatment of social deviance and control is colored by the image of the physician as a benevolent and disinterested figure, assumed to be self-possessed, attentive, devoted, and bent on accomplishing a task of such paramount importance as to transcend his own immediate interests and in some sense even the immediate interests of his patient. Of course, to allow imagery of this sort to influence a paradigm is to run the risk of introducing uncontrolled associations into that paradigm.

When we consider the paradigms used by Parsons, we find not only that they are not all general to the same degree but also, even more important, that Parsonian theory itself is a multistoried edifice within which it is necessary to work both "upward and downward" between the different levels. To the extent that the paradigm of social deviance and control makes sense and is empirically valid, it might be said to be a "concrete theory," to use Robert Blanché's term. George Homans's belief to the contrary notwithstanding, one does not proceed from the more general theory to the more concrete particular merely by "downward" movement from the empyrean of principles to certain specific propositions. Different paradigms may be said to be similar or related, though not deducible from or identical to one another. It would be absurd to confound the roles of educator and physician on the pretext that both have to do with mechanisms of social control. It is hard to see what might be meant by saying that one could be "deduced" from the other.

What did we mean when we said above that certain paradigms were "similar" or "related"? To answer this question we must look at the two distinct levels of theory to which the paradigms in question refer. The first level of theory consists of propositions involving such notions as permissiveness, supportiveness, and so forth, as we have seen. Of course, the content of such notions varies according to the context in which they are used: permissiveness does not mean the same thing in the educational as in the medical context, owing to cultural differences between their respective professional traditions and to inherent differences in the logic of the task appropriate to each. What Parsonian theory asserts, however, is that there is an isomorphism between propositions concerned with social deviance and control in the two contexts. The second phase of the analytical regression consists in moving from the "medium-range" paradigms (social deviance and control, socialization, social change) to a more general level of theory concerned with the fundamental choices available to the actor, or with the fundamental conditions under which groups live and develop. "Deduction" plays no greater role in this stage of the analysis than in the previous stage, if deduction means a "downward movement" from the general to the particular.

Isomorphism of paradigms, equivalence of axioms, exploration of hypotheses and their implications: if one hopes to grasp what is at stake in the discussion, the different moments of the theory must be clearly distinguished from one another. There is no reason to limit the elaboration of a theory to "working downward" from the general to the particular. Theoretical work in fact follows a far more complex path. It involves a number of interrelated approaches: somewhat schematically, these might be grouped under the two heads "working downward" and "working upward." Parsons was well aware of this, and he gave a balanced and excellent description of his methods when he wrote that "what is at present available in my more abstract writings is not a mature system of theory in Homans' sense." Mark well the modesty and serenity of this concession. For my part, I would be tempted to argue that, in Homans's sense of the term, there is no such thing as a satisfactory system of theory, nor can there be one so long as it is stipulated that theory must be purely deductive. Again, Parsons saw this point quite clearly, as when he wrote of his own theory that "the process by which it, such as it is, has been arrived at has most emphatically not been one of having sat down and formulated the basic axiomatic principles and then deduced their logical implications and checked these against known facts" [1970a, p. 868].

We are now in a better position to justify the comparison made earlier between the theorist and the judge. Like the judge, the theorist must deal with a variety of cases. Though he is not responsible for their existence, he cannot avoid sitting in judgment of them. His judgments invoke an existing body of law, or "theoretical scheme," as Parsons calls it, which, "though its premises were not defined with complete precision and henceforth assumed as fully given in a logically complete sense, has had considerable clarity, consistency, and continuity." Thus it is hardly surprising that the logical purity of the theoretical scheme is quite inconsistent. In parts it approaches the clarity of an axiomatic system. Other parts are richer in content but less pure in their logic, closer to the empirical and hence still confused and ambiguous. Thus it is not surprising to find that "a wholly unrealistic abstract kind of formalized theorizing" coexists with an "'esoterically academic' kind" of journalism in the work of one and the same theorist.

Chapter Four

The Political Subsystem

The four-function paradigm makes possible an explicit formulation of the problem of how sociology is related to each of the other social sciences. On the question of the relation of economics to sociology, Parsons had this to say: "The [institutionalist] movement—of which Veblen's negative critique was the Bible—boiled down to a view that traditional economic theory, say from Adam Smith to Marshall, should be discarded because *by itself* it fails to explain adequately a large proportion of the concrete facts of economic life. . . . The only alternative to such a conclusion which seemed adequate [at the time I wrote *The Structure of Social Action*] was stated most cogently by Pareto. Its essence is that economic theory as an abstract system dealt with some of the *variables* which determine concrete social behavior in the 'economic' as in other spheres. Economic theory therefore must be supplemented by one or more distinct abstract theoretical schemes dealing with *other significant variables.* Pareto himself formulated these other variables as 'residues,' 'derivations,' and the division of society into unequal classes. These *plus* the economic variables are the variables of his general sociology. Our view now is distinctly different. . . . Economic theory should . . . be regarded as the theory of typical processes in the 'economy,' which is a sub-system differentiated from other sub-systems of a society. The specifically economic aspect of the theory of social systems, therefore, is a *special case* of the general theory of the social system. . . . The peculiarity of economic theory, therefore, is *not* the separate class of variables it employs but the *parameters* which distinguish the special case or class of cases we call economic in the use of the general variables of social theory from the other important types of special case" [1956, pp. 5–6].

From reading the work published in 1956 by Parsons in collaboration with Neil J. Smelser under the title *Economy and Society,* the first thing to emerge is the importance of intersectoral analysis. Let us begin by associating each of the functions (A, G, I, L) with a subsystem of the social system. "The economy is the primary sub-system specialized in relation to the *adaptive* function of a society. . . . The goal-attainment sub-system focuses on the *political* (in a broader sense) functions in a society. . . . The integrative sub-system of the society relates the cultural value-patterns to the motivational structures of individual actors in order that the larger social system can function without undue internal conflict and other failures of co-ordination. . . . The pattern-maintenance and tension-management sub-system stands relative to the society as the land complex stands relative to the economy. . . . Paterns of value orientation . . . for any system . . . are most nearly constant and relatively independent of the urgency of immediate goal needs and the exigencies of adaptive and integrative problems imposed on the system" [1956, pp. 47–50].

Corresponding to each subsystem is an *output* or symbolic product that the subsystem makes available to the other subsystems. Wealth, which is the output of A, "is a generalized capacity to command goods and services, either as facilities or as reward objects for any goal or interest at any level in society. Power is the generalized capacity to mobilize the resources of the society, including wealth and other ingredients such as loyalties, 'political responsibility,' etc., to attain particular and more or less immediate collective goals of the system. Correspondingly, solidarity is the generalized behavior of system units in accordance with the integrative needs of the system, to check or reverse disruptive tendencies to deviant behavior, and to promote the conditions of harmonious co-operation" [1956, p. 49].

Of the various possible intersectoral exchanges, we shall content ourselves with pointing out those that involve the adaptive function A. We shall consider the following bilateral, symmetric relations: $\overleftrightarrow{AG}$, $\overleftrightarrow{AI}$, $\overleftrightarrow{AL}$. $\overleftrightarrow{AG}$ has to do with the relation between the economy and the polity, which involves the decisions made by the executive authorities in the society as to how resources should be mobilized and allocated. $\overleftrightarrow{AI}$ is concerned with solidarity and conflict regarding members of organizations with an economic function, while $\overleftrightarrow{AL}$ pertains to motivations of the economic actors and to the common values that govern their relations with the firms for which they work. To reiterate, these relations are bilateral and symmetric. For example, economic efficiency (A) may be enhanced by the action of the polity (G): the political authorities can use tax incentives, say, to make business more (or less) efficient. Correspondingly, the increase in productivity (A) will have an effect on the capacity of the polity (G) to attain collective goals, which Parsons refers to as the "effectiveness" of the social system.

Inputs and outputs have a dual character. Not only are they goods and services but also symbolic media. Money is a symbol, the value and significance of which depend on the conditions under which money may be exchanged for other symbols, namely, power (associated with the polity, G), influence (associated with the integrative subsystem, I), and value-commitments (associated with the pattern-maintenance subsystem, L).

In *The Structure of Social Action,* economics, political science, and sociology are said to be "distinct analytical sciences" of equal generality. Political science deals with two phenomena neglected by economics, "coercive power" and the relative distribution of power within society [1937, pp. 767–68]. Thus political science is the theory of power, understood as a constraint imposed by certain members of society on others. Basically, political science tries to explain the existence of conflict (in its extreme form nothing other than Hobbes's "war of all against all") over control of the collective resources. Though Parsons regards Hobbes as the founder of political theory, he refuses to wear the straitjacket of Hobbesian theory, which he regards more as a teaching device—useful for formulating the "problem of order" in rigorous terms—than as a satisfactory description of the state of nature. Hobbes shows clearly that order is problematic, but we must not let this blind us to the truth of another, equally important proposition. So long as a distinction is maintained between the exercise of power and the use of force, it must be conceded that power is always exercised in accordance with rules and that these rules determine the distribution of power within society, in such a way as to preserve social unity. Thus political order is to be sharply distinguished from the reign of force, for the latter tends to eliminate the individual, whereas the former, by making the individual a citizen, tends to perpetuate his existence as such. The idea that order may be benevolent runs counter to contemporary interpretations of the state, according to which, so long as society remains divided into classes, the state cannot possibly be anything other than the "instrument of domination" of one class by another. By contrast, classical theories of the state generally recognize that order is problematical on the one hand and beneficial on the other. With this in mind, we come next to what Parsons calls "normative regulation" and the notion of legitimacy, that is, the values and beliefs that govern the distribution of power. Using these ideas, we can distinguish between the social phenomenon of *power* and the natural phenomenon of *force.*

In 1963 Parsons[1] wrote that, broadly speaking, there are two schools of thought concerning political power: "A major tendency is to hold that somehow 'in the last analysis' power comes down to [either coercion or consensus], that is, 'rests on' command of coercive sanctions, *or* on consensus and the will to voluntary cooperation" [1969, p. 353]. Parsons rejects both these "polar solutions," as he calls them. Consensus and force both play a part in the political process. Though neither can be regarded as unimportant, neither can we be satisfied to strike an eclectic compromise of some sort by setting one alongside the other. The theorist who hopes to advance beyond the flashes of insight of which the naïve observer (who frequently has more worthwhile things to say than the doctrinaire ideologues with their one-sided exaggerations) is capable must explain how the various elements and dimensions of power are systematically related to one another.

Consensus, Force, and Power

The four-function paradigm marks a new point of departure in Parsons's thinking about power, an advance over the views set forth in *The Structure of Social Action*. In this new perspective power is no longer viewed simply as a form of constraint imposed by some individuals on others but is constraint that can and should be leigitmated by invoking common values and beliefs. Power is a social process by which collective goals are defined, implemented, and attained. The goal-attainment function G was defined accordingly. It should be noted, moreover, that this function is a part not only of the social system but of any action subsystem. In the personality or "psychological system," for example, it makes sense to speak of a "tendency to seek goals" [1959, p. 632] of two kinds: affective, which involves differential evaluation of cathected objects, and cognitive, which involves the capacity to elicit and organize information pertaining to the cathected objects. Similarly, we also find the goal-attainment function in the context of the cultural system, where it is reflected in norms (cognitive, moral, or expressive) that give validity to goal-attainment activities.

From the standpoint of the social system, the goal-attainment function is simply the polity [1969, pp. 354–56], which is to be taken in a broad sense and not limited to government, political parties, and the like. For Parsons, power is a capacity to impose constraints, but that capacity must be judged in relation to the attainment of collective goals which it makes possible. At this point in the argument, the nature of these collective goals has yet to be spelled out. To my mind, there are three aspects of such goals. One aspect has to do with possible alternative uses of the collective resources, among which choices are to be made. Another aspect relates to such benefits as security and liberty, which each actor seeks for himself but cannot obtain without collective organization. Still a third aspect of collective goals has to do with their place in a consensus; they may elicit the commitment of the entire collectivity.

Whatever definition we choose of the "collective goals," they share several features in common. Collective goals always tend to achieve stability and viability, to produce or "reproduce" the system of action. Although failures of socialization may impair solidarity and turn out individuals with disturbed personalities, stability is generally reinforced when the actor achieves gratification from the actual possession and enjoyment of the cathected object. In other words, when goal-selection and attainment are positively sanctioned by success, a relatively stable cathexis tends to be established between actor and goal. When goals are validated in this way, the actor's range of choice tends to narrow, and he will most likely try to maintain or consolidate certain "system states" already achieved: preservation of the status quo becomes the goal of his activity.

The different variants of the goal-attainment function are to some extent analogous to one another. Whether we consider the individual quest to attain a goal or the effort to determine what is intellectually right, morally correct, or aesthetically pleasing, we are looking at different modalities of a single stabilizing process, reflecting the tendency of the sytem "to remain in the optimum consummatory state. . . . For most empirical systems, this is a radically unrealistic assumption [however, and] therefore we derive the tendency to change the state of the system and its relation to the situation in the direction of a closer approximation to the consummatory state" [1959, p. 632].

The goals toward which the goal-attainment function is directed are set by the sensibility of the actor and by the socialization process. Attainment of them brings pleasure and hence reinforcement of the goal structure. The goals are not, however, rigorously determined by either the physical environment or the biological structure of the actor. A hungry man can alleviate his hunger in any one of several ways. He may choose a particular one of several unavailable dishes, for instance, or compose a dinner menu tailored to his taste. Because the actor is to some extent free to choose such combinations, goal-attainment is not a strictly mechanical function.

In consequence, collective goals can be attained only if the actors in the collectivity are willing to make choices and commitments. As we have seen, however, the collective goals define a stable system state that brings gratification to the individuals involved and so tends to "reproduce" itself, owing to the reinforcement mechanism whereby expectations, goals, and accomplishments are interrelated. How can these two points of view be reconciled? If we were to adopt the second, we would be giving a "consensus" interpretation of the goal-attainment function. This interpretation is spelled out in some detail in the many analogies to cybernetics that may be found in Parsons's post-1955 work. On this view the polity is said to consist of a variety of regulatory mechanisms, which, taken together, ensure that the actions of various individuals will automatically converge in such a way as to realize system states valued by all.

Though widely current, this interpretation is, I believe, utterly mistaken. In the first place, Parsons rejected any and all one-sided theories in which power is based only on consensus. Furthermore, Parsons was never satisfied to speak of cybernetic regulation in general. Indeed, when he did discuss cybernetic regulation, he focused not so much on the effects of regulation as on the importance of symbolic modes of communication. The term "cybernetic" may, roughly speaking, be used to denote mechanisms of regulation, conscious and unconscious, that govern or "control" any system exhibiting (at least semi-autonomous) goal-seeking behavior. In a more technical, and consequently more restrictive, sense, cybernetics may be defined as the "entire field of control and communication theory, whether in the machine or in the animal."[2] As for the relation between communication and control, a point stressed by Karl Deutsch in particular,[3] a small expenditure of energy (the sound I make in uttering a command or the infrared radiation emitted by a hot furnace) may be enough to trigger a rather substantial subsequent expenditure of energy. As Georges Th. Guilbaud has pointed out,[4] the relation between the thermostat and the furnace is "not perfectly symmetric": in the return segment of the circuit (i.e., from thermostat to oven), what matters is not so much the quantity of energy transmitted back to the oven by the thermostat but rather its form, its modalities, its velocity: in short, the information on the state of the system transmitted from thermostat to furnace. The cybernetic circuit is closed, not because action equals reaction but rather because the symbolic "control" effectively does what it is supposed to do. Cybernetics does, of course, focus attention on self-regulating mechanisms. The importance of such mechanisms, however, had long been clear from the work of the biologist Cannon on homeostasis and the internal stability of living organisms. The point to be made about arguments of the cybernetic type in sociology is not so much that social order is regulated by mechanisms analogous to those found in machines or living organisms but rather that regulation is effected by means of symbolic communication.

By treating politics as a function of the collective goal-attainment subsystem of the social system, Parsons was shifting his emphasis: in *The Structure of Social Action* the accent had been on competition for power and inequalities among the competitors, but now it fell on collective goal-attainment mechanisms. The goal-attainment function cannot, however, be defined in purely cybernetic terms: resources other than symbolism and information are pertinent. Indeed, force looms somewhere on the horizon of every system of power. Every political system seeks to approximate an optimum consummatory state in which all individual goals are realized. Arrival at this state may be delayed, suspended, or prevented for some or all of the members of the group, however, by forceful intervention. Strict "reproduction" is therefore highly unlikely, unless information exerts strict control over energy. Symbolic resources, whose importance for political action will be apparent later in this discussion, come under the head of the polity (G) rather than the cultural subsystem (L), the latter being defined as a code or set of codes "more stable than are the concrete symbolic uses of the code in the course of communication." Strictly speaking, however, programmatic "reproduction" is no more likely to exist in cultural systems[5] (which, Parsons points out, are "analogues of genes") than in the polity, as will be seen clearly in the section on the normative system.

Power cannot be defined in terms of force any more than in terms of consensus. Parsons's polemic against C. Wright Mills is well-known. Although it is frequently cited, there is reason to doubt that the issues at stake are always clearly understood. It is wrong to think that Parsons is merely concerned to discuss Mills's contentions about the growing concentration of power in American society. "For him [Mills]," writes Parsons, "power is power that some people exert *over*, or, rather, *against* others: A can exercise power only at the expense of B."[6] On this view of the matter, power is a two-person zero-sum game. Such a conception of power is compounded out of the old rift between "the elite and the masses," which stems from Machiavelli, and the life-and-death struggle between the "exploiters" and the "exploited," which is the legacy of Marxism. Parsons acknowledges that under certain conditions it is true that power over the collective resources is acquired by one group at the expense of another group. But he denies that power always comes down to the will of the stronger, those with a monopoly of the means of production, for example. Power is "productive" as well and may add to the sum of public welfare in such a way as to benefit even the most disadvantaged members of society, though of course the benefits accruing from the exercise of power may be distributed in a highly unequal manner. National security, natural beauty, and clean streets all figure in the public welfare without being monopolies of the ruling class. Such items of welfare need not be products of violence and coercion of the sort practiced by oriental despots with their grandiose public works built by slave labor. Faithful to the teaching of the classics, Parsons writes that "power is the capacity to mobilize the resources of the society to realize goals to which a public commitment has been, or can be, made." The polity is the *association* of individuals as *citizens* obliged to cooperate in common endeavor. While coercion is sometimes necessary to bring about effective cooperation, it does not follow that coercion is advantageous only to those who employ coercive means. The authorities may have to force citizens to contribute to the public welfare by obliging them to pay taxes, but this does not imply that the resultant welfare redounds solely to the benefit of the "ruling class."

Still more egregiously misinterpreted than the polemic against Mills's cynical realism is Parsons's insistence on "the place of force in the social process."[7] Force is not merely an impediment that nature throws into the actor's path to thwart his will. "Force is a 'way,' not necessarily always a 'means'—in which one unit in a system of social interaction may act toward another, whether the unit be an individual or a collectivity. Within this framework, then, force is the use of control of the situation in which 'alter'—the unit that is the object of 'ego's' action—is subjected to *physical* means to prevent him from doing something ego does not wish him to do, to 'punish' him for doing something that, from ego's point of view, he should not have done, . . . or to demonstrate 'symbolically' the capacity of ego to control the situation, even apart from ego's specific expectations that alter may desire to do things that are undesirable from ego's point of view" [1967, p. 266]. Force forestalls and deters, sanctions and punishes. Apart from its preventive and punitive uses in specific contexts, force may be used symbolically, in a "show of force," as one says, in which force is effective without actually being used. In many cases the mere threat of force is enough to discourage would-be antagonists. A show of force is a force in its own right; fairly intricate symbolic manipulations of force are possible.

Without an adequate treatment of force, no theory of power could hope to explain why, in the final analysis, people obey orders. "Someone says, 'Come,' and we come. Someone says 'go,' and we go. We obey the tax collector, the policemen, and the sergeant."[8] What Bertrand de Jouvenel has called the "mystery of civil obedience" becomes a little less mysterious if we consider the cost of failure to obey. But civil obedience is more than fear of the policeman; the fear of punishment alone does not explain why people obey rules. Self-interest, the desire to identify with prestigious models, and the respect attaching to certain symbolic figures must also be taken into account. Power is more than force, though it is true that ultimately power can always appeal to force.

What is there in power, then, that makes it more than mere force? One way to gain insight into the problem is to compare the rule of a tyrant to the services of a professional who is bound by a code of ethics. There are tyrannies in which the "ruling class" tries to monopolize all the resources of the collectivity. But classical thinkers from Plato to Rousseau have looked upon monopolies of this kind not as the essence of politics but rather as degenerate and perverse cases.[9] Parsons is closely akin to classical thought in this respect; I would contend, in fact, that he carries the argument one step further. In Parsons's view, those who see politics as a life-and-death struggle are describing a situation that, whenever it is found, which is seldom, is unstable; what is more, it is not found in all social groups or in all relations of power within a given society. An employer exercises power over his workers that may give rise to exploitation. It does not necessarily follow that the same is true for the power of the doctor over his patient, the teacher over his pupil, or the father over his son. Even societies riven by class war have survived, the prophecies of certain Cassandras to the contrary notwithstanding; perhaps this is to be explained by the fact that even in such societies safe havens remain, in which what Rousseau called "gentle authority"[10] sits enthroned, and in which the Parsonian account of the therapeutic relationship still makes sense.

There is more to obligation than naked force. When violence is done to me, I can always give in. But even if I choose to confess in order to avoid torture, I remain convinced that I am innocent or in the right, like Galileo before the Holy Office. In other words, ego may be able to compel alter to do what he wants by the use of force, and sometimes this may be enough to achieve the results ego is after. But alter can still tell the difference between coercion by violence and moral or political obligations that bear the stamp of *legitimacy*. This does not mean, however, that the use of force is always illegitimate. Recourse to force may be fully justified by the shortsightedness or selfishness of the person against whom it is used. Abstention from the use of force is no more the criterion of legitimacy than the use of force is the criterion of illegitimacy.

Power as Interaction and as Symbolic Process

Power is more than just consensus, and more than mere force, as we have seen. Mere lip service to the coexistence of both viewpoints is not a satisfactory way of reconciling them, however. Parsons attempted to explain how consensus and force are functionally related in all systems of power. To that end he introduced a distinction between power as interaction and power as symbolic exchange. From the standpoint of interaction, power is seen as involving a series of initiatives followed by sanctions by means of which ego attempts to get alter to behave differently from the way he would have behaved had he been left to himself. From the standpoint of symbolic exchange, "power . . . is generalized capacity to secure the performance of binding obligations by units in a system of collective organization . . . and the medium used [to obtain this capacity] must be symbolic" [1969, pp. 361–62]. How are these two levels of analysis related?

In interaction terms, power is a strategy that ego adopts in order to enlist alter's cooperation, in spite of himself if need be, in the attainment of ego's own goals or of goals for the attainment of which ego has assumed responsibility. How does one go about "reorienting" the actions of a particular individual so that he or other actors will behave in ways other than they would have done had no reorientation been attempted? There are two answers to this question. On the one hand, ego may try to manipulate alter by controlling his situation, either by actually modifying that situation or by making such a modification appear likely, in order to increase the likelihood that alter will act in accordance with ego's wishes. On the other hand, rather than modify the situation, ego may attempt to influence alter's intentions. For instance, he might try to do this by manipulating symbols having a certain significance for alter, so that alter will look upon what ego wants him to do as a "good thing" for himself.

The above discussion may be taken to define what Parsons calls the "channel variable": ego may exert power either through the "situational channel" or the "intentional channel." There is a second variable appropriate to the analysis of power in terms of interaction, which pertains to the sanction-type ego uses to secure alter's cooperation. A sanction that works through the "situational channel" is positive if it changes the situation to alter's advantage, and negative if it leads to a deterioration in alter's objective condition. As for the "intentional channel," the positive sanction is "the expression of symbolic 'reasons' why compliance with ego's wishes is 'a good thing' independently of any further action on ego's part, from alter's point of view, i.e. would be felt by him to be personally advantageous, whereas the negative sanction is presenting reasons why non-compliance with ego's wishes should be felt by alter to be harmful to the interests in which he had a significant personal investment, and should therefore be avoided" [1969, p. 362]. Parsons sums up this discussion as follows: "I should like to call the four types of 'strategy' open to the ego respectively (1) for the situational channel, positive sanction case, 'inducement'; (2) situational channel, negative sanction, 'coercion'; (3) intentional channel, positive sanction, 'persuasion'; and (4) intentional channel, negative sanction, 'activation of commitments'" [1969, p. 363].

It is of course incorrect to suppose that ego's efforts are always crowned with success. Nor does every bout in which power plays a part end after the first round. Alter can sometimes manage to duck ego's blows and avoid being taken in by his feints. To shift from boxing to a Pentagon metaphor, alter may come up with a "second-strike capacity" credible enough to convince ego not to take action against him, assuming that ego is not simply reckless. If alter feels threatened, he can enlist the aid of allies, mobilize more quickly than ego, or even call up fresh reserves, to continue in the military vein.

Changes in the balance of power and even its possible tipping are of less concern to Parsons than the carrot and stick that the adversaries use in an attempt to affect each other's decisions. "Sanctions," as we have hitherto used the term, referred either to the rewards alter could expect for going along with ego's wishes or to the punishments he could anticipate for going against them. These rewards and punishments may take the form of goods and services supplied to or withheld from alter by ego, as the case may be. Attitudes of approval and disapproval may also serve as sanctions, approval when alter lives up to ego's expectations, disapproval when he does not. The foregoing discussion, then, makes clear how power may be analyzed in interpersonal terms. Bear in mind that ego and alter have both internalized role-models to which they try to make their behavior conform, symbolically at least. Accordingly, sanctions imposed on one of them by the other will call for similar self-imposed sanctions, which will reinforce the effect of the original sanction on behavior.

But power, as we began by saying, is not only a form of interaction; it is also a symbolic relation. People will obey the law even if no flesh-and-blood policeman is in sight. Moral imperatives need not be called constantly to mind by a scolding martinet in order to be effective. Coercion and influence are forms of power that do not necessarily require face-to-face contact. Power is an exchange, but the exchange is not a barter. Other actors take part besides those who are exchanging face-to-face and other resources are involved besides those immediately at hand.

Our problem here is reminiscent of the one the economist must deal with when he shifts attention from Crusoe-Friday transactions to a full-blown market. What makes the transition possible is the institutionalization of monetary symbolism, at least two effects of which may readily be seen. First, the introduction of money broadens the nexus of exchange considerably. Money can serve as a true symbolic *medium* only where exchange breaks free of its purely ascriptive underpinnings, in contrast to potlatch-type transactions between kinship groups. In addition, strict controls on the quantity and quality of goods and services exchanged must be lifted. When these conditions are met, the freedom of the trading parties is enormously enhanced.

> In exchange for its lack of direct utility money gives the recipient four important degrees of freedom in his participation in the total exchange system: (1) He is free to spend his money for any item or combination of items available on the market that he can afford; (2) he is free to shop around among alternative sources of supply for desired items; (3) he can choose his own time to purchase; and (4) he is free to consider terms which, because of freedom of time and source, he can accept or reject or attempt to influence in the particular case. By contrast, in the case of barter, the negotiator is bound by what his particular partner has or wants in relation to what he has and will part with at the particular time. [1969, p. 360]

Thus money is a symbolic medium with a "generalized capacity": "Money is, as the classical economists said, both a medium of exchange and a 'measure of value.' It is symbolic in that, though measuring and thus 'standing for' economic value or utility, it does not itself possess utility in the primary consumption sense—it has no 'value in use' but only 'in exchange,' that is, for possession of things having utility" [1969, p. 360].

On the one hand, monetary symbolism makes possible an enormous increase in the volume of transactions. But, as Parsons observes, "The other side of the gain in degrees of freedom is, of course, the risk involved in the probabilities of the acceptance of money by others and of the stability of its value. . . . Money is a symbolic 'embodiment' of economic *value,* of what economists in a technical sense call 'utility.' A dollar has no intrinsic utility, yet signifies commodities that do, in the special sense that it can in certain circumstances be substituted for them."[11]

Depending on what sum of money must be handed over in exchange for a basket of goods with use value to the final consumer, holders of liquid assets may find themselves at an advantage or disadvantage. They will adjust their "cash balance" to reflect changes in the relation between the value of money and the value of real goods. Suppose there comes a time when no commodity is available at any money price. With such extreme inflation money literally ceases to be convertible into goods. It is no longer acceptable. The symbolic system then collapses, since money, which has no intrinsic utility (no one can eat bank notes), has also lost its exchange value.

Parsons never said that the monetary system is "the same" as the political system. Both code and message are different in the two cases. Wherever symbol users are found to have a "generalized capacity" to exchange goods and services, communicate ideas, or issue orders, however, it is legitimate to ask whether the symbolism involved is a mere *flatus vocis,* or whether it contributes to the free circulation and enhanced availability of collective resources. Orders can always be ignored. Someone says "come," and we come; someone says "go," and we go—sometimes: this is the voice of Authority speaking. But we might just as well cite the sarcastic prediction Harry Truman made just before Eisenhower's inauguration: "He'll sit here and he'll say, 'Do this! do that!' And nothing will happen. Poor Ike—it won't be a bit like the Army."[12]

We have thus far analyzed power in terms of role-expectations. If we now extend this analysis by looking at the strategies ego uses to try to make alter's behavior serve his own ends, we shall gain an even clearer idea of just how tenuous power is. Possible ineffectiveness is not the only risk associated with the use of symbolism. Recourse to symbols may cause errors and create chances for deception. Sometimes we mistake one word for another or confuse the meanings of two different words. Someone may warn me to "watch out for the tiger," but if I hear "cat" instead of "tiger" I may open the door expecting to find a purring pet instead of a hungry beast, with possibly fatal consequences. Or someone else may cry "wolf!" even though no wolf is about: a case of deception. In the same way, ego may reach mistaken conclusions about alter's intentions, or he may deliberately or inadvertently deceive alter about his own intentions. In either case the equilibrium of the game will be upset and the ensuing escalation may get out of hand, at which point ego and alter will no longer have the slightest idea what to expect from each other.

If ego attempts to manipulate alter, he may end up by putting himself at alter's mercy and setting off a chain reaction that neither can control. This sometimes happens when a "show of force" is made, in the hope of avoiding the actual use of force. Such a show of force may fail to work as a deterrent. Ego may be vulnerable to counterattack. If he is cautious, he will therefore avoid threatening the use of force as far as he possibly can—unless he is certain of having the advantage. But who can boast of such certainty, since, as Rousseau says, "not even the strongest man can rule forever."[13] If, moreover, the state of affairs is such that no order can be carried out except under compulsion and the eye of the police, society will expend, not to say waste, too much of its energy on defense and repression. Thus it is in every way preferable not to have to use force, or even threaten to use force.

That symbolic systems are tenuous and unstable is particularly obvious when we look at the symbolic medium of money and credit. The banker is a case in point: depending on how well he estimates the amount of liability he may prudently balance off against his cash and paper reserves, he may either get rich or go broke. In general, a monetary system is judged to be in good shape if it is solvent. Solvency is not to be construed in static terms, however. More than a daily comparison of the money supply with the volume of demand for money is involved: the anticipated state of the system at some future date must also be considered. Even if I am able to verify that my banker's accounts are in balance for the time being, the news that six months from now he will very likely be in trouble will cause me to withdraw my funds at once. If other depositors make the same calculation, bankruptcy will inevitably follow. As Merton has said, expectation can be a self-fulfilling prophecy.[14] "The bank does not simply act as custodian for its depositors' funds." The banker is a money merchant who invests part of the money on deposit with him: this is the way he makes money, but he may also lose money in the same way. "[The bank] lends a certain proportion [of its deposits] to borrowers on contractual terms that enable the latter to 'spend' them so long as they are presumptively in a position to repay at the term of the loan, and of course pay interest and any other charges" [1969, p. 426]. The banker "transforms" his clients' liquid reserves into capital that can, through investment, increase the economy's output and productivity. But this "miracle of loaves and fishes," as Parsons calls it [1969, p. 385], takes time and involves risk for the depositors.

To ensure that the system will remain stable between the time of deposit and the time of withdrawal, two conditions must be met. Obviously money loaned out by the bank must be repaid by the agreed due-date of the loan. In the meantime the other depositors must play along by not withdrawing their funds from the bank. No one bank loans out more than a fraction of its deposits, which has presumably been carefully calculated. In addition, each bank is to some extent secured by the banking system as a whole, since all banks have reserves in addition to deposits in the form of shares of stock and cash receivable that can be turned to account if necessary, as well as because the Federal Reserve can always be called upon to provide additional funds through rediscount.

By facilitating novel combinations of resources, the monetary system can apparently enhance the value of the various "inputs" to the system. The banker mobilizes his depositors' idle cash reserves and puts them to use in ways that no depositor would have been capable of undertaking on his own. But the system is still inherently fragile, because its efficiency depends on accurate prognostications by lenders and entrepreneurs, on their good faith, and on the cool-headedness of third parties. Accordingly, the risk of a collapse is ever present, sometimes more serious and sometimes less but never entirely eliminated. Overnight, the pyramid of credit may reveal itself to have been a house of cards, should one category or another of borrowers or lenders, or, still more ominously, all categories at once, find that their commitments exceed what the liquidity in the system can support. At this point a chain reaction begins; depositors flock in ever greater numbers to the teller's windows to "cash in" their symbolic assets, thus bringing on a crash by trying to protect themselves from one.

The foregoing description of a "financial crisis" is obviously stylized. It has an obsolete ring to it, since none of the ups and downs the economy has been through since World War II has seen so dramatic a breakdown of the banking system. But by highlighting phenomena associated with credit and banking, Parsons was able to bring out a basic condition of equilibrium in any social system: the relation between assets and liabilities, expectations and achievements.

The capacity to generalize is best understood by looking at language, the fountainhead of all generalization. Not even language, though, is capable of unlimited or indefinite generalization. In a syntagm,[15] for example, one element cannot represent another element arbitrarily, since the possible associations are by definition not arbitrary. To put it another way, the connection between a particular word and a particular thing *is* arbitrary, but the relation between words and things is determined by the structure of the system of communication. "[A] language must be understood to involve two aspects: on the one hand, the use of language is a process of emitting and transmitting messages . . . that have specific reference to particular situations; on the other hand, language is a *code* in terms of which the particular symbols constituting any particular message 'have meaning.' In these terms, a message can be meaningful and hence understood only by those who 'know the language,' that is, the code, and accept its 'conventions'" [1969, p. 406].

Linguistic symbols have at least one property in common with monetary symbols: the former have no intrinsic expressiveness, the latter no intrinsic final utility. The word "dog" does not bark, nor is a bank note edible. Provided the message is suitably encoded, however, language does convey an extraordinarily wide variety of information. Just as money withdrawn from circulation ceases to represent goods and services, so a message may fail to make sense to the person receiving it because it cannot be translated into concrete mental operations. This can occur in at least three circumstances. The person addressing me may speak a language I do not understand. Or he may use technical jargon, so that I understand neither the messages (the basic concepts) nor the code (e.g., the logical procedures). Or, finally, the "speaker" may be aphasic or insane. In none of the three cases can I get anything out of what is being said to me. Still, there are differences. In the first two cases, for example, I could learn the foreign language or jargon, whereas I cannot learn to speak the language of the schizophrenic. His use of linguistic material has as little value for my purposes as a wheelbarrow full of devalued bank notes (or nearly so, at any rate).

It bears repeating that we are not saying that "linguistic inflation" or, more generally, disorders in the emission of linguistic symbols are the "same" as monetary inflation, or that the absurd demagoguery of utopians who promise that tomorrow man will shave for free or be reconciled with nature and his fellows is the "same" as counterfeit currency. What the comparison suggests is that ultimately all symbolic systems are subject to the same constraint: when circumstances require it, we must be able to regain control over physical objects where we had relinquished control in exchange for the ability to use a symbolic medium, which gave us a generalized capacity to substitute, combine, and exchange resources.

The Normative System and the "Intrinsic Gratifiers"

From the preceding analyses two propositions emerge. First, no normative system is inherently effective, certainly not unaided. Second, beyond norms we must look for values, though collective preferences cannot be taken to guarantee automatic obedience and conformity.

As long ago as *The Structure of Social Action,* Parsons stressed the peculiar effect of norms on individual behavior. Reacting against

Durkheim's positivism, Parsons emphasized the difference between norms and laws of nature. Moral and even legal obligations are not constraining in the same way as the laws of gravity. Parsons does concede that Durkheim had also seen that the constraint that lends force to a rule could come from within, that certain norms could be "internalized." Hence the effectiveness of the normative system could be explained by learning, or "moral education," to use Durkheim's terminology.

Because of the great importance accorded by Durkheim to internalization of norms, his views are said to bear a close resemblance to Freud's concept of the relations between culture (Superego) and personality (Ego):

> Durkheim's insights into this subject slightly antedated those of Freud. Durkheim started from the insight that the individual, as a member of society, is not wholly free to make his own moral decisions.... In the end [he concentrated] on two primary features of the phenomenon: first, that moral rules "constrain" behavior most fundamentally by moral authority rather than by any external coercion; and, secondly, that the effectiveness of moral authority could not be explained without assuming that, as we would now say, the value patterns were internalized as part of personality. [1964, p. 19]

Parsons tempered his praise with the observation that, unlike Freud, Durkheim was not very explicit about the psychological mechanisms whereby norms were internalized through assimilation of values.

The fact is that norms are very seldom clear and explicit. Their relation to values is largely problematical. Taken together, these two assertions make it plain that to explain obedience or conformity by internalization or assimilation is entirely inadequate. Two things distinguish norms from values: norms are less general, and they lay down explicit constraints. They prescribe specific kinds of behavior, and the context of that behavior helps to clarify the content of the norm. Durkheim long ago suggested distinguishing moral rules according to their degree of generality.[16] "Some apply indiscriminately to all men.... But duties of another kind exist too. These have to do not with our human nature in general, but with particular qualities not found in all men."

Two major types of anomie exist, and which type will occur in specific circumstances depends on what kinds of "duties" are the object of dereliction. On the one hand, there are duties that are defined in very vague and imprecise terms. No clear-cut or effective sanctions exist to enforce them: for a recent example we may point to the so-called issues of "human rights." On the other hand, there is a second class of duties, of which it may be asked whether they are in fact duties or, rather, obligations associated with certain economic or professional functions that wrap themselves in the cloak of morality in order to be accepted as legitimate. We see obligations of this latter type in the codes of ethics of the various professions, for example.

Accordingly, it is appropriate to ask two questions about any normative system: Under what conditions are the norms actually applicable? And under what conditions are they deemed legitimate? In *The Structure of Social Action* Parsons concentrated on values, or, as he then said, "ultimate ends," as underpinnings of the normative system. In his critique of utilitarianism, drawn largely from Durkheim [1937, pp. 308–24], Parsons points out that only under certain conditions can we say that the precept that an individual should pursue his own self-interest is a norm: namely, if—and only if—the individual has been socialized in a certain culture (secular, preferably Puritan, culture) that holds certain ends to be paramount and, furthermore, has a place in a nexus of role-expectations such as to sanction and reinforce the motivational orientation acquired in the socialization process. Thus norms, unlike values, "involve a reference to a situation," but this is only a preliminary consideration. Three further "specifications" must be added:

> The first specifies the categories of units to which the norm applies; this is the problem of jurisdiction. The second specifies what the consequences will be to the unit that conforms and to the unit that does not conform to the requirements of the norm . . .; this is the problem of sanctions of enforcement. Finally, the third specifies that the meaning of the norm shall be interpreted in the light of the character and the situations of the units to which it applies; this constitutes the problem of interpretation, which is roughly equivalent to the appellate function in law.[17]

In other words, two limitations are imposed on what might be called the automaticity of the normative system: first, some leeway is allowed for interpretation (which must, of course, be sanctioned by the requisite authority), and, second, account must be taken of the degree of congruence between the normative system and the reference system of values.

Characteristic, then, of sociology's contribution to our understanding of social cohesiveness and integration is the attempt to explain these phenomena in terms of the actor's adherence to a common system of values, which we find in both Durkheim and Weber. Parsons, however, is well aware that the *conscience collective* or common value system does no more than prescribe broadly general orientations, which are largely indeterminate. In the first place, these values pertain only to the society "as a whole" and do not "distinguish normative judgments which refer to differentiated parts or subsystems within the society" [1967, p. 8]. The constraints imposed by "values" are not to be contrasted only with the constraints imposed by "things," as the "spiritual" is contrasted to the "material" or the internal to the external. Value constraints are far less definite, and their effects are far less predictable. The reason for this ambiguity or indeterminacy of values has to do with the fact that they should not be treated as *things* or even as *objects*. Parsons writes:

> There seem to be in the literature of social science, two main approaches to the problem of conceptualization [of values]. One of these, which I reject, is what I like to call the "Chicago" approach, which I think originated in the work of Thomas and Znaniecki. This takes its departure from the dichotomy of "attitudes" and "values." In this formulation attitudes are properties or characteristics of *actors*, while values pertain to the *objects* to which the actors are oriented. The crucial difficulty with this concept lies in its identification of the distinction with the actor-object (or situation) dichotomy as *concretely* conceived. . . . I should like to contrast this with a view that derives, I think, mainly on the one hand from Max Weber, and on the other from American anthropology, especially Clyde Kluckhohn. This is the view that a value is not a category of concrete object or a property of one but is, to use the anthropological word, a "pattern." . . . I therefore accept the first part of Kluckhohn's well-known definition of values as *conceptions of the desirable*.[18]

To impress upon the reader his rejection of any "realistic" conception of values, Parsons goes on to compare values and evaluations: "*Evaluation* is a process by which certain modes of *relation* between actors and objects are established. The special case of values and the process of evaluation with which this analysis is concerned is that in which the system of reference is the same on *both* sides of the evaluative relationship" [1969, p. 441].

The "modes of relation" established by evaluation result in the attribution to objects of qualities such as good or bad, beautiful or ugly, or, more generally, desirable or undesirable. "The bases of cultural legitimation," consequently, "transcend direct contingencies of influence, interests, and solidarity."[19] Questions about how power is actually transmitted may arise in at least three ways during the evaluation process. First, we may judge a given situation "undesirable," thereby impairing or challenging the claim of the existing authorities to legitimacy. Second, a nonexistent state of affairs may be deemed "desirable," thereby impelling people to enlist the aid of others who feel the same way and share the same goals in order to try and bring that state of affairs about. Finally, our evaluations may bring us to make commitments, take sides, identify friends and foes, and so involve us personally to one degree or another in the life of the collectivity. Thus evaluation has effects of three kinds: it may incite opposition to the undesirable, induce efforts to attain the desirable, and mobilize resources for either purpose; it should be readily apparent, therefore, that evaluation is hardly to be confused with "reproduction" of an immutable order, though in the long run it may help to establish a consensus.

In purely realistic terms, what makes a command structure effective? To answer this question we have to discover what might be called the *absolute* incentive or disincentive. Force is the quintessential negative sanction. But the effectiveness of a system of power in which force is the only available resource would be severely limited. Symbolism is also essential. Can we set down an interpretation of power in "real" terms alongside an interpretation in "symbolic" terms? However we finally decide to answer this question, we must begin by determining the scope of each approach, and the conditions under which either may be applied. The two interpretations are not mutually exclusive. Each contains several interrelated levels of analysis, with a hierarchy of two-way controls between the various pairs of levels.

To understand the nature of the "absolutes" on which the symbolism of power ostensibly rests, let us first consider the contrast Parsons draws between the symbolic systems of money and influence. The viability of the monetary system (money itself, according to Parsons, being the institutionalization of one of the four types of interaction of which every social system is composed) depends on two related conditions. First, the economic actors must have confidence in the institutions in which they deposit their funds. Usually this feeling of confidence is all-embracing and undifferentiated; when we try to analyze it, we find that it is based primarily on a favorable judgment of the banking system. Even the depositor least well-versed in economic matters understands that the solvency of his own bank is related to that of other banks and ultimately to that of the Federal Reserve System as a whole. If our average depositor carries his analysis a bit further, he will observe that money is completely acceptable as "legal tender for all debts" only if "it is convertible into objects of rock-bottom economic security."[20] This is the meaning of the old adage,

"The dollar is as good as gold," which, alas, has proved overly optimistic. Given a certain rate of exchange, however, what makes money a "hard currency" in the final analysis is not the amount of gold stored at Fort Knox but the "effective functioning of a ramified system of monetary exchanges and markets." A monetary system is worthy of confidence to the extent that it provides for the regular transformation of "liquid assets" into "real assets."

A typical "basket" of goods and services has an intrinsic capacity to satisfy a set of specific needs: food, housing, clothing, transportation, health. Parsons, for the time being adopting the "realistic" interpretation of the economy (i.e., peering under the "monetary veil" to find what physical resources and human activities it conceals), calls these goods and services "want-satisfiers." Natural-law theorists in the political sphere follow the same path. Behind the constitutional structure, the theorist is concerned to find out how certain public goods, such as liberty and equality, considered as prior to and transcending the normative structure, are distributed.

Unfortunately, this notion of "want-satisfiers" does not withstand serious scrutiny, whether we are concerned with the monetary sphere or with any other symbolic medium, power and influence in particular. Every symbolic system must meet the "solvency" condition. But there is no need to construe that condition in narrowly realistic terms as requiring direct convertibility of symbols into material items. In the case of influence, where such convertibility is not possible, we see this clearly. To understand what influence is, says Parsons, we must begin by comparing it with other varieties or modalities of collective action and asking what it symbolizes. Power symbolizes the effectiveness of collective action; money symbolizes that which is useful to the collectivity, that is, that which can be consumed by a firm, a household, or an individual. Influence may be defined as the set of symbols capable of "bringing about a decision on alter's part to act in a certain way because it is felt to be a 'good thing' *for him,* on the one hand independently of contingent or otherwise imposed changes in his situation, on the other hand for positive reasons, not because of the obligations he would violate through noncompliance" [1969, p. 415]. In other words, influence is a means of persuasion, institutionalized and quite broadly applicable. Persuasion is distinct from power in that it relies neither on force nor on threats. Nor is persuasion to be confused with moral obligation (what Parsons calls "value-commitment").

Is there, then, a category of "intrinsic persuaders," in the sense that there are "intrinsic want-satisfiers" or that power is intrinsically compelling? "The most obvious member of this category is 'facts' from which alter can 'draw his own conclusions.' Ego, that is, can persuade by giving alter information which, given his situation and intentions, will lead him to make certain types of decisions. It seems probable that information is indeed the proper parallel to commodities, with a special kind of information—the announcement of firm intentions of action on the part of significant others—the parallel to services."

Parsons is forced to concede, however, that neither ego's intentions nor the information he provides are "intrinsic persuaders" in the strong sense of the term. In the first place, ego's intentions must be at once specific and authentic. Alter may not find benevolence or condescending charity convincing. Second, the information ego provides may in some cases not be pertinent to alter's needs—alter may find it redundant, incomplete, or even incomprehensible.

The "backing," as it were, for influence as a symbolic medium comes not from the intrinsic character of the intention or validity of the information but from the reciprocal commitment of ego and alter, that is, alter's confidence in ego. But this commitment is based on institutionally sanctioned role-expectations. Take, for example, the case of the patient who must decide whether the surgery advised by his doctor is wise. Suppose that, to aid him in his decision, the results of laboratory tests are made known to the patient. The layman cannot readily comprehend such information. Let us further suppose that the surgeon is absolutely convinced that the operation must take place without delay. If he were to support his opinion with detailed technical arguments, he would risk wasting a great deal of time, and for nothing. Nor would he do himself any good by trying to persuade the patient of his "good intentions." The critical point in the process, says Parsons, comes "when [the patient] 'accepts' [the doctor's] advice, i.e., makes a commitment, [whereupon] the surgeon may proceed to plan for the actual operation with a high probability that the patient will 'go through with it.' ... This, of course, is normally reciprocated by the physician's commitment to continue to supervise the regimen. The 'initial' commitment, however, is the primary lever by which the persuader, the physician, exercises continuing control over his patient's behavior" [1969, pp. 431–32]. With their initial commitment, both physician and patient agree to accept values that make it desirable for both of them, though for different reasons, to work toward restoration of the patient's health. The availability of this "lever" depends on the physician's prestige or credibility with the public—including both his colleagues and his clients.

To reduce the question of influence solely to the "intrinsic persuaders" would amount to taking a behavioristic view of interaction. For an orthodox behaviorist, to say that ego exerts influence on alter is to say that ego is a source of gratifications for alter, that he satisfies alter in the ways expected of him. But such an oversimplified view, on which the arguments of several authors rely,[21] is riddled with obscurities. First of all, the vehicle of influence in social interaction is not always a satisfaction actually provided but rather the promise of such satisfaction. Accordingly, we must abandon the appealing simplicity of the face-to-face confrontation between experimenter and pigeon of which Skinner is so fond. As soon as expectations enter into the discussion, the natural questions to ask are those pertaining to the nature of information and the intentions of the recipient, which is the line Parsons takes. To treat the problem of influence in terms of principles such as "effect," "reinforcement," and "repetition" is to oversimplify the situation drastically, ignoring the "competence gap" between ego and alter and assuming on alter's part certainty as to the effects of ego's initiatives and a correct interpretation of ego's intentions.

For the Skinnerian pigeon to which the experimenter provides a quantity of feed, the message is explicit. The pigeon, moreover, will eat as long as it is hungry and stop eating when it is satiated. For the patient facing an operation, the prospect of a cure is more problematic, and the intentions of the doctor are less obvious than those of the experimenter, who, from the pigeon's standpoint, is merely the purveyor of stimulant. The experimenter has much more complete control over the stimuli to which the subject is exposed than has the persuader over the rewards he dangles before the eyes of his counterpart, the "persuadee." The Skinnerian pigeon is quite literally unable to escape the clutches of the experimenter. His only freedom lies in satiety; the persuadee, on the other hand, can always turn for gratification to another persuader.

If there is no such thing as an "intrinsic persuader," what makes influence work? That it does not always work is the first point to be made. The patient can refuse treatment, for example. But the fact that influence is generally exerted within the framework of an institution is of paramount importance. A person who wishes to persuade another person of something can mobilize a number of resources, the first of which is his *prestige,* related to his *status.* "The information that it is the considered, responsible opinion of a reputable physician that patient X *ought* to undergo a given operation is a crucial factor in X's decision whether or not to make his commitment."[22] Suppose the influence in question is exerted in a bureaucratic organizaton. The persuader will then have at his disposal another resource: his authority,[23] defined as "the aspect of status in a system of social organization . . . by virtue of

which the incumbent is put in a position legitimately to make decisions that are binding, not only on himself but on the collectivity as a
whole and hence its other member units" [1969, p. 372].

Influence depends on the mobilization of resources that are institutional in character and hence exist prior to the attempt to use
them in exerting influence. These resources are not arbitrarily
selected. Differences of competence between persuader and persuadee notwithstanding, the latter must regard the former as sharing
the same allegiances and adhering to the same values as himself. Accordingly, influence often involves ambiguity of some kind. The persuader must be seen on the one hand as wiser and more capable, on
the other hand as a member of the same *Gemeinschaft* [1969, p. 417].
If these two requirements are to be reconciled, the persuader must
take care, in using the various resources available to him (prestige,
authority, wealth), not to jeopardize the primary ties of solidarity
between him and the persuadee, even though he may be set apart
from the persuadee to some extent by his knowledge or competence.

Influence, then, can be studied as a process that produces outputs
by combining various inputs (these outputs are decisions capable of
commanding the loyalty both of those who make them and of those
who must carry them out, as well as of the collectivity for the sake of
which the decisions were taken). From this study emerges a conception of symbolic media (and, consequently, of power as well as influence) according to which inputs circulate from one to another of the
four cardinal points of the social system, being exchanged for one
another at the subsystem boundaries. The symbolic function does not
rely upon a one-to-one correspondence between a symbol and a concrete datum. It does not provide for direct conversion of words into
things but rather for the allocation of very broadly defined capacities.
The symbolic function helps to implement certain values but does not
represent a collection of desirable, interesting, or relevant objects in
the sense that a photograph represents a landscape or family group. It
was because early linguists began by looking for such a one-to-one
correspondence between words and things that they emphasized the
arbitrariness of the linguistic sign. To understand the symbolic function, we must look first at the transactions it sets up among the various
media as well as within the interaction system. We made preliminary
use of this method when we attempted to study economic action in the
broader setting of social action in general. Now that we have identified
symbolic media other than money (power, influence, commitment),
we can show how these various symbols circulate and how they are
exchanged for one another.

Exchange, Control, and Symbolic Code

In *Economy and Society* Parsons carried out the analysis of inter-dependence on two levels. He first considered the process of differentiation within the economic subsystem and, at the same time, sketched the relations between the economy and the other subsystems. By defining economic action as comprising all procedures for optimizing the utilization of the four factors (land, labor, capital, and organization) and subsuming these four categories of classical economics under the more general categories of the A G I L scheme, Parsons succeeded in bringing to light a series of bilateral relations between households and consumer goods markets, households and firms, and firms and banks. Each of these relations corresponded to a particular category of income, as in classical economics: wages, profit, interest. Something new, however, does emerge from Parsons's "generalization," namely, that the recipients of the different kinds of income do not conform to the same "logic," and, more important, that even within a single category the logic is not homogeneous. The logic of economic action must conform to the varying constraints imposed on the economic agents by their membership in distinct subsystems. The wage earner is at once a member of a firm and of a household. In the former context he cannot completely reject the logic of the organization (G) and of capital (A); in the latter he can invoke the logic of needs and aspirations (L).

Let us turn now to the transactions between the economic subsystem and the other subsystems, in particular between A and G (economy and polity).[24] The political powers (i.e., the authorities that exercise control over and allocate the collective resources) tax a portion of the income of firms and households, consume a portion of these taxes to support public services, and transfer another portion of the tax revenue to households and businesses. Thus the actions of the authorities affect the economy in two ways: by placing public goods directly at the disposal of firms and households, and by redistributing wealth from rich to poor as a consequence of the imbalance between the taxes collected and the subsidies (broadly understood) doled out.

What interests Parsons in this exchange is not so much to know "who profits from it" as to describe it as a social relation. Leaving aside the financing of the state's repressive apparatus (only a portion of the state's total activity), the obligatory exchange of resources between firms and households on the one hand and the state on the other has an impact on two characteristic dimensions of the social process: its effectiveness (i.e., its capacity to achieve goals either of particular collectivities or of the political collectivity) and its productivity (i.e., the optimization of the various resources that it controls). Thanks to the taxes the economic agents are obliged to pay, the political sub-system is capable of achieving collective goals for the definition and implementation of which it is responsible. The productivity of the economic subsystem is in turn increased by the public goods and subsidies that flow into the economy at the behest of the political authorities: firms make full use of the factors of production, and household consumption increases demand for the various categories of goods (final, intermediate, and capital).

Making the economy dynamic in this way would be impossible in the absence of credibility of two kinds. When a company director or the head of a household pays his taxes, he must have confidence that his lost income will be "put to some use." Without such confidence, taxes would be mere tribute. Conversely, when the political authorities provide subsidies and services, the assumption is that public funds are to be allocated and used in the "common interest." If such an assumption is without basis in fact, official subsidies become mere tools for corrupting the clients of the government—by lining their pockets. If the relationship between households and firms on the one hand and the government on the other is to be based on something other than extortion and corruption, both groups of actors must feel that they are engaged in a common task, namely, increasing economic productivity and political effectiveness. But an actor who succeeds in "establishing credit" thereby obtains *power* over other actors who need to secure his good will if they are to attain their own ends. Similarly, the banker with idle cash reserves needs to curry favor with prospective borrowers. The borrower thereby obtains power over the banker, since he can refuse to borrow if he finds the terms of the loan unacceptable. On the other hand, the borrower may find it necessary to grant the lender the "right to intervene" in his affairs in order to win approval of the loan. The lender will then in return grant the borrower certain rights over a given sum of money for a specific length of time. In France there even exist certain "joint ventures" in which private firms cooperate with the government. Both parties agree to a bilateral "right to intervene" in the administration of the joint undertaking, which thus comes close to being a cooperative, if not a democratic, enterprise.[25]

If we now turn our attention from bilateral interchanges between A and G to the broader domain comprising all bilateral interchanges in which G in involved, we begin to form a picture of G's relation to the system as a whole, a schematic description of which may be found at the end of the article entitled "Voting and the Equilibrium of the American Political System."[26] Let us look first at the relation $\overrightarrow{AG}$ (and its inverse $\overrightarrow{GA}$): this relation involves what Parsons calls the "mobilization of collective resources." These resources may be evaluated in monetary terms (if one wishes to measure their impact on the productivity of the system) or in power terms (if one seeks to evaluate their contribution to the effectiveness of the system, i.e., its capacity to attain its collectively determined and collectively pursued goals, whatever they may be). The relations $\overrightarrow{GI}$ and $\overrightarrow{IG}$ describe the two-way interchange between the decisions taken by the central authorities and the demands issuing from peripheral interest groups. Accordingly, they may be evaluated either in terms of influence or in terms of power. The decision makers, along with those subject to their decisions (often the same people who asked that the decisions be made), are caught up in a circle of mutual dependency. Because the leaders take decisions pertaining to issues in dispute, they give a boost to the affairs of some while thwarting the interests of others. Because they have the power to make decisions, leaders are sought out and courted. On the other hand, those awaiting decisions on disputed issues are not totally without power over the decision makers. Where decision-making responsibility is bestowed by election, as in pluralist democracies, the authority of the "rulers" depends on the will of the "ruled." We find the same to be true even in bureaucracies, though there the situation is less clear-cut and often in conflict with the spirit of an organization in which roles are hierarchically allocated. Many a subordinate has managed to restrain the impulsive actions of his superior or even water down strong measures promulgated from on high. Conversely, if the support of a subordinate is instrumental to the implementation of a decision taken by his superior, the subordinate's cooperation will be actively sought out. Finally, we come to the relations $\overrightarrow{IL}$ and $\overrightarrow{LI}$, which involve the values that may be invoked by the political authorities to legitimate their decisions, or, conversely, the values that may be employed in challenging the decisions of the authorities.

All these exchanges are two-way transactions. Like the economy (A), the polity (G) gives as well as receives. Hence collective goals that are attainable through political action cannot be adequately defined from a strictly political standpoint: the political subsystem is open to the other subsystems. "Collective system goal-attainment . . . has been defined as the tendency of an action system to change the relation between the system itself and certain features of its environment in the direction of a fuller meeting of one or more functional needs of the system."[27] In other words, politics is not merely a game among politicians who, under conditions of more or less unbridled competition, seek to maximize the quantum of power they manipulate, that is, the quantum of constraint they are capable of imposing on their rivals. This "realist" view, which is to be found in both the Machiavellian tradition and in the radical populist tradition exemplified most notably by C. Wright Mills among our contemporaries, is not entirely false. But it is incomplete. As such it threatens to mask a more fundamental aspect of political action, which, being "problem-oriented," is organized around "social problems" whose origins lie outside the realm of political competition for power. These social problems involve either the relations of the polity with the other social subsystems or the relations of the social system as a whole with its environment, understood in the broadest possible terms: the environment of a social system, as we shall use the term here, includes not only the physical surroundings and other societies but also the biological, psychological, and cultural characteristics of the individuals who make up the society.

Rather than a two-way interchange, it would be better to speak of generalized interchange. For the time being we shall limit our analysis to political transactions *within* the social system, that is, to a description of the circulation of inputs and outputs between G and the other subsystems. To that end we shall proceed as we did in the case of economic transactions. The classical and neoclassical economists believed that once the veil of money was lifted one encountered the "real" inputs and outputs: not physical quantities, such as tons of steel or bushels of corn, but the four factors of production, namely, land, labor, capital, and organization, to each of which corresponds a distinctive "share of income." Exchange between these factors takes place not in the form of barter (which is obviously impossible) but rather via the medium of money. Let us look at the labor factor and its circulation. To begin with we may compare it with the function of the social system to which it bears the nearest resemblance, namely, the adaptive function (A). We may then seek to establish a relation between the way the wage-earners sell the labor factor (their labor-power) on the labor market and the way in which they buy the products of the labor process (consumer goods). We may be interested also in the connections between this primary exchange between inputs and outputs and the circulation of inputs and outputs from the L (cultural) subsystem, which contribute to the definition of the workers' tastes, aspirations, and "practice." At the same time, that "practice" may be either reinforced or obstructed by the way the inputs and outputs from L are used and controlled. We can take the same approach in dealing with the factor "capital," which bears a close relation to the political function: investment is a decision taken by managers. In a still more fundamental sense, investment occurs at sporadic intervals, at peaks in the economic cycle, owing to innovation by Schumpeterian entrepreneurs. Finally, organization, in the sense in which the term is used by theorists of the firm, bears a close relation to the integrative function: to organize is to allocate differentiated roles within a hierarchy while establishing solidarity among the persons assigned to play the various roles. To define the organization function from a systematic (or systemic) point of view is therefore to analyze the transactions between that function and the other functions and subsystems.

Double interchange is thus seen to involve a circulation of inputs and outputs. But the starting and ending points of the process have yet to be spelled out. Unless we do this, the direction of interchange remains indeterminate. Wage labor is of interest to the entrepreneur only because it constitutes one of the factors of production. From the point of view of the individual household, the labor sold by the family head to the entrepreneur is primarily viewed as given in exchange for the consumer goods the household must buy on the marketplace. What the household "produces" (or "supplies") is labor, which is a "factor of production" from the standpoint of the firm. What the firm "produces" is in its eyes "utility" of one form or another (money income corresponding in "real" terms to goods and services), and these utilities are "factors" for the maintenance, replacement, or extension of the labor force. Even if the direction of flow is spelled out for each process, our model is still too simple. Three further specifications are needed if we hope to lessen its inadequacy. The first thing to note is that relations between the two sectors (firms and households) are not strictly bilateral. The equilibrium between the labor market and the consumer goods market is not determined solely by the secular trend of the retail prices-wages ratio. It also depends on prevailing conditions in the capital market. Second, exchange is not limited to exchange in real terms: to the extent that money raises or lowers expectations of the economic actors, exchange is influenced by broad judgments (optimistic or pessimistic) of the economic conjuncture. Finally, exchange may result in a surplus or a deficit. Summarizing, then, we may speak of generalized exchange when we have to do with a situation in which all actors and sectors are involved, exchange takes the form of a symbolic relationship, and a net product is the result.

What *inputs* influence the functioning of G? What *outputs* does G produce? The answers to these questions are complicated by the fact that, in each of the exchanges—and combinations—in which G is involved, we must distinguish not only between inputs and outputs of G but also between inputs and outputs of G relative to A, I, and L, designated respectively G_a, G_i, and G_l. To that end it is useful to designate by G_A, G_G, G_I, and G_L the respective subfunctions of the political system.[28] G_A pertains to that aspect of the polity concerned with the "mobilization of fluid resources" and consequently figures in combinations whereby the effectiveness of collective action is increased and the relation of society to its environment improved. G_G pertains to the selection of those social goals to be attacked by the political authorities and to ways in which those goals might be attained. G_I governs the employment by the central authorities of loyalties and interests that arise within peripheral units of the system and clamor to be heard. G_L has to do with legitimation of the procedures and orientations selected by competent political authorities. Looked at from a different standpoint, however, G_A is seen to produce an output p_1 by increasing the resources available to the productive system. Similarly, G_G produces an output p_2 that might be called the "operational capacity" of the social system; G_I produces an output p_3, leadership aptitude on the part of political leaders and heads of associations and pressure groups; and, finally, G_L produces an output p_4 which activates legitimate expectations in the direction of their realization. Each combination involving G is characterized by an input and an output p, and also by an input stemming from, and an output destined to, the other function with which G is combined.

Three inputs emerge from the analysis of the exchanges between G and the other subsystems: control of a share in productivity (localized in A), interest demands (which form in I), and legitimation (in L). To acquire power one must increase one's control over the resources turned up by the economic actors and assign those resources to other uses than those envisioned by the actors producing them. Second, one must be in a position to facilitate the satisfaction of demands originating on the periphery and unable to attain their ends on their own. Finally, one must be in a position to give the appearance that the actions one has taken are compatible with one's status and responsibilities. Accordingly, three *outputs* of power may now be distinguished. For A, the output of power is the possibility of "allocating fluid resources." For I, the output of power enhances the capacity of the leaders to fulfill their "leadership responsibilities." For L, the output of power enhances the capacity of the "moral authorities" to stimulate mobilization and commitment. To exert power is therefore to hold out the prospect of additional income to the economic actors, new roles and responsibilities to government officials and representatives of interest groups, and new opportunities for "service to the collectivity" to the moral authorities.

To the extent that power combines inputs and outputs associated with functions of different kinds, we may speak of power as a "combination"—the stability and effectiveness of which depend on the degree to which the elements entering into the composite are heterogeneous. The productive resources supplied by the economy (A) and transformed into public services stimulate the society, so to speak, and increase its capacity to attain its goals. Interest-group demands are first encoded by the central political authorities, then re-encoded in the form of decisions and transmitted back to the source, leaving behind as net product the support of the interest group for the decision-making authorities. The quest for legitimacy on the part of the political authorities (as well as possible challenges to that legitimacy) gives rise to legislation setting forth the jurisdiction and relative status of each component of the hierarchy of authority. The outputs of G are in turn elaborated in each of the other subsystems, A, I, and L, in ways analogous to the elaboration we have described of the various inputs to G.

The decomposition of each combination into inputs and outputs throws the inadequacy of a strictly bilateral analysis into sharp relief. We are led to the idea of a crisscross pattern in which we distinguish between inputs and outputs from A, G, I, and L in each transaction involving a bifunctional pair, $A\rightleftharpoons G$, $G\rightleftharpoons I$, $G\rightleftharpoons L$. Are we to view this taxonomy as defining a matrix of intersectoral relations? However that may be, it does enable us to understand why power cannot be reduced to a composite of inputs and outputs. None of the three factors—control over the productivity of the means of production, legitimation of authority, interest-group demands—is power in the strict sense. Only through symbolic mediation can one of the three become power. "Power," writes Parsons, "is the *means* of acquiring control of the factors in effectiveness; it is not itself one of these factors, any more than in the economic case money is a factor of production; to suppose it was, was the ancient mercantilist fallacy" [1969, p. 356].

Power, let it be said once more, is a *general* capacity of control, in essence symbolic. To equate it with the resources that it may command is to commit the error of reification. The following passage describes the output aspect of power, showing how power makes services available to individuals and to society as a whole.

> The political control of productivity makes it possible, through
> combinatorial gains in the political context, to produce a surplus

above the monetary funds committed, by virtue of which under
specified conditions a premium can be paid at the monetary level
which, though a result of the combinatorial process as a whole, is
most directly related to the output of available services as an
economic phenomenon, i.e. as a "fluid resource." [1969, p. 357]

The resources of power against which the political authorities draw
can accordingly be considered from two different vantage points.
From a *monetary* point of view, power is seen to be useful for increasing the income of firms and households. In *real* terms, on the other
hand, it provides opportunities for employment to a work force that
would otherwise remain idle—the "service" rendered by management
in industry or by bureaucratic officials being the offer of jobs, for
example.

To say that the "real" products of power are services—far from
implying that those products belong to a category of material or physical objects standing outside the social interaction system—means simply that they bring about an increase in productivity as a result of the
initial exertion of power, and that that increase is controlled by the
authorities exercising power (at least the authorities strive to maintain
such control). To characterize an input or output as "real" is not the
same thing as to regard it as a physical object. It is rather to assign that
input or output a place in the combinatorial process by means of which
the cohesiveness, effectiveness, and efficiency of the social system are
enhanced, and to associate it with one of the four functions, namely,
that with which it originated.

To complicate matters, if the factors are not consumed where they
are produced, it may be asked whether they can be consumed any-
where or, alternatively, must be consumed according to strict criteria
of location or order. Two examples will help make the point clear.
First, let us go back to the case of the patient who hesitates to have an
operation but in the end decides to take his surgeon's advice. The
surgeon cannot operate without the patient's consent, so that the first
priority is to *persuade* the patient that the operation is necessary. To
put it another way, the doctor can exert his power only if he already
has a certain amount of influence beforehand. Consider a second
example, that of a banker who decides to lend money to an industrialist who intends to make certain investments. Parsons emphasizes
that this act is *political* [1956, p. 125], for at least two reasons. First,
the firm's productivity will be increased as a result. Hence attainment
of the collective goals for which the industrialist is responsible will
be facilitated. But at the same time the firm's power will be enhanced.
Second, the beneficiary of the loan incurs certain obligations toward

the lender. The borrower agrees not only to repay the loan by a set date but also may accord his creditor the right to watch over his business affairs during the period of the loan. At the very least, borrower and lender will have reached agreement beforehand as to the general nature of the investment program for which the loan was sought. There has been an expenditure of power along with the expenditure of money, in contrast to the previous example where the expenditure of power was made possible only by a prior expenditure of influence.

Hence the order in which expenditures are made, as well as the list of beneficiaries, is not arbitrary. Neither is it strictly determined. The patient can "function" without influence; the banker can "function" other than via the monetary medium. The "typical" situation, however, is that the patient cannot be operated on without his consent (say, by administrative fiat) and that the banker will not authorize the payment of funds for long-term investments merely because the prospective borrower happens to be a friend or a member of the same church or political party as the banker. If we consider the doctor-patient relationship from the point of view of the patient rather than that of the doctor, we may find that the relative positions of power and influence in the hierarchy are different, perhaps even inverted. Similarly, in the banker-investor relationship, the banker controls liquid assets, while the investor at best can hold out a prospect of long-term profits. Each input and each output must, therefore, be looked at from the standpoint of two different media (and never just one), as we saw clearly in the case of services. On the one hand, services come under the head of power, because their production increases society's capability to achieve its members' common goals; on the other hand, however, when the head of a household is employed, the flow of resources at the disposal of that household is increased and optimized. "Service . . . is the point at which the economic utility of the human factor is matched with its potential contribution to effective collective action" [1969, p. 358].

Whenever power figures in a given input or output, a problem of *hierarchy* arises, because a quantum of power is being combined with a quantum of some other factor, and it must be decided which of the two has priority. In organization theory hierarchy is conceived as an ordering of jurisdictional priorities: Who gives orders to whom? Within a given jurisdiction, who has the last word?[29] To the extent that any system of power establishes priorities (concerning the use of resources) and defines collective goals, it takes the form of a hierarchy. More generally, at the social system level, the question of hierarchy brings us back once more to the question of choice, which lies at the heart of the theory of action. When power, as input or output, enters into combination with another input or output, we must decide whether power is dominant or dominated, controlled or controlling. This is readily seen in the case of constraints, which may either be subordinated to a symbolic medium or play an independent and arbitrary role.

For example, the "opportunity for effectiveness" that the government provides to firms and households is an input (stemming from G) that induces actors (situated in A) to invest in the one case, to accept jobs in the other. Accordingly, in the relation on which we are now focusing, $\overrightarrow{AG}$, power takes precedence: it is the driving force. Considered in isolation, however, this relation tells us nothing about the origin of the quantum of power thus expended—unless we have some way of tracing the evolution of the symbolic medium through successive states, from the moment of inception of the quantum in question to the moment of its final consumption. Consider now the combination $\overrightarrow{IG}$. Policy decisions also involve a power input. They increase the capacity of interest groups to achieve their objectives. But such decisions are made pursuant to demands issuing from the periphery. Thus power must have been subordinate to influence for a while. Let no one be misled, however, into thinking that interest-group pressure "rules" the government. In the relation $\overrightarrow{GL}$, power appears as mediated through I and A. Indeed, the "legitimation of authority" requires a certain degree of solidarity between rulers and ruled (this is where I comes in) and a certain degree of effectiveness in the instrumental relation between society and its environment (involving A). Accordingly, we cannot accept the claim that there is any one-sided—or even two-sided—determination of politics by the economy (the factors of production), since any power channel involves more than two categories of activity, and each such category is itself subdivided into inputs and outputs.

Power, therefore, is not one thing. The social order is not the same as a chain of command in the military. Not only are resources other than constraint and dissuasion available for attaining social goals, but constraint and dissuasion are themselves merely elements in an exchange, the recourse to physical force being not so much a moment in the actual process as a condition of that process. What has to be explained, therefore, is when the recourse to force occurs or can possibly occur. This would enable us to identify the nature of the force used by the place it occupied in the sequence of phases and in the interchange between symbolic media.

To that end, it is possible to localize G in two ways, in accordance with one or the other of the two possible courses taken by the social process. To begin with, we remind the reader that, on the basis of the observation of small discussion groups, Parsons was able to specify the sequence of phases as A G I L. In the group process, A is the phase during which the participants take their positions with respect to the task confronting them (or the task they have chosen for themselves). G is the moment at which responsibilities are assigned. I marks the creation of group solidarity and L the constitution of a tradition, an esprit de corps or collective identity. This model recapitulates the stages of a learning process, with its double aspect of adaptation and assimilation. At the disposal of the group and each of its member individuals are regulations for controlling their interpersonal relations, the relation of each individual to the group, and relations between the system of action and its environment. In the sequence A G I L, G plays the part of a disciplinary and allocative function. Once the question "What is this all about?" has been asked, there is a need to decide which individuals are most capable of discharging given tasks and how the various tasks are to be ordered within the group's plan of action. In the sequence A G I L the political function is seen to play its part only after a "technocratic" instrumental identification of the objective problems. At this point, let us assume that the problem the group was facing has been resolved and the learning phase completed. Now we find that the order of the phases, the order in which regulations are implemented in confronting a new problem (during another meeting, for instance) is different—the reverse of the order in which they were learned.

Instead of the sequence A G I L, we find the sequence L I G A, which reflects the primacy of internalized dispositions (what Parsons calls "cybernetic" regulations) over the exogenous constraints or conditions of action.[30] In this second sequence, G comes after L and I. In other words, the political function operates within a framework of cultural references and among "socialized" actors already bound by ties of solidarity. Hence it is "controlled" from within (i.e., by the system of values and norms) rather than from without (i.e., by the constraints of the external environment).

In such circumstances we may speak of cybernetic control. What interests us here is not so much the analogy between society and the thermostat as the importance of the attributes and attainments of the social system. But Parsons is cautious. He does not speak of "reproduction" pure and simple but rather invokes a "strain toward consistency." He holds that the social system manifests tension when there is too great a divergence between interests and beliefs. This tension is kept within limits or eliminated by conscious or unconscious, mediated or unmediated efforts to reestablish a certain minimum degree of compatibility among the elements of the system. It is in this ultimately restrictive sense that any tradition, once constituted and internalized, tends to preserve and to reproduce itself. We previously observed this phenomenon of continuity and reproduction in the case of motivation. We are now in a position to understand the "reproductive" aspect of culture. Is it permissible to look upon the political system as wholly regulated by repetition of the motivational cycle and cultural reproduction?

The need-dispositions (motivations) that govern our behavior were originally internalized during the socialization process. The law of effect, furthermore, ensures that there will be a fluctuating equilibrium (mutual contingency) between need-dispositions on the one hand and socially defined and sanctioned norms on the other, in consequence of which individual behavior will be confined within relatively stable limits more or less broadly defined by the norm. The mechanism of motivation via need-dispositions is certainly not as simple and strictly determined as the mechanism of the thermostat (which is strictly determined by virtue of its simplicity), but it does exhibit two characteristics that may be termed "cybernetic." Motivation is internally regulated by the laws that govern its own function, and this internal regulation is linked to feedback mechanisms that limit the variability of individual behavior.

Do the symbolic models stored in L have the same attributes as motives? Before cybernetic metaphors became fashionable, Parsons was already applying the homeostatic metaphor to cultural systems. He himself tells us that the possibility of using the idea of homeostasis from biology to analyze action and interaction had always interested him [1970a, p. 849]. As Anatol Rapoport has pointed out, biologists look upon homeostasis as a process involving a specific set of mechanisms so constructed as to produce predictable effects. For example, there are mechanisms for maintaining the concentration of sugar, salt, oxygen, and carbon dioxide in the blood within a certain tolerable range. Similarly, in the higher vertebrates there is a mechanism for maintaining a nearly constant body temperature.[31] And yet if homeostasis means self-regulation and internal stability, one of its consequences, as Alfred Emerson reminds us, is variability. To put it another way, homeostatic mechanisms maintain relatively constant levels of certain characteristic features (such as salt content, sugar content, and internal temperature) of organic structure and so reduce the variability of those characteristics, but at the same time increase the variability of other characteristics of the species, thereby broadening the scope of individual competition. Sex, according to Emerson, "is not an increase of reproductive efficiency but an increase in controlled variability which is necessary if natural selection is to operate in an evolutionary process. Sex, then, becomes the homeostasis of variability."[32]

What Parsons calls "pattern-maintenance" bears a close resemblance to Emerson's version of the concept of homeostasis.[33] Cultural models are supposed to be stable; what is more, they are held together by a "strain toward consistency." It does not follow from their consistency and stability, however, that such models necessarily reproduce identical copies of themselves indefinitely, or that their meaning is the same when they enter into the experience of individual members of the group as motives.[34]

For each living creature (and for the species as a whole)[35] homeostatic equilibrium is characterized by "the maintenance of certain independence relative to the environment," where this result is obtained, of course, through a certain degree of interindividual variability and by more or less pronounced differences between genotype and phenotype. To control individual behavior the cultural system possesses no such mechanisms, certainly not mechanisms providing for such tight control. A moral norm is effective only under a number of fairly restrictive conditions. It must first of all be internalized. What is more, the social authorities must take responsibility for imposing external sanctions to enforce respect for the norm. In both cases these requirements must be compatible with the context in which the particular system of action is embedded. Finally, in a more fundamental perspective, we may look at the norm in two ways: from the actor's standpoint as a recommendation or command, or from the observer's standpoint simply as a *possible* model for action, whether or not that possibility is realized. Realization of the norm requires that the consequences of its being applied (or not being applied) be made clear to the actor, that is, mediated, in terms of his own motives and the attitudes of others toward him. A distinction should therefore be made between cultural systems and social systems, since they are actualized in different ways. Kroeber and Parsons put it this way: "We suggest that it is useful to define the concept *culture* for most usages more narrowly than has generally been the case in the American anthropological tradition, restricting its reference to transmitted and created content and patterns of values, ideas, and other symbolic-meaningful systems as factors in the shaping of human behavior and the artifacts produced through behavior. On the other hand, we suggest that the term 'society'—or more generally, 'social system'—be used to designate the specifically relational system of interaction among the individuals and collectivities."[36]

As a consequence of this distinction, society cannot be treated purely as an expression of culture, regarded as a repository of values or ideas; conversely, neither can culture be treated merely as the reflection of social relations (of production or domination). Even if the two systems are mutually contingent, as Kroeber and Parsons insist, what is necessary to ensure the consistency and stability of one will not be the same as what is necessary for the other. The social process of domination, therefore, is not enough to explain cultural reproduction—nor vice versa. Having stated this important proviso, we may say that the cultural subsystem exerts control of some sort over the three other subsystems—it is now up to us to explain the nature of that control.

To that end, we must first understand that the L subsystem (like every system) is differentiated, and, furthermore, that the symbolization process is heterogeneous. Intrinsically, the cultural subsystem is differentiated into ideas or beliefs, moral norms, judgments involving taste, and basic models out of which we construct our experience. However these facets of the cultural subsystem articulate with one another and with the various facets of the other subsystems, cultural control is essentially *symbolic*. What precisely is meant by this multifarious term? The existence of a symbolic control, no matter what the sphere in which that control is exerted, requires four conditions to be met [1970*a*, p. 849]. First, we assume that specific *values* (utility for money, collective effectiveness for power) pattern the choices of the actors. Second, the actors must possess *interests* by means of which those values can be put into practice. Third, there must be a *definition of the situation*. And, finally, it must be possible to distinguish between legitimate and illegitimate procedures by reference to a framework of norms.

Two different points of view are combined in this conception of symbolism. In the first place, we are extending the characteristics of language to expressive phenomena in general. "Language . . . is not an isolated phenomenon. In the field of social interaction, many mechanisms have properties so similar to those of language that it is not too much to say that they *are* specialized languages. Mathematical and artistic symbol systems are cases in point" [1969, p. 407]. In this sense language consists of a variety of mechanisms for controlling, by means of codes, the regular emission of messages. In this standard definition, due to Jakobson and Halle,[37] we once again encounter the elements that entered into our earlier definition of symbolism. In both cases the specific references to a particular situation (the information content of the message, the interests of the actors involved in the communication) are controlled by the rules that govern the transmission and reception of the message. This last point leads directly to Jakobson's very strict notion of code: a code is "a fixed transformation, usually term by term, by means of which a set of information units is converted into a sequence of phonemes and vice versa."[38]

Jakobson also asks whether the codes are strict enough to "match signified to signifier, signifier to signified" in messages expressed in different media as well as in messages between one medium and another. Stated differently, this question boils down to asking whether the media can constitute genuine sanctions, that is, control ego's conduct as effectively as do alter's attitudes and behavior toward ego. Let us try to answer this question in formal terms, that is, hypothetically rather than categorically. In other words, the question we shall attempt to answer is not whether symbolic media actually do constitute effective sanctions, but rather under what conditions they might do so.

It is in this hypothetical frame of mind that table 3 in Parsons's paper on power should be read [1969, p. 402]. Let us agree to treat the social structure as a language or a symbolic function. The distinction between the message (i.e., a collection of elements pertinent to a specific situation) and the code (i.e., the procedures whereby those elements are endowed with meaning) then becomes applicable to the analysis of the social structure, or, perhaps better, to the analysis of the four functions, which we have set down in the order L I G A, since we are concerned with structure from the point of view of the cybernetic control exerted by L, the pattern-maintenance and cultural-reproduction function. We are then faced with a series of "correspondence problems." Is there "matching," to use Jakobson's term, between message and code? This rather sweeping question may be broken down into a number of subsidiary questions. Focusing first on the code, a distinction may be made between the values or range of interests whose expression it makes possible and the procedures it sets in motion. Consider, for example, the second line in the table, which has to do with the integrative function (I). On the left-hand side of the page we read that influence has to do with the "solidarity" value and employs a procedure ("coordination standard") identified as "consensus," that is, the technique of agreement. The distinction being made here bears a close resemblance to a distinction we make spontaneously when, for instance, we look at dance as language and try to "decode" it. The spectator's perception is affected by such values as grace and suppleness, though he is also aware that the dancer is adept in the use of certain techniques. If we now turn our attention to the right-hand portion of the table (still looking at the line pertaining to "influence"), we find that the message may be viewed either as an input or as an output, that is, from the standpoint of the emitter or encoder on the one hand, the recipient or decoder on the other. For example, the "outputs" controlled by the message I are moral commitments and political loyalties; this control, moreover, is exerted through two "inputs," membership in certain groups or social movements, and participation in the political decision-making process. Accordingly, the symbolic inputs and outputs under the control of I are messages sent or received by A and L. To ensure a sufficient level of overall correspondence in the system, the code (i.e., the value-principles and coordination standards that govern the influence function) must control the circulation of messages in communications subsystems other than I. The symbolic system must therefore not only allow for a whole series of "code switches"[39] but also clearly specify the hierarchical ordering of the various codes.[40]

Are these conditions satisfied or not? If they are, we may treat the social structure as a language in the strict sense of the word. But this is not always the case. Symbolism need not take algorithmic form: there are symbols besides those that stand for operational rules such as +, −, etc. A symbol can also be an image. When Parsons speaks of "the father as a symbol," he is suggesting a definition of symbol quite different from the algorithmic definition. "We may define a symbol," writes Parsons, "as an *object*—which may be a physical or social object, event, aspect of a concrete object, or a class or complex of any of these—which has acquired *meaning* for one or more actors involving a reference to meaningful entities other than the symbol-object itself. . . . We are here interested primarily in . . . what I shall call an 'expressive' as distinguished from a cognitive symbol. This is always an aspect of the meaning of any symbolic object, but we will speak of an expressive symbol when this aspect has primacy over the cognitive. A symbol is expressive in this sense in so far as its meaning *has reference* not to other objects as objects but to the motivational state or states of one or more actors."[41]

Typically, the problems associated with expressive symbolism have to do on the one hand with the kinds of equivalences such symbols establish between the motivational states of the actor emitting them and the motivational states of the recipient who decodes the message, and, on the other hand, with the type of relation that is established between the sphere of immediate experience and the specific field to which the message relates under certain explicit conditions. The symbolism of the father is built up out of significations of many different kinds, stemming from a wide variety of situations with which the individual must deal during the socialization process. Parsons first observes that the father is the person who intervenes in the mother-child social microsystem, the intruder who "constitutes the symbolic focus of the pressure from the outside world which is responsible for breaking up the 'paradise' of the child's state of blissful security with his mother" [1964, p. 40]. He is also the rival who, for part of the time, claims the attentions and affections of the mother. In addition, he is worthy of admiration and respect because he is strong and all-powerful. He is a source of encouragement and protection and at the same time a source of punishment and discipline. "The father then tends both to personify the 'higher' demands or requirements to which the child is being asked to live up, and thus to require a high order of respect and authority, and, at the same time, he is the primary target of the aggression (and anxiety) generated in the process. . . . The father tends to mean both that which is respected and to be, on the one hand, emulated, on the other, obeyed, and at the same time an object of anxiety and hatred. . . . This level of ambivalent orientation to the father can be symbolically generalized in a number of respects." The symbolism of the father governs the transfer of emotional and motivational states from one sector to another of our social life. Within the family context, the father represents—in an anticipatory sense for the child, who has as yet no direct experience of it—the demands of the working and professional world. In the economic context, where the father is responsible for the upkeep of the household, he stands symbolically for economic exigencies not reducible to marketplace logic. In this respect the father symbol serves to mediate between A and L, giving priority to either one or the other depending on the situation and circumstances. Within the domestic unit, the father enters into three series of relations: with his wife, with his male children, and with his female children. From these relations the participants draw a repertory of extremely labile attitudes, closely related to one another in spite of the fact that at first sight they seem to contrast (love/hate) or to relate to different persons. Transference makes possible free substitution of one of these persons for another. Mindful that the ambivalence of symbolism is rooted in the socialization process, the ends and tendencies of which are not entirely under the control of the individual subject [1964, pp. 50–51], we must recognize that symbolic control is fraught with ambivalence and uncertainty whenever it relies on concrete, personalized symbolism, as in the case of a charismatic figure.

It does not follow, however, that the symbolic function is at the mercy of individual whim, even where expressive symbolism is involved. Every symbol is a "bundle" of significations. But this bundle is hedged about by the lines of force of action, by the ribs of the structure of action. This explains why the symbolic content of the father role, for example, depends on the system of social relations in which the role figures. If relations between the outside world and the household are controlled not by the mother's husband but by her brother, then the relative importance of discipline and permissiveness in the father's role is reversed: the father becomes a sort of older brother, while the mother's brother is seen and responded to in ways typical of the paternal position in patrilineal systems. The context shapes the content of the symbolic function; to the extent that it is possible to compare the requirements of one context with those of another, it is also possible to compare the symbols themselves.

Parsons later came to regard symbolic indeterminacy as related to what he calls "interpenetration"[42] of the subsystems, which he felt was of great importance for analyzing systems of stratification. "If, on the one hand, cultural symbolism is largely the projection of our childhood experiences...it is nonetheless true that the real father—as opposed to the father of symbolism and imagination—is the projection into the family of the main structural models of the global society." The symbol gives simultaneous expression to all aspects of the social structure, though with widely varying degrees of precision and intensity. The equivalences thereby established between diverse elements of the system are not always specified by term-by-term transformations defined by explicit codes. Not indeterminate, these equivalences are nevertheless problematic, in a sense to be clarified below.

Inflation and Deflation in Symbolic Systems

Symbolic control can be effective only if two conditions are satisfied: first, the messages must be strictly subordinate to the codes, and, second, the codes themselves must be hierarchically ordered in such a way that those that ensure the maintenance of the integrity of the system take precedence over those that have to do with the solvency of the system or the utility of its members. These two conditions are not always met. To convince ourselves of this, we need only think of certain phenomena associated with deviance and control, to which we may add processes of social change, the subject of the next chapter. What deviance, social control, and socialization have in common is that in all three, when we focus on the level of individual behavior, we find both rigidity and imprecision in the codes, disparity between the codes and the motives of individuals, and a need to employ resources associated with identification and transference in order to discover new value-orientations, orientations exhibiting a higher degree of complexity or differentiation than is ordinarily found in the interaction process. As we shall see when we come to the analysis of change, many important characteristics of symbolic systems cannot be explained in terms of a lack of congruence of some sort between codes and messages on the one hand, and individual motives and interests on the other.

Economists have long observed how the monetary mass alternately expands and contracts, as well as how certain other key economic variables (prices, incomes, production levels) fluctuate. Such a cycle typifies the inflation-deflation process. Following Schumpeter, Parsons describes this process as the breakdown of the "circular flow," that is, of the invariant cycle of exchange between households and firms that we would expect to find if the tastes of the consumers and the coefficients of the production function remain constant under conditions of equilibrium.[43] By definition, the circular flow produces no net product or surplus. Thus any attempt by one economic actor (or category of actors) to improve his lot can only be made at the expense of another actor (or category). Game theorists refer to such a situation as a two-person zero-sum game. In real terms, everything that is produced is either consumed or invested; in monetary terms, the monetary mass is exactly balanced by the value of goods and services available on the market. Given such a situation of strict solvency (balance between monetary costs and receipts), any expenditure by an economic actor, be he consumer or producer, must be compensated by a corresponding income or revenue. Strictly speaking, there is no such thing as credit. Thus the only thing that one actor can claim over and above what the market allows in return for his contributions is what he can take from another actor. Either there is no surplus, or else one category of actors lays claim to a surplus that is nothing other than the fruits of the exploitation of other actors. The only way to break out of the circular flow and its concomitant struggle for advantage is through credit. Credit, however, is not simply a matter of making additional resources available to actors who can make good use of them. Under these conditions, giving credit requires depriving some actors of resources over which they formerly exercised exclusive control. As Parsons conceives of it, however, credit is not a transfer of preexisting real resources from one category of actors to another, but rather involves the creation of additional resources, or the laying of odds that additional resources can be created.

In what sense does credit create inflationary risks? The firm receiving credit must be able to pay back capital and interest within the terms of the contract. For the economy as a whole, the risk of expanded credit is that rather than bring about an increase in productivity it will merely lead to depreciation of the value of money. Deflation occurs when the profit outlook has deteriorated to the point where entrepreneurs would rather hold on to their liquid reserves than put them to work, even though the factors of production are underemployed from the standpoint of the national economy as a whole.

Inflation and deflation, we are told, tend to undermine confidence in the system. This effect is psychological in the sense that it is the result of incorrectly anticipating the behavior of various categories of actors. Psychological, however, is not synonymous with subjective, to say nothing of random or capricious. What a banker or businessman predicts about the future is not the consequence of his personal whim. Economic prognostications, even if ultimately proved wrong, are interpretations made by certain economic actors of the behavior of their partners or competitors. What is at issue is the relevance of the message and the strictness of the code. The modification of the relations between incomes, costs, and prices or divergence between the rate of profit and the rate of interest induces errors of calculation that may cause disastrous decisions to be taken. Examples of such malfunctions in the economic codes are not far to seek. In an equilibrium situation, an increase in the relative price of a product reduces demand for that product. In an inflationary situation, however, price increases encourage further increases, while in periods of deflation price decreases lead to other decreases. A simple explanation in psychological terms sees the cause of these phenomena in the propensity of the actors to extrapolate trends, which they recognize and diagnose only belatedly. American psychologists have described what they call the "bandwagon effect," where undecided voters jump on the bandwagon of the party they think will win. Apart from the widespread occurrence of cumulative phenomena such as these, we may also mention the irrational consequences for the collectivity of behavior that is rational when looked at from the point of view of the individual. In a deflationary period, the entrepreneur is well-advised to liquidate his assets. If, however, all entrepreneurs simultaneously cut their expenses in order to build up their cash reserves—most notably by laying off a part of the work force—the monetary mass will contract as a result of decreased consumption and investment and the corresponding increase in precautionary savings, with the result that entre-preneurs desperate to increase the amount of cash on hand find that they have only worsened their cash positions.

Money, therefore, is not neutral: variations in both the mass and the velocity of the monetary reserves influence the prognostications made by the actors and so affect their plans for production, saving, and consumption. Though we cannot go into the details here, it is worth mentioning that these prognostications can be thrown off by changes in the structure of production costs, in the behavior of the authorities in charge of money and banking, and in the "tastes" or "needs" of the consumers. When this happens, the erroneous predictions can be either corrected and compensated for, or perpetuated in a cumulative process. In any event the instructions embodied in the code will no longer be valid. If the actor follows them anyway, the results he will obtain will be the opposite of those he had bargained on.

Economists have traditionally asked themselves three sorts of ques-tions. They first inquire as to the origins of the process, and then seek to explain why, once begun, it tends to build cumulatively. Finally, they examine what kind of linkage may exist, as there is reason to believe, between expansion and contraction: Does crisis inevitably follow expansion? Is depression necessarily followed by recovery? Of the two great economists whose work had the most direct impact on Parsons's thinking, Keynes and Schumpeter, the former was mainly interested in cumulative processes in economics (particularly in the fact that recovery from depression was not assured, especially if re-covery is defined as full employment of all factors), while the latter was mainly concerned with the possibilities of innovation as a way of escaping from the "circular flow." We may ask, as Parsons did, whether the three questions mentioned above (creation of "value added" by means of a novel combination of factors, expansion and contraction of the symbolic system, and the cumulative character of the process) do not also arise in connection with other media.

The question of the "value added" by the symbolic media is par-ticularly important where power is concerned. Parsons argues that if power did not create added value it would be nothing other than a two-person zero-sum game. This being the case, we must choose. We cannot contend both that power is a life-and-death struggle and that it is the symbolic realization of collective ends, as we originally defined it. Now, ends are not collective merely because the political au-thorities have the responsibility of attaining them, but also in a less obvious yet quite fundamental sense. To begin with, let us assume that the situation is one of barter between candidates seeking votes and interested individuals or groups. A voter can transfer his allegiance from one candidate to another only at the expense of the candidate forsaken. The only change a candidate can make in his platform is to alter the relative priority of the various issues. If the candidates are not free to change their platforms and the perferences of all voters are fixed, the electoral competition boils down to one candidate "stealing" votes from another, while individual voters or blocs of voters can at best hope to see their particular demands given higher priority than those of others. Now, this is not the way things actually work, for two reasons. First, the voters' preference schedules are not always explicitly defined. Second, the issues in the platform are not fixed, nor are their relative priorities. The uncommitted vote, therefore, must be taken into account, along with such unforeseen circumstances as may arise between elections.

These two sorts of uncertainty considerably enhance the power of the politician. He is no longer bound by a strictly bilateral contract with each voter (or bloc of voters). He will make certain commitments to the majority (necessarily heterogeneous in composition) and perhaps also to the "nation as a whole." His commitments do not relate exclusively, or even principally, to specific issues but rather to a general policy orientation. Thanks to the indeterminacy in the number and priority of issues, the electorate produces a "net product." Furthermore, the demands of the voters are generalized in the sense that they cannot be reduced to a sum of individual demands but are rather transformed into the expectation that a certain policy—including not only those demands but also demands stemming from other social sectors—will in fact be adopted. Those in office find that their commitments undergo a similar transformation; once elected, a politician no longer holds fast to promises made to one sector or another but rather supports certain major policy "options," which in his view are likely to promote national prosperity and a bright future. The value added by the electoral process consists in the generalization, or, rather, the collectivization of supply and demand (i.e., decisions and interests), which adds a true increment to the fund of power, just as the transition from a barter to a money economy enhances the productivity of the factors of production.

The successful candidate enjoys not only more power but also more influence. "Another component of the freedom of elected leadership . . . is the freedom to use influence—for example through the 'prestige' of office as distinguished from its specified powers—to embark on new ventures in the 'equation' of power and influence" [1969, pp. 389–90]. Attracted by new faces in power or by campaign promises, previously inactive lobbyists and other interest groups will seek out new officeholders because they are visible, wield or promise to wield power to good effect, and enjoy the mandate of the electorate. The power vested in the newly elected official raises new expectations and demands on the part of persons or groups previously on the fringes of politics, if not excluded altogether from the political process. Because of such expectations, officeholders can extend their influence to an even greater degree. With growing influence they are not only encouraged to take action but also equipped with the means to do so, not only on issues with which they are personally identified but also on related, broader issues affecting the political system as a whole.

What makes the production of surplus power possible is the ability of politicians, even before they have been elected, to generalize the demands made on them and, once in office, to turn the prestige of the position into effective levers for attaining their platform goals. Influence may be analyzed in the same way. Clubs and pressure groups use the influence of their prestigious members, which they accept on deposit, "like banks," Parsons says. But the influence of an individual member of the Rotary Club, say, is specific: it is based on his position and the prestige that goes with it and is applicable primarily within his particular profession. The eminent Dr. Smith has influence with other physicians. Mr. Jones, the architect, carries great weight with his fellow architects. But influence extends beyond its source. Because Dr. Smith enjoys high esteem as a physician, his fellow citizens rate him relatively high on the scale of influence. Taken as a whole, moreover, the influence of the Plainville Rotary Club exceeds the individual influences of all the Smiths and Joneses who belong to it.

It may be objected that neither Smith's nor Jones's influence can be measured very accurately. The objection is not conclusive, however. It is true that an individual's power is not amenable to quantification in the way that his money income is. But we can determine where and over how many people his power is exerted. Similarly, an individual's influence may be rated by counting the number of people who, after consulting with him on a certain issue, changed their views or reversed their decisions to reflect his advice.[44] Let us call influential individuals "persuaders." Persuaders who belong to an organization or hold a prestigious post may find their personal influence enhanced by virtue of their position. The leaders of clubs and pressure groups may be able, temporarily or permanently, to make use of some or all of the influence of the group's members. The Plainville Rotary to which Smith the doctor and Jones the architect belong, for example, can bring their personal influence to bear in other spheres. The club leaders can transfer influence earned elsewhere—in business, medicine, architecture, or journalism, for instance—and placed with them "on

deposit," as it were, to politics, for example. The total volume of
influence in circulation is increased as a result of "recycling" originally
specific types of influence through the network of associations. Ultimately, in the hands of politicians in a position to translate influence
into decisions, that influence can be turned into power.

Intuitively, the creation of a "value added" is most readily understood in the area of "value-commitment." The charismatic prophet or
hero, filled with unshakable conviction *(Gesinnung),* "typically emphasizes that [his] demands are not for the fulfillment of routinely
established obligations, but for something new. Weber repeatedly
quoted from the Gospels, 'It is written, but *I say unto you*'" [1969, p.
467]. The charismatic message inspires commitment and mobilizes a
following, but by the same token it jeopardizes the very code in which
it was couched. Commitment to a prophet, unlike power and influence, is not channeled through established institutions. The
prophet does not represent his followers in the way that the president
of the Plainville Rotary Club represents his members, or the con-
gressman from the second congressional district represents the voters.
Thus the prophet can deal more freely with language (code and messages) and with his audience than can the banker or politician. But this
does not mean that what he has to say is necessarily new or effective.
Taken together, though, the elements that go to make up charisma (a
leader, a church, a gospel) *can,* and sometimes do, yield something
more than the sum of the parts.

Charisma has a "multiplier effect," the propagation of which may be
traced both within the social system and at the point where the social
system articulates with the personalities of the actors to whom the
prophet's message is addressed. The prophet's ability to win followers
depends on his capacity to serve as a symbol with which they can
identify. That capacity comes down to an ability to transform promises
into realities, sometimes deceptive realities—to bring about an in-
carnation of the vision. The greater the tensions between the prophet
and his group on the one hand and traditional society on the other, the
easier it is to transform charismatic "influence"[45] into political power.
The charismatic multiplier effect, the cause of which is to be looked
for in the way in which charisma operates through the channels of
power and influence, is further enhanced by the close relation (as we
saw in our treatment of socialization) between moral questions and
questions relating to the personalities of the actors—the prophet himself or his followers in the present case [1969, p. 468].

Commitment, particularly in its charismatic form, produces an
added value by increasing power and influence, benefiting not only
those directly concerned but society at large as well. As we have seen

in the case of money, symbolic systems are not neutral; they are not "reflections." Symbolic combinations are not merely rearrangements of the elements that enter into them. The nature of the elements themselves is changed, and in consequence "something" is added.

The problem of surplus arises in symbolic systems in two ways. First, in relation to the material substrate of meaning: How do vibrations engraved in a wax or plastic disk give expression to the *allegro vivace* that the composer penciled in the margin of the score of his symphony's final movement? How does the listener's impression of grace and vivacity come to be associated with his perception of sounds, rhythms, and tempi? Second, how does one symbolic system B produce a surplus in comparison with another system A—where does the surplus come from? This question will be taken up again in the next chapter, which deals with evolution and change. For the time being we must confine our attention to the question of how symbolic systems malfunction—by surfeit or deficiency—and the related question of how in the long run such tendencies may be compensated.

To understand inflation and deflation we must look first at how the "surplus" is created. Two conditions must be met if there is to be a surplus ("value added," net product). First, resources must be reallocated. Then, what is implicitly anticipated in the reallocation plan, a hoped-for profit, for example, must be sanctioned and confirmed by the distribution of inputs and outputs once the plan has been put into effect. Because a chance must be taken, there is always room for error. This is quite clear in the case of money and credit. The creation of a surplus (a complex matter to pin down precisely, since, apart from the interest paid to the bankers and the profit of the entrepreneur, one might wish to include the increase in real wages and the decrease in cost to the consumer) requires that a portion of the funds on deposit with the bank be placed at the disposal of entrepreneurs, who will in turn acquire factors whose share in the output can be determined only after the investment process is complete. At the end of the cycle, everyone has to get back at least as much as he laid out, and with luck something will be left over to be shared out. Suppose that the banker or the entrepreneur (or both) was overly optimistic; it will then be impossible to recover the funds advanced—at least not at their *real value*. But inflation is essentially a macroeconomic concept. It is in the economy as a whole that we see such symptoms of inflation as a rise in the level of relative prices or a shift in the relation of prices to interest rates. Inflation is due essentially to unduly optimistic prognostications as to the ultimate productivity of the factors at the end of a term fixed by the due dates of the loans advanced, at which time new loans must be negotiated to keep the expansion going.

> The increments of effectiveness that are necessary to imple-
> ment new binding policies that constitute an addition to the total
> burden on the collectivity cannot simply be willed into being;
> they require organizational changes. [1969, p. 391]

If the anticipated changes do not actually come about by the end of
the fixed period, the wager will be lost. There will be no net product,
only debts that cannot be repaid.

Inflation is the result of unfounded confidence based on inaccurate
judgments of what the future holds. For the system it leads inevitably
to insolvency. Parsons's description of the contraction phase of the
cycle is based on Keynes's concept of the cumulative increase of
underemployment. Deflation is an inability or unwillingness to honor
obligations.

> Hence, it comes to involve some restriction of the degrees of
> freedom that a unit may enjoy in the sphere of value implementa-
> tion, especially by shifting responsibility from the unit to some
> outside agency, e.g., the "law." [1969, p. 463]

When the "crisis," in which Parsons's description is a crisis of liquidity, first breaks out, the deflationary process is like a row of falling
dominoes. Later, it stabilizes in a kind of vicious circle in which the
only way to solve one person's problem is at the expense of someone
else, and the only way to rebuild depleted cash reserves is to cut
production.

American politics in the 1950s illustrate the effects of the "boom-
and-bust" cycle described above. After the Second World War the
American government took responsibility for a variety of activities
that previously had been left to other hands. "After 1945 our strength
grew too quickly." America was forced to abandon its isolationism in
view of the power vacuum that developed in Western Europe, owing
to the French collapse in 1940, the weakness of a victorious but
exhausted Great Britain, and the partition of Germany, not to mention advances in military technology. But the federal government did
not simply increase its foreign commitments. Internal developments
and the quest for full employment forced the federal authorities to
take an increasingly active role in the economy. The postwar years
were consequently marked by galloping inflation in governmental
commitments of all sorts. McCarthyism may be explained as a reaction
against the failure to live up to the promises implicit in those commitments.[46] Public suspicion of all governmental activity was aroused:
foreign aid to Europe was seen as assistance unwisely lavished on
corrupt peoples, while welfare was attacked as an inducement to sloth

and indolence. Subsequently, with the disappearance of the last vestiges of confidence in government, elected officials, community leaders, and, more generally, the "establishment," distrust turned to mass
hysteria: many saw "a stab in the back." In the end there was a falling
back on native values—"the American way of life"—and a concomitant rejection of everything foreign.

The ebb and flow of charisma is a subject familiar to historians of
religion. We may draw a parallel with the expansion/contraction cycle in
the economy: corresponding to the phase of expansion is the phase of
conquest, the "Promise" ("Thou art Peter, and upon this rock I will
build my Church") or sense of mission from which the belief in the
future of the prophet and his followers derives. After the charismatic
boom comes the slump, the phase of contradiction, which takes the
form of absolutism and fundamentalism. Commitment ceases to be a
matter of belief in some future good for which the followers of the
prophet are willing to work, to spread the news ("Let Thy Kingdom
come."). "It is written" once more assumes unquestioned precedence
over "I say unto you." Those who hold the sacred tradition in trust
anxiously turn their attention to upholding the letter of the law and take
countless precautions lest the law's purity be tainted or exposed to alien
influences. With the deflation of charisma society turns back to its
traditional forms, but at the same time there is a heightening of aggressive and authoritarian tendencies among its members.

In each of the major symbolic media we can observe fluctuations that
affect the social system. Alternating waves of expansion and contraction
accompany malfunctions in the symbolic codes. We are now in a position to describe briefly how these malfunctions may occur and to
suggest an interpretation of them. The most striking and best understood type of symbolic malfunction occurs in the economic medium.
The "normal" meaning of certain "messages" (such as a rise in prices) is
twisted and distorted. Instead of regulating exchange and reestablishing
equilibrium, the messages are interpreted literally, with the result that
runaway inflation is only worsened or, in the case of deflation, the
downward spiral only becomes more precipitous. In general, symbolic
malfunction takes the form of a failure of "values" to mesh with what
Parsons calls "coordination standards." In the case of influence, the
characteristic value is "solidarity." I can persuade alter because both he
and I feel or know that we belong to the same *Gemeinschaft*. The
coordination standard is consensus. At this point two difficulties arise.
Coordination standards and procedures are not always effective. Even
between partners in good faith, consensus is not easy to achieve. What
solidarity requires may be open to different interpretations. Worse,

one of the two partners may have it in mind to deceive the other. A shrewd ego can play on alter's sense of solidarity to "manipulate" him. We find a similar situation with power and value-commitment.

Do the codes malfunction in the same way for all the symbolic media? To ask a more radical question, does the notion of code have the same meaning for all the media? We encountered this question earlier when we discussed polysemic symbolism: Is the symbol an image or an algorithm? The rules of economic calculation are like codes in that the procedures they lay down are comprehensible to whoever makes use of them, even for nefarious ends, regardless of the consequences for ego, alter, and the collectivity. In other words, the meaning of the rules is clearly defined independent of the circumstances in which they are used; it is not left to be determined by special features of the context. This explains why we find such rules of calculation embodied in more than one form, as either norms or instructions. Does the same hold true when we turn from economics to charisma or influence? Both these media have a generalizing capability. But this capability is more wrapped up with its source than in the economic case. The authority of the prophet is bound up with his person, while the individual who attempts to exert influence over another individual must be like him in some respects.

Finally, the stability of the code is determined by the relationship between the "energy" elements (the motivations of the actors) and the "information" elements.[47] Though elliptical and imprecise, this statement makes clear that there are many different kinds of "codes," each with a different capacity to "control" the social system and a different likelihood of serious malfunction. One danger in the use of any code is the possibility of its use by an ill-intentioned individual. So long as the system is stable enough to discourage would-be interlopers, however, this danger may be minimized. If the sanctions contained in the official message are actually applied, while those contained in the interloper's message go without effect, the attempted sabotage of the system will misfire harmlessly, with no consequences more serious than those attributable to normal errors of transmission. More worrisome is the development of expectations with no symbolic counterpart in the media. We find instances of such a disparity between the motivations of the actor and the resources provided by the symbolic media in therapy, socialization, and the analyst/analysand relationship (e.g., helplessness, abandonment, rejection, hostility). It is possible to overcome such deficiencies but only with additional resources (information or energy elements), as we have already hinted in the discussion of socialization, and as we shall soon see even more clearly in the theory of social change.

Chapter Five

Social Change

Parsonian sociology has been accused both of confusing the idea of social equilibrium with that of cybernetic regulation and of altogether neglecting the phenomenon of social change. Both these accusations are without foundation. What is more, there is such an obvious connection between them that, if one is shown to be baseless, the other must be dismissed also. If the actor is held to be influenced by what he has learned and internalized, is it necessarily the case that the society that "inculcated" those lessons "manipulates" him in every respect? Does society impose rigorous constraints on individuals in the sense in which the natural environment was thought by nineteenth-century biologists to impose rigorous constraints on living creatures?

From our inquiry into the nature of power we have learned first of all that the effectiveness of both constraint and symbolism is limited. At first sight, power appeared to be a modality of the relationship between ego and alter. "Do thus and so," one of them says to the other, "and you can expect a good result. But don't do otherwise or you'll regret it." On this view, the accent is on the interpersonal nature of the relationship. Two things are lacking, however. First, no account is taken of the effects on the *couple:* ego *and* alter. For example, consider the case of two neighbors who together remove a tree blown down by a storm and blocking their street. Suppose that one of them, a lumberjack by trade, takes charge of the operation. His skill gives him power over his partner. It is advantageous to both of them, however, as well as to any traveler who happens by, that their common goal—clearing the roadway—be attained. If power were no more than a kind of interpersonal sanction, we would find it only on the microsystem level of interaction. Because impersonal relations exist, however, it is clear that microsystems are not closed. Suppose Tertius happens to drive down the road cleared by ego and alter. He benefits from their work, though he has taken no part in it and may be entirely unaware of what they have done. If, rather than consider power from the standpoint of interaction (focusing on the types of interaction involved, whether persuasion or constraint), we look instead at the achievement of the objectives to which ego and alter have committed themselves, objectives that transcend their direct relationship, it becomes clear why we might want to define power as an increase (or decrease) of collective effectiveness involving the use of symbolic media: increase of control over physical resources, facilitation of actor-to-actor contact and exchange, and legitimation of previously suspect or contested procedures.

Now, the codes associated with the various symbolic media vary widely in precision and efficiency. It is less easy to lay down explicit rules for exerting influence than for wielding power. The code governing charismatic commitments ("Sell whatsoever thou hast, and give to the poor . . . and come, take up the cross and follow me," to cite the Christian version) is quite different from that governing buying and selling in a bazaar, to say nothing of the Stock Exchange. What is more, once bureaucratization or a return to traditional ways has brought about a "routinization" of charisma, the successors of the charismatic hero or saint will find their freedom of action severely limited in comparison with his—though not altogether lacking. The theologians of the new doctrine will still have some latitude when it comes to establishing the code and spelling out the message handed down by the prophet.

Symbolism does not reproduce a copy of reality; it is not a reflection, as is sometimes said. Instead, symbolism enables us to anticipate what the effects of certain stimuli would be by considering them in hypothetical rather than real terms. Symbolism thus enables us to generalize, at once extending our control over the environment and standardizing the mechanisms by which we exert that control. Dostoevski's well-known dictum that "money is freedom coined" can also be applied to the other Parsonian media (power, influence, commitment), although, to be perfectly accurate, we should say "freedom institutionalized," that is, freedom exercised in accordance with certain rules.

Equipped with the resources of the various media, the actor makes choices among the possible eventualities that he is able to discern when he views his own situation according to the normative framework. Accordingly, a distinction must be made between "cybernetic" control by the symbolic media and operant conditioning. On the surface this would seem merely to recapitulate the critique of behaviorism with which Parsons began his work. But between *The Structure of Social Action* and the papers of the 1960s on power and influence, the theory of action had advanced in another, equally important respect. Continuing his criticism of psychologism and culturalism, Parsons came to the view that actors were endowed with a capacity to choose, a view that contrasted not only with behavioristic determinism but also with other forms of determinism based on the motivations of individuals and on cultural models. That we behave in conformity with norms can no more be explained solely by "internalization" of norms than by invoking natural constraints, whether physical or biological. Every actor has some room for maneuver, some leeway to gamble, to experiment with his freedom of choice. He has a strategic capacity, however minimal it may be. What he cannot do is renege on decisions once made, pick up his chips, and drop out of the game. He must put up with the consequences of his decisions when alter capitalizes on them to make some countermove. So far we have said nothing that was not said in *The Social System* under the rubric "double contingency." In view of the double contingency principle, individual behavior is limited not only by ego's dependency on a particular alter with whom he happens to be engaged in a relationship, but also, owing to the existence of impersonal relations and to the broadening of the field of applicability of the norms, by the need to deal with a generalized other. This restriction on behavior is aggravated by the existence of expectations and sanctions of many different kinds, and at the same time by the variety of media through which such expectations and sanctions are expressed.

Power may be described in two ways: in terms of society's hold (both positive and negative) on the individual, by means of which he is induced to work toward the achievement of common goals, and in terms of the strategies that the individual adopts for his own ends (whether cooperative or competitive). There are three possible interpretations of violations of the norms by individual actors. One is that they are only making errors of no great significance. Another is that even though they may be violating the norm in significant respects, they do so without jeopardizing the integrity of the normative structure as such; indeed, their very violations add to the richness and complexity of that structure. Finally, they may be changing the system in ways that signal its eventual breakdown or lay the groundwork for its replacement by something new. According to the analyses of socialization and social control and deviance in *The Social System*, a wide variety of malfunctions may occur in the interaction process and in the control mechanisms that ensure that the behavior of the actors will conform to the norms. These malfunctions may be of an idiosyncratic kind, some of which are essentially random and insignificant both for the individual and the group, while others, though insignificant for the group, are important for the individual. Noncontagious, essentially private forms of deviant behavior belong to the latter category. At this point we might do well to consider certain types of adolescent behavior that seem bizarre to adults. Some such behavior ceases to appear "irrational" if regarded as a phase in the learning process. The learning process (meaning not only the goal but the process qua process) endows apparently aberrant behavior with meaning. But this meaning, as set forth in the guise of a norm, is not necessarily the same as the subjective sense the actor makes of his own behavior pattern. The actor builds up his own meaning over the course of his life in the process of establishing connections between his expectations and the consequences that actually ensue.

Norms change, not only in the eyes of the actor who, as he grows older, learns new ways of behaving and new codes, but also in the eyes of the observer, whose comparative observations of the same society in different states over an extended period of time reveal that the normative system itself has been rather profoundly altered. Since the symbolic media exert control over behavior in ways that cannot be reduced to enforcement of conformity, whether by means of external sanctions or internalized manipulation, it must be admitted that the relation between the actor and the normative system is a dynamic one. Not only does the norm operate through the socialization process to bring about changes in the actor; the actor's manner of interpretation also brings about changes in the norm.

Normative change is a possibility inherent in the interaction process. But what kind of change does the norm undergo? A gradual alteration? A radical break with the past? Partial, local change? A change that amounts to an innovation, applicable in circumstances other than those peculiar to its origins and amenable to combination with previous innovations incorporated into a relatively substantial tradition of change? Most theories of social change make use of two dichotomies: endogenous/exogenous and continuous/discontinuous. By concentrating on innovation, Parsons teaches us how to distinguish between modifications in the interaction system and changes in the normative-symbolic structure. His approach also helps us to avoid the dilemma that besets others: having to choose between reproduction ad infinitum of the status quo on the one hand, and the providential occurrence of a radical break, out of which something altogether unforeseen is supposed to emerge, on the other.

Change and Differentiation

In his autobiography [1970*a*, pp. 850–51], Parsons observes that it was around 1963 that evolutionary problems once again took on a special importance for him. In that year he took part along with Robert Bellah and S. N. Eisenstadt in a seminar in which those problems were discussed.[1] Parsons has left us with a very clear description of his own reasons for being interested in the subject: "This line of interest, of course, constitutes a continuation of my concern with Weber's comparative and historical perspective, particularly in its relation to the nature and problems of modern society." Social scientific thinking about these problems can draw on work already done on comparable questions in the biological sciences.

Unlike many sociologists, physiologists do not make the mistake of confusing change with evolution. The relation between a living thing and its environment is constantly changing in one respect or another, and life might even be defined as those changes that enable the living thing to sustain itself as a relatively independent and self-subsistent being by means of controlled exchange with its environment. Evolution is change of quite another order. Evolution involves the emergence at a specific moment in time of a trait or complex of traits necessitating a radical modification of the relation between the individual or species and the environment. Heredity will pass these new traits on to subsequent generations. Accordingly, Parsons argues, we must distinguish "between the physiological processes by which the state of the individual organism is maintained or changed, and evolutionary processes involving change in the genetic constitution of the species" [1970*a*, p. 851].

This distinction had already been discussed in *Economy and Society* [1956, p. 247]. It made possible a contrast between "processes within the system" and "processes of the system." The former involve fluctuations around an equilibrium position. Saying that a system has an equilibrium position, however, is not the same thing as saying that it is static. "The rates of inputs and outputs are not assumed to be constant. . . . But . . . such changes are in general relatively small in magnitude and short in duration. The 'equilibrium' conception is that such relatively small changes tend to be 'counteracted' by the effects of their repercussions on other parts of the system, in such a way that the original state tends to be restored."

Processes of the system differ from processes within the system in three ways. First, the changes they bring about are greater in magnitude and longer in duration. Second, the restorative mechanisms lose their effectiveness: the system no longer returns on its own to its initial position. On the contrary, it diverges ever more widely from its equilibrium state, and before settling into a new state passes through "periods of disequilibrium and/or unstable equilibrium." Finally, processes of the system bring about a *qualitative* transformation of the system and its institutional structure.

In order to see these "changes in the state of society" in more concrete terms, let us introduce a new distinction, which revolves around the difference between norms and values. Certain changes *of* society take place without posing a threat to the common values. Change is confined to the area of norms and procedures. On the other hand, change may involve both values and norms, since changes in values will require a reworking of the norms. The change in this case will be more arduous and time-consuming. It took centuries, for example, to introduce Christian values into the ancient world, and reworking of the whole institutional structure was required.

By way of example, let us consider a very important, though limited, institutional transformation, which first emerged in industrial firms in the United States and has since spread to nearly all capitalist societies: separation of the ownership of the means of production from the power to make decisions. Parsons accepts the view of Berle and Means that the owners of large businesses no longer run them, but he does not interpret that view in the way that has subsequently become popular. What Parsons takes from the work of Berle and Means is not that the "managers" are becoming a "new class" or a "technocratic elite," but something rather less sweeping. "At the time of the large-scale introduction of the corporate form of organization soon after the middle of the nineteenth century, and certainly before that, the control of the business firm lay overwhelmingly in the hands of the same 'people' (e.g., household units) who legally owned . . . the property employed as capital in the enterprise. . . . [Today] the locus of real control may, of course, vary from a group of 'insiders' on the board to career managers not on the board at all" [1956, pp. 253–54]. The separation of ownership and control was accomplished by "dispersion of voting stock ownership which had come to be held primarily as an investment" and by the rise of "managers," many of whom owned no stock at all.

It would not be unreasonable to say that this transformation marked the beginning of a new age of capitalism, characterized by a new distribution of the power of decision-making. How is this change to be explained? Parsons points first of all to the strength of the resentment aroused in the last decade of the nineteenth century by the enormous fortunes that the great tycoons who profited from the uncontrolled

phase of industrial expansion that followed the Civil War had managed
to amass. Because of the intensity of the wave of "populist"[2] feeling,
"the Vanderbilts, Harrimans, Morgans, Carnegies, Rockefellers, [and
so forth] . . . failed to consolidate their position as the dominant *class* in
the society."[3] American industrialization in the period 1865–80 *might
have* given rise to a closed ruling class, set apart from the populace in
the European manner. This did not happen. Limits were placed on the
power of the tycoons, but only because that power had stirred up
resistance of many varieties: moral outrage in the "muckraking" press
and protests from regions and industries hurt by the monopoly of the
oil, rail, steel, and coal barons. Another factor, perhaps the most
important of all, was the abundance of skill and talent that could find
no employment within the restrictive framework of the family firm.
Protest against the established order was one aspect of the change;
another was the emergence of new kinds of institutions. There is,
however, no reason whatever to think that these new institutional
forms were somehow "final causes," that they *caused* the crisis.

American business did in fact change, and by changing it managed
to survive and grow. Vague at the outset, the role of the capitalist later
split into two roles: in the place of the solitary capitalist we now find
both owners and managers. The analogies cited by Parsons (with "binary fission," e.g.) help to remind us that differentiation is a cardinal
point of the theory of action. Differentiation in the form of splitting or
proliferation of roles provides the actor with an escape from the dilemma he faces when he must contend with adversaries holding views
diametrically opposed to his own.[4] In the socialization process, for
example, the incest taboo forces the child to forgo the familiarity he
once enjoyed with his mother, thereby setting tenderness apart from
sensual gratification. When a growth process encounters obstacles,
however, differentiation is neither an inevitable result nor an optimal
solution to the problems to be faced. The mere fact that tycoons,
engineers, and the general public enter into a period of tense relations
no more guarantees that a transition to a "higher form" of organization
will take place than the troubles of adolescence necessarily presage a
happy adulthood.

What is more, the separation of ownership and control goes hand in
hand with another process, which might be called integration through
cybernetic regulation, not to be confused with mere segmentation.
"Since the 'managerial revolution' the functions of 'ownership' and
'control' have become differentiated in American big business in the
sense that distinct units of organization usually perform these functions. . . . [But] the division of the original Standard Oil Company

into several regional Standard Oil companies" was not an example of genuine differentiation. Indeed, the "new companies [were] approximately the same as each other and the 'parent' company." This is what we mean by segmentation. By contrast, in a process of true differentiation, "the new units are neither structurally nor functionally equivalent, but each contributes different specialized ingredients to a more general function" [1956, p. 256]. Furthermore, the various "specialized contributions" are subject to evaluation by common criteria and to the control of a common authority. They are distinct, individual parts of a new whole, in which they figure as interdependent elements of a hierarchy controlled by a common system of values.

The new relations between the two groups are viable only if they have been suitably redefined or "restructured." Managers are no longer under the thumbs of the owners, but this does not necessarily mean that the owners disappear or become mere figureheads. Managers and owners may enter into a kind of "cooperative" relationship. The former head of a family firm may decide to "specialize" in public relations or "public service," or he may strike out on his own in new business ventures, particularly in banking. He is hardly expelled from the firm, but rather assumes a new role within it, responsible for planning, coordination, and innovation. "The typical Board of Directors of a large corporation probably approximates the result of restructuring, for it represents both sets of interests [ownership and control] without any clear-cut primacy relation" [1956, p. 269]. This common locus for information, discussion, and decision-making serves to coordinate the differentiated activities by bringing together the various parties involved and providing avenues for cooperation. Differentiation is thus not merely a matter of altering existing activities but involves the actual separation of the newly created units. The various fragments of the organization coexist side by side, however, and are parts of one system, which exerts control over all of them.

An example of structural change, quite characteristic of the industrialization process in general, appears in Parsons's 1960 article entitled "Some Considerations on Social Change."[5] Reverting to views worked out in his earliest writings, he treats a phenomenon that he deems vitally important in industrial growth, namely, differentiation of the range of activities once carried on within the household (involving relations between a married couple and their children and forebears), which gradually come to be distinguished from economic and professional activities proper, the latter being carried on outside the home, in a workplace at some distance away. From his outside occupation the individual earns the income necessary to buy what he needs on the consumer goods market. In this separation of domestic and professional roles we find certain features similar to those we noted above in connection with the separation of ownership and control in the business firm. The differentiation of domestic and economic functions gives rise to tensions and problems of several kinds, which the sociologist may view in three different ways: from the standpoint, first, of roles; second, of the family (a special kind of collectivity); and third, of society as a whole, given society's need to exert greater control over both domestic and productive units.

To look first at roles, we may consider, for instance, the father in his capacity as teacher. Because under modern conditions the best part of his time is spent outside the home, he can no longer be the guide who, "in the good old days," used to apprentice his son to a craft. The absent father relinquishes this role to the mother or schoolteacher. If we now consider what changes have taken place within the nuclear family, we find that it is not enough merely to observe that the household is no longer a self-sufficient unit of production and consumption: work, which now takes place not at home but at a place of business, is done under completely different conditions. The producer loses his independence and comes more and more to work under the close supervision of the "capitalist" and his foremen. What is more, since apprenticeship and professional training are no longer family functions, the only possibilities for acquiring a skill are on-the-job training (controlled by the "capitalist") and formal education at school. At a later time the government intervenes in the role of regulator of working conditions (e.g., by setting the length of the working day and standards for the protection of workers, especially women and children) and educational standards. School attendance, for instance, when made compulsory through early adolescence, has a twofold effect: influencing the supply of labor, while at the same time shifting to outside institutions the burden of responsibilities traditionally borne by the family.

From the initial differentiation follow a welter of consequences. The family as an institution enters into a period of crisis, the resolution of which must be sought outside the family. In this enlarged context, institutions of social control must cope with five problem areas or sources of tension, which Parsons lists as follows [1970c, p. 106]:

(1) a loss of function by the kinship unit, (2) a new pattern of organization of the functions which have come to be dissociated

from the kinship unit, (3) a substitution of new ways of taking care of the needs of the kinship unit which are occasioned by the loss of service to it, (4) a way of organizing the terms of their relationship including the handling of the risks entailed in "cutting loose" from kinship in favor of employment in the new organization, and (5) a way of balancing the legitimation of both units at both the collectivity and role levels so that the inevitable component of conflict of interest is "contained" within a pattern of mutual contribution to higher-order system functioning.[6]

Segmentation is one thing, differentiation another. In order for differentiated elements to coexist and cooperate within the same normative context, the differentiation process must take place under the control of one or more of the regulatory mechanisms that we encountered previously in connection with the socialization of the individual and the control of deviance. The initial conditions of the differentiation process are comparable with those we observed in all the critical phases of individual development. In Parsons's terms, there is an overabundance in A (excess of instrumental and adaptive capacities) and a shortage in G (of capacities of allocation and coordination). Factors available in A remain idle because G has no way of putting them to use. The resulting malaise threatens to continue so long as no opportunities for employment have been created by initiatives taken in G. The captains of industry might have become a ruling class had they barred new blood from entering their ranks, but this might have provoked a strong reaction on the part of those excluded as well as the general public.

The analysis of tensions characteristic of the first phase of change suggests a comparison between individual socialization and institutional change. But such a comparison must be undertaken with caution. It makes no sense to say that a society in a transitional period encounters the same problems as a child or adolescent undergoing socialization. In rapidly changing societies many individuals do indeed find themselves confronted with new tasks and roles. But each of these individuals has reached a particular stage of life. Learning the role of a factory worker means one thing when the person being trained is himself the son of a worker and has just left school, and another thing when that person is a farmer's son who is obliged to learn a new trade because he has been forced to sell the family farm at the age of 30, after spending 15 years of his life working in the fields. What is more, occupational roles, such as those of the worker or the farmer, each with its own specific content, are quite different—they are more specialized and specific—from such broad cultural roles as male, female, youth, adult, or retiree. Thus it is easy to see why socialization, from which we learn primarily roles of the second kind, is not equivalent to learning in general. Nevertheless, the socialization of an individual and the learning of new roles both rely on similar mechanisms in order to deal with analogous problems.

Only if two conditions are satisfied can the individual learn: first, he must be motivated to learn by the prospect that he will be deprived of desired gratifications if he continues to act as he has acted in the past; second, he must be endowed with capacities that will enable him, if he has the opportunity, to behave as the new model requires. Societies undergoing change must meet the same requirements. The tensions associated with change are created by obstacles to the employment of new inputs. But such tensions also encourage people to press on with the process, so as to make new resources available, in new combinations. Like individual learning, social change takes the form of a kind of dynamic instability, a tendency to narrow the gap between the costs (of giving up old habits and old ways of doing things) and the expected benefits. Change often involves a danger of careening out of control, just as socialization involves dangers of deviance and regression.

Accordingly, the paradigm of social control, which is based on the familiar notions of permissiveness, support, and denial of reciprocity, can shed a good deal of light on processes of change. Is innovation treated permissively enough to allow the innovator the freedom he needs to experiment and to take the risks associated with experimentation? Or is he ridiculed as an inveterate fool, even before he has been given an opportunity to prove himself? Permissiveness is a rather diffuse criterion. A more positive requirement is support. Can the innovator rely on the *support* of certain groups, and if so, which ones? Finally, *denial of reciprocity* is central to the question of profit, and Parsons, following Schumpeter, sees such denial as the source of the "crucial reward" in the dynamic of innovation. The innovator lays claim to a portion of the surplus stemming from his innovation, and if he takes more than his share, no one can object, at least not initially. But "the prospect of profit does *not* account for the *genesis* of the motivation to innovate" [1956, p. 266]. Or, rather, the prospect of profit is an effective motivation to innovate only if profit is legitimate within the society's system of values: the question to ask is, How do the other parties involved, as well as the general public, react to the profit reaped by the innovator? Profit is "essentially unstable" [1956, p. 269] in amount and manner of production. Each innovation threatens to make earlier innovations worthless. Finally, the innovator's rewards are affected by a principle of justice implicit in the denial of reciprocity, which justifies the advantage the innovator receives, provided that his behavior is in conformity with the system of values.

Programs and Short Cuts

The order in which the phases of a process occur affects the nature of that process. There is a normal order, or "program," disruption of which disrupts social control. In the socialization "program," for example, a "short circuit" in the normal course of the program manifests itself in the appearance of neurosis. Smelser finds like instances of subversion of symbolic controls in the history of the industrial revolution, in particular in his study of the textile industry in England. The period he focuses on is one that saw a crisis in the adaptive function and definition of a new code of rights and obligations in the G function. The disequilibrium first spread in G (either within the management of the productive units or in the administrative bodies of society as a whole), then in I (in both primary workers' groups—the home, the family, or the workplace—and such worker associations as guilds and unions).

The malfunctioning of the traditional controls can be explained either by the emergence of exogenous factors (such as technological innovation or an unexpected influx of money into the economy) or by changes in endogenous factors (feelings, beliefs, practices). The malfunction may result in either a breakup or a breakthrough. In either case we find that the control network has been short-circuited. Smelser begins by laying down the "normal" sequence of tensions and resolutions, a sequence of seven phases leading to the elaboration of a new normative system. In stage 1, characterized by dissatisfaction, the producer is not satisfied in either of his roles: family head or entrepreneur. This dissatisfaction relates, on the one hand, to the level of profits, the organization of work, and the structure of the market, and, on the other hand, to the scarcity of the resources available to the family and the difficulty of "earning a living."[7] Stage 2, the stage of turbulence, is characterized on the ideological level by the surfacing of negative attitudes as well as by more and more acute hostility between traditionalists and reformers. Utopian schemes first make their appearance during this stage. Stage 3 is witness to the mobilization of "repressive" agencies (courts, police, local organizations), which attempt to hold back or co-opt the reform movement. In stage 4 "new ideas" begin to overcome the handicaps of censorship. Instead of being looked upon as shocking and outrageous, the novel solutions

201 **Social Change**

are recognized, at least by certain social groups, as having some "positive" value by virtue of their novelty. In phase 5, specific solutions are sought for specific problems, but the scope of these solutions is still limited. Phase 7 sees the consolidation of the results achieved in phase 6, the effects of which are extended to the entire society.

This sequence of stages is reminiscent of the maturation of a normal personality. Under the guidance of a benevolent, enlightened, and self-possessed teacher, the normal individual gradually increases his control over circumstances without provoking extreme anxieties. The teleological cast to Smelser's model must not be exaggerated, however. Many sociologists who exhibit nothing but scorn for "psychologism" do, of course, envision change as a process guided by an invisible hand or by the ruses of History/Providence in one guise or another; it is supposed, in either case, that change has a purpose, namely, to replace an obsolete social order with a new order, presumably more efficient and satisfying. The slogan that "societies only set themselves such problems as they can solve," from which the evolutionist optimism of vulgar Marxism takes sustenance, is vitiated by any of a number of objections. To begin with, this view of the matter holds that "society" possesses a consciousness of its problems and resources, whereas in fact such consciousness exists only in the minds of a small minority of society's members, and even then in a highly deficient form. What is more, the suggestion implicit in this unfortunate slogan is that a "problem" once given always admits of one solution and one solution only, and that this one solution is optimal (or at least that the search for a solution continues so long as the optimal solution has not been attained).

Now, the notion that such a thing as the "one best way" exists leads to impossible paradoxes, which we are in no way obliged to accept. To defend such a view, at least where historical development is concerned, is to heap sophism upon sophism. The argument bogs down in a series of dilemmas: either History has no meaning, or else, if it has a meaning, it can only consist in the gradual "becoming" of the Subject of which History is the history.[8] This might make sense if History were totalized, if it were complete, and if all its moments were equally present in the consciousness of the Subject of history or of whoever speaks in its name. For sublunary creatures such as ourselves, however, such a view has the disadvantage of assigning to an abstraction, Mankind, which in reality is no more than a collection of individuals or a cultural repository, a destiny modeled on what the individual actor takes to be his own destiny. To avoid sophistry of this kind, we have only to admit that a process need not have just one meaning but may well have several. To interpret the meanings appropriate to each moment we need neither interpret the entire process as though all its moments coexisted in time nor wait until the process has run its course.

A process need not *necessarily* lead to the emergence of a certain form, even if that form is "higher" than the one existing when the process began: such an outcome is only one of a possible range of outcomes. Furthermore, even if the process arrives at a point where the new form is quite likely to crystallize, relatively severe instabilities may yet occur, and even the possibility of regression cannot be ruled out entirely. The course of the process may be detoured so as to break off progress temporarily or even halt it permanently. In attempting to explain such anomalies in the normal sequence of events, Smelser was led to his concept of "collective behavior":[9] "an uninstitutionalized mobilization for action in order to modify one or more kinds of strain on the basis of a generalized reconstitution of a component of action." An abnormal sequence of events threatens the equilibrium of the entire symbolic-normative system. Certain new forms of behavior will not be institutionalized, while some old forms will lose their institutional legitimacy, gradually or abruptly. Noninstitutionalized forms of behavior will proliferate, since many kinds of behavior will no longer have institutional sanction, while others will not yet have been sanctioned.

When this happens, change takes the form of crisis, and the actor will feel a tension between his goals and his resources. In such a situation, one temptation is to look for a solution in the form of a "miracle cure," although this might, from a logico-experimental standpoint, seem relatively or totally inefficient, if not downright harmful. As Smelser says, "Collective behavior is the action of the impatient." This impatience tends to embitter conflicts and to lead the collectivity down paths that do not culminate in its self-proclaimed ends.

The danger of a short circuit in the normal sequence of events (whether due to fixation or to regression) is inherent in processes of change, just as dangers of early or late development, which may have an impact on personality, are inherent in the socialization process. Ongoing differentiation of a normative structure is only one of the elements we must keep in mind when diagnosing changes *of* society. Differentiation may help to resolve earlier conflicts, or it may lead to confrontations among the individuals assigned to play the newly differentiated roles. What is more, whether differentiation carries with it solutions or is pregnant with new problems, it affects the performance of the system, which may be either enhanced or degraded. Hence differentiation cannot be treated solely as a process; the effects of that process must also be considered.

These efforts may be distributed throughout society as "impersonal relations," or they may be relatively localized in peculiar new combinations of resources. This was clear to Parsons as early as *The Structure of Social Action:* "The properties of the system of action are emergent only when the relations between the actors have attained a certain level of complexity." Furthermore, "It is impossible to say, on the basis of data describing an isolated rational act directed toward an immediate goal and in a context of strictly specified conditions and means, whether or not that act is rational." Such a judgment is possible only from the standpoint of the whole within which the act in question occurs, through the complex of ends and means of which it is an element. From the notion of a whole or system, which *The Structure of Social Action* attributes to Whitehead, we move to the notion of a combination, defined as the addition of an element to a collection of other elements, by means of which that collection is transformed into a system. What is important in this definition is the idea of discovery, of "something new," or, as Schumpeter called it, "innovation," a term that has passed into common usage. Two features distinguish innovation from circular flow (which Parsons calls change *in* society). First, innovation is neither marginal nor incremental. What is more, the inputs, the ingredients that enter into combination, receive their values ex post in the light of the innovation. This is what Parsons is hinting at when he speaks of "adaptive upgrading." Adaptive upgrading is a kind of change in which "the participating people, as well as the collectivity as a whole, ... become more productive than before, as measured by some kind of output-cost relationship" [1966, pp. 22–23]. The change may involve individuals, particular collectivities, or society as a whole. Role adaptation can occur in such a way as to increase the productivity of the individual role without "upgrading" the collectivity within which it is played. The collectivity may even suffer an overall decline of efficiency. Similarly, it is possible for certain individuals to become more "productive" at the expense of other individuals, with no net change in the cost-output ratio for society as a whole. This ratio, incidentally, may be calculated in terms of any set of costs or outputs of A, expressed in real or monetary terms.

Parsons does not neglect what might be called the nonadaptive aspect of adaptive upgrading. Differentiation is not always accompanied by progress. The recessive aspects of change (to which sociologists refer as anomie or disorganization) must not be forgotten.

Relatively complex institutions are frequently rejected by societies onto which they have been grafted. Seemingly promising innovations—or perhaps one ought to say inventions—sometimes do not take hold. What seemed about to take off may crash in flames.[10] The explanation is not far to seek. Indeed, "adaptive upgrading . . . requires that specialized functional capacities be freed from ascription within more diffuse structural units. There is, then, a reliance upon more *generalized* resources that are independent of their ascriptive sources. For these reasons, differentiation and upgrading processes may require the *inclusion* in a status of full membership in the relevant general community system of previously excluded groups which have developed legitimate capacities to 'contribute' to the functioning of the system. . . . A system or sub-system undergoing a process of differentiation, however, encounters a functional problem which is the opposite of specification: the establishment of a version of the value pattern appropriate to the new *type* of system which is emerging. Since this type is generally more complex than its predecessor, its value pattern must be couched at a higher level of *generality* in order to legitimize the wider variety of goals and functions of its sub-units." Furthermore, "Any given value system is characterized by a particular type of *pattern,* so that, when it is institutionalized, it establishes the desirability of a *general type of social system.* By what we have called specification, such a general variation is 'spelled out' in its implications for the various differentiated sub-systems and the various segmental units. Hence the value orientation appropriate to a particular collectivity, role, or norm-complex is not the general pattern of the system, but an adjusted, specialized 'application' of it" [1966, p. 23].

The sociologist cannot treat change as though it consisted in a sequence of instantaneous modifications following one another in an arbitrary order. On the other hand, there is no such thing as the famous "direction of history": change is no more a trend in a certain general direction than it is a miscellany of unrelated events. Philosophers, of course, tend to find in the labors of historians only what they are looking for: the nominalist will cull such historical facts as "the marquise went out at five o'clock" or "John Lackland visited here," while the Comtean, Hegelian, or Marxist will discern the laws of history, in the light of which the past and future of mankind acquire a meaning. The mind-set of the sociologist is different: his choice is to treat societies as systems of action governed by internal controls and certain conditions in the external environment. Accordingly, when the sociologist undertakes to compare two different states of an institution or society, he will consider the relations that constitute it as a system and ask how these are affected by changes in one of the system's characteristic dimensions (or functions). What happens to G, for example, when there are changes in A, I, or L? How can the nature of such changes be spelled out?

Thus Parsons analyzes change in terms of functions, variables, and cybernetic controls. On the A level, change is a process of upgrading. On the G level, a process of splitting, opposition, or exit—as we have seen in the case of capitalist firms that introduced a separation of ownership and control. On the I level, a process of "inclusion"—where this term, which will be defined shortly, refers to the entry of new individuals or groups into society as well as to the consequences of such entry for the normative controls. On the L level, change is a process of legitimation (by specification and generalization combined). As for the variables, it is not hard to identify which of them are pertinent to the theory of change. Upgrading requires that technical roles be assigned to the most capable and motivated individuals. It therefore presupposes a certain mobility of the factors, with the risks attendant thereupon. The "freedom from ascription" mentioned in the long passage cited above harks back to the quality/performance and universalism/particularism variables. Inclusion involves expansion of the domain in which the normative system holds sway. Hence the universalism/particularism variable is involved. Inclusion does not—at least not immediately—pertain to all roles played by newcomers, however. Such persons may, for example, be affected by inclusion in their roles as producers, consumers, or citizens, and yet find themselves only indirectly concerned in their roles as fathers, husbands, or members of a particular political party or church. "The more diffuse structural units" that result from the inclusion process have to do with the specificity/diffuseness variable. To the extent that these new units are "societal communities," however, they function in quite different ways from the modes prevalent in the familial or territorial groups that predominated in earlier forms of organization. The specificity/diffuseness variable cannot, therefore, fully describe their functioning. As we shall see later on, the quality/performance variable is also necessary to explain the nature of the new "solidarities." To sum up, then, we have found that each of the phases of change (differentiation, upgrading, inclusion, specification) is characterized by a pair of fundamental variables. What remains now for us to do is to look into the way the different phases fit together to establish a general trend. This will enable us to follow the sequence of *states* through which a particular society must pass as it undergoes change.

The Evolutionary Universals and the Diaspora

According to Max Weber, History "is not a cab which one can have stopped at one's pleasure."[11] Change is not a process in which we can intervene as we please, at least not if we care about having some reasonable likelihood of success. The phases of change are systematically interrelated and occur in a certain order, although the sequence of events may be affected by the occurrence of what we earlier referred to as "short circuits." There is a logic to the order of change, though not the implacable logic of the steamroller. The fact that a process is systematic does not imply that it is totalizable—at least not in the sense in which one speaks of a "concrete totality," that is, an integrated system of interaction such as Parsons's "societal community." The group consisting of all persons who have benefited from the innovations that have accumulated over the course of history is not a "concrete totality," for example. In other words, in the absence of absolute knowledge and a universal state, "mankind" is not a sociological but a cultural category,[12] that is, a relatively consistent set of symbolic codes and traditions to which one or more meanings may be given, independent of the system of interaction in which the codes originated, and which in principle are comprehensible by any actor whatsoever.

The two societies whose innovations in religion, thought, and politics have had the greatest impact on the development of mankind, namely, Israel and Greece, exemplify what Parsons calls "seed-bed societies," the nature of which it will be worthwhile to examine further. Israel and Greece, "though having relatively small consequence in the society-systems of their time and place, were the agents of cultural innovations that have proved of the highest significance for a wide range of societies which were not their direct evolutionary sequels" [1966, p. 96]. In neither the biological nor the genealogical sense are we the heirs of the Jews of antiquity or the citizens of Periclean Athens. Though there may be no very strict or clear-cut line of descent linking them to us, or perhaps even linking them to those who nowadays boast of being their heirs, we are nevertheless indebted to both the ancient Greeks and the ancient Jews for what is uniquely and preeminently valuable in our tradition. This twin miracle, as it might be called, raises two sorts of problems, according to Parsons. First, what made innovation possible must be explained: How were the idea of monotheism and the concept of "secular" science and philosophy arrived at? Second, how did they spread and endure beyond the times and places in which they actually figured in relations of exchange and domination? As to the first question, such radical innovations in culture could only have been born and could only have flourished within the great empires of the era. They could only have arisen within tiny minorities within those empires, minorities cut off from the outside world. These minorities, moreover, had to possess an unshakable sense of their identity, capable of resisting assimilation.[13] As for the spread of the innovations, the more easily they could be dissociated from the societies in which they originated, the more readily they could become widely diffused.

How do innovations associated with a particular time and place become "evolutionary universals," to use Parsons's term?[14] The diffusion of such institutions as parliaments (which originated in England) and business organization along modern lines (which originated in northwestern Europe and North America) raises problems analogous to those associated with the spread of monotheism in its Jewish, Christian, and Islamic forms. What must be grasped in each case is how a contingent and particular combination of circumstances is transformed into a universal or universalizable formula.

An evolutionary universal is "any organizational development sufficiently important to further evolution that, rather than emerging only once, it is likely to be 'hit upon' by various systems operating under different conditions" [1967, p. 491]. The problem implicit in this definition is similar to the one the biologist must deal with in order to explain how an innovation such as vision first occurred and subsequently spread to new species. In this case, too, we may speak of universals, though these differ in at least one respect from sociological universals: they cannot be treated as the product of symbolic interaction. Vision was a mutation of the utmost importance in the history of living things, because of the range and kind of information about both proximate and remote environments that it made available to creatures. This crucial innovation occurred in several distinct species independently and under different conditions—not without analogy to the independent discovery of the theory of action by Durkheim, Weber, and Pareto. Furthermore, while vision resides in anatomically distinct sites in each of the three orders in which it first appeared—mollusks, insects, and vertebrates—the organs involved all exhibit the same biochemical mechanisms, based on vitamin A. Whatever its mechanisms or structures, vision "seems to be a genuine prerequisite of *all* the higher levels of organic evolution."[15]

Parsons introduces the idea of prerequisites cautiously and in a roundabout way. Unlike the theory of socialization, the theory of prerequisites involves no continuous sequence of dialectically interrelated phases. Going over Parsons's list of historical-social "universals" will help us to understand their nature. We can classify the universals into three categories. One contains universals in the strong sense of the term, such as religion, social organization through kinship (with the incest taboo), language, and technology. These symbolic and normative organizational forms are "features of even the simplest action system," and, furthermore, "no known human society has existed without *all* four in relatively definite relations to each other" [1967, p. 495]. This being the case, we may treat these four features as functional prerequisites of any societal community, where the latter term is to be understood in Parsons's sense.

To say that the "evolutionary universals" are prerequisites might mean one of two things: either that without them there would be no society at all, or else that societies in which they occur have a decisive advantage over societies in which they do not. Parsons plainly had the second meaning in mind when he wrote, "An evolutionary universal, then, is a complex of structures and associated processes the development of which so increases the long-run adaptive capacity of living systems in a given class that only systems that develop the complex can attain certain higher levels of general adaptive capacity" [1967, p. 493].

This description is applicable to the second category of universals, which I shall call "quasi-universals": bureaucracy, money, and the market. No human society has ever existed without language, an incest taboo of some sort, and some level of technology, however minimal (gleaning, for instance). But there have been and still are societies without bureaucracy. There are others in which money plays no role. Nor is there any fixed evolutionary scheme according to which a bureaucratic phase must precede the inception of markets. Owing to the "adaptive upgrading" of societies equipped with a bureaucratic apparatus to facilitate the mobilization and utilization of collective resources, such societies have a decisive advantage over their competitors. Hence bureaucratic forms of organization will ultimately be copied and spread widely, if someone does not first have the inspiration to reinvent them. Certain forms of organization have become universal because the seed-bed societies in which they first took root obtained a competitive edge as a result; in addition, these organizational forms acquire a certain independence of the societies that supported them initially, which makes their transmission by symbolic means possible; in other words, they can be passed on without direct interaction, merely by remote insemination.

There is a third, intermediary category of evolutionary universals, which includes the related phenomena of stratification and legitimation. While not prerequisites of the same degree of universality as language or technology, stratification and legitimation are less contingent than bureaucratic organization or a money economy. There is no society that is not stratified, or at least differentiated, but the principles of stratification are so varied that it is hard to say what is universal about them: a class system such as we find in the original capitalist societies and the sort of hierarchy prevalent in certain Pacific tribes have so little in common that to say that stratification is universal is to say very little. In treating both stratification and universalization, therefore, we must understand that we are not looking at universal attributes so much as at a process of universalization whereby a variety of groups, activities, and decisions tend to be subsumed under a single hierarchy of values. To say that a society is stratified is to say that there is a prestige system (or several prestige systems battling for preeminence) that establishes *differences* in value between one position and another of significance to individuals and groups in the society. The society, accordingly, acquires a certain (arguable) unity, the unity of an ideal system, whether already established or to be established by collective action. In these terms, then, legitimation is the process whereby the prestige system on which the system of stratification is based comes to be established; the legitimation process sets forth the conditions under which an act of alter's can be recognized as legitimate by ego, particularly if ego is in a position of authority. With such recognition of the legitimate act goes mutual recognition by ego and alter of their subsumption under the same "we." In Parsons's own formulation, "explicit cultural legitimation" is "the emergence of an institutionalized cultural definition of the society of reference, namely a referent of 'we' . . . which is differentiated . . . from other societies, while the merit of we-ness is asserted in a normative context" [1967, p. 501].

Stratification and legitimation are not "universals" in the sense that language and technology are universals, nor are they "universals" in the sense that bureaucracies and markets are. They are "universals" to the extent that they give rise to comprehensive systems that make it possible to classify most types of actors and actions. But they are more dependent on the content of social systems than are such symbolic media as language, religion, social organization on the basis of kinship, or even technology. Universals like stratification and legitimation highlight the importance as well as the ambiguity of the process of inclusion, which is one particular mechanism of universalization of value criteria.

The Process of Inclusion

The phenomenon of inclusion is central to the theory of change. Inclusion defines one characteristic dimension of change and is one of its central mechanisms. A consideration of the inclusion process will also help us to distinguish between those aspects of change that have to do with values and those that have to do with norms. So long as our attention is focused on the "evolutionary universals," that is, novel and autonomous combinations that spread from seed-bed societies to other societies, the distinction between norms and values is of relatively little importance: the evolutionary universal involves change in both norms and values at the same time. Jewish monotheism entailed a revolution in both norms (pertaining to the nature of the law and of political authority) and values (pertaining to the relations between the sacred and the profane). But the separation of ownership and control, which was of the utmost importance for the normative system of the capitalist firm, did not jeopardize the basic values of American society but rather consummated the *inclusion* into the group of decision makers of actors previously denied access thereto. In analytical terms, inclusion is a broadening of the area of competence and responsibility of certain actors, which is accomplished by a redefinition of the normative system. Of course, the emergence of an evolutionary universal is also accompanied by redefinition of traditional roles in the areas of law, economic activity, politics, and religion. If the emergence of an evolutionary universal fundamentally alters the way factors of production are combined, inclusion of the zealous partisans of the change in question may even lead to the destruction of society. While problems of inclusion always occur in connection with the emergence of evolutionary universals, such problems may also arise in other circumstances.

Parsons analyzes the inclusion process associated with the immigration of various ethnic minorities to the United States, which came in several waves. The difficulties of including the new groups may be envisaged according to Smelser's model. The problem then becomes one of relating those difficulties to the overall process. At the beginning of the process society is assumed to be in a more or less stable state. During the course of inclusion social relations within the society are redefined, and the eventual result is said to be a new and more or less enduring state of equilibrium.

In its ethnic composition American society was initially relatively homogeneous. "The core was surely white, Anglo-Saxon and Protestant (WASP)."[16] Outside this central core group, of course, there were certain minority groups, such as the black slaves, the Catholics of Maryland, a few Jews, and some Dutch. A problem of inclusion arises when a compact minority group seeks to gain access to the "societal community" and to obtain full citizenship. A necessary condition for the establishment of a societal community is that social identity must cease to be based on ascription. The citizen must be defined other than by his membership in a particular family, professional, ethnic, linguistic, or religious group. The political community to which the citizen belongs straddles all these boundaries. When I say that I am an American, I mean that regardless of my occupation, race, or religion I am a member of a unique and distinctive community to which I owe allegiance, a community that transcends the fundamental, narrow, primordial relations that bind me to my workmates, neighbors, friends, and relatives in the course of everyday life. Furthermore, the societal community is not based solely on authority and constraint. Because it does not rely on domination alone, on *imperium* pure and simple, a societal community presupposes a certain distinction between the government and the society. When I say that I am a citizen, I am saying that I am more than a mere subject, that I participate to some degree in the power that the collectivity exerts over its members. Finally, the members of the societal community are free to come and go as they please, to enter or leave the community's territory. In negative terms, the societal community may be defined as a type of society that cannot be reduced either to ascriptive ties or to mere acquiescence in governmental edict or to enforced residence in an assigned locale. What ethnic minorities want is to move from a society of the first kind (ascriptive, coercive, discriminatory) to a society of the second kind. Parsons calls inclusion "the process by which previously excluded groups attain full citizenship or membership in the societal community" [1967, p. 429], and he compares this with the nineteenth-century acquisition by disadvantaged groups in English society of rights of three kinds, which, following T. H. Marshall, Parsons calls civil rights (or legal rights, namely, the right to enter freely into contracts, under the same conditions for all, which presupposes the elimination of ascriptive particularisms), political rights (the right to vote), and social rights (the right to enjoy a certain level of well-being regardless of income).

One way to describe inclusion is as a debate or confrontation between the officials of the "central" authorities and representatives of "peripheral" groups, the course of which depends on the supply and demand curves of each of the participants. What do the groups seeking inclusion want? What are they offering or contributing? Demands must be judged in the light of the degree of mobilization of the group making them. Supply must be judged against the capability of the group, as determined by the qualifications of its members, to contribute to the collective endeavor. As for the "central authorities," or, as Parsons puts it, "those already in" [1967, p. 436], they can grant relatively limited recognition to demands for inclusion, or hold out more or less indefinitely against such demands. For their part, the one nonnegotiable demand is that their own interests, privileges, and beliefs be accorded some consideration and not condemned out of hand.

The process that Parsons takes for his model—the political and social history of England in the nineteenth century, as interpreted by T. H. Marshall—is one that involved not mortal struggle but compromise. If, in this case, it proved possible to change the relations among the various social groups and allow newcomers access to the inner circle without thereby provoking social disintegration, the reason has to be that it was possible to achieve at least an implicit consensus between "those already in" and their new rivals for power. This by no means implies that the values or interests of capitalists and workers are, or should be, identical. In order for new members to gain access to decision-making power by inclusion achieved through compromise, a necessary, though hardly sufficient, condition is that the candidates for inclusion be in a position to support their demands by appealing to certain fundamental, uncontested common values, thereby accomplishing three things: (1) justification of the demands for inclusion in the eyes of the aspirants themselves; (2) conquest of public opinion; (3) outflanking the opposition by portraying the adversaries as selfish, petty, or even criminal.

Thus the first result of invoking the common values is to justify whoever is invoking them, whether in behalf of change or of the status quo. "Mere affirmation of values is not enough" [1967, p. 454], however, as Parsons is quick to point out. Cries of outrage against injustice may provoke unrest and turmoil but are powerless to bring about change by themselves. The "indignant," as Riesman calls them, have little likelihood of success as long as they remain isolated. A consensus arrived at through praise lavished upon the great principles that are being flouted under the prevailing disorder can be turned into the basis for effective action by the desire to maintain or establish "a single community with full membership for all."[17]

At the risk of belaboring the obvious, we may say that ultimately inclusion is possible because everyone feels an attachment to the old mansion, society, those on the outside trying to get in just as much as those already inside. In view of this attachment, all are compelled to work toward a "more perfect union"—which means that those inside must squeeze together a bit to make room for the newcomers, or else that everyone has to pitch in to build a new addition. In other words, inclusion has an impact on the processes of differentiation and role-redefinition as well as on adaptive upgrading. The inclusion process affects the normative system and the decision-making organs of the society. Values may be spelled out more fully than before, but they are not set aside. Irish, Jews, and Blacks all invoked the American way in support of their demands for first-class citizenship.

The Adjustment of Norms to Values: The Case of the United States

We now come to a point of the utmost importance, having to do with values and their relation to the process of change. On the subject of differentiation, Parsons wrote, "During . . . differentiation, the *main value system* is assumed to remain stable. The change, that is, is not in the value-content of the pattern-maintenance cell of the system in question, but in the number of sub-systems and their structural and functional relations to each other" [1956, p. 256].

One characteristic feature of Parsons's analysis of change is that he assumes that values remain constant in the short run. To justify this assumption is the fact that, as we have seen in our study of the inclusion process, values are invoked even though they are flouted. For example, that basic tenet of the American faith, "All men are equal in the eyes of the law," was used by the most radical advocates of civil rights in their fight against discrimination and for first-class citizenship in the societal community.

As for the stability of values, we find a particularly clear exposition of Parsons's views on the matter in his discussion of David Riesman's well-known ideas about the "changing American character."[18] According to Riesman, the "American character" or culture has passed through three phases. It was first "tradition-oriented," then "inner-directed," and, finally, "other-directed." About the tradition-oriented phase we shall be brief. "Character" in Riesman's sense may be defined, in terms of the interrelation of the personality of the individual and the culture in which he has been socialized, as a mode of interaction in which each influences the other. During the traditional phase, character was strictly determined in minute detail by immutable behavioral models. With the rise of the inner-directed character, behavior was no longer governed by venerable authority but rather by universal and abstract principles. The transition from a culture in which traditional duties were underscored day after day by the regular round of festivals, the rhythm of the changing seasons, and the stages of the life cycle, and in which the content of those duties was fixed by a man's rank in the hierarchy of occupation and status, to a culture in which duties were seen as imperatives derived from the relation between the moral conscience (as organon of a duty imposed on all men by virtue of their being creatures of reason or sons of God), on the one hand, and the empirical consciousness (of our passions and interests), on the other, marks the break with the Catholic tradition of old and the advent of the Puritan whose obedience to God demanded that he seek greater mastery over himself and nature. Finally, other-directedness, which emerges with the development of consumer society and the spread of modern techniques of communication, corresponds to the decline of the Puritan model. The direction that the Puritan sought within himself in the depths of his conscience, the harmony he strove to maintain between his conscience and God's law, are supplanted in his other-directed successor by the desire for approval, social recognition, and a feeling of consonance between one's own behavior and the behavior of others.

Each of these phases is supposed to correspond to a different system of values. The inner-directed individual holds work, striving, saving, reflectiveness, and self-contained decision making in high esteem. The other-directed individual is disdainful or contemptuous of these Victorian virtues. He appreciates "popularity," however indiscriminate; he consumes more than he saves; and he prizes the subjective certainty of being right less than the approval of his peers. Riesman is at pains to back up his analysis of values with a discussion of institutions and types of social milieus. The inner-directed Puritan lives in a close-knit family in which the father is the central figure. Persons of different age and sex are subjected to the authority of an all-powerful paterfamilias. In the workplace the Puritan is a boss. He is an entrepreneur who is lord and master of a small-scale production unit, distinct from the domestic unit. His power at work is absolute, neither shared with anyone else nor limited in any way. The congruence of values and institutions is clear. Active individualism, which exalts toil, abstinence, innovative spirit, and initiative, as well as the conviction that one is acting as God and the Law expect, serves to justify the ambition of the individual to assume responsibility and exercise it to the full, without concern for pleasing or persuading anyone else. By contrast, consumer society is a completely different world—in family and workplace alike. Instead of a hierarchy in which the older generation takes precedence over the younger, and men over women, we find greater equality. As for relations between the young and the old, one might go so far as to say that the young—adolescents, anyway—tend to impose their tastes on their elders. At work, the growing complexity of the various tasks means that constant attention must be paid to questions of mutual adjustment, coordination, and negotiation. Finally, the ever-growing number of enticing consumer goods increases the other-directed individual's dependence on material rewards and pleasures as status symbols indicative of his capacity to gain acceptance and recognition.

Parsons and Riesman are in agreement on a good many points. Who can deny that the present day differs from Victorian times in such matters as the structure of the family, business management, and styles of symbolic communication? But to explain these transformations, is it necessary to assume that they were accompanied by a wholesale renovation of values, with the replacement of Puritanism by permissiveness and compromise?

Parsons questions Riesman's sweeping generalizations in at least two points. He suggests, first, that Riesman employs the notion of consumption too broadly. Is it correct to think of purchasing household appliances as consumption? The very term "consumer durables" (used by econometricians to describe such goods) is suggestive of the ambiguity inherent in this sort of purchase. A washing machine, for instance, is indeed destined for use by a final consumer, and in this respect differs from capital or intermediate goods. Such purchases "are, for the household, factors of production, and otherwise serve as instrumental facilities that in part replace labor-input" [1964, p. 230]. The same argument applies to education and perhaps even to leisure-time activities. The increasing sums of money allotted for education may be interpreted as indicative of a desire for higher status, as Riesman acknowledges, but we may also see in them a desire for "upgrading," which in turn may lead to obtaining more prestigious and better-paid work.

As for changes in the structure of the family and the socialization process, Parsons makes similar criticisms. "What Riesman interprets as the abdication of the parents from their socializing responsibility can therefore be interpreted in exactly the opposite way.... The requirement of preparing the child for high levels of independence, competence, and responsibility means that as socializing agent the family cannot do its job unless it emancipates its children from dependence on the parents, an emancipation that precludes parents from being too definite role-models for the child's own life course" [1964, p. 217].

Where Riesman thinks he sees a radical change of values—the transition from Puritanism to a certain kind of hedonism, characterized by abundance and dependence—Parsons emphasizes the stability of the American value system, which he defines as a variety of "instrumental activism" [1964, p. 196]. Not redundant, these two words taken together are said to define a peculiar form of culture:

> The term "activism" . . . [is] meant, as a characterization of a
> set of values for a social system, to refer to an orientation to active
> mastery of its external situation in an empirical sense of situa-
> tion. . . . We interpret active mastery to mean essentially the
> *mobilization* of resources, among which the commitments of indi-
> viduals occupy the key place, in the interest of a mission for the
> society that is not defined as the "gratification" of individual
> wishes in the usual psychological sense. [Unlike communist value
> systems, however], the American value system does not imply the
> primacy of [collective goals]. Its values place the *unit* of the
> system, in particular the individual, in an instrumental position.
> *His goal* cannot be self-indulgence or the maximization of the
> gratification of his personal wishes, but must be achievement in
> the interest of the good society. The society itself does not,
> however, tend toward a specific goal, but rather to a prospect of
> progressive improvement of the level of realization of its values.[19]

Two comparisons will help to clarify the essential nature of *instrumental* activism. First of all, a distinction must be made between instrumental activism and so-called hedonistic instrumentalism, which has been held to be characteristic of American society, most notably by Sorokin. Pleasure is not the legitimate end of technical mastery, the goal of which transcends immediate gratification. Here we touch upon the essentially religious foundations of the American value system. The only justification for the mastery of nature is God's will, which "commands us to build his kingdom on earth": this is the significance of instrumental technical mastery. In secular terms, this principle translates into an obligation for individuals to "achieve," to strive toward "self-realization."

This last feature of instrumental activism distinguishes it from what might be called collectivist activism. Our activities are aimed at ends other than the realization of our desires. It does not follow, however,

that society can impose goals directly on the individual actor. Just as
God acts through the general will and issues impersonal command-
ments, society, too, lays down the rules of the game but leaves it up to
each actor to play out his own hand. Nothing is rigidly spelled out in
detail, and society has nothing to say about how the individual should
go about his work, what he should do first and what last. When all is
said and done, the only obligation the actor has to society is to assert
his independence, that is, to work toward his own self-realization as an
individual governed by law, while respecting alter's right to work
independently toward *his* self-realization.

Parsons contends that this ideal of personal achievement has been a
constant in American culture. Observed by the earliest European
travelers, most notably de Tocqueville, it is still in evidence today,
according to Parsons, as the basic principle of American law. But this
individualism is institutionalized.[20] It finds its expression within, and
under the control of, the institutions that socialize the individual and
govern his activities. If the institutional framework changes, norms
and values must be readjusted to one another.

The Charismatic Breakthrough

If we reduced change to the process of inclusion, we would be moving
in the direction of an incrementalist theory, and it would not be terri-
bly difficult to find a place for violence in such a view. What is really at
issue is not whether Parsons has given us a "revolutionary" or a "conservative" theory, but rather how he explained the "innovations" to
which he attached so much importance. For this he relied heavily on
the idea of a "breakthrough," which he took from Max Weber's
sociology of religion.[21] Innovations, or breakthroughs, exhibit two
characteristic features: they appear sporadically, and their scope is at
least potentially unlimited, as a result of the "chain reactions" they set
in motion. In the opening pages of *The Protestant Ethic and the Spirit of
Capitalism,*[22] Weber emphasized the fact that "in western civilization . . . cultural phenomena have appeared having *universal*
significance and value." The fortuitous conjunction of singular occur-
rences in science, technology, and law gave rise to something unique.
But what was originally peculiar to western civilization has become
part of the cultural heritage of all mankind. Democracy, capitalism,
the experimental method, and applied science all have *universal* scope.
These innovations did not merely shift the balance of power in favor
of the societies in which they first came to light. They also have
meaning independent of the conditions under which they developed.

Weber endeavored to associate these innovations of western genius with the evolution of religious beliefs, broadly understood as world views, and their related practices. In this context change took the form of a discontinuous series of events. Although puritanism took over and further developed the ascetic theme that was part of the "vital center" of Christian tradition in the fourteenth and fifteenth centuries, it did not carry on or gradually transform the moral and religious outlook of Catholicism. It was something "different," something new.

To understand what kind of breakthrough the Reformation was, a description of the crisis that preceded it is necessary. That crisis developed when an earlier consensus broke down, in part because the dominant values had grown weak and spiritless, in part because alien values had emerged and been invoked in support of a radical challenge to the old order. Under the circumstances two resolutions were possible. Either the new elements must be suppressed and bridled, or they must succeed in "breaking through." An initial "breakthrough," however, could not by itself ensure the success of the new ideas, which might turn out not to be viable or might aggravate the social crisis, temporarily or permanently. Still another possibility was that the new ideas would have taken hold for a while, seemingly to stay, only to vanish in the end, much as grafted organs are sometimes rejected by the host body after a period of time. In any case, the fate of major cultural innovations of this sort is determined on the level of religious orientations (understood in the broadest possible sense), that is, of ultimate principles, the principles that serve as the basis for the answers the culture and the society give to the root questions and fundamental problems of human experience. What is essential in this concept of religion and its relation to social change is not only, and certainly not primarily, the role religion plays in consolidation and reproduction, but the capacity of religion to introduce radically new and original inspirations and to acclimate those novelties in the prevailing social climate.

At this point, it may be asked under what conditions religious ferment will bring forth new social forms, and why, in different circumstances, it produces only ephemeral turmoil, heat without light. "It is within this framework," writes Parsons, "that the place of Weber's key concept of *prophecy* is to be understood. The prophet is above all the agent of the process of breakthrough to a higher, in the sense of a more rationalized and systematized, cultural order, an order at the level of religious ethics.... It may be remarked that [the] individualistic emphasis in Weber's treatment of the concept of charisma has tended to obscure the fact that he treated it not *only* as a quality of an individual person, but also of a normative *order.* The latter reference, for example, is a necessary basis for making use of the important concepts of lineage-charisma *(Gentilcharisma)* and charisma of office *(Amtscharisma)."* Although charisma appears in association with spontaneity and affectivity, it is related to the process of rationalization, now defined not as a collection of techniques but as "the systematization of pattern or program *for life as a whole,* which is given meaning by an existential conception of the universe.[23] Understood in this way, the connection between charisma and rationalization[24] enables us to see what is ambiguous about charisma (and hence what is unpredictable about social change). The prophet's course may veer in one of three directions, toward the role of "law-giver," teacher, or "mystagogue." In the end his actions may become indistinguishable from the actions associated with one of these role-types. Nevertheless, what the prophet does is in a fundamental sense distinct from what any of the other three does, because their roles are defined with reference to institutionalized expectations, whereas the prophet, who announces a new *order* of things, has broken with the conventional and expected forms.

Still, the prophet as Weber sees him is neither a destructive nihilist nor a solipsistic creator enamored of his own marvelous uniqueness and convinced that he is at once the origin and the measure of all things human and divine. In the light of the well-known distinction between the exemplary and the ethical prophet, it is possible to relate the prophet's actions to a context that exists prior to his arrival on the scene, and hence to understand how and to what extent his actions can produce lasting effects. The exemplary prophet evokes and embodies a model, which the prophet, as the adjective suggests, rather exemplifies than imposes. When one says that Saint Francis of Assisi or Buddhist monks "preach by example," one means that, within the limits of finite existence, they participate in something that transcends or, better still, overwhelms them: *In eo, vivimus, movemur et sumus.* With their sense of mission and moral obligation, they do not merely invoke a normative system that is to be brought down to earth, but address themselves directly to the individuals and groups on whom they intend to rely for the establishment of the kingdom of God.

If the prophetic message is to find an audience and become a source of inspiration, the prophet's public must meet certain requirements. Weber attempted to determine which social categories—peasants, artisans, bureaucrats, intellectuals—were most "sensitive to exemplary and to ethical prophecy." He further sought to determine a priori, as it were, what kinds of messages the charismatic prophet might be expected to carry. To put it another way, prophetic messages are not products of the inspiration of the prophet alone but also depend on the structure of the relationship between the prophet and his audience. Only certain kinds of messages are apt to be promulgated, propagated, and heeded. There are two extreme types, delineated by the "basic dichotomy . . . between the conception of an immanent principle of divinity which is part of the world from eternity and to which in some sense man can 'adapt' himself and the conception of a transcendental divinity, in principle fundamentally separate from the world, controlling it from above and, in the extreme case, conceived as having created it *ex nihilo*" [1967, pp. 53–60].

The source of the breakthrough lies first of all in a "discrepancy" between expectations institutionalized in normative systems and the actual practice of the actors [1967, p. 61]. This cognitive dissonance need not *necessarily* find resolution. The new message may meet with an echo, but it may also be swallowed up in the din of daily life. The novelty of the prophet's message is not enough to guarantee it a hearing.

"During . . . differentiation, the *main value system* is assumed to remain constant" [1956, p. 256]. Does this assumption hold true for the analysis of charisma? It is clearly valid for short-term analysis of change. But such a setting is frequently too narrow. It must be broadened to allow role-differentiation to proceed far enough so that new values will emerge. Not all change, however, conforms to the model of the charismatic breakthrough. Not condemned to be either tragic or tiresomely repetitious, history can also accommodate the merely prosaic. Any alteration in the structure of society that is more than just fluctuation around an equilibrium position fixed by institutionalized norms will jeopardize the stability of the norms themselves. To explain changes in the norms, it is by no means necessary to assume that the fundamental values of society have been overthrown. Change may amount to no more than a spelling out in detail of existing norms, whether legal or merely customary, so as to make them more satisfactory to individuals in the society. The organic growth of the normative system, reminiscent of the growth of common law through accretion and amendment, is quite different from the discontinuous process punctuated by so-called *coupures* (breaks) said by some recent French authors to typify the succession of social types and phases of history. History is more than a series of leaps and jumps. It also allows for accumulation (by differentiation of what already exists) and diffusion (by transmission of evolutionary universals from the seed-bed societies to other societies with the capacity to take advantage of their heritage). Tendencies implicit at the level of values are actualized in the system of norms, thus adding to the society's wealth of resources. Protest gives way to specification of the norms. The "American way," for instance, was spelled out in detail in the form of antitrust legislation after populist criticism, invoking egalitarian principles, had pointed an accusatory finger at the concentration of wealth and power in the hands of a few and at the laws regulating the conduct of capitalist business, which had permitted this concentration to occur.

Is specification the *only* way for values to change? In the long run, breakthroughs are possible—provided we are agreed as to what a breakthrough is. Such values as abstinence, thrift, and a technical-experimental orientation are clearly not "specifications" of medieval values. Apart from being rare, such drastic changes on closer inspection turn out to be modulations and recapitulations rather than entirely new departures. To take the values of nascent capitalism, for example, though contemporaries may have looked upon them as radically new or even scandalous, capitalist values in reality merely made explicit certain points that had been adumbrated as long ago as the earliest Christian writings, only to vanish subsequently into oblivion. Puritanism, after all, is bound up with an aggressively ascetic and egalitarian strand of Christian thinking, which we find running throughout the early history of the church. When asceticism moved out beyond the circles in which it had first grown into prominence, however, certain of its previously latent tendencies were reinforced by contact with allied value systems. From the "secular" leanings of the early capitalists asceticism acquired a pragmatic and instrumental tinge, the peculiar facets of which were given prominence by Max Weber in his discussion of *innerweltliche Askese* (innerworldly asceticism).

After centuries of obscurity and silence, the ascetic theme re-emerged. But in its puritan form it was embellished, like the continually recurring *"petite phrase"* of Vinteuil's sonata [in Proust's *Remembrance of Things Past*—trans.], by the lush harmonies of its new context. Change takes place in time but is more than a sequence of events. The difference between the asceticism of Diogenes and that of Calvin is not accounted for solely by the passage of time. Time is only a dimension in which a sequence of different combinations is possible. To call a moment in time a *coupure* is as arbitrary as to periodize history by centuries or millennia (though it may be conceded that individual lives span more moments than they do centuries). The theory of action is not based on the *individual* actor, any more than the theory of social systems is based on "concrete totalities." The long run has no more reality than the short run. "Heavy" history has no more reality than "immediate" history. Both are expressions of the different "interests" of historians, who put the same material and the same analytical categories together in a variety of ways. The prophet works his effects in the short term, and so does the reformer who here and there makes decisions that change the ways in which capitalist firms do business, say, decisions whose consequences extend beyond the context in which they were made to have an impact on the larger society for many years to come.

Life and Death: The Identity of Values

Our analysis of change must provide answers to two sets of questions. First, what is it that changes? Norms or values? What functional relations are conducive to change in one rather than the other? Second, if values do in fact change, as the analysis of charisma suggests, what is the nature of that change? Is it a specification of existing values or a radical break with the past? Much light can be shed on these questions by recent developments in medical practice and ethics and in the values associated with medicine. As we have seen, medical practice is not merely a set of techniques whose efficacy is guaranteed by science (i.e., logico-experimental knowledge). Doctor and patient alike become involved in a relationship in which each forms socially and culturally sanctioned expectations of the behavior of the other. What justifies the different but complementary obligations imposed on doctor and patient is the goal that both share, namely, the restoration of the patient's health. Health—its maintenance and restoration—is thus deemed a paramount value. Health may, of course, be looked upon as both good in itself and for the community at large. People have to be healthy if they are to do their assigned tasks. "From the sociological standpoint, health is the condition which ensures our optimum capacity to perform those tasks valued by society."[25] Beyond the social justification is the religious principle that makes health a paramount value and imposes strict limits on what the doctor can and cannot do, while at the same time establishing a goal for his efforts. Christian tradition emphasizes the dignity of human life, which is literally a gift from God. Medical practice is thus consecrated and at the same time made subordinate to certain ultimate ends, expressed as beliefs and norms. Since life is something we have received from God (which we can transmit but not create), we are not at liberty to deprive anyone of it, not even ourselves. Life being a gift from God, the physician's labors have a place in an essentially religious context. The doctor cannot refuse the benefit of his ministrations to the person too ill to care unaided for the sacred gift entrusted to him. "If the role of the physician involves not simply high status and honor but also a potential and frequently activated charisma of office, it derives these qualities from a fiduciary responsibility for maximizing those basic human gifts which individuals actually receive" [1972, p. 387].

When coupled with the instrumental activist orientation that is a salient feature of Western cultures, the emphasis on the sacredness of life means that the modern practitioner must accord overriding value to his obligation to save his patient's life. The physician's task is thus very clearly spelled out, so that the doctor is immune to ethical doubt and protected against outside interference. He is guided by a single rule: save the patient, even if salvation only means prolonging a life of cruel suffering, a life so drastically curtailed that the patient himself might be tempted to end it.

This conception of the physician's role is at present undergoing change. Nevertheless, the religious principle that life is of preeminent value continues to be upheld. Advances in medical technology have changed the way we think about death, while at the same time giving us the means to interfere with the process of dying to a greater extent than ever before. It is not only that the average life span has been extended, so that even rather remarkably long lives are no longer as unusual as they once were. More than that, it is now possible to prolong life artificially, in some cases for rather long periods of time. "There are patients of whom it can reasonably be claimed that they have died more than once." As the physician increases his control over life and death, he is becoming more and more uncertain of what he ought to be doing. "Sometimes the decision to 'allow' a patient to die by removing the artificial supports of life seems to be the most reasonable recourse, although it is a decision which physicians generally try to avoid" [1972, p. 399].

For reasons connected with the evolution of technology, morality, and law, the old principle, "Save the patient at all costs," is no longer the categorical imperative it once was. Can we say that the religious value attaching to human life has been repudiated if it is true that doctors no longer regard the survival of the patient *at all costs* as a peremptory requirement? "Fundamentalist" practitioners argue that we can, and they oppose this change with the same determination they bring to the fight against liberalization of the abortion laws. Thus we have entered a period of crisis with regard to a crucial point of medical ethics, which threatens to provoke a radical reinterpretation of the physician's role, while at the same time burdening him with heavy new responsibilities. Parsons does not deny that such a crisis is upon us.

What he does deny is that the change it presages will necessarily mean a radical break with past values.

To begin with, it should be noted that more "responsible," more active attitudes toward life and death are not merely a consequence of scientific and technological hegemony, itself a consequence of the instrumental orientation that predominates in Western societies. "The impending, inevitable death of a patient need not be taken as a defeat of treatment. . . . The relativized ethic also renders the boundaries of medical ethics more flexible. . . . The physician must take more responsibility for admitting the medical significance of ethical considerations structured in other sectors of the moral system. The recognition of the consummatory significance of death is one example of the new penetration of medical ethics by a religio-moral perspective having essentially non-medical origins" [1972, p. 403].

What is required of both doctor and patient is what Parsons calls "the transcending of death." Progress in science and technology has increased the powers of medicine, but with these increased powers have gone increased anxiety and fear, which can be overcome only by spiritual attributes, that is, by a combination of sharpened perception and firmer discipline. Advances in medical technology can help us to die in tranquillity and with our eyes open. Parsons feelingly cites the dying words of Pope John XXIII: "My bags are packed, I'm ready to go." Ideally, death should bring home simultaneously to doctor and patient the meaning of the words, "His work is done" [1972, p. 405].

Though clearly at odds with the old dictum, "Save the patient at all costs," this view is perfectly compatible with recognition of the preeminent dignity of human life. In other words, a change in norm is compatible with constancy of values. In this respect, the crisis in medicine that we have just examined yields conclusions identical with those Parsons drew earlier from his criticism of Riesman: namely, that we must be careful not to confuse changes in norms with changes in values. Now, however, we can carry this one step further. Respect for life is not a value that stands alone. It can be reconciled with either a mystical and passive orientation or with an activist orientation. The activist orientation, moreover, has two forms, one strictly instrumental—and, in the case of the more extreme advocates of "heroic measures," compulsive—in character, the other aimed rather at achieving greater awareness and control in regard to one of life's most critical moments. No one who respects life will squander, indulge, or take chances with it. To respect life is to try to make one's own life testify to that respect in the fullest measure possible. But if life is so many things at once, to say that the value of life never changes amounts to saying that the value of life is completely indeterminate, does it not?

There is what we might call a "vital center" in our values from which they derive a certain identity, even if in many respects they change with time. But to grasp that identity we must look at the system as a whole rather than at the value-orientation of one particular individual. What gives life its value is not the prominence given to individual *survival* at any cost, but rather the effort to make appropriate and dignified restitution of the gift of life entrusted to all of us and passed on by some of us. The idea that individuals pass on the gift of life is an abstract one. It gives rise to yet another idea, that there is an *exchange* and hence a bond between the living and the dead, which can be made manifest only by way of a highly complex system of symbolism, in which religious ideas, coupled, or, rather, mingled, with biological ideas, have an essential place. In the Christian tradition such exchange takes place not only between successive generations of men but also between men and God, creating a bond that is expressed in a particularly dramatic way through the symbol of the messiah who comes down to earth to die for mankind. Death thus becomes a symbolic event, which expresses in both immanent (biological) and transcendent (religious) dimensions the solidarity of all men, who are bound together through time and conditioned by the circumstances of their existence. Catholicism has singled out two images to represent this solidarity, the images of the blood and the body of Christ, both central to the sacrament of the eucharist, in which the death and sacrifice of Christ are reenacted. The blood represents the continuity of time and symbolizes what is passed on from generation to generation; the body of Christ, an essential part of the symbolism of the Church, represents the solidarity of the faithful and, ideally, of all mankind in its simultaneous aspect.

Christian symbolism, constructed as it is around the crucifixion and resurrection of Jesus, makes death the central event in which the debt contracted in accepting the "gift of Life" is finally repaid. Accordingly, death is conceived in two different ways: it is "the sacrificial death of Jesus by crucifixion . . . a kind of 'supreme sacrifice.' On the other hand, the death of the individual can be conceived as not merely paving the way for his entrance into 'heaven' but also as a sacrifice for the redemptive benefit of humanity in general. . . . This represents a major upgrading of the religio-metaphysical status of man" [1972, pp. 377–79].

The value of human life is based on the fundamentally religious idea that death is not merely a biological fact but has a meaning in that it provides man with an opportunity to return with dignity, with *piety*, the gift that has been conferred upon him. The essence of religion, Durkheim thought, was "life taken seriously" but the life at issue is not *my* life as an individual but the life entrusted to me, upon which my dignity as a human being is based. Life has still another, complementary aspect: obligation. Life is not merely "something" that we have received and must one day give back, but also "something" to be made to bear fruit. This aspect of life may be "seen in the Calvinist conception that it was man's mission to build the kingdom of God on earth." From this point of view, death is the consummation, "signalling the completion of the *task* for which [man] was placed in the world" and given the gift of life. "This conception is beautifully symbolized in a phrase in the Episcopal funeral service, 'His work is done.'"[26]

The stability of values is explained by the persistence of combinations of differentiated, even antagonistic, elements, which coexist in a variety of relations and under a variety of conditions, not because they chanced to come together in one fashion or another but rather precisely because they are differentiated from one another and complementary or antagonistic in their intricate relationships. Accordingly, it has proved possible to bend the old dictum, "Save the patient at all costs," without violating the fundamental principle, that the value of human life is paramount. One might even contend that, with the availability of new technologies for coping with life-and-death situations more effectively than ever before, the religious principle of the dignity of life is being upheld more firmly than ever, because it has now become possible to adapt that principle to actual conditions. By focusing on the example of the doctor and his obligation to save his patient's life, we have been able to gain some insight into the ways in which values may be inflected, varied, and given new substance by being brought to bear on a new set of circumstances. Different precepts can be shaped by the same "symbolic mold." But when sociologists tell us that the manners, rules, or customs associated with some social or cultural system have changed, by what criteria can we decide whether we are still looking at the same system or have more or less imperceptibly shifted our attention to something "new"?

The Vital Center of the Christian Synthesis

Parsons's treatment of the evolution of Christianity makes it possible to give at least a partial answer to the preceding question.[27] He gives prominence first of all to the *continuity* of a long-term trend. He also stresses the importance of what he calls the *diversity* of the ingredients that entered into the Christian synthesis. The analysis of so complex and long-lived a phenomenon will give us a better understanding of the solidity of the "vital center" of the Christian synthesis, a center that was itself differentiated, intricate, even shot through with conflict at the outset, but that ultimately, thanks to its complexity, was able to serve as a stabilizing element in a number of different combinations of other elements.

Christianity differentiated itself initially by breaking its ties with the two traditions against which it rose in protest, though it was at pains to preserve and assimilate the important contributions in the legacy of both Judaic and Greco-Roman culture. Against both of these traditions Christianity claimed to be a universal religion that brought the "good word" to Jews and Gentiles alike. "To use the terms loosely, they had been 'ethnic,' 'civic,' or 'national' religions. . . . Christianity arose as a sect within Judaism, at a time when Palestine was Hellenized and Romanized—certainly the members of the elite were culturally quite Hellenized. . . . These questions [of differences between the early Christians and the rest of the Jewish community] reached a crux when St. Paul initiated the church's historic break with the traditional Jewish community by declaring that the observance of Jewish law had no bearing on a convert's status as a Christian" [1968, p. 428]. Christianity originated, then, in discontinuity and conflict, a situation reenacted by each new convert: *conversion* is a strictly personal act, at once a breaking-off and an engagement, which forges a bond between each new Christian and his church and savior, while at the same time severing all of his prior ties and allegiances.

Christianity did, however, carry over from the two traditions out of which it arose certain basic elements, which it recombined to form a new synthesis. From Judaism it took the idea of a unique God, "the *sole* creator and governor of the world . . .[as well as] the theme of human imperfection, in acute contrast with the transcendence and thus in some sense the glory of God, [which] is sharply accented in Judaism and became the basis of the Christian doctrine of sin." From the Greeks and Romans Christianity borrowed the idea of a natural world consisting of phenomena of many kinds, which reason, aided by experience, could comprehend. The notion of the *cosmos,* moreover, was not limited to what would later come to be known as *physical* nature: "It also had relevance to human relationships, and in this connection, especially among the Stoics, the ideal of human society came to involve the ordering of these relations in accord with the 'order of nature.' The fullest institutionalization of this universalistic conception came with the systematization of Roman law, which by including both the *jus civilis* ... and the *jus gentium* in a single, coherent legal system, transcended the parochial particularism that characterized previous conceptions of social order" [1968, p. 427].

Incorporating elements borrowed from two different, and, in many points, antagonistic, traditions, Christianity was neither a reconciliation nor a syncretism, but a genuine synthesis. The combination of a universalistic with a transcendentalist orientation (in terms of pattern variables, one would be tempted to speak of affective neutrality) gave priority to what Parsons calls a "transcendental-activistic attitude," which emerged as a compromise between the components peculiar to the Christian synthesis. Not only is Christianity a transcendental, monotheistic religion; the central notion of Christian theology is that man has a divinely ordained active mission in the world: God created man "in his image," in order to work his divine will on earth. Such an activist orientation is not unique to Christianity. We find it also in other "people of the word": the Jews and Muslims. But the Jews, after a brief existence as a small, politically independent kingdom, were dispersed over the face of the earth in groups too small, too weak politically, and too isolated from one another to exert any appreciable influence on the political development of human societies. Islam, on the other hand, effected so thorough a fusion of the religious authority with the government of a rapidly expanding empire that it was unsuccessful in controlling the institutional conditions under which social change took place, and so failed to direct change along the lines laid down in a broad way by the Islamic religion [1968, p. 427].

The "transcendental-activistic" orientation is the "vital center" of the Christian synthesis. Its development was not linear, however. Each of the several elements of the Christian synthesis has at one time or another enjoyed relative prominence, only to fall back later into relative obscurity; the relations among the elements have changed over time, and occasionally their relative priority has shifted and even been inverted at certain stages. At times one element or another has even dropped out of sight altogether. In support of his claim that the activistic orientation has been a constant of the Christian cultural system, Parsons makes three main points. First, this orientation is the basis of the separation of church and state, on which the claim of the church—particularly the Roman Church—to independence rests. Second, the church's freedom from dependence on ascriptive ties, whether of the kinship or ethnic group variety, is in a sense implicit in the strictly individualistic conception of conversion. After Constantine made Christianity a state religion, however, the problem of the political independence of the church arose once more, though in terms different from those in which the early Christian sects had known it. The development of monastic orders—this is Parsons's third point—was the defensive reaction of the Christian church to the danger of subordination to the state apparatus—a danger with which the Eastern Orthodox Church dealt far less effectively than did the Roman Church: "The religious, as members of the orders, became the elite of the church. Their withdrawal from the world, symbolized above all by the vows of poverty and chastity, insured [their] independence from secular ties. . . . The vow of obedience can be seen as assuming selective obedience to religious authority, specifically of the abbot, and hence protection against non-religious influences and pressures" [1968, p. 432].

The activist aspect of the Christian synthesis manifested itself at two critical moments. The first was when, in opposition to Byzantine monastic traditions, which were dominated by the contemplative ideal, the Rule of Saint Benedict "instituted a regime of secular useful work for its members, labor in agriculture and in crafts, as a religiously valued ascetic exercise—as Weber particularly noted" [1968, p. 433]. The second came during the Reformation, when the activistic and ascetic orientation—*innerweltliche Askese* in Weber's terms—was re-affirmed in a striking way: a man's occupation, or what the Stoics had called the *officium,* became central to his Christian life (this is what Max Weber referred to as the *Beruf*). But while the Reformation reaffirmed and in a sense realized the activistic orientation that was already apparent in the earliest writings in which we find the Christian synthesis expressed, it also destroyed one of the pillars of that orientation, the primacy of the clergy over the layman. Reformation produced an "upgrading of the Christian laity. This was effected by ending the individual's dependence on sacerdotal mediation. The individual soul stood in *immediate* relation to God through Christ. . . . The [church] exists only in the souls of those who by faith are its true members in the eyes of God. The visible church has become 'secularized'" [1968, p. 436].

The Reformation did break with the past, but only with the immediate past. It "broke" the primacy of the ecclesiastical hierarchy. But at the same time it took up and embellished in the process an old theme, one that runs throughout the history of Christianity, which we find in the primitive church and even more prominently in the organization of the monastic orders: the theme that worldly asceticism is a necessary condition for the "coming of the Kingdom of God." The break in Christian history marked by the advent of Calvinism and Puritanism was also a reaffirmation of the message of early Christianity. One feels almost tempted here to mention Schumpeter's discussion of "cycles" or "waves" of innovation in the "capitalist process of creative destruction."[28] Of course Schumpeter never clearly recognized that these phases of creativity occurred within a unified whole: an evolving economic, cultural, or social system. So long as the central values and symbols of transcendental activism remain intact, even the most seemingly dramatic changes, such as the transition from the medieval church to reformed Christianity, are mere twists and turns in the discontinuous building process of a single tradition.

How can we tell how solid the essential "vital center" of any particular tradition is? Although Parsons gives no explicit answer to this question, two remarks are in order. First—this may seem to be a tautology—the transcendental-activistic orientation, the "vital center" of Christianity, remains stable as long as it survives ruptures and discontinuities in the tradition. Behind this trivial truth, however, are hidden several propositions of considerable importance. First, we had best be extremely cautious about making predictions: the owl of Minerva flies only at night. Our awareness of the "vital center" keeps us from making the same mistake as the legions of pseudoprophets who rise to proclaim a "crisis of civilization" whenever problems are encountered, and at the same time gives us a solid start on analyzing crises that have actually occurred. Each of the crises through which Christianity has passed was associated either with a modification in the external environment (as in the Constantinian era, when the Christian sect, previously the victim of state persecution, was invited to join in the rule of the empire), or with a modification in the internal environment (as in the changes in the relations between the laity and the clergy during the period prior to the Reformation). Each of these crises can be analyzed in terms of the categories we have had occasion to use previously: *upgrading* of religious society (or of one of its components), *differentiation* (of religious from political society, or of the laity from the clergy), *inclusion* (definition of the conditions for membership in the Church according to criteria that became less and less particularistic and ascriptive as time went by), and, finally, *legitimation* (i.e., congruence of the solutions arrived at with the stable and repeatedly reaffirmed central core of the transcendental-activistic orientation). Each crisis, moreover, corresponds to a distinctive type of religious organization: the strict hierarchy of the post-Constantinian church is clearly different from the type of organization prevalent in the Puritan sects.

At what point does the system cease to have sufficient momentum to meet a new crisis and carry on? At what point do the problems in the internal or external environment become so severe that rather than "breakthroughs" they produce "breakups," to borrow from

Toynbee? Parsons devoted little attention to breakups: we shall see later on that his prognoses for industrial society and for the United States were optimistic. Still, he did make a remark—in passing, it is true—that can help to put us onto an interesting trail. This had to do with what Parsons regarded as the petrification of the Islamic world, for which he saw two causes. First, Muslim societies did not succeed in differentiating the political from the religious. Hence they had a hard time secularizing innovations and assimilating them to the tradition of Islam. We can look at this remark in two ways. In the more obvious interpretation it serves to underscore the threat to the unity of a social or cultural system posed by innovations, which the system tends to reject as foreign bodies. But there is another, more positive interpretation: that the capacity of a social system to control change depends on the resources it possesses *initially,* which, by the action of differentiation and opposition, can ultimately bring forth new fruit. One reason for Christianity's rapid spread was that it was born in a highly differentiated and articulated environment. From its dual legacy of Jewish and Greco-Roman tradition, Christianity took a wide range of subtly differentiated solutions to its potential dilemmas, a broad spectrum of strategies for consolidating the complementary (and contrasting) strands in its heritage and for making them prosper.

Chapter Six

Industrial Society

Sociology took shape in the nineteenth century as an inquiry into the nature of industrial society. The elaboration of a comparative and analytical theory of society revealed the naiveté of earlier investigations into the future of capitalism, the transition to socialism, and the coming of the positive age. At the same time, the founders of sociology, Durkheim, Weber, and Pareto—whose teachings Parsons set himself the task of systematizing—helped to heighten awareness of the uniqueness of the Western type of society and its historical tradition, a singular development in the history of mankind, and yet, opinions to the contrary notwithstanding, a development fraught with implications for mankind in general.

Parsons's earliest published work[1] is devoted to a discussion of the origins of capitalism as seen by Weber and Sombart, both of whom may, in spite of their differences, be regarded as critics of Marxist doctrine. From the first Parsons rejected the distinction between socialism and capitalism, and in this early work the word "capitalism" is placed in quotations as if to underscore its ideological rather than scientific character. This explains why he preferred to characterize societies like the one we live in as "industrial societies" rather than "capitalist societies."

Industrial society, however, has been criticized not only by the left but also by the right. Conservative ideologues described the early days of industrialization as the disintegration of traditional society, pure and simple. Disintegration, they contended, went hand in hand with a sharp intensification of social conflict and a heightening of hedonistic appetites, cynicism, and self-interest. On the first point conservative, or, rather, reactionary, critics were in agreement with socialists. For both left and right industrial society was a society riven by mortal conflict. On the second point the two ideologies diverged and sometimes conflicted. As heir to the Enlightenment, socialism refused to see in the glorification of *Gemeinschaft* an ideal and in the traditional social order something worth going back to. Reactionary criticism, critical of the myths of individualism, which it associated with hedonism and libertinism, could not believe in the prospects of freedom and fulfillment held out by utopian socialists: a radiant future in which men would ultimately be reconciled with themselves, their fellows, and the world of nature.

In opposition to both the socialist, especially the Marxist, and the reactionary interpretations of industrial society, Parsons developed his own conception. He seems never to have taken the reactionary view very seriously, except in its "fascist" version of the thirties and forties,[2] which he looked upon as a benighted and brutal attempt to deny the complexity and ambiguity inherent in the functioning of industrial society. Behind the nihilistic despair and violence of fascism, however, there is a philosophy of the evolution of Western civilization and of the place of individual values therein that is largely independent of ideological commitment, since it may be found in the work of both the theorists of the decline of the West (generally right-wing) and the theorists of alienation (generally left-wing).[3]

One sociologist who insisted most vehemently on the connection between what he regarded as the decadence of Western civilization and the rise of sensualist individualism was Sorokin. We shall begin by examining Parsons's criticisms of Sorokin's ideas about the historical development of Western civilization, not only because those ideas stand in marked contrast to the ideas of Parsons but also because Sorokin's approach—in which society and civilization, social structure, and values are all mixed up together—diverges sharply from Parsons's, with its emphasis on differentiation of the social system and the cultural subsystem.

Neither Sorokin nor Marx

Parsons's views on industrial society are to be contrasted, on the one hand, with the view that industrial society is no more than a boiling kettleful of individual demands and interests (i.e., a sort of generalized anomie) and, on the other hand, with the view that class conflict is all-important.

According to Parsons, Sorokin's position is based on two equations: first, that religion is equivalent to the system of values, and, second, that the system of values is equivalent to society. The history of Western society, as Sorokin sees it, is summed up in a sequence "of three fundamental types of cultural orientation—the 'ideational,' 'idealistic,' and 'sensate.'"[4] Parsons explains Sorokin's view as follows:

The ideational pattern is one which gives unquestionable primacy to transcendental and other-worldly interests in the religious
sense. Reality itself is defined as ultimately beyond the reach of
the senses, as transcendental. The goal of life must be to reach the
closest possible accord with the nature of transcendent reality, and
the path to this must involve renunciation of all worldly interests.
Broadly speaking, otherworldly asceticism and mysticism are the
paths to it. . . . The opposite extreme to the ideational pattern is
the sensate. Here, the empirical, in the last analysis the "material,"
aspect of reality is taken as ultimately real or predominant. In
practical conduct the implication of a sensate view of the world is
to make the most of the opportunities of the here and now, to be
concerned with worldly success, power, and—in the last
analysis—to put hedonistic gratifications first of all. The idealistic
pattern is conceived as intermediate between the two, not in the
sense of a simple "compromise," but rather of a synthesis which
can achieve a harmonious balance between the two principal components. This basic classification is then used as the framework for
outlining a developmental pattern leading, in the history of a
civilization, from ideational to idealistic predominance and in turn
from idealistic to sensate. . . . Sorokin tends to regard the contemporary period, exemplified particularly in the United States, but
also in the Soviet Union, as close to the peak of the sensate phase
of development and destined for a general breakdown comparable
to that of Greco-Roman civilization before a new ideational pattern can become established.

Parsons objects to Sorokin's view on several grounds. In the first
place, "transcendental orientation in the sense of other-worldliness"
does not seem to be an adequate measure of the "degree of religiousness." Asceticism and mysticism are not the only possible religious
orientations. What is more, some kinds of asceticism, such as Max
Weber's *"innerweltliche Askese,"* are genuine religious orientations and
yet do not require "the reduction of all desires to participate positively
and actively in worldly activities like political or economic functions. . . . Western Christianity belongs in the category of orientation
which is high in degree of religiousness, with a predominantly innerworldly orientation so far as the field of expected action of the individual is concerned. . . . This . . . becomes most clearly evident in
'ascetic Protestantism.'"[5] In other words, Calvinism contributed, in
Weber's terms, to a "disenchantment" of the world, that is, to a "de-
sacralization" of the natural world and of human experience in general, because it led to at least a partial secularization of economic and
political relations. Nevertheless, the question of salvation, individual
salvation, remained central for the Puritan. Suppose we concede, for

the sake of argument, that for the medieval Christian the world was an undifferentiated whole, which disintegrated and was partially secularized in the Reformation. Still, man retained the sense of something sacred, namely, his relationship with God. Calvinism is, in the full sense of the word, a *religion* of the individual. Hence there is no reason to suppose, as Sorokin does, that individualism is exhaustively descriptive of the sensate phase. Accordingly, the fact that individual autonomy is taken as a fundamental and, as it were, religious value by industrial society is no reason to regard that type of society as morally degenerate, given over to the most debased forms of sensuality.

The final objection Parsons makes to Sorokin's arguments is that Sorokin failed to see the difference between a "radically individualistic" doctrine—the doctrine of the state of nature as understood by Hobbes or Plato's Callicles—and another variety of individualism, this one not "anarchistic, but what we have come to call an 'institutionalized' individualism. . . . Instead of a single 'line' of relationship between an ultimately transcendental God and man, God became related to man *through* the Christ figure who was both God and man, and Christ became the head of the Church, the 'essence' of which was formulated as the third person of the Trinity, the Holy Spirit."[6] This differentiation of the persons of the Trinity has implications beyond theology: it implies "differentiation of the church from secular society, a differentiation *within* the religious system itself, in the broadest respect between the aspect of devotion and worship on the one hand, and the aspect of the Christian's relation to his fellow men on the other. The Christian community was constituted by the fact of common faith and common worship, but the contexts in which worship was paramount were differentiated from the context of love and charity which bound the community together in bonds of human mutuality," whether in a Church, a sect, or a congregation.[7] For the Puritan, action is impossible without the mediation of these institutions, just as, in the profane order—as we shall see later on—political and economic action is impossible without the mediation of such institutions as contracts, property, markets, and suffrage. It is therefore unreasonable to reduce the individual to instinctual drives or calculated interests and thereby cut him off from socially available resources.

Reactionary critics of industrial society say that if individuals are officially recognized as independent, anomie of desire is the inevitable result. By granting such recognition, they argue, a society prepares the way for its own destruction. At bottom the reactionary critique is based on the belief that industrial society functions exactly as the utilitarian model says it does: that isolated individuals pursue their own self-interested ends, using means chosen at random. Accordingly, industrial society represents a return to the state of nature, to the war of all against all—in this respect reactionary criticism echoes the pessimistic side of the utilitarian tradition—which is then open to reinterpretation in the light of social Darwinist teachings. To ward off such a disastrous outcome, the reactionary critics propose a restoration of some sort of "organic society," based on the negation of individualism. As to the future of individualistic society, Marx and the Marxists are every bit as pessimistic as their reactionary adversaries. The inspiration of the "classless society" is different, however, from that which animates the partisans of the *"back to Gemeinschaft"* movement. The idea of a classless society is largely informed by utopian thought, in one degree or another an ever-present ingredient of the Enlightenment tradition from which socialist thought derives.[8]

In Parsons's view, the Marxist interpretation of history incorporates all the problems left unsolved by utilitarianism and compounds them with its own concept of a class struggle pared down to one essential element, the mortal conflict between capitalists and proletarians. "Marx introduced no fundamental modification of the general theory of human social behavior in the terms of which [the Utilitarian] school of thought represented. He did, however, unlike the Utilitarians, see and emphasize the massive fact of the structuring of interests rather than treating them as distributed at random. The structure of the productive forces which Marx outlined for capitalist society is real and of fundamental importance. . . . The fundamental fact is certainly correct. . . . Marx, however, tended to treat the socioeconomic structure of capitalist enterprise as a single indivisible entity rather than breaking it down analytically into a set of the distinct variables involved in it." In other words, Marx saw the "structure" of interests that the Utilitarians had failed to see, even as he took over their views with regard to the motivation of human action. But rather than describe how that structure is differentiated, he compressed all the subtleties into a simplistic opposition between those who own the means of production and those who possess nothing but their labor power.

In *Sociological Theory and Modern Society* Parsons included an essay critical of what he took to be the Marxist conception of capitalism, in which he made three main points. First, he rejected the notion of the class struggle and the reduction of all social relations to a mortal confrontation between the "bourgeoisie" and the "proletariat." He next attacked the theory of the takeover of power and the leap to freedom *(Sprung in die Freiheit)*. And, finally, he denied the validity of the Marxist notions of "interest" and "false consciousness."

The first criticism is based on a number of arguments, all of which attack the inadequacy of Marx's view that capitalist society comes down to a confrontation between two classes, capitalists and workers. As Marx describes it, the capitalist firm is a petty monarchy, in which the capitalist owner exercises all management responsibilities, while the employees have no control whatever over the means of production. In Parsons's estimation, such a simplification is clearly unwarranted. To begin with, there has been a steady differentiation of the role of the capitalist. Though the owners have not entirely lost control over the means of production, today that control is exerted under far more complex conditions than in the days when the capitalist was a jack-of-all-trades, at once owner, manager, and engineer. Now economic actors of several kinds (old-line stockholders, sources of new capital, bankers and entrepreneurs, and technicians of many varieties) all have something to say about the operation of the business. The workers, for their part, are *organized,* frequently with the approval and support of the government, in unions. Organization has increased the workers' bargaining power considerably, and in contract negotiations they are frequently able to make the employers pay handsomely for concessions. Ongoing processes both inside and outside the firm have led to a relative increase of power for the workers, and what was originally a duel between the owners of the means of production and the suppliers of labor has given way to a far more complicated system, in which the "employees," as a group including besides manual laborers many different kinds of workers, are far from being left without any workable strategy.

Turning now from the microcosm of the firm to the stratification of industrial society as a whole, we find that the idea that society is composed of just two classes, capitalists and workers, is every bit as tenuous in this context as in the previous one. Marx held that there would most likely be a "polarization" of all social categories not directly engaged in the process of production around one or the other of the two main antagonists. But, in fact, the "middle classes," professionals, service workers, and peasants are unwilling to join either "camp." By way of self-consolation, Marxist "science" may insist that "objectively the interests of small businessmen should impel them to join with the proletariat." But in that case it must be allowed either that the prophecy will come true only at some indefinite future date or else that individuals are for the time being blind to their own true interests, which requires a theory of "false consciousness" of some sort to explain why this should be so.

Parsons caps his critique of the worker/capitalist dichotomy in Marxism with an attack on what for him is the fundamental weakness of Marxist sociology: the inadequacy of its analysis of the functions of the social system and its persistent refusal—despite the embarrassment Marx himself sometimes felt in the face of the implications of his position—to accord a lawful status to the various functions revealed by the analysis. "Marx did not discriminate analytically between what we would now call economic and political factors but because in the special case being analyzed they seemed plausibly to operate in the *same direction* he treated them as 'aspects' of the same factor" [1967, p. 109]. The "polarization" thesis, untenable except by rhetorical artifice, was the price Marx had to pay for his obstinate refusal to admit a functional pluralism. Between the rejection of pluralism on the theoretical level and the polarization thesis on the sociological level, Marx found himself forced into a vicious circle from which he was never able to escape.

Because of its resolute reliance on the "logic of dichotomies," in which only "exploiters" and "exploited" matter, Marxist thought has been forced to deny the authenticity of both individual and collective ends. So long as "capitalist exploitation" continues, Marxists suppose, such notions as the "general will" or "common good" will remain as ridiculous as the idea of individual interest in "bourgeois economics," which they regard as a mere "mystification." This brings us back to the Hobbesian state of nature, to the war of all against all,[9] except that now, instead of an undetermined number of antagonists, there are only two classes locked in a struggle to the death and supposed to be motivated by self-interest, like the Hobbesian individual. "The state is nothing other than the executive committee of the 'bourgeoisie,' and will never peacefully hand over power to the workers' movement." It is true that the Marxist tradition includes "democratic socialists of the Bernstein persuasion [who] believed that even in capitalist societies the normative order of political democracy was sufficiently firm and independent of the capitalists' interests, so that it could reasonably be relied upon to provide the opportunity for the advent of socialism." But the orthodox Marxists rejected even this much of a concession, typical of revisionism, as flying in the face of the rigorous "logic of dichotomies."

If the state is nothing but the instrument of the "ruling class," then no state is legitimate, that is, entitled to promulgate norms applicable to all persons, no matter what their individual interests. The laws of the state would then be nothing more than a "reflection of the class structure," a "bourgeois trick." Against the pseudorealistic approach, which shunts aside the problem of the social order, Parsons put forward a body of ideas that he took from Durkheim, who treated the normative order as a condition of cooperation and coexistence, although it is of course true that the norms are at best imperfectly representative of the values of society at any given moment. Taken literally, the Marxist "logic of dichotomies" precludes understanding of how society works: history becomes a tale told by idiots—who are also "watchdogs" [the allusion is to the title of a book by Paul Nizan, *The Watchdogs*—trans.]—unless one assumes that History has a palpable meaning and direction, a supposition all the more dubious in view of the fact that the divination and interpretation of that meaning and direction are functions reserved exclusively for the high priests of the Revolution.

For Marxists, civil obedience under a capitalist regime is exclusively the consequence of coercion and manipulation. The "logic of dichotomies" forces Marx to draw a radical distinction between the fact of "exploitation" and the fictions of "bourgeois law." It also prevents him from explaining the transition to socialism as anything other than a leap into freedom *(Sprung in die Freiheit)*. This way of putting things ill conceals a contradiction not at all dialectical in nature, since it by no means contains all the preconditions for its own resolution. If socialist society requires a sharp break with capitalist tradition and practice, how can the "exploited" leap to freedom except by seizing power themselves, unless it is seized for them in a violent uprising led by the "vanguard" of the workers against the "ruling class"? Such a dramatic turn of events can only be an act of historical providence, a sudden grace that would do away with the class struggle and establish a utopian harmony [1967, p. 118]. To prepare the way for the leap to freedom, Marx, or, rather, the Leninist version of the Marxist tradition, calls upon the dictatorship of the proletariat, established and administered by the unique "vanguard party of the working class." In the social-democratic tradition, of course, it is supposed that a reign of terror can be avoided. But the social democrats who flatter themselves by thinking this to be true are rooted more in the culture of democratic liberalism than in the Marxist tradition itself. How could there be reformism if there were no form of political competition in capitalist society other than class struggle between "bourgeoisie" and "proletariat" leading to extermination of the former by the latter?

The reason why Marxist thought often lapses into obscurity is that it is obsessed with the "logic of dichotomies" according to which the behavior of the two antagonistic classes can be explained by their opposing "interests." This fascination with the "battle of giants" has one final consequence for Marxism, possibly the most deleterious of all: because the "scientific," "objective" character of the class struggle thesis must be preserved at all costs, it is impossible for a Marxist sociologist to gather objective data about social reality. If all aspects of social life are dominated by *Realfaktoren,* which ultimately come down to a stark opposition between relations of production of two kinds, then it follows not only that there is a "bourgeois world-view" opposed to a "proletarian world-view"—the point would seem to be unarguable—but also that there are two kinds of social science, one proletarian, the other bourgeois, each of which is *directly* determined by its position relative to the process of production. Now this is an absurd contention, because, taken literally, it destroys itself: if whatever we say is absolutely conditioned by objective interests, whether we are aware of it or not, then we may as well shut up and let the "class interests," in the person of their chosen representatives, slug it out with one another.

Using Weber's well-known distinction between *Wertfreiheit* (value freedom) and *Wertbeziehung* (value relevance), we can escape from this impasse.[10] According to Parsons, what must be recognized is that the role of the scientist is sometimes independent of other roles the scientist may be called upon to play, while at other times the two kinds of roles are interdependent. Scientists are influenced by the conditions and circumstances in which they must act. "[Only] naïve empiricism [holds] scientific knowledge to be simply a reflection of the reality of the external world. . . . Scientific investigation is never purely an occupation of the ivory tower and its products are not 'immaculately conceived.'" Weber's notion of *Wertbeziehung* makes this clear. The idea of *Wertbeziehung* implies that "the scientist himself, as a total human being, must find his commitment to his science meaningful in terms of his values," that "values must be relevant" to the knowing subject. But what values? The commonly held values of the society to which the scientist belongs, of the culture in which he has been socialized? Or the values of the particular group (his profession or scientific discipline) with which he is identified? Parsons speaks in the first case of the "value-science integrate" and in the second case of ideology. The value-science integrate involves what Parsons calls a "primary selectivity":

> "Even apart from limitations on the empirical resources available for validation, no social science integrated with the value system of a society can give answers to *all* the possible significant problems of societies, but only to those which have meaning within this integrate."[11]

This "primary selectivity" is a less serious problem than what "may be called 'secondary selectivity' to distinguish it from the 'primary type,'" for, as Parsons tells us, secondary selectivity "shades off into

distortion. . . . The criterion of distortion is that statements are made
about the society which by social-scientific methods can be shown to
be positively in error, whereas [primary] selectivity is involved where
the statements are, at the proper level, 'true,' but do not constitute a
balanced account of the available truth." Rather than say "true at the
proper level," it would probably be more correct to say "neither true
nor false," as Parsons himself suggests when he speaks of the "nonlogical" sphere. "It is clear that both secondary selectivity and distortion in an ideology violate the standards of empirical social science, in
a sense in which the value-science integrate does not." It is a true
statement that real per capita income in France has increased between
1945 and 1975, in the sense that it is possible to confirm or refute an
empirical statement. But to be interested more in questions of income
distribution than in questions of increases in average productivity is a
legitimate preference on the part of the researcher, the origin of which
lies in the value-science integrate with which he operates.

The task of social science is not merely to uncover distortion,
which, like other sciences, it does by insisting on the hygienic practice
of verification, but also to bring to light the kinds of selectivity typical
of the cultural system, though not by rejecting or disallowing in advance research results obtained by scientific methods, duly controlled.
All knowledge is relative to the value-science integrate, but this does
not mean that selectivity equals distortion. The Marxists, with their
class-conflict rhetoric, make just such an equation, however, at least
when they are railing against "bourgeois science." "Proletarian science," on the other hand, is apodictically certain, as we hardly need
mention.

If we hope to find an appropriate framework for dealing with problems of stratification in capitalist societies, with the nature of politics,
and with the role of the sociologist, then we have to rid ourselves of
the simplistic assumptions that caused Marx's thinking to ossify. His
genius was often agile enough to make it appear that he had found his
way out of the labyrinth of his own making. This does not alter the fact
that his reputation is based on such popular but fundamentally regressive ideas as the class struggle, the dictatorship of the proletariat as
precursor of the leap to freedom, and the determination of knowledge
and consciousness by material interests. Marx left his exegetes an
impossible task: to bend the two-class model sufficiently to accommodate certain irrefutable facts and eliminate certain patent logical difficulties, while at the same time refraining from open attack on the
model itself, lest the whole edifice of "scientific socialism"[12] come
tumbling down like a house of cards.

The Individual and Individualistic Society

At the center of industrial society in the view of Marxist ideology is "alienated man," whereas reactionary ideology gives pride of place to "anomic man." Certain features are common to both images: the individual is "manipulated" via his own desires and "exploited" by the violence of alter. In his very first work Durkheim wrote that anomie, which he then viewed as a dissolution of collective norms and values that went hand in hand with heightened individualism, was not "a natural and inevitable product of the division of labor, but rather something that arises in unusual and abnormal circumstances."[13] Is industrial society, as it has existed in the West for more than two centuries, such an "unusual and abnormal circumstance"? It would no doubt be difficult to maintain this position seriously.

Later in his career, Durkheim himself left us a more radical argument against interpreting society in general solely in terms of alienation and anomie. As it happens, he was speaking not of advanced industrial society but rather of so-called primitive society. Were the Australian aborigines, the Melanesians, and the American Indians puppets of chimera and fantasy? Durkheim attacks the notion that they were, and on precisely the ground where it seemed most firmly established: in the area of totemic beliefs. Indeed, we cannot help looking upon religions based on plant and animal worship as "an inexplicable hallucination."[14] But that hallucination has "a foothold in reality," according to Durkheim. Was "primitive" man the victim of some master magician, as we ourselves are said to be? Primitive men looked upon pieces of wood that stood for animals or plants as gods; are we not supposed to obey laws that are merely masks for the interests, whims, and arbitrary desires of the "ruling class"? In characterizing religion as "an inexplicable hallucination," Durkheim was conceding a point to empiricists for whom any concept not based on actual perception is an instance of "hallucination." On this view of the matter, society, too, would be a "hallucination," but, Durkheim tells us, a hallucination grounded in the reality not of a thing but of a system of relations. As a good rationalist, he goes no further than this, for although there may be reason for skepticism concerning the "reality" of religious imaginings, at least as they appear to us, it would be absurd to doubt the reality of the social fact. It may, of course, be doubted that a society is in reality as its ideology depicts it or that it conforms to its system of values. In other words, society is not always as it should be. But it is possible to treat society as a reality without regarding collective representations as scientifically valid assertions.

All we need do is distinguish between objectivity and reality: the point is that collective representations give us access to a "reality" that we can come to know as an "object" only through suitable scientific research. In short, we need only treat society as an interaction process the meaning of which the actors involved derive from norms and values.

Under what conditions and within what limits is it possible for an interaction process to exist that makes sense to the actors involved? As regards industrial society, both Marxists and reactionaries hold that all interaction comes down to either violent confrontation or compromise between material interests, of which the actors have at best a "mystified consciousness." Parsons's approach is entirely different. Rather than ask whether the individual is alienated, Parsons investigates the conditions under which he is able to act in an institutional context. Without stretching the term unduly, it might be said that Parsons's approach is "critical" in the Kantian sense. Parsons himself suggests as much, in regard not to the problem of the social order but rather to that of the objectivity of knowledge. The two problems are related, however. Parsons begins by distinguishing between what he calls the "Kantian problem" and the "Weberian problem." At the heart of Weber's thinking on the objectivity of sociological knowledge is the *suspicion* "that no matter how fully any given empirical propositions are validated, their inclusion in a body of knowledge about society is never completely independent of the value perspective from which those particular questions were asked and to which these propositions constitute answers."[15] The Kantian problem is quite different. In Kant's estimation scientifically valid facts do exist. Under what conditions may a given proposition be regarded as scientifically valid? The same question may be asked of the social order. The Weberian "suspicion" is this: a society might be other than what it is, because its values are contingent and so their legitimacy is open to doubt and ultimately to revocation. Nevertheless, we do find order of some kind in society: under what conditions will that order be perpetuated or, alternatively, changed? The latter problem corresponds to Kant's. The two questions are related insofar as both validity and reality criteria are constructed *pari passu* with the growth of sociological knowledge.

Suppose that in every society, and hence in industrial society, there is an order in some way meaningful, that is, an order that makes meaningful interaction between the members of the society possible. This order will have a significance that is not simply a matter of statistical regularities observed from outside the system, but that relates also to the way the actors themselves interpret their interaction. How can the observer reconstruct the meaning of an interaction? Under what conditions is he warranted in regarding as more objective than the actor's interpretation of his own conduct the meaning reconstructed by way of analysis, which brings to light the elements of the interaction and their systematic interrelations in the context of an overall synthesis? For the time being we shall leave this question unanswered. The point is merely to emphasize that interaction cannot be analyzed exclusively from the point of view of the system. The point of view of the actors themselves must also be taken into consideration, if only because, without some motivation of the actors, the "system" would not hold together.

Accordingly, an explanation of how the system functions must include the individual. Parsons, of course, uses the term "actor" rather than individual, and he is careful to point out that the actor may be either an individual or a "collectivity." The expression "collective actor" risks being misleading if it suggests that collectivities are actors in the same sense as individuals. Risen from the ashes, hyperfunctionalist sociology, which for some unfathomable reason likes to call itself "critical theory," attributes to abstract types such as capitalism the psychological determinations it refuses to attribute to the "alienated" or "mystified" individual. The individual is seen as a stooge controlled by an evil genius of some sort, whereas the "system" is all-knowing. Transferring to the "collectivity" the attributes that classical psychology vested in individuals, hyperfunctionalism gives the "collective actor" the lead role in that grandiose melodrama, History. Parsons understands the term "collective actor" in a totally different sense. No reification of the collectivity is implied; what emerges instead from Parsons's use of the term is a relativization of the individual. Neither the collectivity nor the individual is "real"; they are not self-subsistent entities. If, however, the observer can associate a set of intentions with a center or source, in which intentions are amalgamated into a means-ends chain in view of their anticipated consequences, then it is legitimate to speak of an "actor."

Accordingly, the term "actor" may be applied to an organization as well as a physical person. In this sense, it is quite legitimate to say that "General Motors wants to capture 25 percent of the Japanese market, that it aims to eliminate Ford from competition," and so forth. This is a kind of shorthand, which means that of all the possible outcomes that the executives of GM might choose, it is possible to impute a certain objective (control of the Japanese market, elimination of Ford) to the particularly aggressive strategy that the company has actually chosen to use against its competitor. To the extent that it can be said to have a strategy or strategies, General Motors is a collective actor. To speak of a "collective actor," then, commits us to the following two propositions: first, that the actor is characterized by his strategic capacity and, second, that the more diversified and better integrated his resources are, the greater that strategic capacity will be.

In delineating Parsons's position, it is not enough to stress the primacy of the relational orientation in his conception of the individual or collective actor, as we have done above. Prominence must also be given to the fact that his brand of individualism has nothing to do with utilitarian individualism. Parsons himself has termed his version "institutionalized individualism." As long ago as *The Structure of Social Action,* the importance of the individualistic orientation and the many strands of Western tradition entwined within it were given great prominence. "Probably the primary source of this individualistic cast of European thought lies in Christianity. In an ethical and religious sense Christianity has always been deeply individualist. That is, its ultimate concern has been with the welfare, above all in the next world, of the individual immortal soul." Beyond Christianity, though, Western individualism has secular origins, at once Roman and Greek. The contribution of Roman law to the idea of the individual was the delineation of a sphere within which the individual, as property-owner or party to a contract, had rights over things and could oblige others to act in certain ways, as they could oblige him in return. As a member of a family, furthermore, the individual was allowed some freedom in the employment of his patrimony. These rights could be invoked by one individual only because they were recognized as applying to all. What is more, their secure exercise depended on the backing of the state. Ultimately, Roman law embodied the distinction between self-orientation and collectivity-orientation. Rather than treat these two orientations as mutually exclusive alternatives, however, the law laid down the institutional conditions under which the subject was free to act as he might choose. A man is master in his own home because, under legally established limits, he is free to enter into contracts, to buy, sell, take a wife, and come and go as he pleases. From the Greek tradition came an enhanced idea of the powers of the individual. Philosophy in the Socratic-Platonic tradition recognizes the individual as the subject who makes judgments, who distinguishes between true and false, good and evil. But the Greek, especially the Athenian, is also a citizen, a subject who has something to say about the ends of collective action. As philosopher and as citizen, Western man in the humanist tradition is an *individual,* not in the sense of a self-sufficient entity but rather in the sense that he acts in certain specific, institutionally defined ways.

However divergent the pagan humanist and Christian traditions may be, both recognize in the individual a capacity to make decisions, and both see him as the recipient of a message that "passeth his understanding" but is intended for his scrutiny. History makes sense only in relation to what some individual person can feel or understand of it or do with it, that is, in relation to his preferences, his goals, and his resources. This way of putting things is ambiguous, because the individual is seen as having a spiritual destiny or as identified with certain activities and rights. It is essentially this ambiguity that the third component of the individualistic tradition, utilitarianism, unsuccessfully tried to eliminate. In the utilitarian view, the individual is not merely a soul with a spiritual destiny, a judge, a citizen, a person endowed with certain rights, but also a consumer or producer, who selects and combines scarce goods in order to achieve the highest level of gratification that the resources at his disposal will permit. The crucial contribution of utilitarianism, for which exchange and the division of labor are the central concepts, was the discovery of utility as the fundamental relation between man and thing as between man and man, the latter being important to the extent that men can negotiate over what relations they will set up with one another, with the object of turning their desires into objects for consumption by means of production. Technical and economic activity, then, is carried on within two main frames of reference: the means-ends chain, as the passage from Weber that serves as epigraph to *The Structure of Social Action* makes clear, and the need-dispositions and gratifications of technicians and producers, who will put the resources at their disposal to use only in order to attain ends that in one way or another bring them gratification.

Because utilitarianism emerges out of the explicit attempt to naturalize and secularize human action, to reduce it, as Hobbes tried to do, to a question of passions and interests, it leads ultimately to an untenable interpretation of individual action: on the one hand, utilitarians argue that the individual can attain his goals only with the cooperation of other individuals, while on the other hand each individual defines his goals only in opposition to the goals of others, or at best in indifference to them. Caught between the objective conditions of his situation, that is, the division of labor, and the affirmation of his subjectivity, that is, his desires, the utilitarian individual is trapped: he must confront on the one hand the fact that his ends are essentially contingent, so that ultimately his action does not matter at all, and on the other hand the fact that his goals are incompatible with the goals of others: this is just another way of saying that violence and anomie are the only possibilities.

This is the impasse in which utilitarian individualism finds itself and which Parsons described with unfailing force and lucidity. Let us beware, however, of discarding the baby with the bathwater. This is the mistake made by sociologism in the Durkheim mold, at least in its more polemical versions. Durkheim failed to take sufficient precautions against falling into the trap of interpreting society as an entity distinct from the individuals who make it up. "The crudest version of this interpretation is that [society] is a spatially separate object. . . . It is quite clear, for instance, that society does not commit suicide in the sense in which that term is used in Durkheim's monograph" [1937, p. 367]. What utilitarian individualism fails to comprehend is the nature of collective ends, which it either pretends to ignore or treats purely as aggregates. This does not mean that the utilitarians were not clearly aware of the crucial importance of the means-end relationship for explaining human action. What was needed was an explanation of that relationship more comprehensive than the utilitarian explanation, in which specific resources were matched to discrete, identifiable gratifications. In my view, this is what Parsons attempted; a determined critic of utilitarian individualism, he has nevertheless given us a profoundly individualistic theory of action.

Two remarks will help clarify the nature of Parsons's conception. To begin with, individual and society are both equivocal terms. Either they are abstractly conceived, that is, exclusively in terms of their attributes, as though they were self-subsistent entities, or else they are conceived relatively, that is, as elements defined by the place they occupy in the system of action. In the relativistic view, the intuitive notion of the individual falls into two parts. On the one hand the individual is the role-playing actor, while on the other hand he is the personality within which motivations and orientations are coordinated. But the individual is never a unity closed in on itself, cut off from other people—in a word, autarchic. Accordingly, when Parsons points to the "elementary unit" of the system, he is careful to stress that it is not to be looked for in the individual but rather in what he calls the "unit act," or, in a slightly different sense, the role. It is in the unit act that an individual reveals himself as an actor in an interaction in which he takes initiatives vis-à-vis alter, and in which alter takes initiatives vis-à-vis ego. It makes no sense to speak of unit acts without reference to an actor, ego, and his partner in the interaction process, alter, the two of them mutually contingent, as we have seen. The sociologist must be equipped to search, even under the carapace of the most rigid of institutions, for this vital sap of mutual dependency, the form of which may vary from one context to the next: cooperation and consensus in some cases, conflict in others; sometimes hierarchy, other times equality.

On the most elementary level, the role is a relation or even a system of relations between two or more persons, which is treated by each of them as a part of his environment, and which as such may aid or impede them in the attainment of their goals; in other words, the role may be a source of either gratification or frustration. The collectivity, for its part, is "the system composed by the interaction of the two [or more] participants, so far as it shares a common normative culture and is distinguishable from others by the participation of these two [or more actors] and not others."[16] To bring out the relativity of sociological categories, Parsons points out that "we often speak of a role or collectivity as if it were a concrete entity, but this is, strictly speaking, elliptical. There is no collectivity without member roles and, vice-versa, no role which is not part of a collectivity" [1966, p. 19]. We may speak of the collectivity that consists of doctor and patient, but only insofar as we invoke the norms to which both are subject and the values that legitimate those norms. Even though medical ethics may not be what we are fundamentally interested in, without a knowledge of medical ethics we cannot properly interpret the interplay of doctor and patient roles. We may describe the role that each actor plays, but our description makes sense only in relation to the therapeutic process. The observer decides what point of reference to choose. But his choice does not relieve him of the obligation to consider all the independent variables, even if some of them happen to fall outside his area of immediate interest.

It was along these relativistic, or relational, lines that Parsons's thinking developed. We find the earmarks of the relativistic approach even at the most general level of theory, that is, in the theory of action, where it accounts for the distinctions between personality, society, and culture. Within each of these three spheres we again find the relativistic approach at work. To take society, for instance, relativism figures in the relationship between the role and the collectivity, which is defined in terms of norms and values. If one were blindly to follow this procedure, however, knitting together as extensive as possible a chain of relevant data, the result might be no more than an amorphous list of "interesting" questions. Pluralism often does just this: there is this, but also that, and then again this other thing, and so on. Parsonian individualism is not content to set down one "factor," the individual, alongside another "factor," society, in the name of common sense. Rather it seeks to establish the relations and mediations among the various terms deemed relevant to the analysis of the action process. Now, choice is the essence of action. Accordingly, the key to analyzing systems of action is the consistency or compatibility of preferences. On the level of collective systems, aggregative individualistic models very quickly reveal their ambiguity. Aggregation by addition is permissible if and only if preferences relative to a given eventuality are weighted equally in the sum. Suppose that each voter has one vote that may go to either A or B. Such preferences may be added. But as soon as we relax the conditions a bit, say by taking account of the intensity of each voter's preference or by including additional possibilities in the range of choices, aggregation becomes more complex. Straightforward addition is no longer possible. Instead, we must analyze the conditions under which the basic preferences of each individual are compatible with one another.

The idea of compatibility, that is, of order, is central to Parsons's thinking. As we have seen, this idea is important in the concept of the individual actor, and equally important, though naturally in a more complex way, in the concept of the collective actor. In Parsons's view the actor makes choices and combines resources. He makes choices because he cannot have everything. In this sense the utilitarian notion of costs and benefits remains valid, but it must be generalized to include not only goods and services but also less tangible rewards. The utilitarians improperly define the cost-benefit ratio in strictly material terms. They also pretend that each actor can calculate the ratio of benefits to costs. Parsons dismisses these two assumptions but is no less insistent on the importance of choice than the utilitarians and other theorists of action who attempted to generalize the economic model. *Homo parsoniensis* not only makes choices but also combines resources. The idea of "combining" resources is particularly important. Parsons aimed his critique of behaviorism at the claim that the actor merely *reacts* to the situation. Instead, he argues that the actor rearranges the elements of the situation according to an order that the actor himself establishes. What is more, the individual does not face a situation that is shut off from the rest of the world. As we have frequently had occasion to point out, situations are delineated by boundaries, and these boundaries can be crossed. Hence ambiguity and anomie are inherent dangers in any situation, but there will also be possibilities of transforming the available resources to meet the needs of the moment, because the actor can play in more than one game at a time.

As an actor who makes choices and combines resources, *homo parsoniensis* is bound by the logic of compatibility. There are two aspects to this logic: dichotomies and combinatorics. On the most basic level, choice is mutually exclusive: there are only two sexes (male/female) or two age classes (adult/child), and no individual can belong to more than one at a time, any more than a person can be in both Paris and Bordeaux at the same moment. The pattern variables are said to be strict dichotomies of this type when taken individually. But we can also combine two or more pattern variables, thereby relaxing the condition of compatibility. Suppose we take two pattern variables and let one describe ego's expectations, the other alter's. If we then require that the combination meet stability conditions defined with respect to both internal and external environments, we obtain the four functions, which, as we have seen, are prerequisites in every system of action. A unit act cannot simultaneously be both universalistic and particularistic. But a social system is simultaneously adapive *and* integrative. The social system is not characterized by the presence of one or another of these two functions, to the exclusion of all others, but rather by the way in which the two functions are actually combined and the way their combination affects the combinations of the remaining two functions, that is, the overall hierarchy of the system.

When we say that *homo parsoniensis* makes choices, we are not contending that he is condemned to choose between the mutually exclusive alternatives of either doing or not doing something, or that he creates the alternatives between which he must choose ex nihilo. The actor's alternatives and the form of his choice are defined by the situation. At a given moment, not all the possibilities open to one actor will be open to another, whose past experience is different. To begin with, an actor's range of choice is limited by his own preferences: certain goods and services, certain possible outcomes will not interest him. The goods, services, and outcomes that do interest him, moreover, may be obtainable only at prices he cannot afford. "You can't have your cake and eat it, too," is a common way of putting the limitations imposed on our action by scarcity. Scarcity also makes itself felt when we analyze hypothetical means-ends linkages: "If I want to obtain such and such a result, I will need certain resources, and to have them, I will have to give up certain other resources."

Institutions may be thought of as imposing constraints and restrictions on the actor's range of choice. Eventually, of course, the legitimacy of these restrictions is open to criticism. Now, the problem is to explain the conformity of individual motives with social norms. There are quick and easy ways of doing this, just as there are quick and easy ways of explaining sleep, like the ad hoc theory that attributes it to a *virtus dormitiva*. Parsons's approach eschews this sort of theorizing, since he explicitly regards the effectiveness of an institution as depending on its legitimacy. Parsons does focus primarily on institutionalization, that is, the process by which norms and values are internalized (where norms are seen as immediate and self-evident specifications of values, hence as legitimate). But internalization is not enough to ensure conformity. Accordingly, the theory of institutions is more than the theory of institutionalization. Internalized values are at once too general, too ambiguous, and not sanctioned effectively enough to ensure that actual behavior will conform to their idealized prescriptions.

Institutions do not provide the actors with a ready-made repertory of solutions but rather with a "repertory of roles." With such a repertory at hand, an actor confronted with a range of related problems can decide which of the various courses of action open to him to choose. Thus when Parsons and Smelser speak of the "institutional structure of the economy," what they mean is that goods and services are allocated so as to ensure that the adaptive function of the economic subsystem is compatible with the other functions of the social system. For the individual actor, the "institutional structure of the economy" establishes criteria for deciding how to use the resources at his disposal. One additional restriction is always implicit, however: namely, that the potential benefit of such employment of resources be compatible with what the actor takes to be the requirements imposed on him by virtue of his participation in the other subsystems of the system of action.

In the economic subsystem, Parsons and Smelser [1956, p. 44] identify four functions: investment (A), production (G), organization (I), and employment (L). These functions are governed by various rules and standards, which define the terms of trade between the different parties to the exchange. Accordingly, "a central feature of the economic process involves coming to terms with those who control factors of production and inducing them to utilize or permit utilization of these resources for economic purposes. . . . Contract thus constitutes the institutional framework for the basic economic process of exchange" [1956, pp. 104–5]. Different types of contract are associated with each of the four functions mentioned above: loan contracts with banks to obtain the funds needed for investment (A), contracts between producers and customers (G), contracts between producers and suppliers of goods and services (I), and contracts between producers and employees (L) are typical examples. It is around these activities that "the institutional structure of the economy" crystallizes.

Investor and lender, job-seeker and employer are all governed by rules, the purpose of which is broader than merely to curb capriciousness and greed. Rules are also useful for establishing criteria for choosing between two alternative uses of the resources at hand. Consider, for example, an employment contract, first from the standpoint of the employer and then from the standpoint of the employee. Unless the job in question is offered on a "take it or leave it" basis, the employment contract does more than state the availability of a certain kind of work. In addition, it will usually specify the rate of pay, the skills required, the duration of employment, and a detailed job description (pertaining to matters of discipline, security, and training, for instance). Implicit in the contract are criteria for determining whether it makes sense to substitute machines for "living labor," or whether production ought to be curtailed or halted because both machinery and labor are too costly. From the job-seeker's point of view, the contract is a way of determining whether the prospective job will meet his needs in regard to difficulty of the work, ease of access, hours, job security, and potential for advancement. In some cases hiring is not contractual because the worker is obliged to accept whatever job the employer offers—or die of hunger (such a worker may legitimately be called a "proletarian," which use may be contrasted with the many rhetorical uses of the term). But such extreme situations are obviously exceptional. The hiring institutions do not in general set up "take it or leave it" situations, although it should be borne in mind that the position of the employer is not equivalent to the position of the worker in this respect. What the institutions do is to lay down a range of eventualities of varying degrees of probability and varying levels of gratification, among which individuals may choose according to their own preference schedules.

Investment contracts may be analyzed in the same way [1956, pp. 123–39]. Ultimately, of course, investment comes down to a "yes or no" decision: "I will borrow or I will not borrow," or, from the banker's point of view, "I will lend or I will not lend." But the banker who decides not to lend to certain capitalists, or, rather, to lend to them only at a rate of interest so high as to persuade them (or at any rate most of them, particularly the more cautious and less enterprising) not to borrow, need not leave his funds idle. He may limit his loans to industry in order to reserve more funds for federal or local governments, or for individuals and households. To put it another way, only in exceptional cases does the institution put a stop to all loans. It may well establish criteria that hinder our plans by making the cost of carrying them out too high, by imposing a high rate of interest, for example, or inflated wages, or a high discount rate on future income. But if the interest rate is too high, I can opt for increased liquidity through reduction of stocks, or even cut prices in order to boost sales, reckoning that inflation will reduce the real value of my debt by the time it comes due. Similarly, if the real wage offered by an employer is too low, I can draw on my savings or go into debt in order to upgrade my skill level so as to qualify for a better-paid position.

How stark the alternative will be in any particular case will depend on the full spectrum of alternatives open to me, that is, on the resources at my disposal. If the choice facing me is one between unemployment and a "pauper's wage," and I have only a few dollars in my pocket standing between me and starvation, I may still be metaphysically a free being. But in the domain that interests us here, that of action, I am trapped: I have almost no room to maneuver. To be assured of freedom I must have a wide range of resources at my disposal, and a wide range of situations in which those resources can be brought to bear. Money, as we have seen, is important precisely because it lends itself to a virtually unlimited range of uses, and this is true also of symbolic media in general. Calculation in monetary terms makes it possible to establish priorities and hence to choose, provided the key indices of the various alternatives can be expressed in a form amenable to calculation. Money, however, is a resource only for those who possess a certain amount of it. And the number of uses they can put their money to obviously depends on the amount of money they have.

The judgment I make of an institution will depend not only on what constraints it imposes on my actions but also on my preferences, on the resources the institution allocates for my use, and on the range of alternatives that it makes available to me. Accordingly, judgments of any particular institution will vary from individual to individual, and no institution will be wholly approved as gratifying or wholly condemned as frustrating by everyone. The theory of deviance and social control can help to explain why a particular institutional allocation of resources and activities will in one case be felt to be intolerable, in another rectifiable, in still another as signaling the need for a radical transformation. Institutional analysis is also applicable to resources and activities in the political sphere. "Supply/demand" transactions between rulers and ruled are of course different in nature from supply/demand transactions between employers and employees. Still, it is legitimate to speak of a "political market" if by that one means that, as in the labor, consumer goods, or capital markets, there are actors of several kinds involved in the bargaining, the terms of which

determine the final allocation of certain collective resources, most
notably of the funds collected by the authorities (in the form of taxes,
for instance). Neither government nor citizen is permitted, however,
to appeal to private interest to justify "demands" on the "political
market." To violate this prohibition would lead to corruption of the
political process. A citizen will, of course, look to his own interests in
deciding which of two parties or candidates to vote for, just as the
physician will be aware that the fees he pockets for his services provide for the welfare of his family. But the primary frame of reference
within which the doctor-patient relationship is defined and regulated
is that of the "therapeutic couple," with its collectivity-orientation.
Similarly, considerations of private interest may influence the citizen.
Unless he is completely cynical, however—*après moi le déluge*—he
will not deem legitimate a solution beneficial to himself in the short
run if in the long run it will mean disaster for the collectivity.

Such problems are central to politics, whereas in economics they
seldom arise. There is no need to assume that the economic actor who
saves or spends "wishes" to bring about an optimal allocation of factors as seen from the point of view of the collectivity. It is extremely
difficult, however, to base policy decisions on a purely cynical set of
assumptions. Individualistic economic theory as Parsons interprets it
is applicable to all "Pareto-optimal" equilibrium situations. Political
theory must proceed more delicately, for its purpose is to specify the
conditions under which the collectivity-orientation takes precedence
over the self-orientation for the actor as citizen.

Even if "economistic" interpretations of politics are ruled out, it is
possible to establish political analysis in terms of resources and their
utilization on firm grounds. In the political subsystem, or "polity," as
Parsons and Smelser call it, we again find the four functions. Let us call
the adaptive function within the polity the *administrative function,*
which we shall denote A_G. Its purpose is to effect a "double interchange" between the center and the periphery: resources are pumped
into the periphery from the center, and the center redistributes all or
part of what it receives back from the periphery in return. We shall
call the goal-attainment function within the polity the *political
decision-making function,* G_G, the purpose of which is to choose goals
for the collectivity. Similarly, I_G will denote the *support function,* by
which "demands" are conveyed to the decision makers before decisions are reached, and decisions are transmitted to the public before
being implemented. L_G, finally, is the *legitimation function.* The polity
must deal with differentiated functional problems involving bureaucrats, voters, government officials, ideologues (in search of legiti-

macy), and lobbyists for various pressure groups. The political institutions constrain these various categories of actors in fairly specific ways. At the same time, the institutions provide certain resources and lay the groundwork for a reasonably open-ended spectrum of uses of those resources.

Citizens have certain political resources at their disposal. To confine our attention to modern democracies only, the citizen is a voter. Through universal suffrage he has access to the symbolic medium of power. The situation is analogous to the one that obtains in the economic subsystem, where the actor's power depends in part on the amount of money at his disposal. Thus, at the grass-roots level of political institutions, we find once again the individual actor and his gamut of choices. But what choices can voters actually make? They cannot register their opinion of every theoretically possible utilization of the collective resources, not only because the information available is at best incomplete but also because most of the possible choices are not spelled out explicitly. Hence the voter is not a rational individual, in the sense the term "rational" is used in marginalist economics, particularly in the theory of consumer behavior. The complete range of possibilities on which he will base his choice is not available to him. In addition, he does not connect any definite set of consequences with any particular choice. Finally, for any particular decision, he does not have a rank-ordering of the various consequences from the most desirable to the least desirable. But, as March and Simon, from whom the foregoing analysis is paraphrased, have clearly shown,[17] the fact that decision makers lack both complete information and adequate prognoses, as well as transitive preference schedules—in short, the fact that decision makers are not "rational" in the strict sense of the word—does not mean that they have not tried to rationalize their choices. Nor does it mean that their choices would not have been worse had they not tried to rationalize them, the imperfections in the decision-making process notwithstanding. Parsons, following Pareto, stressed the importance of the residual category of the "non-logical," which is not covered by the distinction between the logico-experimental and the illogical. In Parsons's commentary on Pareto nonlogical decisions are those in which symbolism played a preponderant part. It might be worthwhile also to compare nonlogical decisions with "reasonable" decisions, which are not to be confused with rational decisions, although they may under certain conditions approximate to rationality.[18]

Voters, then, are certainly not rational. They are sometimes reasonable, however, that is, capable of weighing various eventualities against their own preferences and of giving their vote and their support (i.e., their resources) to the candidate judged most likely to bring about the desired state of affairs. It is in relation to the institutional definition of the possible alternative uses of his resources that the "reasonableness" of the voter must be judged. Reasonable decisions are possible because the rules of the game reduce the range of possibilities and hence the degree of uncertainty associated with choice. Such decisions are taken only after candidates and issues have gone through several preliminary stages of sorting out. Only a limited number of issues are actually presented to the voter, and for each issue only a limited number of strategies are possible. The number of candidates and parties to choose from is also small. The range of choices is thus not open-ended: issues not germane to the election (or at least treated as such by the institutional system) outnumber the issues that are germane (i.e., the questions that the system allows the voter to consider).

When the range of choice is so curtailed as to embrace but a single alternative, the problem of the inconsistency of collective preferences is sidestepped. But is not the voter's freedom of choice simultaneously eliminated? This would no doubt be so if the choice between the Republican and Democratic candidates for president were really the choice between tweedledum and tweedledee that radical critics of the American system contemptuously contend it is. Are the party platforms, as these critics believe, really only minor, nay, imperceptible, variations on the same theme? Are the rival candidates mere figureheads who might equally well be replaced by two other nonentities? Parsons sharply rejects this line of thinking. In commenting on the work of Lazarsfeld,[19] moreover, he is at pains to point out that the two-party system lays down not only lines of consensus but also lines of cleavage. The majority of American voters of both parties are in agreement about many values. Democrats and Republicans are closer in their ideas about the purposes of politics than are, say, the Left and the Right in France. There is also a powerful consensus on the rules of politics and the respective powers of the president and the Congress, a consensus that cuts across party lines. Nevertheless, Republicans and Democrats do part company on important issues, and the policies of Democratic administrations since the New Deal have been different from those of the Eisenhower and Nixon administrations.

The choice available to the American voter is limited in scope but nonetheless real. Defining the limits of that choice more precisely will give us greater insight into the nature of the choice itself. According to Schumpeter's well-known theory, the voter does not really choose the policy that the government is supposed to carry out on his behalf, but rather he chooses the personalities who will govern him (his masters, Rousseau would say). Parsons's argument is more subtle. The voter, according to Parsons does not merely choose a personality—a future president of the United States, for instance. In opting for a man he also opts for a program. Of course, this program is not an actual "contract," politicians' promises to the contrary notwithstanding. It is inherent in the very nature of the office of the presidency, which extends over a four-year term, that the candidate can at best commit himself to a general policy line, not to a specific policy. An elected official is different from a proxy in civil law. Still, even if he wanted to break his campaign promises and abandon the individuals and interest groups that made his election possible, he would have a hard time doing so. Although no actual contract exists, the elected official is bound by his promises, and his commitment is the counterpart of the power and freedom of choice of the voter. What is more, the voter is not unaffected by his candidate's victory or defeat. A victory for the Democratic Party carries with it certain implications for subsequent allocations of collective resources. Public expenditures for social security, for example, would have been less had Goldwater been elected rather than Johnson, the father of the "Great Society." As things turned out, of course, it may well have been true that inflation robbed the "poor" of the "phoney benefits" that Johnson and the other "socialist demagogues" in the Democratic Party had promised them. Whether or not such was the case is of no importance for our purposes; all that matters is that a Johnson victory was in fact perceived by an appreciable proportion of the electorate as implying a future different from that which would have followed a Goldwater victory.

The voters do perceive differences between the platforms of the two parties; they make comparisons and express their preference for one or the other. There is no reason to believe that this perception is due solely to manipulation. There are, however, limits on the choices open to the electorate. For one thing, the outcome of the election must not be such as to jeopardize the peaceful coexistence of the two parties. The logic of the two-party system imposes a clear-cut verdict, which is tolerable only because the losers are not afraid that what they see as their vital interests will be drastically affected by the victory of the opposing party. If the victory of a certain party meant the extermination of X, it would only be logical to expect X to do everything in his power to prevent that party from winning. For a two-party *political* system to operate normally, the clash of interests must not be in the nature of a life-and-death struggle. The two-party system and the idea of a loyal opposition, therefore, are not compatible with the idea of the class struggle as conceived by orthodox Marxists. A priori, it is of course impossible to define just how far the winner could go in abusing his power before the coexistence of the opposing groups and interests would become impossible. The difficulty is particularly acute in the political realm, where, as Albert Hirschman has pointed out, "exit" is hardly practicable because the costs are so high: as Danton said, "One does not carry one's fatherland on the soles of one's shoes." In consequence, negotiations, usually implicit, over just what "going too far" means are among the most delicate aspects of the art of politics. This judgment has more to do with such moral virtues as moderation and wisdom than with theory. Consensus rests on the existence of such limits, whether readily apparent or not. When political reckonings take explicit account of them, utilitarian analysis is no longer adequate. A utilitarian individual who happens to be in the minority and yet remains in the group, even though the majority has just gone against his own interest, is attributing to the perpetuation of the body politic a value greater than the personal benefit he has been forced to sacrifice. By the same token, a utilitarian individual who belongs to the majority but is persuaded not to take undue advantage of victory shows himself convinced that harmonious relations with his fellow citizens, even those with interests opposed to his own, are of greater value than whatever immediate benefit the strict letter of the law might permit him to reap.

"Public-spiritedness" thus limits the voter's freedom of choice. His freedom as a citizen requires such a prior limitation of his freedom to choose. This is the meaning, or, rather, one of the two meanings that Parsons attributes to consensus. Looked at in one way, consensus consists of a web of constraints that limit the range of choices theoretically available to the individual. But consensus is also solidarity, sometimes rather somberly described as "being condemned to live with one another." Parsons was never tempted to reduce politics to consensus. The survival of the body politic does, however, to some extent take precedence over the immediate self-interest of each citizen, at least under certain circumstances; hence the need to preserve the consensus sets limits on what individuals can presume to demand.

Thus far the member of the political system has been treated as though he were defined by a single role. Our arguments have all been based on the implicit assumption that the citizen is simply a voter and that all his power resides in his vote. In reality, the citizen takes part in many political activities other than the relatively infrequent elections in which he casts his vote. He may also be a member of a club or organization of some sort and take an interest in the goals set by the group. As a parent of a school-age child, a user of public services, a taxpayer, or, more generally, as a person approving or disapproving of the way the government is being run, the citizen may take an interest in a wide variety of issues of great importance in determining the allocation of collective resources and the broad outlines of public policy, even though they have no direct bearing on the fate of the incumbent administration.

The citizen, like the consumer and the entrepreneur, is never completely defenseless. Neither all-powerful nor totally powerless, his position is comparable to that of an individual in an organization. Each echelon in a hierarchy, except for the very highest and the very lowest, sits between two other echelons. The statement that A has more power than B means not only that A can compel B to carry out his orders but also that more echelons in the chain of command are subject to A's orders than to B's. It also means that decisions taken by A are pertinent to a greater number of situations than are decisions taken by B. This does not mean that B has no area of responsibility at all, however. Power need not be allocated on an "all or nothing" basis, except where, as Hobbes imagined, a tyrannical sovereign has gathered all power into his own hands, leaving none to the other members of the body politic.

Parsons sets forth the institutionalized freedoms at the disposal of the individual within the political and economic order as follows.[20] "The consumer . . . has the following degrees of freedom: (1) in accepting money, e.g. in exchange for labor services, he is not *ipso facto* committed to buy what he wants to spend it for from any particular source of supply—he can 'shop around'; (2) he is not committed to any particular composition of the 'package' of items for which he spends it, but can select in terms of his wants at the time; (3) he is not committed to any particular terms of exchange but can shop and/or bargain over prices; and (4) he is not committed to any particular time of expenditure of his funds, but can extend his expenditures over time. . . . Political differentiation . . . creates degrees of freedom analogous to those of the market as follows: (1) The analogy of economic source of supply is leadership agency, e.g. a party as the agency taking responsibility for collective decision-making if given requisite political support. A 'free electorate' has a choice between such agencies and is not ascriptively bound to any one by its legitimacy. (2) The political analogy of products is policies. . . . The individual or group . . . is free to allocate such influence as he has between a significant range of alternatives. (3) The political analogy of [cost] is the obligations entailed by commitment to a collective decision or policy. . . . (4) In the political as in the economic case, differentiation makes it possible for leadership and followership both to enjoy greater flexibility with respect to time." These freedoms may be curtailed by the existence of monopolies, or even by market imperfections less drastic than monopoly, by deterioration of product quality, or by erosion of purchasing power due to inflation in the case of the economic consumer. Similar malfunctions occur in the political system. For one thing, there can be concentration of political power in the hands of a closed elite group, that is, an oligarchy, with a concomitant elimination of electoral choice. For another, we sometimes find "inflated" promises being made by politicians and a widening gap between political rhetoric and "reality," which can endanger individual liberties. Are oligarchic and monopolistic tendencies in modern society so clearly in the ascendant that the last vestiges of true democratic choice are rapidly being eliminated? However that may be, we cannot accept the view that "society" exerts an unlimited power to constrain the individual externally and manipulate him internally. In what Parsons calls institutionalized individualism the individual comes equipped with certain preferences, and certain resources are available to him; given the constraints under which he must operate, he will choose to make certain uses of those resources. All of this is fair game for sociological inquiry. Only through research can we judge the relative degree of individual freedom, of power or impotence, exhibited by the system under various conditions and in different circumstances.

Stratification and Legitimation

Is it appropriate to characterize industrial society as an instance of institutionalized individualism? "The more complex and pluralistic a society becomes, however, the more dependent its functioning comes to be on freedom of unit decision and on generalized mechanisms which facilitate and guide those decisions."[21] Indeed, the individual is characterized by his capacity to make choices and decisions. The greater the number of alternatives open to him, the more the functioning of the society depends on his capacity to make choices. As for the mechanisms, the "generality" of which Parsons stressed in the passage cited above, we may think of them not as having been put together to meet the needs of specific situations but rather as institutions, consisting of a reasonably consistent set of rules, internalized to a degree sufficient for the purposes at hand. The structural complexity of modern society is attested by the large number of highly specialized occupations we find within it. By now this sort of observation is a familiar commonplace, a reformulation of the idea of the division of labor with its concomitant broadening of the market.

More interesting is Parsons's observation that the division of labor tends to sever the close ties that bind the individual in traditional society to his family and village. Along with this loosening of "ascriptive" solidarities go great dangers for the individual. The stockpile of resources that he amassed within the framework of traditional society are no longer of much use to him. In his new environment, in which economic pursuits have been sundered from domestic activities, the individual is faced with choices for which traditional society in no way prepared him. Traditional societies, then, are far more "programmed" than are modern societies. In the former, individuals can scarcely do anything they are not supposed to do. Relatively few choices are open to them, and those that are are specific and explicit. The deviant is hit with strict and unavoidable sanctions. Even if the structure is complex, as in some cases we know it was from the wealth of rules governing marriages, the individual has very little room to maneuver.

As the burgeoning division of labor increases the range of available resources and their potential uses, the nature of conformity undergoes a change. Conformity can no longer be ensured by a fixed, one-to-one correspondence between available positions in the society and roles that actors have been trained or brought up to play. The fact that my father was a blacksmith does not necessarily mean that I will become a blacksmith as well. Even if family background and parents' status are indices that can be used to give fairly accurate predictions of the level of prestige, power, income, or status to which an individual is likely to rise, that individual may well be doing a job the nature of which differs radically from the sort of work his father did before him. Even at a given status level, the individual may well find a wide range of different employments over the course of his life. Traditional society offered relatively few "programs," and these were relatively simple in nature. Such elementary activities as consuming and voting, which institutions such as the market and mass democracy are said to "program" in industrial societies, actually give access to a far wider range of possible outcomes than traditional societies make available, and the ways in which these outcomes may be attained are not fixed, but hypothetically free, not to say randomly distributed.

The repertory of roles that an individual is capable of playing constitutes his "capital." With this capital the individual can earn a living, win recognition from alter, and obtain gratifications associated with his role-status. A role is two things: on the one hand a fund of resources at hand or mobilizable if needed, on the other hand a set of rules covering the use of those resources. The resource/utilization dichotomy is of interest for analyzing the "wealth," both real and symbolic (i.e., property, privileges, riches, and honors), of the actor playing a given role. Different types of societies are characterized by the kinds of resources they make available, as well as the utilizations of those resources that they make possible, as David Riesman observed in *The Lonely Crowd,* although he makes too much in that well-known work of the distinction between the inner-directed and the other-directed individual. In actuality, every actor's fund of resources includes the "responses" of alter (and hence every actor may be said to be other-directed) as well as the judgment of his own conscience (for which reason every actor may be regarded as inner-directed). We respond to the external sanctions with which alter greets our initiatives, and we also respond to the internal sanctions imposed by our own consciences (in accordance with the internalized norms on which our critical self-judgments are based). The relative importance of internal as opposed to external sanctions depends on the number, consistency, and stability of the available roles, as well as on the common values and their effect on the values associated with clusters of more specialized activity. Furthermore, external and internal sanctions may both be either real or symbolic. To arrive at a judgment of how free the individual is in industrial society without resorting to clichés about "manipulation," we must determine what resources are available to each of the several categories of actors and what uses may be made of those resources (where both resources and utilizations may be symbolic as well as real).

The hierarchy of roles and the way in which they are allocated are the central topics of the debate over social stratification. Parsons approached the question from two angles. He first attempted to use the theory of action to deal with the problem of social stratification. He also tried to show in what respects the types of stratification found in industrial societies, and, more particularly, in certain nations, such as the United States, are unique. We shall begin our discussion with a few general remarks about the problem of social stratification. "All the components of systems of action and of the situations in which action takes place are subject to the process of evaluation, as desirable or undesirable, as useful or useless, as gratifying or noxious."[22] Within what frame of reference is such an evaluation carried out? Evaluations may be made with reference to values of three kinds: the idiosyncratic values of the evaluator, the values of some group of which he is a member, or the values of society as a whole, that is, of the "group of groups," comprising all groups and activities in which the individual takes part. When the latter frame of reference is invoked, Parsons speaks of the "paramount value system." The paramount values are not necessarily the values of the ruling class; indeed, the power of the ruling class is frequently challenged in the name of the paramount values. What is more, the power of the paramount values is by nature different from the power of one class over another. Bear in mind that values are frequently no more than vague indications of what a society holds to be desirable. They are effective only if backed up by a system of internal and external sanctions, at once hierarchical and inter-dependent, material and symbolic.

The system of stratification does not "reproduce" the value system in either the Platonic sense in which the copy reproduces the model or the biological sense in which the species reproduces itself from gener-ation to generation. There are at least two reasons for rejecting the so-called functionalist theory of social stratification. To begin with, Parsons holds that the actual distribution of resources, jobs, and re-wards does not reflect the system of values in any simple way, because in many respects the distribution is in contradiction to or conflict with the paramount value system. It is not *in order to* embody the ideal that society is what it is; indeed, in many ways society stands in contradic-tion to its own basic principles. Because the value system is relatively indeterminate, moreover, it will be useful for making judgments only in a small number of situations, potential or real. Though some of these situations may be deemed of little or no interest from the col-lective standpoint, yet they may be judged extremely desirable or undesirable by certain individuals but in the light of their own, and not the common, value system.

Let us define the system of stratification as a hierarchy of posi-tions, each of which has a meaning—but not necessarily the same meaning—for two or more actors (and not as a set of several individual situations). What is the nature of the "units" that enter into this classification, both as subjects and as objects? Parsons stressed the following point: they are not individuals, but actors, that is, persons playing certain roles. We do not perceive these persons immediately in terms of their contributions to the "system" or the compensations they receive from it. Alter does not directly grasp ego's relation to the system but rather ego's relation to him, or to some other actor with whom he interacts: that is, evaluation is made first of the "particular properties" of the actor in the interaction process.

Once again we find the familiar quality/performance dichotomy. Alter may be judged either by the qualities we ascribe to him or by what he achieves through his performance:

> Qualities are those properties of a unit which can be evaluated independently of any change in its relations to objects in its situa-tion, but may be ascribed to the unit as such. Thus when we say a man "has an I.Q. of 120" we describe a quality usually called "in-telligence." When, however, we say "he gave the right answer to

the question" we describe a performance, which is thus a process
of change in his relation to a situational object, the questioner,
which can be ascribed to his "agency."

A person is not defined solely by his qualities and performances but
also by his "possessions." "Possessions," according to Parsons, "are
situational objects which are intrinsically transferable and to which an
actor (individual or collective) in a social system has a specific relationship of 'control' such that he has in the institutionalized case
rights to their use, control or disposal differentiated from those held
by other units in the system. . . . Possession in turn may be of two
primary orders of significance in social systems, either of which may
have primacy. On the one hand they may be 'facilities,' i.e. means-
objects relative to instrumental goal-attainment processes, on the
other hand 'rewards,' i.e. objects which either are objects of direct
gratification or are symbolically associated with such objects."

Every system of stratification sets up a hierarchy of qualities, performances, and possessions, and also of individual and collective actors, to the extent that the actors are seen as having control over those
possessions, as authors of those performances or as bearers of those
qualities. The evaluation process involves neither rigorous scrutiny of
particular cases in the light of common values nor subjective, cir-
cumstantial judgment. The objectivity of the stratification can be
understood only in relation to the interaction process itself, a process
that begins and ends with an evaluation by the actors of what they are
contributing to and taking from the common fund. Like every interaction process, the evaluation process involves the evaluator and evaluee
in a symbolic relationship, that is, a relationship in which ego and alter
see and judge each other in a number of contexts, broader in scope
than the context of their interaction proper. By what standards are the
contributions and rewards of ego and alter evaluated? "On the basis of
recent theoretical work," Parsons tells us, "it seems possible to treat
the standards on the basis of which both object-qualities and performances are evaluated as reducible to four fundamental types which
correspond to what we believe to be the four dimensions of action
systems." In other words, the stratification standards will be derived
from the four-function paradigm (A, G, I, L). Each of the four functions, it will be recalled, combines two of the pattern variables. To put
it another way, the standards involved in determining the hierarchy of
qualities, performances, and possessions enable us to find the place of
an act or actor in relation to the functional prerequisites of society, as
reflected in the fundamental dichotomies that enter into the definition
of the social functions.

To illustrate what we mean, let us look first at the adaptive function, A. When alter evaluates ego in relation to this function, his judgment is based on ego's "technical competence." In other words, the results of ego's action are judged in relation to a norm that combines universalism and performance. The correlative sanction is approval or disapproval, which corresponds to the combination of specificity with affective neutrality. Turning next to the goal-attainment function, G, we find that the evaluation of ego's qualities, performances, and possessions is made in the light of his commitment to the collective goals as well as the legitimacy of his own goals in relation to those of the group. Evaluation focuses on the responsibilities that ego assumes. Performance and particularism govern the judgment of the way he discharges those responsibilities. The corresponding sanctions recognize his participation in the common undertaking, judged according to the combination of specificity with affectivity. As for the integrative function, I, individuals are judged by their loyalty. It is ego's performance in manifesting his solidarity with his partners that shows his loyalty (particularism-quality). The corresponding sanction, according to Parsons, is "acceptance," which, in pattern-variable terms, is defined by the combination of diffuseness with affectivity. Ego "is recognized as one of us, as belonging to our group." Finally, the value associated with the latency function, L, is "cultural value-commitment," made manifest by the intensity of ego's commitment to the beliefs and values of the group (quality plus universalism), and sanctioned by alter's esteem, corresponding to the combination of affective neutrality with diffuseness.[23] Accordingly, the system of stratification should mete out rewards and punishments to individual initiatives and life-styles on the basis of their "technical competence," "system-goal commitment," "loyalty," and "cultural value-commitment."

Is this description accurate? Nowhere do we find a strict correspondence between qualities, performances, and possessions on the one hand and functional prerequisites of the system on the other. Strictly speaking, to expect to find such a correspondence would be utopian, as Parsons demonstrates with three arguments. There is, first of all, a difference between power and authority, which throws into relief the discrepancy between the real hierarchy and the ideal hierarchy. The second argument focuses on the relation between the evaluation mechanisms and the symbolic function. Finally, the discrepancy between the common values of the society and the values intrinsic to each of the groups that make it up forces us to recognize that the integration of the system of stratification and the coherence of the evaluative process must be regarded as problematic.

In every system of stratification we find discrepancies between the actual and the ideal allocation of possessions and rewards, where the ideal allocation is determined by the legitimate evaluation standards. The stratification judgment, as it might be called, involves comparisons of two kinds: (1) the contributions (performances or qualities) of individuals in class X have greater value than the contributions of individuals in class Y, (2) the rewards (possessions or compensations) of individuals in class X have greater value than those of individuals in class Y. Each type of comparison presupposes the existence of precise, general standards of evaluation applicable to both the contributions and the rewards of the status groups being compared. Quite often we may find that class X enjoys a greater advantage over class Y in terms of money, power, popularity, or prestige than its contributions would seem to warrant. This discrepancy between the ideal hierarchy and the actual state of affairs is usually explained as being due to the power that one group exerts over another.

We have defined the power of a group as a highly generalized capacity to realize its goals. In setting forth this definition, Parsons emphasized the connection between power and effectiveness. He did not, however, deny the possibility of conflict over control of this "generalized capacity" and the ability to manage the use of resources that it guarantees. Nor did he deny that in some cases conflict may take the form of a struggle to the death. What he does assert is simply this: that the two-person zero-sum game is not the right place to begin to understand the relation of power. The exchange relation and the division of labor are far better for the purpose, provided we take into account the possibility of exploitation inherent in them. Accordingly, we have reason to look to power—understood now not as a generalized capacity to achieve collective goals but rather as a product of the disaffection of certain members of the society who do not scruple to confiscate the fruits of cooperative endeavor—as one cause of the discrepancy between the actual and ideal distributions of qualities, performances, and possessions. "Power," says Parsons, "we may define as the realistic capacity of a system-unit to actualize its 'interests' (attain goals, prevent undesired interference, command respect, control possessions, etc.) within the context of system interaction and in this sense to exert influence on processes in the system." Looked at in this way, power is the capacity of an *individual*[24] or, more generally, of a "system-unit," to achieve his (its) own ends, even at the expense of others. This capacity is not necessarily illegitimate, but it may become so. In any case it is an expression of ego's competitiveness, which presupposes "the permission of other actors to allow any one

[ego] to do things which are more or less out of line with the common value standards."

Parsons adds that "there is no reason to believe that all of the units in the system conform or are expected to conform equally with the common value-standards." A second reason for the discrepancy between the real and the ideal stratification is the disparity between the mechanisms of evaluation in the narrow sense and the mechanisms of evaluation in the broad sense. When I say that X is technically competent, I may be basing my judgment on direct observation of his competence to solve a specific set of problems in an interaction context: I may say, for example, "Dr. X is a good doctor, he saved my life." But such an evaluation can be seriously awry. In the first place, I may overestimate the degree to which my particular case was serious or unusual, and hence overestimate the merit and skill of the physician. My cure may not have been very difficult—it may even be that I would have gotten well if left solely to the devices of *vis medicatrix naturae:* Ambrose Paré was no doubt wise to observe, "I treated him, God cured him." Rather than base my judgment on my own experiences or on those of my friends or neighbors, however, I may say instead that "Dr. X is a very competent doctor. He is a resident at Massachusetts General Hospital." In this case my judgment is based on the institutional guarantee, the *credentials* of Dr. X. Of course, it may well happen that even a physician whose office walls are festooned with diplomas will err in making a diagnosis and prescribe a treatment that will worsen, rather than cure, his patient's malady. In point of fact, evaluation in this case is a complex process, which combines our personal experience, the reputation of the physician, and the prestige of the institutions with which he has been associated. All these factors enter into our judgment of the competence of a doctor, and, more generally, of any kind of "professional."

The degree to which an individual or category of individuals contributes to the attainment of collective goals gives rise to judgments where the logic is comparable to judgments of technical competence. A variety of signs will attest to X's successful performance as manager of a certain firm, for example. A business that seemed about to go under may once again be a going concern, now that X is manager. But X's effectiveness as manager may also be presumed in view of his place in the hierarchy, his credentials, his background, and his training and education. In the area of administrative, political, or managerial efficiency—wherever the capacity to assume responsibility is involved, in other words—diplomas and the like are invaluable but ambiguous credentials. Even though an unquestioning faith in credentials, diplomas, and the like may result in error from time to time, such a faith is indispensable to the modern organization. It is essential that the leaders of an organization be accepted as leaders without having to put their reputations constantly on the line. Initially, at least, instructions from the leader must have the benefit of the doubt, as it were—though his subordinates may later go over his head, of course, to seek redress; in other words, the leader's instructions must at least fall into what Chester Barnard has called the zone of indifference, in which subordinates accept unenthusiastically, but without open resistance or principled hostility, whatever orders are conveyed to them from "authorized sources," that is, from persons whose hierarchical position entitles them to issue such orders and see that they are carried out. The presumption that in the absence of proof to the contrary the leader is qualified to exercise his responsibilities is a precondition that must be satisfied if any organization is to function. Until confirmed by success or called into question by failure, the only warrant for this presumption is the institutional backing that the leader can invoke. Matters are further complicated in politics and government because the criteria of success and failure are less clear-cut than the criteria for judging the technical competence of an expert or professional. The paradox—evidence of the tenuousness of bureaucratic power—is that the only guarantee of (and limitation on) the authority of the leadership is the institution, which cannot function unless its leadership enjoys the necessary measure of authority.

Problems still more difficult are encountered in connection with the evaluation of loyalty (unless we happen to be dealing with a group in which all the members know one another and all the explicit objectives are unanimously supported by the membership). If the group is split into factions or even distinct strata, then loyalty to one faction may be regarded as hostility to another. It is not, of course, beyond the realm of possibility that all sides will recognize certain standards. Of a member of a rival faction, for example, it may be possible to say that "while he may not be with us, he's still the right kind of fellow," as judged according to the commonly accepted standards. Evaluation in this case is shifted from the domain of loyalty (I) to the domain of cultural value-commitment (L). When we do this we grant L priority over I in this particular instance. In a similar vein, people sometimes say, "He's not with us, but he's a decent sort, not one to deal any low blows." As one moves from the area of organizational responsibility and efficiency to the area of group loyalty and cultural value-commitment, the evaluation process thus shifts from relatively specific mechanisms for judging technical competence and its contribution, to the outcome of the interaction process, to more and more hazy kinds of judgment. The farther one moves from A toward L, the more evaluation shifts from the realm of the logico-experimental and institutionalized instrumentalism toward the realm of symbolism.

Such shifts become readily apparent when the problem is to classify individuals or categories judged to be equal in prestige. How do we establish the equivalence of disparate sets of diverse qualities, performances, and possessions, particularly when different standards of judgment apply to each? Prestige, which we take to mean the conformity of an actor and his actions with the common values, is evaluated in an extremely diffuse context, unlike competence, which is evaluated in a specific context. The prestige rating is a sort of overall grade measuring the whole gamut of intrinsic and extrinsic attributes of an individual or category of individuals. In evaluating prestige we content ourselves with giving an *overall* grade: X ranks higher than Y on the scale of prestige. By contrast, when I say X has more *money* than Y, more *power* than Z, more *influence* than W, I could, if necessary, justify my judgment by pointing to such criteria as wealth, organizational rank, membership in a variety of different associations and groups. It is true that power, influence, morality, even money, are not easy to measure. To say that X is wealthier than Z may mean that X spends more than Z, for instance, or that X has more capital than Z. The order of precedence might be reversed if I were to focus on current income instead. But when I rate X as more prestigious than Y, it is because I believe the way he manages his resources, acquits himself of his responsibilities, and participates in the group conforms more nearly to what I am entitled to expect from him than the way Y does these things. Reality may falsify my judgment in two respects. For my judgment is based on symbols and images, and the relative weight I ascribe to those symbols and images is arbitrary and unsteady.

The system of stratification gives at best a very imperfect ranking of the actors and their qualities, performances, and possessions. The classification is ambiguous because the standards used have very different degrees of precision and may give conflicting readings. Even more important, it is open to challenge and apt to provoke controversy. The prestige attributed to any given individual is ultimately dependent on the *weight* assigned to his intrinsic and extrinsic attributes in the general mind. X may not be very rich and yet enjoy a great deal of prestige. He may be known, for instance, for his commitment to his job and its responsibilities. I therefore rate him higher in prestige than Y, who is a millionaire exclusively interested in his business affairs. Two further conditions are worth spelling out explicitly. In order for X to be judged prestigious, it is not enough that he be committed to a cause or group. The group to which he is so devoted must itself be valued highly. Commitment and loyalty are prestigious only if their object is valued. Nothing assures us, however, that the rank-order of various groups will accord perfectly with the hierarchy of common values. For example, a society may place a high value on "collectivity-orientation." At the same time it may rate businessmen highly as a group, even though they are oriented more toward being "kings in their own castles" than toward philanthropy and public service.

Hence we must be wary of a misleading culturalism, the view that social stratification is merely an expression of the common values of the society. There are three points to be made against this tempting but dangerous fallacy. The first is one with which we are already familiar: so broadly general are the common values that they may be interpreted in quite different ways by one group or another. Second, with every group a hierarchy of activities is associated. Even if the group rates one or more common values as first and foremost, the context in which those values are put to work exerts an influence on their interpretation, heightening their ambiguity. For example, the meaning of individualism, broadly understood as implying priority of the autonomous, responsible actor, is not the same in the family context as in the organization. Finally, since each group looks at the common values through its own lenses, some values may be upheld in one group while being contested in another. Parsons sums all of this up as follows:

> The *organization* of value-standards relative to each other is analyzed as follows:
> 1. Characterization of *paramount* value pattern. . . . This defines the content of the Latency cell of the figure, when applied to the system as a whole.
> 2. The system will then be differentiated into "primary" subsystem:
>   *a)* One of these will most directly institutionalize the paramount value system (the one whose norm type defines this latent cell, e.g. the occupational system of the United States)
>   *b)* Others will be differentiated from it in relation to exigencies of (1) situational adaptation, (2) system and unit goal attainment, (3) system integration, (4) cultural pattern-maintenance and tension management. Structural lines need not correspond *directly* to this classification, i.e., structures may be "multifunctional."

As Parsons sees it, stratification raises a problem of evaluation, that is, of order. How is this order defined? How is it realized? If all transactions took the form of actual interaction, then the status ordering would merely reflect the distribution of contributions and rewards that the participants themselves had worked out and judged valid. To achieve such a result it is not enough that the group be small and that its members know one another. They must agree also on the relative value of their contributions and rewards. The more numerous and ambiguous the standards of evaluation, the more fragile this consensus will be. Accordingly, the more ardently conflicting interests invoke these standards for conflicting purposes, the more open to challenge the standards themselves will be. Thus as the group becomes more extensive and differentiated, the less able the actors will be to resolve conflicts as they arise using only the resources and sanctions intrinsic to the interaction process; when this happens, the only possible way to achieve a coherent evaluation will be to resort to the common values, which everyone recognizes as applicable to all actors in all circumstances.

Thus conflict has two aspects: on the one hand it is a discharge of hostile tensions, while on the other hand it may be likened to an appeals process in the courts, in which attention shifts step-by-step from the original source of trouble to the tribunal to which the actors appeal their case in the hope of settling their differences, either by compromise or confrontation. Recourse to the court of appeals has the effect of raising questions about the common value system itself, this being the broadest of the several frames of reference within which the meaning of the conflict may be understood.

Stratification is a classification of actors and their intrinsic and extrinsic attributes according to common value-standards. The term "value-standard" refers both to the paramount values on which the hierarchical ranking of the different groups is based and to the values of each group. In the case of American society, the *paramount* values are relatively stable. "In our system," says Parsons, "the primary value-focus is universalism-performance," embodied in what he calls "instrumental activism." The word "paramount" here is no mere stylistic flourish. It means more, for instance, than saying that answers consistent with instrumental activism are given more frequently in questionnaires filled out by Americans than by Frenchmen. These values are paramount because they tend to maintain their authority even when called into question by individual deviance (against which sanctions may be mobilized) or inequities in the hierarchy of groups or functions. Thus "paramount" is not a vague term chosen to replace some more rigorous notion, such as statistical frequency. The paramount value system incorporates mechanisms of social control by which a certain structure or configuration of society *tends* to perpetuate itself.

Since the "primary value-focus" is, as Parsons says, universalism-performance, priority is accorded to adaptive activities, hence to the groups that carry on such activities: businesses, organizations. In consequence there is an economistic and productivist bias. No single logic controls the activities of any group, however. An industrial firm, for instance, must first and foremost meet certain productivity requirements; it cannot survive for long unless it makes enough money to cover its costs. But the firm must also take other constraints into account. It must, for example, deal with the demands its workers make in response to their household needs. Parsons's version of pluralism asserts more than the existence of a plurality of group-types deriving from the plurality of functions. In each type of group, all four functional prerequisites manifest themselves simultaneously. The cohesiveness of the group is assured by according priority to one of the four functions, thereby bringing all four into equilibrium. Stability is not an automatic consequence of the plurality of functions and activities, however. It depends, rather, on how effectively the paramount values can be put to use in arbitrating whatever conflicts arise.

Second in the rank-order of precedence in the American value system is the cultural function (L), defined by universalism in conjunction with quality. We have defined L as the function of storing up symbols (universalistic in nature) associated with collective capabilities and experiences (quality). Parsons justifies his assignment of so high a place to this combination by pointing to the importance accorded both religious and secular education in the thirteen colonies, which had so impressed Tocqueville. Still, the cultural function is in some sense subordinate to the adaptive function in the United States, although this by no means signifies that one has absolute precedence over the other. For instance, the fact that science is recognized to be socially useful—an article of faith in the United States—in no way implies that science is in thrall to capital. U-Q is not subordinate to U-Per in any hierarchical sense; the hierarchical metaphor is as little apt to explain the relations between the functions as is the Marxist theory that the superstructure reflects the material reality. Rather, the predominance of U-Per over U-Q in American society is reflected in the fact that intellectual and scientific work is not regarded as autonomous and completely self-sufficient, unlike, say, the Platonic tradition, where theoretical work is held to suffice unto itself. The predominance of instrumental activism does not override the special standards applicable to the roles of intellectual and scientist, however. Moreover, intellectuals enjoy a certain latitude owing to the weakness of the governmental (or collective goal-attainment) function G. In the United States collective goals are limited (in contrast to individual initiative, which is afforded very wide latitude), relatively un-integrated, and at times contradictory. "The positive position of government is relatively weak, and also dependent on its articulation with other functions." Unlike Gaullist France or prewar Germany, the preservation of the state, to say nothing of its grandeur, is not a goal so peremptory that it may be invoked legitimately in opposition to the interests or aspirations of particular groups. Because the holding of office in the United States is decided by election, and because the actions and decisions of the office-holders are subject to judicial review, the governmental function is subordinate not only to a very broadly defined notion of the general interest (embodied in a constitution, which is not so much a code of governmental conduct as an expression, in theory, anyway, of the quintessential spirit of the laws and customs of the country) but also to the constant pressure and influence of the various groups within the society.

Schematically, we may summarize the hierarchy of American values as follows: (1) A (universalism, performance); (2) L (universalism, quality); (3) I (particularism, quality); (4) G (particularism, performance). The two pattern variables that are essential to the analysis of the value system are universalism/particularism (U/P) and performance/quality (Per/Q), which occur in combination as U-Per, U-Q, P-Per, and P-Q. The variables yield information about the value pattern when we examine how they enter into combination or opposition and what relative weights are ascribed to them by various groups within the society. A and L, that is, broadly speaking, economic and cultural activities, are associated with U, while I and G, that is, governmental and political activities in the broad sense, are associated with P. What "universalizes" an action is its adaptive dimension, evinced by its availability or by the availability of its product, for use as an object of exchange, or its cultural dimension, evaluated by its suitability for inclusion in the symbolic repertory of the society. What "particularizes" an action, on the other hand, is its political dimension, that is, its contribution to the success or failure of a common undertaking, or its reinforcement of the solidarity of the group. A group sets itself apart (particularizes itself) by concentrating on its own ends or on the establishment of a space within which its members can coexist. On the other hand, a group enters into relations with the rest of society by placing material or symbolic objects in general circulation.

These may have value for other groups as well, as is evident in the case of economic goods, and still more evident when we look at the ideas, sentiments, and symbols placed in circulation by the "seed-bed societies." A society such as the United States, which gives U priority over P, values the economic and the cultural and devalues the political and, more concretely, governmental institutions, which the European continental traditions shift over to the universalistic sphere.

The major problem besetting this analysis, as Parsons repeatedly emphasized, is that there is never a rigorous correspondence between functions and variables on the one hand and groups on the other. The governmental institutions fulfill certain adaptive functions, and the predominance of G in such institutions is only brought about by a series of intersectoral transactions (with A, I, and L), which we attempted to outline above. Another possibility is that governmental authorities will take on responsibilities that more highly differentiated and decentralized societies leave to capitalists, as we see in underdeveloped economies where an effective entrepreneurial class is lacking. Similarly, we find central governments taking over the responsibilities of regional or local leaders or agencies. The fewer the resources controlled by the latter, the more readily such takeovers can be accomplished. What in France the bureaucracy—whether royal, Jacobin, Napoleonic, or Gaullist—is determined to do itself is elsewhere left to the initiative of interest groups and citizens' organizations. In both the economic and the administrative spheres we find that action is governed by a specific logic. Any group that wishes to engage in economic or bureaucratic action must take the appropriate logic into consideration, even though the influence of that logic within the group may be tenuous at best.

Each function, too, has a logic of its own. Since, in a given group, a given function is at best paramount and never absolutely predominant, a compromise must be struck between the logic appropriate to that function and the logic appropriate to each of the other functions with which it happens to be associated. In addition, some accommodation must be reached between the logic of the paramount function and the hierarchy of common values. Consider the case of an American university [1973]. The professors are only one of several groups with an interest in how the school functions. Administrators, students, research sponsors, and financial interests are also involved. Because the university is a cultural institution, however, in which the professors as a group may legitimately lay claim to paramount status, demands made by the professors, as well as their objections to the demands of other groups, will usually win the support or tacit approval of the other parties involved. Then, too, the university stands in a certain relation to its environment, which supplies the school with resources and its graduates with jobs. The university is regulated to some degree by the common value that we have dubbed "instrumental activism," and this tends to guarantee the academic freedom of the institution (against financial institutions, churches, local governments, and political or ideological groups). The subordination of knowledge to public utility (often defined in ways objected to by scholars) is thus not the strict and one-sided relationship that radicals often profess to see. Implicit in that subordination is a problem of compatibility among the ethics of several specific groups and the common value system. The conditions under which this compatibility is established are not immutable, however, nor are they very strict. Social utility need not have the last word, because scientific progress seems to require academic freedom as a precondition, and also because the public utility is at best a rather vague governing concept, the content of which is open to a wide range of interpretations, particularly in American society, in which collective ends are neither very explicitly defined nor very effective as constraints.

As a key to analyzing social stratification, the notion of compatibility is more useful than the idea of domination by certain interest groups, or the idea of cybernetic control of the system by the value component. In other words, neither power nor authority provides an adequate conceptual framework for social stratification. The people at the top are not there because *somebody* put them there or because they put themselves there, nor are they there because that is their proper and legitimate place. Priority is not accorded to certain activities because the "culture" dictates that it must be so. The rank-ordering is merely a necessary compatibility condition reflecting the fact that various social activities coexist in unstable equilibrium. A rank-ordering or hierarchy is just a relatively precise criterion for ensuring compatibility among the heterogeneous elements of a system. Textbook examples aside, we would have a hard time spelling out the compatibility conditions associated with a given social system. Malthus's law of population, for example, shows that geometric growth in population is not indefinitely compatible with arithmetic growth in the food supply. But is the growing proportion of intellectuals in the population compatible with the perpetuation of property relations? With authoritarian management in the factory? With authoritarian government or an authoritarian educational system? The fact that the authorities have done nothing to plan for or to cope with this trend hardly makes these questions easier to answer; we can only wait to see if tensions rise to the breaking point.

In spite of the difficulty of spelling out compatibility conditions in detail, the analysis of compatibility has proved feasible and fruitful. Basically, the elements of each social situation are treated as a system, which to one degree or another is stable. The analysis becomes hypothetical and progressive and regressive at once, to extend Max Weber's terms. Two complementary approaches are taken. First, we ask whether the elimination or change of one or more elements of the system would entail breakdown of the system or leave it intact. Second, we ask whether the nature of a particular element would or would not change if we were to insert it into another system. The first question is central to functional analysis proper, the second to comparative analysis.

Is the absence of democratic competition compatible with the functioning of industrial society? Are certain combinations of values incompatible with modernization and industrialization? These questions have been of great importance in the theory of economic development. They are to blame for the fact that the most highly ideological forms of that theory reached an impasse in the early 1960s, when it was common to hear well-meaning liberals maintain that democracy is necessary to economic development. A subtler analysis of compatibility would have refuted this claim. Comparative analysis of compatibility brings out the wealth of different combinations into which particular elements may enter. Consider the adaptive function (U-Per), for example. In the American value system it ranks first, as we have seen. It may also rank first in quite different value systems. Suppose that instead of the rank-order A L I G, such as we find in the American case, we have A G L I or A I L G. The former corresponds to the adaptive function in a bureaucratic centralist and technocratic system (where I ranks lowest among the functions). The latter corresponds to an adaptive function closely attuned to the requirements of group allegiance, not so much technocratic/bureaucratic as corporative.

Compatibility analysis can also shed some light on the legitimation process. Characteristically, Parsons uses this expression often, while the term "legitimacy" is scarcely to be found in his writings.[25] No social order is legitimate, but every order seeks legitimation. The legitimation process tends to bring about a congruence between the common values and the actual practice of the society. Parsons defines the political aspect of legitimation as "a mechanism of *allocation* of authority to different subcollectivities and statuses within them, by virtue of which they are 'put in a position' to acquire and use power" [1969, p. 488]. Legitimation also has a cultural aspect. Certain social situations come to be qualified (or disqualified) as being (or failing to be) in conformity with the norms and values. The legitimation process is a way of implementing that which is deemed desirable and appropriate, or else it brings to light the conditions that stand in the way of that implementation. In societies that value instrumental activism and rely not so much on the action of governmental institutions as on cultural and economic exchange to implement that value, impediments of several kinds may thwart the achievement of equality of opportunity, power over resources, and satisfaction with the outcomes of collective action. Appropriate and effective rules are needed to ensure the circulation of goods, ideas, and personnel from one subsystem to another within a differentiated system. These rules are essential for distributing the prizes among the various competitors, but the rules themselves may become prizes in conflict of a higher order. The legitimate common values thus establish no hard-and-fast line that actors dare not violate. Legitimacy itself may become problematic, for it is restricted in two ways, and only the legitimation process makes it possible to get around those restrictions. First, there has to be some way of *justifying* particular decisions. In the political sphere, for instance, there has to be a process for justifying specific laws and regulations as in conformity with the constitution, which is held to embody the notion of what is "legitimate." Second, the constitution itself is not immutable, not an irrevocable "supreme authority," particularly in the United States, where very broad legal and moral principles are inextricably intertwined in the articles of the Constitution with rules setting forth in detail how governmental institutions such as the Congress, the Supreme Court, and the executive branch shall operate. The general principles are not fixed once and for all but are rather subject to continuing judicial review and to criticism from citizen groups and private individuals who "take their case to court."

The idea of a "final appeal," then, is meaningless, except in the purely procedural sense, because it is nonsense to say that the common values, as embodied, for instance, in the Constitution, are a fixed and final arbiter, unless it be supposed that the Constitution is a self-validating document whose prescriptions are unwavering and wholly determinate. We do make such a supposition when we attempt to *justify* particular decisions on the basis of general principles. But often the principle adduced is not enough to justify a decision that in other respects we have good reason to regard as legitimate. General principles, common values are indeed a last resort, but a last resort that need not have the last word: when this happens, it becomes necessary to turn the principles against themselves. In a way, the metaphor of the court of appeals is a dangerous one to have chosen, because it gives the idea that the social order is a closed system, a finite hierarchy with a single line of authority and rank-order. It is true that the process of justification (and hence also of protest) is one that ultimately forces judges, plaintiffs, and defendants alike to appeal to the common values. But there are no guarantees that those values will yield an appropriate and unassailable resolution of the problem. Somehow such a resolution will then have to be worked out, or, if that proves impossible, a rough and ready compromise will have to be found.

Legitimacy is not bodied forth in a set of rules indelibly inscribed on holy tablets. Rather, it is a term we apply to principles that justify certain procedures. A vague way of putting it, obviously, but not altogether without implications. To say that certain rules are legitimate does not mean that they prescribe a unique and, as it were, mechanical way of cutting to the heart of any set of problems but rather that they establish a framework for dealing with conflicts. Legitimacy is not a condition but a practice, a living tradition, of which the common law provides an example in the juridical realm. More generally, the evolution of certain industrial societies, England and the United States, for example, offer more ample illustrations of the concept.

The common values are a "last resort" only to the extent that they are invoked to settle differences between groups involved in the legitimation process. They must provide points of reference precise enough to guide action but flexible enough to withstand necessary changes in the conditions that produced the conflict in the first place. Such an interpretation was put forward by Parsons in his article "Equality and Inequality in Modern Society, or Social Stratification Revisited" [1970d]. What we have been calling "instrumental activism" provides American society with a rationale for legitimation. But this vital center is subject to very powerful tensions that propagate throughout the social system, while at the same time the tensions that have been accumulating in the rest of the system affect the vital center. The U-Per combination gives rise to two compatibility problems. First, under what conditions can it coexist with the other combinations (U-Q, P-Per, U-Per), given its precedence in the hierarchy? Second, is the combination itself intrinsically consistent?

The U-Per combination means that certain attributes of the actor are valued: his ability to take initiatives (Per) and his capacity to accept interpersonal evaluations of himself and his achievements (U). The context in which both of these capacities make themselves felt is a relatively decentralized one, since the political function is ranked last in the functional hierarchy. Only in exceptional circumstances are governmental institutions supposed to take over for failing actors or substitute collective preferences for private ones as registered and aggregated by the impersonal mechanisms of the economic and cultural markets. However moderate government or other intervention may be, the actor must nevertheless come to terms with the other actors and the constraints imposed on him as a result of working cooperatively with others. The meaning of Parsons's notion of "institutionalized individualism" lies in reckoning with constraints of this sort (which are compensated for by the regularity and predictability that the actor can count on in return for accepting the limits they lay down).

Initiatives and constraints are defined institutionally in terms of freedom and equality. The legitimation process in American society is carried on in the name of these two common values: freedom, that is, space within which the individual's own decisions and preferences reign supreme, and equality, that is, an absence of discrimination against the individual's qualities and performances. The simultaneous implementation of both of these values is made more difficult by the fact that they may come into conflict with each other, and above all by the fact that the subsystems in which they are embodied are a precarious combination of requirements intrinsic to the subsystems themselves with divergent, if not contradictory, requirements.

Following Parsons, let us ask how equality is defined for each of the four functions. The term "equality" may be taken in several different ways. When we say that American citizens are all equal before the law, we mean that all have the same rights, which they are entitled to exercise under the same conditions, whether in entering into contracts, receiving public subsidies and services, or taking part in politics and government. This equality is associated with a status, that is, a set of qualities, shared by all members of the community. These rights are all very different in character. The only thing they have in common is that any member of the community (except for convicted felons and certain others) is entitled to exercise them, regardless of the value of his own accomplishments. Any American citizen can buy or sell goods, marry, vote, or run for office. These civil and civic rights have a long history. The right to enter into contracts in civil law under conditions equally applicable to all inhabitants of a country, for example, was not won overnight, as the existence of slavery in the United States until the time of the Civl War makes clear. To take another example, the French legal system was based on estates and privileges until the late eighteenth century, to say nothing of the many forms of segregation that have lasted into the second half of the twentieth century.

Such social rights as the right to health or to an education regardless of wealth or ability have had to wait even longer for recognition.[26] As rights, the essence of which is equality, these could be claimed on strictly universalistic grounds. Justice also has another dimension, however. To the extent that it is deemed appropriate to apportion reward to effort or responsibility to capacity, for example, justice may necessitate an unequal distribution. Turning now to the four-function paradigm, we may ask when equality rather than proportionality is paramount, and when it is the other way around; we find that in fact elements of both egalitarianism and proportionalism are present in all four subsystems. In the polity, for instance, both requirements make themselves felt simultaneously: there is strong pressure for equal participation, but at the same time the hierarchical principle implies that the most important decisions must be left to a small number of officials, perhaps even to the president alone. "One man, one vote" and equal voting rights for all on the one hand; on the other hand, Aristotle's maxim that while many deliberate, one decides. In the economic subsystem we find the same tension. It is not possible to provide the same remuneration to productive and unproductive factors. On the other hand, it is impossible to let a worker die of hunger because his productivity falls below the cost of his upkeep. As for L, the egalitarian orientation rules out elitism. But in the cultural sphere the very nature of research, teaching, and thinking results in a certain asymmetry between teachers and pupils, between the initiate and the uninitiate.

The tension between one kind of equality and another has its counterpart in the tension between one kind of freedom and another, paralleling the dichotomy between collectivity-orientation and self-orientation. Ego claims the right to take initiatives in return for accepting their consequences: the "freedom to pursue unit interests," as Parsons puts it. He also claims the freedom to make "value commitments" and to "allocate commitments." These claims are by no means peremptory, however, any more than the choice between egalitarianism and proportionalism is one of "either/or." In fact, ego can assert his independence only if he takes account of two constraints: "constraints by collective decisions and sanctions," and "constraints by moral authority in the community." Like the demand for equality, the demand for freedom has two aspects. Ego wants to be free to do as he likes with the products of his industry and talent. In one case his claims have to do with his possessions and performances, in the other with his qualities. What is valued in the first case is initiative, in the second originality and spontaneity. As was the case with equality, freedom coexists with constraint in all four subsystems: work discipline *and* freedom to do as one pleases with the products of one's labor (A), hierarchical authority *and* freedom of participation (G), group solidarity *and* affective identification with its members (I), respect *and* internalization of values (L).

To determine that a system of stratification is legitimate is to hold that it is consonant with our value judgments concerning qualities, performances, and possessions. It is possible to deem both "inequality of valued achievement" and "freedom to pursue unit interests" worthwhile at the same time: this is the case with meritocracy. To take another example, we may well find that both the hierarchical principle and the unequal distribution of power in the collectivity are held to be valuable. These combinations are stable because they associate congruent forms of freedom and equality. We may look upon these stable combinations in several ways. They can be judged, first of all, in relation to the logic of the subsystems in which they are embodied. For example, the adaptive subsystem has a logic more proportionalist than egalitarian in nature. Then, too, when different values come into conflict, a positive value can be used as a principle for legitimating a negative value. In meritocracy, for example, ego's "freedom to pursue unit interests" may be used to counterbalance what might be adjudged an excess of inequality in performances and rewards, which might otherwise be resented and disallowed as intolerably inhuman.

The legitimation process, as we are describing it here, does not simply assume the existence of conformity between norms and actual practice, between the ideal and the actual distribution of rewards. As Parsons himself tells us, his approach differs in this respect from that of the early functionalists, like Kingsley Davis. In Parsons's view the system of stratification is not the expression or the embodiment of a supposedly self-subsistent system of values. Why limit discussion of problems of stratification to legitimation of inequalities and impediments to freedom, as though disparities in wealth or prestige and obstacles standing in the way of initiative were invariably functional, designed merely to "reinforce" the common values. The question of legitimacy may be asked about equalities as well as inequalities. In the early days of functionalism, when meritocracy was the primary focus of research, status inequalities were considered to be obvious necessities. "Now," Parsons wrote in 1970, "the tendency is to emphasize the respects in which societal units, but especially persons, are and should be treated as equals, and to place the burden of proof not only on the explanation but above all the justification of components of inequality" [1970*d*, p. 19]. At first sight this may seem a surprising statement. Does Parsons want to challenge the "scientific" approach of the early functionalists, who were trying to explain stratification as they found it, and substitute instead the ideological bias of so-called critical sociologists?

By recognizing that constraint and inequality are invariably open to challenge and in need of legitimation, Parsons is making a large concession to "critical" sociology. Critical theory has revived Hobbes's old idea that social order is always problematic. For Hobbes the problem was to figure out how the rulers came to have their authority over the ruled. For Parsons the problem lies in the process by which resources and roles are allocated, in all its multifarious aspects. In contrast to the approach taken by "social contract" philosophers and so-called critical theorists, however, Parsons does not question the existing order in the name of values that we ourselves are said to have posited. The questions he raises are immanent in the social process, since interaction always involves evaluation. These questions are neither wholly unconscious nor wholly voluntarist. A system of stratification does not "produce" itself any more than it "reproduces" itself. In industrial societies in which the U-Per combination is paramount, the system of stratification emerges from the confrontation between the "desirable" goals of freedom and equality and the exigencies of hierarchy and meritocracy. Functionalists regard stratification as a "fact of nature" and as legitimated by common values. In "Equality and Inequality," Parsons looked upon stratification as "a dual 'dialectically' structured aspect of the 'problem of order,'" constituting both a confirmation of and a challenge to the existing distribution of resources among the actors in society.

Was this use of the term "dialectical" a concession to fashion? It would be quite unfortunate, indeed, if its use led to teleological interpretation of the interaction process according to which the paramount values in their pristine purity would somehow, through interaction, come to be embodied in the system of stratification. In fact, the paramount values are relativized in two ways. On the one hand, one value is always paired with another, and there is always tension between the two (i.e., we always have both liberty *and* equality, and the pair overlaps the three dichotomies, universalism/particularism, performance/quality, self-orientation/collectivity-orientation). On the other hand, values are shaped by the subsystem context in which they are realized.

Legitimation, therefore, is not, as radical critics usually claim, a question of acknowledging the presence of some sort of legitimacy, without which the social order must be regarded as intrinsically perverse. Legitimation is a process, which Parsons explains in his article [1970*d*], particularly in table 5 of the appendix. In the economic subsystem (A) an unequal distribution of wealth may be deemed legitimate *if* it is adjudged the only way of assuring the actors equality of opportunity. In the polity governmental constraint is legitimate *if* it is exercised so as to assure equal protection of the laws to all. Accordingly, in industrial societies of the American type, in which collective goals have relatively low priority, constraint and inequality are conditionally legitimate, and anyone who invokes that legitimacy in order to impose limits on freedom or to curb demands for equality must demonstrate that the necessary conditions are satisfied.

Once the process of legitimation is made explicit, it becomes a subject for discussion, not to mention rhetorical posturing. This is a second sense in which the process must be termed "dialectical." We must then ask whether this dialectic is merely a discourse *about* society, whether legitimation is always utopian or ideological, or whether it will be accompanied by a real transformation of the conditions of interaction. What new opportunities does the legitimation process make available to certain individuals in the society? First, it must be said that change is always accompanied by a process of evaluation. Even if the change is one of major upheaval in the relations of production, such as might result, for example, from technological innovations often incomprehensible to the people most directly affected by them, it will raise questions about the old order. As a result, some will call for restoration of the threatened social order, while others will clamor for its replacement by something new. We are normally largely unaware of the causes and effects of such upheavals, but we experience them as desirable or undesirable. Once the question "What is to be done?" has been asked, we must face the facts: individual and collective resources are scarce, protests difficult to organize, and our efforts likely to lead to unanticipated consequences. Thus our commitment to do something is likely to get us involved not so much in a project with coherent goals as in a kind of quest for a mythical Holy Grail. In Parsons's view, the history of the eighteenth and nineteenth centuries, which saw the conquest first of civil and political and then of social rights, has not brought us any nearer some sort of mystical "end of history," but it did bring about remarkable changes in both the rights of individuals and social conditions. Industrial society is not necessarily the highest form of human organization. It has not turned out to be the embodiment of the individualist ideal that Spencer and the evolutionary utilitarians saw in its future. It has merely provided individuals with resources and opportunities of ever greater scope and diversity, forcing them to make more and more difficult choices in the process.

Solidarity and "De-differentiation"

Radical critics of industrial society refuse to distinguish between two kinds of questions. They argue that the individual is neither happier nor better (in a moral sense) nor freer in industrial society than in traditional society. A reasonable argument, never more clearly set forth than by Rousseau in his first *Discourse* and by Durkheim in his *Division of Labor.* But from it the radicals have drawn all sorts of arbitrary and outrageous conclusions. Because the growing division of labor has not made us happier, they conclude that society is in the grip of an evil genius bent on deceiving us all and busy instilling into us the passions and prejudices that render us slaves. Parsons suggests a different approach: he recognizes the anomie and unhappiness of individuals but seeks to relate those facts to the conditions under which individual actors must make their choices.

Each actor is involved in several games at once, and the rules are different in each of the four subsystems (A, G, I, and L). We see this in the wide variety of "codes," which differ from one another by their intrinsic rules as much as by the types of values they convey. The economic subsystem values utility, that is, a use of individual and collective resources consistent with the preferences of the users. The rule of utility (which Parsons calls the "coordination standard") is solvency, that is, the capacity of the economic agent to balance expenditures against returns at the end of a specified period. This rule is strict. Should it be violated, the subsystem is beset by a cycle of inflationary and deflationary imbalances. The political subsystem values effectiveness. The rule is success, which is different from solvency. It is entirely "rational" to go into deficit in order to attain a political goal, if attainment of that goal is deemed indispensable to the survival of the body politic, the paramount goal. Similarly, cultural integrity (L) is not the same thing as group solidarity (I). To maintain or restore that integrity, those entrusted with the mission of cultural preservation must on occasion run the risk of pitting themselves against certain of their partners. Conversely, in order to maintain consensus, the appropriate authorities may find it expedient to ignore the bones of contention over which the group is divided in order to concentrate on the fundamental commitments that its members share.

Social action is differentiated and may at times give rise to tension and contradiction. The risks are heightened by the fact that each subsector or function is itself heterogeneous to some degree. The logic of solvency is paramount only in the economic subsystem. Within the same subsystem other logics also operate: the logic of success (since the firm is also an organization), the logic of solidarity (since different categories of actors do coexist, their conflicts of interest notwithstanding), and the logic of cultural integration (since workers are also citizens, family heads, residents of particular towns or cities, etc.). Not all these actors have an adequate understanding of the games they are or might be playing. Their capacity to shift attention from one contest to another varies widely from individual to individual and is always limited, even for those most free to range widely and to combine resources of many kinds. Social differentiation is often seen as a source of tensions difficult to get rid of and as an obstacle to free choice.

We find these tensions within each of the four subsystems as well as between one subsystem and another. In the economy there is tension in the solvency/gratuity dichotomy; in the polity, in the effectiveness/participation dichotomy; in the integrative subsystem the solidarity/conflict dichotomy is the source of tensions; and in the cultural subsystem it is the integrity/difference dichotomy. None of these pairs is a contradiction in either the logical or the dialectical sense, by which we mean that the two terms of each dichotomy are neither strictly incompatible nor necessarily conducive to a higher "rationality." The solvency/gratuity dichotomy can be resolved by the introduction of a universalistic standard. For instance, the requirement of solvency can be temporarily eased if a standard is adopted according to which the citizens of a certain country cannot be deprived of a subsistence allowance merely because they are financially insolvent. Ultimately, such a standard can be fulfilled by an increase in productivity to make up the welfare deficit. If these two approaches are combined, we obtain a third resolution of the dilemma. Once increased productivity levels have been attained, the economy can satisfy the overall requirement of solvency and still meet other demands for assistance, either by gratuitous distribution or by remunerating the factors of production at a rate in excess of their productivity. Turning now to effectiveness/participation, we should say first that in drawing the distinction we do not mean to imply that bureaucratic rule is the only politically and administratively effective method. Broad participation in the decision-making process imposes certain constraints on political organizations and bureaucracies, which, even if those constraints do not nullify the effectiveness of political or administrative action, do complicate that action and, more important, make it necessary to reassign responsibilities and realign channels of communication and mechanisms of control. Both democracy (in the Athenian sense) and effective self-management by small, decentralized industrial units are difficult to achieve, for several reasons: the distribution of skills is highly unequal; opinions and interests are often in conflict; motivation to participate varies widely in intensity from individual to individual; and opportunities to make decisions occur largely at random times rather than according to a regular schedule. But merely because participation is difficult to achieve in industrial society, it does not follow that it is either logically impossible or dialectically necessary. What we can say with a good deal of certainty is that it can be achieved only under certain conditions relating to the competence and "capacity" of the participants (in the sense in which Proudhon used to speak of "political capacity") and to the flexibility of the procedures for delegating authority. If these conditions are not satisfied, it is hardly a major theoretical accomplishment to predict a breakdown in organizational effectiveness.

You cannot have your cake and eat it too: this does not mean that we must choose between effectiveness and participation (with a capital E and a capital P), but rather that we must choose the combination of the two best suited to our preferences—neither extreme case being considered a *combination*, since in one we have all participation and no effectiveness, in the other all effectiveness and no participation. Tension, as we have been calling it, is just another name for the embarrassment of riches we face in trying to compare the benefits of different combinations, the costs of which are difficult to evaluate: the question, in other words, is, What kind of trade-offs have to be made as we move along a particularly ticklish set of indifference curves? Such tensions are evident in the economic and political subsystems. To confine our attention to the latter, we shall next attempt to explain how the values of hierarchy, professionalization, and association are combined in political decision making.

Political choices are hierarchical in at least two ways. First, they commit the resources, and potentially the forces, of the collectivity to confrontation with anyone who might oppose the decision taken by the authorities. Such decisions can be made only at the highest levels of government, or at least with the consent and under the control of the highest authorities. In other words, political choices tend to be hierarchical and centralized. But this tendency, which is consistent with the logic of effectiveness, must accommodate two other tendencies that are less apparent in governmental institutions than in the professions and in citizens groups. While political authority is hierarchical (whence power may be defined as the legitimate monopoly of the use of force in a given territory), it also has certain traits in common with associational and professional authority.

An individual qualifies as a member of a profession[27] first of all by virtue of his formal technical training, for example, by completing a university program and receiving a diploma; second, by virtue not only of his technical and specialized competence but also his general skills; and, third, by applying those skills to social ends deemed legitimate and sanctioned by an institution, particularly an institutionalized code of ethics. Accordingly, professional authority can be characterized by the way in which it is acquired and exercised and by the ends it serves. The award of diplomas is controlled either by the profession itself or by the university. In Parsons's view there is little difference between the two cases, so intensive and constant are the exchanges between professional and academic institutions, both viewed broadly. Professional authority is thus based on the certified competence of the person upon whom it is bestowed. What is more, it is not exercised for the benefit of the professional but rather for the sake of his client: a doctor, for instance, would be committing a grave breach of professional ethics if he were to reason that he might serve his interests by prolonging a patient's illness—if not his life. Professional authority is therefore benevolent authority, and, as such, more immediately acceptable as a model than authority based on competence or hierarchy. Professional authority derives from the "competence gap," but the legitimation thus afforded is subject to two conditions: peer approval and client commitment. In view of the former, colleagues in a given profession enjoy parity; in view of the latter, the obligations of the "professional" and his clients to render services are asymmetrical.

Political authority can be professionalized in two quite different ways, which have only one trait in common, namely, that both increase the distance between rulers and ruled, superiors and subordinates. On the one hand, the professional politician is sometimes viewed as a flatterer adept at garnering votes in exchange for service to certain special interests. This is a cynical conception of politics, predicated on a degradation and corruption of the authority of the professional politician, who is ranked with the practitioners of the cosmetic and culinary arts, which Plato accorded a lowly rank in his early dialogues. On the other hand, professionalization may take the form of "technocratic" rule, and even where the ideal of public service is respected, the technocrat who presumes to speak in the name of the common good may find his good intentions challenged as "paternalistic." Technocratic authority must be prepared to justify its decisions to the lay public, even though answers to the layman's questions frequently do not exist.

"Populism," as the term has come to be used in the United States, represents for Parsons the violent reaction of the relatively less competent segments of the populace against the more or less well-intentioned designs of competent authority. With a platform providing for recall of elected officials, direct democracy through popular initiative, and strict control by the voters over judges and civil servants, the populists believed they were fighting a paternalist oligarchy. The point of their demands was to eliminate differences of competence and responsibility in order to regain a kind of primitive unity in which the participants in the political process would regain their equality. In modern regimes this egalitarian orientation is coupled with what Parsons calls an orientation toward "voluntariness." On this view, a law is not legitimate unless it expresses the will of those to whom it applies. As Parsons remarks, this is an ambiguous requirement, to say the least. "This principle can never apply quite strictly to compliance with a normative order or collective decisions, since an element of bindingness is essential to all collectivities" [1969, p. 53]. This "bindingness" is always open to question in voluntary associations, "an alternative to compliance always being resignation." The "exit" alternative, however, is a costly one. Unlikely as exercise of the exit option may be, its mere existence is enough to underscore the fact that civil obedience is conditional. The voluntaristic orientation does not—Sartre's belief to the contrary notwithstanding—induce citizens to swear oaths of loyalty and solemnly declare their devotion to the collectivity. It rather makes the association into a body governed by laws and not by men, a republic, that is, a constitutional regime in which elections decide who will be named leaders, when they will be replaced, and what the scope of their powers will be. Understood in this way, voluntariness is characteristic of all associations designed to achieve common goals under the guidance of the membership, whether political or not.

Political action in modern societies[28] must meet three requirements, two of which are inegalitarian, though in quite different ways, while the third is egalitarian. The two inegalitarian requirements are technical competence and hierarchy. The necessity of the former is felt primarily during the decision-making process, the second during the phase of execution and implementation. We may, moreover, call the first oligarchic or collegial, the second monarchical, despite the fact that nowadays, with divine right seldom invoked, "monarchy" enjoys only functional and delegated authority, as in the case of the chief executive in a modern democratic regime. The third requirement reflects a demand for participation, or, to use Parsons's term, association, stemming from the periphery and directed toward the center. The simpler the society is, the easier this demand is to satisfy. When it is not satisfied, however, the more complex the society is, the more regressive and violent the forms this demand may take.

A similar analysis of the economic subsystem could be given. Turning now to the system as a whole, of which each of the four functions constitutes one aspect, we can gain some insight into the enormous complexity of modern society and the wide variety of conditions and constraints to which it is subject. Hence modern society can never be treated as perfectly autarchic and integrated, nor can it be treated, as Michelet treated France, as a person. We have often had occasion to speak of the social system. The system in question is not a closed system, however. It is open to a physical environment, to a culture, that is, a symbolic capital, and to actors, without whose cooperation it could not endure. The openness of the social system is a central theme in Parsons's thought. We find it in his distinction between society, culture, and personality. We find it, too, in his more recent work on the importance of the external environment, and even of the organism, as distinct from the personality. Hence no complex society can be regarded as a "concrete totality." Still, it is not an abstract collection of terms chosen for the convenience of the observer. It makes sense to the actor, possibly in more ways than one.

A society is an object composed of many compatible cognitive references and affective loyalties. Parsons uses the phrase "diffuse enduring solidarity," which he borrowed from David Schneider, who applied it to the American family.[29] The sense in which it is possible to treat the society of a nation in terms of "diffuse enduring solidarity" can be clarified by taking a look at the modern family or, in certain multiracial societies such as the United States, the ethnic group. The point is not that a nation exhibits the *same kind* of solidarity as a family or a community of immigrants. Parsons uses the word "solidarity" in the Durkheimian sense of "organic solidarity," which he views as standing in radical contrast to Tönnies's notion of *Gemeinschaft*. In the first place, solidarity does not mean identity, as would be the case with two elements distinguishable only by their different locations, or identification, as in the case of a love relationship. Second, solidarity is not to be confused with contiguity, as in a face-to-face relationship: impersonal transactions carried on over long distances and periods of time can exhibit the characteristics of solidarity. Third, solidarity does not exclude the possibility of conflict, a statement for which the disputatious nature of labor-management relations provides abundant evidence; on the other hand, conflict need not imply life-and-death struggle or a danger of social breakdown and disintegration. Parsons attempted to describe ethnic solidarity in present-day American society by relating it to the existence of a common language and common traditions. Ethnic groups are "a transgenerational type of group. . . . Just as in the kinship context an individual is ascriptively the child of his parents . . . the citizen is ascriptively one of the heirs of his forebears in the societal community and will be one of the progenitors of the future community so that many of the consequences of the actions of contemporaries cannot be escaped by future members in new generations" [1975, pp. 60–61].

Solidarity, then, subjects us to a wide range of influences, which affect our present condition in ways unwilled and uncontrolled by us and to which it is frequently difficult to attribute a source, but which we neither can nor wish to repudiate. In a sense solidarity is impersonal; we cannot repudiate our impersonal bonds anymore than we can choose our parents. Similarly, I may reject a political program or denounce it as absurd and yet have to endure its effects along with all those who supported and implemented it. Impersonal relations are indeed real, but obviously this does not imply that they create very solid ties. Our present condition depends on actors we have never seen and will never see, whether because they have long been dead or because contact with them is physically impossible. Our fate is affected by acts not intended to have any impact on us personally. We cannot escape from dependency of this kind without paying a very high price. The problem is not the reality but the legitimacy of this dependency, or, rather, the conditions under which we deem it legitimate. Another problem is to explain how segmentary solidarities can give rise to an all-embracing "diffuse enduring solidarity."

Industrial society, in any case, cannot be regarded as a *Gemeinschaft* in which, to use Edward Shils's terminology, "primordial ties" bind us together in small, closed units, within which individuals come to look upon one another as brothers by blood. If it is held that any society in which solidarity is not based on primordial ties (i.e., on face-to-face relationships or on primary, unconscious identifications) is anomic, then all industrial societies must be regarded as such, because they are based on contracts, markets, and elections. Of course, in Parsons's view, as well as in his interpretation of the views of Durkheim, the division of labor, which increases the number of pertinent impersonal relations, makes the social order problematic, not only for the philosopher but also for the actors themselves, because they must make an ever larger number of choices, the consequences of which are in some cases very difficult for them to predict. But is anomie an inevitable consequence of the increasing number of impersonal relations?

When we speak of impersonal relations, we are thinking of the undesired and in some cases unseen consequences of the actor's dependency on partners on whom his power, influence, prestige, and moral authority are contingent. This dependency may take many forms, but there is no reason to reduce it to the extreme case of complete helplessness or total domination. The very large number of roles that industrial society offers its members is often said to be indicative of the great freedom they enjoy. This is a misleading remark in that it fails to mention the highly unequal distribution of freedom and, what is even more important, of the capacity to make choices, which varies from one social category to the next. For most roles, moreover, the available choices are not "all or nothing" but rather bear on modes of participation and degrees of involvement. Finally, it is possible for an individual to play many different roles without ever taking part in the activities that interest him and without reaping any of the benefits he expects from cooperative undertakings.

What is misleading about doctrinaire pluralism is the assumption that, because there is a wide variety of roles in society as a whole and because those roles seem diverse to those who perform them, there is necessarily some overall compensation mechanism to balance constraints and frustrations against gratifications and rewards. What Parsons calls "role pluralism" must not be viewed with such ingenuous optimism. Indeed, role pluralism has consequences of two kinds, and a priori it is impossible to say whether they are *functional* or *dysfunctional.* For one thing, role pluralism leads to a specialization of interests, qualities, and performances, and thereby widens the range of exchanges between actors, who communicate with one another only via symbolic media. For another, it is conducive to compartmentalization and standardization of those exchanges. In other words, where there is role pluralism each role becomes specialized and the number of roles proliferates, while individual roles are chopped up into sequences of limited decisions, each of which may be of relatively small moment.

It is possible to imagine a world in which role pluralism would set up a stable equilibrium among a wide range of activities and reward each with a just compensation, but equally possible to imagine it responsible for incoherence, isolation, and conflict. Parsons tried to determine the conditions under which role pluralism would be compatible with full (and appropriate) employment of individual resources. Following W. I. Thomas, he stressed the importance of social recognition (recognition of alter by the group) in influencing the way in which we are impelled to take up our roles. Social recognition

sanctions the actor's capacity to cope not only with his current responsibilities but also with the various responsibilities that were his in
early phases of his career. Role pluralism refers not only to the range
of present choices open to an individual with given resources and
talents but also to his persistent capacity to assume new roles as he
encounters them during the course of his life. Looked at both syn-
chronically and diachronically, then, role pluralism is nothing other
than the capacity to "take the roles of others," as George H. Mead
stressed, whether it be an alter with whom one is dealing at present or
another self, a person one has been in the past or will be in the future.

The impersonal relations that go along with role pluralism may be
either positive or negative, depending on the character of the $\overleftrightarrow{IG}$ and
$\overleftrightarrow{IL}$ interchanges. We are used to speaking of the four functions of the
social system, the adaptive function (A) constituting the economic subsystem, the goal-attainment function (G) constituting the polity, the
integrative function (I) constituting the subsystem of primary loyalties,
and the latent-pattern maintenance function (L) constituting the cultural subsystem. It is also possible to attempt to define the functions of
the *system of action,* the broadest possible framework or environment
within which it is feasible to situate the social system. The A function,
then, pertains to the actor-environment relationship, and we may
speak of the intelligence of the actor, or, more generally, of the capacity of the system of action, whatever it may be, to control its environment. Similarly, G becomes a "performance capacity," which, when
implemented, allows the system to attain its goals; I appears as the
"system responsiveness," that is, the capacity of the system to "respond" to the demands made on it by the external environment; L is
the situation, as defined by and for the system. Accordingly, role
pluralism may be defined as a specialized or segmental capacity of the
actor to achieve or realize his ends. This capacity depends in part on
affective reinforcement through responsiveness of the actor to initiatives
taken by his partner and to the responses of his partner to his own
initiatives, in part on the legitimation of his role in the situation as
culturally defined. The critical aspect of the GI relation is the distance
between the actor and his roles: if this distance should become too
large or too small, the result is deviant behavior of either the compulsive or the alienative type. If the actor is too involved with his commitments, fanaticism results; if he is insufficiently involved, indifference and cynicism are the consequences. An actor who was at
once identified with his roles and totally committed to his beliefs
would indeed be oversocialized, as some writers have accused *homo
parsoniensis* of being. The totally detached individual, on the other

hand, would succumb to complete anomie, owing to the absence of affective motivation or cultural commitment.

Following Mead, Parsons places great stress on the distance that in general separates an actor from his roles. The *decentering* of the actor vis-à-vis his roles is extended by *detachment* vis-à-vis his value-commitments. Parsons makes a fundamental distinction between group loyalty and value-commitment. Compared to group loyalty, value-commitment makes moral obligation less dependent on considerations of cost, benefit, constraint, or threat. It should also be noted that, if value-commitments relativize group loyalties *(amicus Plato sed magis amica veritas),* group loyalties also relativize value-commitments. Because value-commitments and group loyalties are not mutually reinforcing, the individual can play one off against the other, as it were, thereby recovering some freedom of action.

Distance and detachment are possible, however, only if the actor possesses a sufficient capacity to generalize. With such a capacity he can behave "as though" certain hypothetical conditions were in fact satisfied; at the same time, he can learn to recognize and respond to goals more complex than mere "intrinsic gratifiers." The capacity to generalize is very unevenly distributed in the population. It is dependent in part on socialization under conditions of decenteredness and detachment, as well as on the actor's ability to come to grips with such conflicts as may crop up between him and alter, which depends on his ability to use symbols. The acquisition of this capacity is thus dependent on both personal and social factors that cannot be counted on to be present in many cases. Accordingly, the risks of "de-differentiation" pose a grave threat, which must be faced.

The concept of "de-differentiation," to which Parsons attached increasing importance in his last works, stems from the psychoanalytic notion of regression: when a developing individual faces choices that will force him to give up certain previously available gratifications, he may fall back on an earlier personality structure, a so-called archaic personality. A comparable process is observable in societies. In the face of growing specialization, increasingly tenuous integration, and the correlative growth of impersonal relations, two reactions may be forthcoming, either simultaneously or in succession: an "authoritarian" reaction, and a "radical" reaction. Characteristic of the former is an inability to tolerate ambiguity, which may in an extreme form result in the impassioned and violent denial of all complexity. It is a reaction that stems from groups whose status is threatened by the demands of new groups for inclusion in society on an equal footing with those already in, on terms to be fixed by negotiation. One example of de-differentiation is the racism of "poor whites" determined to maintain their supremacy; it is a refusal to acknowledge that the performance level of the group discriminated against has in reality been upgraded. The authoritarian reaction, accordingly, is seen to have two aspects: the demand for equality is disallowed while the hierarchical principle is fiercely upheld. The radical reaction, on the other hand, of which American populism offers a particularly vehement example, is intolerant of all inequality, even when it is based on the principle of proportional justice or on a matching of responsibilities to capabilities. The populist obsession with leveling, the propensity to "cut down whatever stands out," results in an idealization of a completely undifferentiated egalitarianism, just as the refusal of the "racists" to countenance the eventuality or even the possibility of upgrading of the excluded group results in the simplest and most primitive of all confrontations, that between the powerful and the oppressed.

De-differentiation is a regressive, violent process focused on one or the other of two utopian ideals: undiscriminating equality or absolute submission to authority. The more complex a society is, the greater the danger of de-differentiation and the concomitant risk of violent regression. Is de-differentiation always regressive? Our rationalist bent would incline us to think so, but for two considerations that have been given considerable prominence in our discussions. First of all, there is the phenomenon of charisma. The teaching of the prophet comes as an ardent rejection of pharisaic subtlety and at the same time as an invitation to recapture the pristine purity of the word. In the second place, there are the developmental phenomena associated with the growth of the individual personality and with social change. In neither of these areas does progress boil down to a series of incremental adjustments. It involves discontinuities, jumps, and risks of stumbling or regression. Often the course of development takes shortcuts, breaks out of well-trodden paths, and establishes new, if tenuous, connections. Bear in mind that for Parsons the actor is someone who combines resources in new ways. He is a manager, but he is also an innovator. He compares and chooses, but he also makes commitments. He has a definite place in the scheme of things, but he is not "boxed in."

What accounts for his not being boxed in? It is not merely because of the destructive capacity with which he is so generously endowed by radical critics, but also because he faces "real" choices, with distinct eventualities contingent on the various alternatives. Failure to grasp this point was responsible for the well-known debate over formal liberties. The radical critics began their attack by declaring "formal" any liberty that does not realize our desires. They also contended that any choice that was not a choice between extremes was nothing more than a choice between "tweedledum and tweedledee." Because the Democrats are no more identified with socialism than the Republicans are with capitalism, they conclude that the American electorate has no real choice. What makes a choice real? Is it merely that I should be free to reject what is offered to me (thereby running the risk that a more powerful adversary will resort to violence to make me do what he has decided is best)? Freedom is more than just perpetual "nay-saying," and more than what we sometimes call "creative freedom," the freedom of the artist to follow his own instincts. The freedom of an individual depends on the roles open to him, and on his capacities to combine and relate them.

The individual actor does not face the dilemma of choosing between constraint or freedom. Nor are all constraints equivalent, so that he will be indifferent whether one or another is imposed on him. Society does not consist merely of constraints, any more than culture is purely arbitrary. One system of values may be said to be arbitrary in comparison with another system of values. Instrumental activism is not more "rational" than Confucian religious traditionalism. The superiority of one over the other cannot be established except on the basis of a dogmatic conception of human nature and the social order. Taking each system in itself, however, we find that both have a logic of their own, designed to achieve compatibility among the various divergent tendencies embodied within them. Only if culture is reduced to a set of proscriptions and prescriptions does it seem to be arbitrary. But culture is inseparable from legitimation. In the legitimation process the content of culture is either reinforced or vitiated by a twofold process of specification and generalization. What drives this process is the desire to achieve compatibility—or dissatisfaction with the existing incompatibility—between the value system and the individual or collective preferences of the actors. Cultural symbolism does not once and for all ascribe meaning to undifferentiated matter. Rather, a number of meanings are suggested by the symbols of culture, and these meanings, as seen by the actors at any one time or in successive periods, may or may not be compatible with one another.

The argument—which takes several forms, all equally unacceptable—that culture is fundamentally arbitrary is based on a misunderstanding. It is true that, taken as a whole, every system is arbitrary and contingent. But what culture can be treated as a whole? From the synchronic point of view, culture is a composite, which must satisfy the compatibility requirement. Diachronically, on the other hand, it must be seen in relation to the legitimation process, not as something dictated by a preexisting notion of what is legitimate. Some would hold that a culture is a closed totality that confines all who come under its sway. On this view, the walls of culture are said to ensure the unlimited power of the "oppressors" over the "oppressed" by incarcerating them. By contrast, we have tried in our approach to distinguish between the system of significations and the nexus of interactions. The importance that Parsons accords to the diaspora shows that in his view the "seed-bed societies" could bear cultural fruit even after a waning secular authority had lost control over the culture. The diaspora quickened the commerce between cultures, which came to know themselves in the shock of mutual encounter and confrontation. Just as culture is not an arbitrary, closed totality, so the history of mankind is neither a linear unfolding of possibilities implicit at the beginning of time nor a "totalization" of innumerable experiences, providentially assured to be convergent. It is rather a process of communication, which takes the form of exchange and contact, as well as conflict and violence, between human groups, which attempt, though never altogether successfully, to achieve compatibility and free exchange with one another.

Everything inclines us to look upon social processes in terms of choices—choices that are significant, even though the goal actually attained may well be different from the goal aimed at. Merely because some kinds of action give rise to unanticipated consequences, it does not follow that they are absurd, insignificant, or the work of an evil genius. We must follow Parsons's lead and learn to treat social action as a set of games, each of which has its own character and logic. The players may employ various delaying tactics and multigame strategies to switch their bets from one game to another. The idea of "totalizing" all the different games going on at any one moment, now or in the past, does not make much sense—except in the mind of God. It would not be a total waste of time, though, to try to describe the games more accurately than do the actors themselves, focusing on the different types of games, the constraints imposed on each of them, and the kinds of initiatives they make possible.

There is no reason to look upon industrial or any other type of society as a battlefield on which two (and only two) classes are engaged in a struggle to the death. The relation between a social group and one of its member elements, whether that element be an individual or a collective actor, can be interpreted as a relation of inclusion-exclusion only at the price of oversimplification. One of the sociologist's tasks is to identify the conditions under which certain processes of polarization may begin. These processes may sometimes continue long enough to pose a threat to the cohesiveness or even the existence of a society. It is quite another matter, however, to assert that the class struggle, in which the well-off are pitted against the oppressed, is the motor of History. When, in 1789, the abbé Sieyès maintained that the third estate was treated as though it were nothing, when in fact it was everything and meant to be something, he was establishing, well before Marx and for a long time to come, the model of class-struggle rhetoric. But we have progressed since Sieyès and Marx, and there is today no excuse for accepting the deceptively simple solutions offered by this rudimentary Manichaeanism.

The problem of institutionalization is central to thinking about industrial society. Institutionalization has a number of different meanings. To begin with, any action shaped by the reciprocal expectations of the actors may be called institutional. One problem that comes up in this connection is that of explaining the conformity between expectations on the one hand and norms and observed behavior on the other. What ensures that there will be such conformity is in part constraint—in some cases force—in the form of sanctions against deviant behavior, in part the calculations made by the actors, who recognize that they have a clear interest in reaching agreement and doing what is expected of them. Institutionalization also relies on internalization of norms, or, rather, of certain norms. The task of the sociologist is to point out these various explanatory principles and bring to light the relations between them. The difficulty of doing this is compounded by the fact that such categories as force, interest, and internalization are far from clear and easy to handle. In industrial societies the characteristic modalities of institutionalization depend on the way in which certain norms relative to production, work organization, and distribution of material and symbolic profits are internalized. This internalization is particularly tenuous in the case of the capitalist firm. The difficulty of institutionalizing labor and management roles is increased by the fact that the constraints and orientations included in their respective frames of reference are learned, assimilated, and internalized in ways that vary greatly from individual to individual.

Finally, the problem of social order always takes the form of a problem of overall compatibility among elementary choices and constraints of quite diverse kinds. The analysis of compatibility is the central thread of sociology. It is applicable to both roles and institutions. Different approaches must be used in different cases, however, and some are more complex than others. To consider roles first, compatibility analysis seeks to discover the conditions under which a "bundle" of differentiated orientations can coexist, along with the constraints imposed on the actors in the interaction process. In addition, the analyst tries to delineate the boundaries of each role, which in some cases are so narrow that the actor is reduced to choosing between mutually exclusive alternatives. The basic point is that ego can neither do nor be everything at once. The narrower the field of action and the tighter the "time-frame" within which action must take place, the more the choices involved come down to strict dichotomies, and the more stringent are the conditions imposed on the functioning of the social system. Differentiation strategies can be used to change the nature of the constraint, and the same end can be accomplished if some actors are willing to lend resources to others. Two actions may seem absolutely incompatible at first in view of the constraint ("you can't have your cake and eat it too"), but a strict prohibition can sometimes be turned into the milder requirement to make two actions compatible by employment of differentiation or loan-making strategies, as we have suggested. Limitations and impossibilities are given prominence in synchronic analysis, whereas diachronic analysis tries to bring to light hidden resources as well as resources that can perhaps be liberated or summoned into existence. Expectations are not merely norms that define and regulate interaction here and now but also hopeful anticipations of general possibilities implicit in future interaction. The diachronic perspective restores what I am tempted to call the *natural* confidence of man in himself and his fellows (taking the word "natural" in its eighteenth-century sense). This confidence may often be unwarranted, but it is invincible so long as men remain convinced that they need not be wolves for other men.

The analysis of compatibility conditions—of coexistence—is more than a method: it is a theory, because it permits us to set forth certain general propositions concerning man as an actor and as a participant in cooperative undertakings as well as man as a sentient, perfectible, and educable being. Compatibility analysis bids us look upon existing instances of compatibility or incompatibility as the end result (or starting point) of a process of compatibilization, thereby placing action at the center of sociological theory. Sociology is invariably a sociology of action, not in the sense intended by those who say that society "produces" itself or the individuals within it, but rather in the sense that social facts can be explained only in terms of the intentions of the actors and of their attempts to achieve mutual compatibility, whether under present conditions or under new conditions that remain to be spelled out. In no way does this imply that the structure of society at any given moment need be consistent with the will or desire of all, some, or any of its member individuals. The paradoxes that result from arguments based on notions of the "general will" attest to the importance of the unanticipated consequences of our acts and intentions. Still more significant, perhaps, as illustrations of these unanticipated consequences are the examples provided by our account of social change. Hence we must abandon faith in all utopian ideas of social order, whether given here and now or projected into the future as goals attainable merely by willing them. No society is all that it claims to be, and none embodies fully all that it proclaims through its paramount value system to be desirable. But neither is any society just a set of constraints, which reproduce themselves indefinitely. A society is neither substance nor will but a set of relations to some extent systematic in nature. Hence it is possible to agree with Parsons that a society is a process of inclusion and exclusion, by means of which a relatively durable symbolic solidarity can be established among the social actors. To that end, the actors must successfully differentiate their projects and establish a rank-order of coordinated goals; they must accept whatever constraints are imposed by the choices that need to be made at once, and yet not forget the prospects that innovation holds open for the future.

Notes

Foreword

1. Talcott Parsons, *Action Theory and the Human Condition* (New York: Free Press, 1978), p. 353 n.
2. For a good recent example, see Parsons's commentary on the Harvard Law School jurist Roberto Unger, pp. 32–44 of "Law as an Intellectual Stepchild" (*Sociological Inquiry* 47, nos. 3–4 [1977]: 11–58).
3. Readers who are puzzled by this example might read Parsons's "Death in the Western World," in *Action Theory and the Human Condition*, chap. 14.
4. Charles Lidz and Victor M. Lidz, "The Psychology of Intelligence of Jean Piaget and Its Place in the Theory of Action," in *Explorations in General Theory in Social Science: Essays in Honor of Talcott Parsons*, ed. Jan Loubser, Rainer Baum, Andrew Effrat, and Victor Lidz (New York: Free Press, 1976), chap. 8.
5. Parsons and Gerald Platt, *The American University* (Cambridge, Mass.: Harvard University Press, 1973).
6. See Victor M. Lidz, "The Law as Index, Phenomenon, and Element—Conceptual Steps toward a General Sociology of Law," *Sociological Inquiry* 49, no. 1 (1979): 5–25.
7. See Parsons's "A Paradigm of the Human Condition," in *Action Theory and the Human Condition*, chap. 15.

Introduction to Talcott Parsons

1. Lon L. Fuller, *The Anatomy of the Law* (New York: Mentor, 1969), pp. 132, 135, 141, 144.
2. George C. Homans, *Sentiments and Activities* (New York: Free Press, 1962), pp. 43–44, 46.
3. Thomas Kuhn, *The Structure of Scientific Revolutions* (Chicago: University of Chicago Press, 1962), pp. 10, 23.
4. Claude Lévi-Strauss, *La pensée sauvage* (Paris: Plon, 1962), pp.

26–29, 198; trans. as *The Savage Mind* (Chicago: University of Chicago Press, 1966).

5. My italics (F.B.).

6. Jean Piaget, *Etudes sociologiques* (Geneva: Droz, 1955), pp. 145–46.

7. Herbert Marcuse, *One-dimensional Man* (Boston: Beacon, 1964), pp. xv, 10.

Chapter One

1. Talcott Parsons, *The Structure of Social Action* (New York: McGraw-Hill, 1937; reissued in 1949 by the Free Press, Glencoe, Ill.). Citations here refer to the 1949 edition.

2. This passage from L. J. Henderson is cited by Parsons in ibid., p. 41. See also the article by Henderson, "An Approximate Definition of Fact," *University of California Publications in Philosophy* 14 (1932): 179–99, which Barber has called the most complete exposition of Henderson's views regarding the "constructivist character of conceptual schemes." See Bernard Barber, *L. J. Henderson: On the Social System* (Chicago: University of Chicago Press, 1971).

3. Parsons is quoting Malthus (1937, p. 489).

4. My italics (F.B.).

5. On the place Pareto attributed to psychology in social analysis, see Guy Perrin, *Sociologie de Pareto* (Paris: Presses Universitaires de France, 1966), esp. pt. 3, pp. 153–69.

6. Pitirin A. Sorokin, *Contemporary Social Theories* (New York: Harper, 1928), pp. 37–62.

7. Vilfredo Pareto, *Traité de sociologie generale*, 2 vols. (Lausanne and Paris: Payot, 1917–19). Cited by Parsons (1937, p. 244).

8. Parsons borrowed the phrase "eternal objects" from Whitehead. See Parsons, *The Structure of Social Action*, p. 763.

9. My italics (F.B.). See Parsons, ibid., p. 31.

10. Parsons italicized "logical." See Parsons, ibid., p. 33.

11. Alfred North Whitehead, *Science and the Modern World* (New York: Macmillan, 1948), pp. 105–6.

12. P. W. Bridgman, *The Logic of Modern Physics* (New York: Macmillan, 1927). Cited by Parsons in the 1949 edition of *The Structure of Social Action*, p. 3.

13. For a discussion of this question, see Parsons (1937), pp. 737–51.

14. Weber defined the social relation as the relation that obtains between the "significant content" *(Sinngehalt)* of the behavior of two or more individuals, by virtue of the influence on one another of their behavior *(auf einander gegenseitig eingestellt),* in consequence of which each orients himself to the others. See Max Weber, *Economy and*

Society, 4th ed., trans. E. Fischoff et al. (Totowa, N.J.: Bedminster, 1968), vol. 1, chap. 1.

15. On this point we are still close to Weber's definition of the group *(Verband)* in *Economy and Society* in terms of the preservation of order, guaranteed by specific individuals.

16. Parsons, *The Social System* (Glencoe, Ill.: Free Press, 1951*a*).

17. Whitehead, *Science,* p. 88.

Chapter Two

1. Max Weber, *Economy and Society,* vol. 1, chap. 1.

2. A. M. Henderson and Parsons, *Max Weber, The Theory of Social and Economic Organization* (Oxford: Oxford University Press, 1947), p. 87. See also the article by Paul F. Lazarsfeld, "Quelques remarques historiques sur l'analyse empirique de l'action," in *Philosophie des sciences sociales* (Paris: Gallimard, 1970), pp. 163–67.

3. Parsons and Edward Shils, "Values, Motives, and Systems of Action," in *Toward a General Theory of Action,* ed. Parsons and Shils (Cambridge, Mass.: Harvard University Press, 1951*b*).

4. Lazarsfeld, "Quelques remarques," pp. 168–69.

5. Edward C. Tolman's essay, "A Psychological Model," is pt. 3 of *Toward a General Theory of Action,* pp. 279–360.

6. Edward C. Tolman, *Operational Behaviorism and Current Trends in Psychology.* Cited by Lazarsfeld, "Quelques remarques."

7. Lazarsfeld. Cited in *Psychology: A Study of a Science,* ed. Sigmund Koch (New York: McGraw-Hill, 1959), 3:738.

8. See Parsons, "On the Concept of Value-Commitments," in *Politics and Social Structure* (New York: Free Press, 1969), pp. 440–42, where Parsons attacks the realist concept of values.

9. Max Weber, *Die Wirtschaftsethik der Weltreligionen,* vol. 1, pp. 237–368.

10. On the pattern variables, the basic material may be found in *The Social System* (1951*a*), pp. 58–67; the joint article with Shils, entitled "Values, Motives, and Systems of Action," in *Toward a General Theory of Action,* pp. 76–77; and another joint article with Robert F. Bales, entitled "The Dimensions of Action-Space," in *Working Papers in the Theory of Action* (Glencoe, Ill.: Free Press, 1953), pp. 66–67.

11. H. H. Gerth and C. Wright Mills, *From Max Weber: Essays in Sociology* (New York: Oxford University Press, 1946), p. 119. The passage cited occurs in the essay on "Politics as a Vocation."

12. As I did in my introduction to a French translation of Parsons's work entitled *Eléments pour une sociologie de l'action* (Paris: Plon, 1955).

13. Weber, *Economy and Society,* part 2, chap. 3 [I have translated from the passage cited in French—trans.].

14. See Parsons, "Durkheim's Contribution to the Theory of Inte-

gration of Social Systems," in *Sociological Theory and Modern Society* (New York: Free Press, 1967), pp. 3–35.

15. Robert K. Merton, *On Theoretical Sociology* (New York: Free Press, 1967), p. 69.

16. Adam Smith, *An Inquiry into the Nature and Causes of the Wealth of Nations,* 7th ed. (London, 1793), bk. 1, chap. 2, pp. 19–25. Cited in *Theories of Society,* ed. Parsons and Edward Shils, et al. (Glencoe, Ill.: Free Press, 1961), pp. 104–5.

17. Parsons, *Societies: Evolutionary and Comparative Perspectives* (Englewood Cliffs, N.J.: Prentice-Hall, 1966), p. 9.

18. Nicolas Troubetzkoy, "La phonologie actuelle," *Journal de psychologie* (1933), pp. 228–32.

19. André Martinet, *La linguistique synchronique* (Paris: Presses Universitaires de France, 1965), pp. 17, 83–84.

20. Similarly, in linguistics, "the very suggestive comparison between the course of acquisition of language and the course of its loss in aphasia has been said by Roman Jakobson to provide confirmation of his views on the nature of linguistic systems in general and of phonological systems in particular." See ibid., p. 97.

21. Troubetzkoy, "La phonologie actuelle," p. 235.

22. Martinet, *La linguistique,* p. 78.

23. Nicolas Troubetzkoy, "Essai d'une théorie des oppositions phonologiques," *Journal de psychologie* (1936), pp. 1–18.

24. Ibid., p. 11. Concerning Troubetzkoy's shift from correlative to proportional relations, see Martinet, *La linguistique,* p. 78.

25. A. R. Radcliffe-Brown, *Structure and Function in Primitive Society* (New York: Free Press, 1965).

26. Claude Lévi-Strauss, *Structural Anthropology* (New York: Anchor, 1967), p. 39.

27. Troubetzkoy, "La phonologie actuelle," p. 231.

28. In the sense in which Ferdinand de Saussure speaks of the *value* of the knight in chess: "By its material make-up—outside its square and the other conditions of the game—it means nothing to the player; it becomes a real concrete element only when endowed with value and wedded to it" (*Course in General Linguistics,* trans. Wade Baskin [New York: McGraw-Hill, 1959], p. 110).

29. In my introduction to Parsons, *Eléments.*

30. Robert Blanché, *L'axiomatique* (Paris: Presses Universitaires de France, 1955), pp. 41–43.

31. The term used by Blanché is *"réalisable"* (p. 42).

Chapter Three

1. In *The Structure of Social Action* (1937), Parsons maintains that this overly restrictive notion is an unfortunate legacy of utilitarianism.

2. Parsons and Neil J. Smelser, *Economy and Society. A Study in the Integration of Economic and Social Theory* (Glencoe, Ill.: Free Press, 1956).

3. Robert F. Bales, *Interaction Process Analysis: A Method for the Study of Small Groups* (Cambridge: Addison-Wesley, 1950), p. 33.

4. Robert Bales uses the same term as Parsons does in *The Social System* (1951*a*).

5. Parsons, "Some Problems of General Theory in Sociology," in *Theoretical Sociology,* ed. John C. McKinney and Edward A. Tiryakian (New York: Appleton-Century-Crofts, 1970*b*), pp. 29–31.

6. Parsons, "An Approach to Psychological Theory in Terms of the Theory of Action" (1959), in Koch, ed., *Psychology: A Study of a Science,* 3:612–711, esp. 631–32.

7. Ibid., p. 633. Parsons's italics.

8. Kingsley Davis, "The Myth of Functional Analysis as a Special Method in Sociology and Anthropology," *American Sociological Review* 24 (1959): 758. Davis quotes Radcliffe-Brown as follows: "Might it not prevent confusion if it [functionalism] were renamed Malinowski-anism?"

9. Raymond Boudon, "La notion de fonction," in *La crise de la sociologie* (Paris: Droz, 1971), pp. 205–15.

10. A. R. Radcliffe-Brown, "On the Concept of Function in Social Science," *American Anthropologist* 37 (1935): 397.

11. Boudon refers explicitly to Parsons as opposed to Malinowski and Radcliffe-Brown. See "La notion," p. 213.

12. Carl G. Hempel, "The Logic of Functional Analysis," *Lewellyn Gross Symposium on Sociological Theory* (Evanston, Ill.: Row Peterson, 1959). A detailed summary of this article may be found in Pierre Birnbaum and François Chazel, *Théorie sociologique* (Paris: Presses Universitaires de France, 1975), pp. 304–31.

13. In Chap. Five, "Social Change."

14. Parsons, "The Present Position and Prospects of Systematic Theory in Sociology" (1945). Reprinted in Parsons, *Essays in Sociological Theory,* rev. ed. (Glencoe, Ill.: Free Press, 1954).

15. Merton, *On Theoretical Sociology.*

16. Dennis H. Wrong, "The Oversocialized Conception of Man in Modern Sociology," *American Sociological Review* 26 (1961): 183–93.

17. Parsons, "Comment on 'Current Folklore in the Criticisms of Parsonian Action Theory,'" *Sociological Inquiry* 44 (1974): 55–58.

18. See the passage from Wolfgang Koehler cited in *Theories of Society* (1961).

19. Particularly with Parsons, Bales, et al., in *Family, Socialization and Interaction Process* (Glencoe, Ill.: Free Press, 1955).

20. Sigmund Freud, *Group Psychology and the Ego.*

21. Urie Bronfenbrenner gives prominence to *ideals, standards,* and *patterns* as important elements in the theory of socialization. The latter

two terms suggest that socialization is not a process of copying or "reproduction" but rather one of flexible control (it is tempting to say "remote control") of the actors by one another in relation to changing motivations. See Bronfenbrenner's "Parsons' Theory of Identification," in *The Social Theories of Talcott Parsons,* ed. Max Black (Englewood Cliffs, N.J.: Prentice-Hall, 1961), p. 193.

22. Parsons, "The Super Ego and the Theory of Social Systems," in *Social Structure and Personality* (New York: Free Press, 1964), pp. 23–28.

23. Parsons cited Piaget as early as *The Structure of Social Action* (pp. 384–85) in discussing Durkheim's concept of moral education. He mentions him in connection with universalism in *Family, Socialization and Interaction Process* (1955), and in "An Approach to Psychological Theory in Terms of the Theory of Action" (1959), p. 658.

24. Peter M. Blau, *Exchange and Power in Social Life* (New York: Wiley, 1967), pp. 171–79.

25. See Parsons, *The Social System,* pp. 294–96, where charisma is discussed in connection with the romantic-utopian element in political and religious movements.

26. See Parsons, "Definition of Health and Illness in the Light of American Values and Social Structure," *Social Structure and Personality,* esp. pp. 274–76.

27. In Freud's work, see first chap. 27 of *Introduction to Psychoanalysis.*

28. See Parsons, "The Father Symbol," *Social Structure and Personality,* pp. 34–56.

29. Robert Dubin, "Parsons' Actor: Continuities in Social Theory," *American Journal of Sociology* 25 (1960).

30. Parsons, "Pattern Variables Revisited: A Response to Robert Dubin's Stimulus," *American Sociological Review,* vol. 25, no. 4 (1960). Reprinted in *Sociological Theory and Modern Society* (1967), pp. 199–221.

31. In expounding the distinction between ego's "orientations" and alter's "modalities."

32. Boudon, "La notion," pp. 167–78.

Chapter Four

1. Parsons, "On the Concept of Political Power," *Proceedings of the American Philosophical Society* 107, no. 3. Reprinted in *Sociological Theory and Modern Society* (1967), pp. 297–354; and also in the recent collection *Politics and Social Structure* (1969), pp. 352–404. References in the text are to the latter collection.

2. Norbert Wiener, *Cybernetics* (Cambridge, Mass.: MIT Press, 1961).

3. Karl W. Deutsch, *The Nerves of Government* (New York: Free Press, 1966), esp. chap. 5.

4. Georges Th. Guilbaud, *La cybernétique* (Paris: Presses Universitaires de France, 1954), pp. 27–28.

5. Parsons and Gerald Platt, *The American University* (Cambridge, Mass.: Harvard University Press, 1973), p. 16.

6. See Parsons, *Structure and Process in Modern Societies* (Glencoe, Ill.: Free Press, 1960), pp. 220–21.

7. Parsons, "Some Reflections on the Play of Force in Social Process." Reprinted in *Sociological Theory and Modern Society,* chap. 9.

8. Bertrand de Jouvenel, *Du pouvoir* (Geneva: A l'Enseigne du Cheval ailé, 1947), p. 31; translated by J. F. Huntington as *On Power* (Boston: Beacon, 1962).

9. Jean-Jacques Rousseau, *Discours sur l'origine et les fondements de l'inégalité parmi les hommes* (Paris: La Pléiade, 1964), 3:184. "Government did not at first exercise arbitrary power, which is nothing but the corruption of government, the end of a long decay resulting in the rule of the strongest, *of which originally governments were the remedy."* My italics (F.B.).

10. Rousseau contrasts "the ferocity of despotism with that authority [he is speaking of paternal authority] which looks more to the advantage of him who obeys than to the utility of him who commands." See *Discours,* p. 182.

11. Parsons, "On the Concept of Influence," in *Politics and Social Structure,* p. 407.

12. Richard Neustadt, *Presidential Power* (New York: Wiley, 1976), p. 9.

13. Jean-Jacques Rousseau, *Du contrat social* (Geneva: A l'Enseigne du Cheval ailé), bk. 1, chap. 3, p. 178.

14. Merton, *On Theoretical Sociology,* chap. 4.

15. See Saussure, *Course in General Linguistics,* pp. 122–27, for a discussion of the distinction between syntagmatic and associative relations.

16. Emile Durkheim, *Leçons de sociologie* (Istanbul, 1950), pp. 7–8.

17. Parsons, "Durkheim's Contribution to the Theory of Integration of Social Systems," *Sociological Theory and Modern Society,* p. 9.

18. Parsons, "On the Concept of Value-Commitments," in *Politics and Social Structure,* p. 440.

19. Parsons, "Theoretical Orientations in Modern Societies," in ibid., p. 43.

20. Parsons, "On the Concept of Influence," in ibid., p. 414.

21. George C. Homans, *Social Behavior: Its Elementary Forms* (New York: Harcourt, Brace & World, 1961), chaps. 1 and 5.

22. Parsons, "On the Concept of Influence," in *Politics and Social Structure,* p. 433. Although Parsons makes no reference here to the "two-step flow" theory developed by Elihu Katz and Paul F. Lazarsfeld

in *Personal Influence* (Glencoe, Ill.: Free Press, 1955), the Parsonian concept also exhibits the distinction between two levels, one of contact between persuader and persuadee, the other of institutional authorization of the persuader and the propensity of the persuadee to credit what the persuader thus authorized has to say.

23. Authority is defined as an attribute of certain individuals and status positions that are assigned political responsibilities and consequently are entitled to support. Parsons, "Authority, Legitimation, and Political Action," in *Structure and Process in Modern Societies,* p. 198.

24. Parsons and Smelser, *Economy and Society* (1956), pp. 73–79. See esp. the table on p. 77.

25. In the United States, banks participate with business firms in similar kinds of ventures, to an even greater degree.

26. Reprinted in *Politics and Social Structure,* pp. 204–41. The table referred to in the text may be found on p. 238 of that work.

27. Parsons, "Polity and Society: Some General Considerations," in ibid., p. 474.

28. As Parsons does in *Economy and Society,* chap. 2.

29. Ibid., pp. 369–71. "The power of A over B is, in its legitimized form, the right of A ... to make decisions that take precedence over those of B, in the interests of the effectiveness of the collective operation as a whole."

30. The distinction between (exogenous) conditions and cybernetic controls is set forth in "The Concept of Society," in *Politics and Social Structure,* pp. 32–33.

31. Anatol Rapoport, "Homeostasis Reconsidered," in *Toward a Unified Theory of Human Behavior,* ed. Roy Grinker (New York: Basic, 1967), p. 228.

32. Alfred Emerson, "Homeostasis and Comparison of Systems," in Grinker, ibid., p. 149.

33. In the discussion following Emerson's essay, Parsons states his agreement with the celebrated naturalist and outlines an analogy between the gene and the symbol, in which he emphasizes the differences between the two forms of control, the latter characterized by internalization and very great generality (Grinker, ibid., p. 154). This discussion is referred to in *Politics and Social Structure,* pp. 6–7.

34. "Cultural systems are in no sense completely integrated. . . . What is more, the actual behavior of individuals ... is *congruent* [my italics (F.B.)] in varying degrees with the significations carried by the cultural system." See Parsons, "Culture and Social System Revisited," in *The Idea of Culture in the Social Sciences,* ed. L. Schneider and C. Bonjean (New York: Cambridge University Press, 1973), p. 35.

35. See Ernst Mayr, *Population, Species, and Evolution,* pp. 10–21.

36. A. L. Kroeber and Parsons, "The Concepts of Culture and of Social System," *American Sociological Review* 23 (1958): 582–83.

37. Roman Jakobson and Morris Halle, *Fundamentals of Language*. Cited in "On the Concept of Influence," in *Politics and Social Structure* (1969), p. 406.

38. Roman Jakobson, *Essais de linguistique générale* (Paris: Editions de Minuit), p. 91. Jakobson is citing C. Cherry in this passage, taken from n. 2 on p. 91. The last part of the sentence is Jakobson's.

39. The term is found in Jakobson, *Essais*, p. 95, who defines it as "the transition from one code to another," with "all the different aspects of translation" that this entails.

40. The task of reading the remaining lines in the table will be left to the reader, using the interpretive scheme proposed in the text.

41. Parsons, "The Father Symbol," in *Social Structure and Personality* (1964), pp. 34–57.

42. Especially in "Equality and Inequality in Modern Society, or Social Stratification Revisited," *Sociological Inquiry* 40 (1970): pp. 13–72.

43. Parsons is citing Schumpeter. See "On the Concept of Political Power," in *Politics and Social Structure,* pp. 386–87.

44. Elihu Katz and Paul F. Lazarsfeld, *Personal Influence.*

45. The quotation marks signify that the Weberian prophet is not a person who exerts influence in Lazarsfeld's sense. Influence is exerted between peers, or pseudopeers. Charisma presupposes a marked disparity between the prophet and his followers.

46. Chap. 7 of *Structure and Process in Modern Societies* (1960) is devoted to the analysis of McCarthyism. Parsons also treated the subject in his essays on the media, "On the Concept of Political Power," pp. 392–94, and implicitly in "On the Concept of Value-Commitments," pp. 463 ff., both in *Politics and Social Structure.*

47. Parsons contrasts "conditions" (high energy) and "controls" (high information). See "The Concept of Society," in *Politics and Social Structure,* pp. 32–33.

Chapter Five

1. See the June 1964 issue of *American Sociological Review,* which contains articles by Parsons, Robert Bellah, and S. N. Eisenstadt and summarizes the contribution of each to the work of the seminar.

2. The reader may wish to consult Richard Hofstadter, *The Age of Reform: From Bryan to F.D.R.* (New York: Knopf, 1956).

3. Parsons and Smelser, *Economy and Society* (1956), p. 254. Parsons's italics.

4. Durkheim wrote, "The division of labor is a result of the struggle for existence, but it is also a tempered resolution of that struggle" (*De la division du travail* [Paris: Presses Universitaires de France, 1960], p. 253).

5. Parsons, "Some Considerations on Social Change," in *Readings in Social Evolution and Development,* ed. S. N. Eisenstadt (New York: Pergamon Press, 1970*c*), pp. 95–123.

6. Neil J. Smelser, *Essays in Sociological Explanation* (Englewood Cliffs, N.J.: Prentice-Hall, 1968), pp. 79–81, gives a very good detailed analysis of the points we have examined in the two examples drawn from Parsons.

7. Ibid., p. 79.

8. This notion, which is central to historicisms of all kinds, is the central thread of Maurice Merleau-Ponty's *Les aventures de la dialectique* (Paris: Gallimard, 1965).

9. Neil J. Smelser, *Theory of Collective Behavior* (Glencoe, Ill.: Free Press, 1952), pp. 71–72.

10. S. N. Eisenstadt, "Breakdowns of Modernization," in *Readings,* pp. 451–52.

11. From the essay "Politics as a Vocation," in Gerth and Mills, *From Max Weber,* p. 119.

12. To my mind, this is the interpretation one ought to ascribe to Comte's saying that mankind is composed more of the dead than of the living.

13. Cf. Weber's notion of a "pariah people," developed for the case of the Jews. See Max Weber, *Ancient Judaism* (Glencoe, Ill.: Free Press, 1952).

14. Parsons, "Evolutionary Universals in Society," *American Review of Sociology* 29, no. 3 (June 1964), mentioned above. Reprinted in *Sociological Theory and Modern Society* (1967), to which the page references given in the text refer.

15. Ibid., p. 492.

16. Parsons, "Full Citizenship for the Negro American." Reprinted in *Sociological Theory and Modern Society,* p. 425.

17. Ibid., p. 455.

18. See Parsons and Winston White, "The Link between Character and Society." Reprinted in *Social Structure and Personality,* pp. 183–235.

19. Ibid., p. 197. See also Parsons's discussion of Sorokin's ideas in *Sociological Theory and Modern Society.*

20. Parsons uses this expression in his article on "Durkheim's Contribution to the Theory of Integration of Social Systems," in *Sociological Theory and Modern Society,* pp. 3–35.

21. Parsons, "Introduction to Max Weber's Sociology of Religion," in ibid., pp. 35–79.

22. Max Weber, *The Protestant Ethic and the Spirit of Capitalism,* trans. Talcott Parsons (New York: Scribner's, 1958), p. 13.

23. Parsons, *Sociological Theory and Modern Society,* pp. 49–50.

24. Ibid., p. 48. The same interpretation is given in *The Structure of Social Action* (1937).

25. Parsons, Renée C. Fox, and Victor M. Lidz, "The Gift of Life and Its Reciprocation," *Social Research* 39 (1972), p. 394.

26. Ibid., p. 383. My italics (F.B.).

27. Parsons's article on "Christianity," in *International Encyclopedia of the Social Sciences* (New York: Free Press, 1968), pp. 425–46.

28. Joseph A. Schumpeter, *Capitalism, Socialism and Democracy* (New York: Harper, 1942), pt. 2, pp. 81–86.

Chapter Six

1. Parsons, "'Capitalism' in Recent German Literature: Sombart and Weber," *Journal of Political Economy* 36 (1928): 641–61; and 37 (1929): 31–51.

2. Parsons, "Some Sociological Aspects of the Fascist Movements," in *Politics and Social Structure* (1969), pp. 82–96.

3. I stress the word "generally," because there is much shifting back and forth between the two groups.

4. Parsons, "Christianity and Modern Industrial Society," *Sociological Theory and Modern Society* (1967), pp. 385–421.

5. By "ascetic" variant Parsons meant Calvinism as opposed to Lutheranism, which he regarded as a mystical variant. Ibid., pp. 390, 404–5.

6. This is the argument developed by Durkheim in pt. 3 of *La division du travail,* p. 393.

7. Parsons uses the distinction suggested by Ernst Troeltsch and Max Weber between the Church and the sect, to which he adds a third term, the "denomination," characteristic of present-day American protestantism, which he refers to as "denominational pluralism."

8. See *The Structure of Social Action* (1937), pp. 488–95, 657–58; *Essays in Sociological Theory* (1954 ed.), pp. 323–26; and "Some Comments on the Sociology of Karl Marx," *Sociological Theory and Modern Society,* pp. 102–37.

9. The comparison between Marx and Hobbes is sketched out in *The Structure of Social Action* (1937), p. 109.

10. Parsons, "Evaluation and Objectivity in Social Science: An Interpretation of Max Weber's Contribution," *Sociological Theory and Modern Society,* pp. 79–102.

11. Parsons, "An Approach to the Sociology of Knowledge," ibid., pp. 139–66, esp. 152–53.

12. According to Parsons, "scientific socialism" has about as much claim to being scientific as does "Christian Science." See "Some Comments."

13. Durkheim, *De la division du travail,* p. 364.

14. Durkheim, *Les formes élémentaires de la vie religieuse* (Paris: Felix Alcan, 1912), pp. 323–24.

15. Parsons, "An Approach," pp. 148–49.

16. Parsons, "An Outline of the Social System," in *Theories of Society* (1961), pp. 41–42.

17. James G. March and Herbert A. Simon, *Organizations* (New York: Wiley, 1959).

18. Regarding this distinction, see F. Bourricaud, *Esquisse d'une théorie de l'autorité,* 2d ed. (Paris: Plon, 1969), pp. 336 ff.

19. Parsons, "Voting and the Equilibrium of the American Political System," *Politics and Social Structure,* pp. 204–41.

20. Parsons, "The Mass-Media and the Structure of American Society," ibid., p. 246–47.

21. Parsons, "Equality and Inequality" (1970*d*), p. 47.

22. Parsons, "A Revised Analytical Approach to the Theory of Social Stratification," in *Essays in Sociological Theory* (1954), p. 386.

23. I am summarizing pp. 412–14 of *Essays in Sociological Theory.*

24. In his article "On the Concept of Political Power," in *Politics and Social Structure,* Parsons stresses the realization of *collective* goals, whereas in the text considered here he is emphasizing the realization of individual ends.

25. "Legitimate order" appears in the index to *Politics and Social Structure,* with only four references.

26. Parsons is here following the analysis of T. H. Marshall in "Social Class and Citizenship."

27. See the article on "Professions" in the *International Encyclopedia of the Social Sciences* (1968).

28. See tables 1 and 2 in "The Concept of Society," in *Politics and Social Structure,* pp. 32–33. See also Parsons, *The System of Modern Societies* (Englewood Cliffs, N.J.: Prentice-Hall, 1971), table 1, p. 6; and table 2, p. 12.

29. Parsons, "Some Theoretical Considerations of the Nature and Trends of Change of Ethnicity," in *Ethnicity,* ed. Nathan Glazer and Daniel P. Moynihan (Cambridge, Mass.: Harvard University Press, 1975), pp. 58–64.

List of the Works of Talcott Parsons
Cited in the Text

References to the works of Parsons given in the text are by year and page. The following chronological list will enable the reader to find the passages cited.

1937.   *The Structure of Social Action*. New York: McGraw-Hill. Reissued in 1949 by the Free Press, Glencoe, Ill. Citations refer to the 1949 edition.

1945.   "The Present Position and Prospects of Systematic Theory in Sociology." In *Twentieth Century Sociology*. Edited by Georges Gurvitch and Wilbert E. Moore. New York: Philosophical Library. Reprinted in *Essays in Sociological Theory* (1954).

1951*a*.   *The Social System*. Glencoe, Ill.: Free Press.

1951*b*.   *Toward a General Theory of Action* (Cambridge, Mass.: Harvard University Press. Edited with Edward Shils.

1953.   *Working Papers in the Theory of Action*. Glencoe, Ill.: Free Press. With Robert F. Bales and Edward A. Shils.

1954.   *Essays in Sociological Theory*. Rev. ed. Glencoe, Ill.: Free Press.

1955.   *Family, Socialization and Interaction Process*. Glencoe, Ill.: Free Press. With Robert F. Bales et al.

1956.   *Economy and Society*. Glencoe, Ill.: Free Press. With Neil J. Smelser.

1959.   "An Approach to Psychological Theory in Terms of the Theory of Action." Pp. 612–711 in *Psychology: A Study of Science*. Edited by Simon Koch. Vol. 3. New York: McGraw-Hill.

1960.   *Structure and Process in Modern Societies* (a collection of essays). Glencoe, Ill.: Free Press.

1961.   *Theories of Society*. Glencoe, Ill.: Free Press. With Edward Shils et al.

1964. *Social Structure and Personality* (a collection of essays). New York: Free Press.

1966. *Societies: Evolutionary and Comparative Perspectives.* Englewood Cliffs, N.J.: Prentice-Hall.

1967 *Sociological Theory and Modern Society.* New York: Free Press.

1968. "Christianity" Pp. 425–46 in *International Encyclopedia of the Social Sciences.* New York: Free Press.

1969. *Politics and Social Structure.* New York: Free Press.

1970*a*. "On Building Social Systems Theory: A Personal History." *Daedalus* 99, no. 4 (Autumn 1970).

1970*b*. "Some Problems of General Theory in Sociology." In *Theoretical Sociology: Perspectives and Developments.* Edited by John C. McKinney and Edward A. Tiryakian. New York: Appleton-Century-Crofts.

1970*c*. "Some Considerations on Social Change." In *Readings in Social Evolution and Development.* Edited by S. N. Eisenstadt. New York: Pergamon Press.

1970*d*. "Equality and Inequality in Modern Society, or Social Stratification Revisited." *Sociological Inquiry* 40 (1970): 13–72.

1972. "The Gift of Life and Its Reciprocation." *Social Research* 39 (1972): 367–415. With Renée C. Fox and Victor M. Lidz.

1973. *The American University.* Cambridge, Mass.: Harvard University Press. With Gerald Platt.

1974. "Comment on 'Current Folklore in the Criticisms of Parsonian Action Theory.'" *Sociological Inquiry* 44 (1974): pp. 55–58.

1975. "Some Theoretical Considerations on the Nature and Trends of Change of Ethnicity." In *Ethnicity.* Edited by Nathan Glazer and D. P. Moynihan. Cambridge, Mass.: Harvard University Press.

Index

Acceptance, 113–14. *See also* Love

Action, 23, 27, 56; as the basis of sociology, 298; social, 51, 82, 83; system of, 38, 39, 47, 132–33, 292; theory of, 33, 52–53

Action space, 15

Action time, 33

Activity/passivity, 119, 224; in Christianity, 228–29

Actor, 50, 292–93; use of term, 244–45. *See also* Ego and alter; Individual

Adaptive behavior, 88, 89, 132; in American value system, 272; in bilateral interchanges, 163; definition of, 92; differentiation of, 92, 198; in group process, 86; relation to economy of, 138, 161–67; in relation to goal-selection, 90, 92, 161–67; relation to other three functions of, 138. *See also* Four-function paradigm

Adaptive upgrading, 203–4

Adequacy, 112–13

Adorno, Theodor, 125

Adulthood, 121; definition of, 115

Affectivity/affective neutrality, 61, 67; in doctor-patient relationship, 69–70; in relation to achievement, 132; in relation to deviance, 121; in relation to integration, 93. *See also* Pattern variables

Alienative deviance, 119, 120, 292

Alter. *See* Ego and alter

Ambiguity, 122

Ambivalence, 177; relation to deviance of, 118–19, 122

America: equality in, 279–80; Riesman's cultural analysis of, 213–26; value structure of, 75, 271–74

"American way," 221

Anomie, 60, 153, 284. *See also* De-differentiation

Approval, 114; definition of, 68, 113

Aristotle, 280

Artist: role of, 74

Asceticism, 221, 234. *See also* Calvinism; Puritanism

Atomism, 25–26

Authoritarianism, 125, 293

Authority, 159–60; hierarchy in, 286, 288; institutional backing of, 267–68; legitimacy of, 287; political, 286–89; professional, 287–88; in relation to deviance, 124

Autonomy, 109

Avoidance mechanisms, 116